CONTENTS

For Meher and Dahlia
            my past
                my present
                    my future
    with love always
                dad

ACKNOWLEDGEMENTS

I am grateful to the many wonderful people who helped in the development of this book.

Ewa Krynsk and Alfred H. Yuen were the first editors to look at the manuscript. Their broad perspective and valuable insights helped shape my story to make it more readable and coherent. Nadia Halim did a line-by-line and word-by-word analysis of the text and made many suggestions that raised it to a higher level. Edna Barker added the final touches and rounded off any rough edges.

I am indebted to Linda Riley, who, at an early stage, took it upon herself to carefully read the manuscript from start to finish. Her comment to me that she "couldn't put it down" was a great boost to my ego and presented me with some reassurance that the book might be of interest to readers outside of my circle of family and friends.

Sorrel Steinberg, besides reading and commenting on the first chapter of the book (originally intended to be the entire book), did research for me in Regina that helped fill in empty spaces, which I otherwise would not have been able to include. Other first chapter readers whose comments I appreciated are Linda Liss, Shelley Yampolsky, and Moshe Shomer.

A lot of discussion and searching went into finding a suitable title. The suggestion by Dr. Sharon Letovsky to call it *Rogue Rabbi* struck a chord, which was echoed by my children, Meher and Dahlia, and by my good friend Brahms Silver. This, of course, was the title selected by my publisher and his staff.

My appreciation to Shula Steinberg and Lynn Sokoloff for providing me with photographs that have been incorporated into the text. Also to Susan Klein of the Archdiocese of Regina who expended considerable time and energy to track down a photo of a Catholic priest I knew when I was a little boy.

Laurie Obornick did a careful reading of the introduction and the blurbs, resulting in changes and supportive comments.

Rabbi Zalman Schachter-Shalomi, Michael Tacon, and Father Paul

Massel were very gracious in their response to my requests for a brief comment on the book. These can be seen on the back cover.

The staff at ECW Press, including Crissy Boylan, Erin Creasey, Rachel Ironstone, and Jenna Illies, have been a joy to work with. Always helpful, insightful, and encouraging, they have taken their calling as literary midwives to heart and left no stone unturned in bringing this work to fruition.

To Jack David, my publisher, I can only say — thank you. You believed in me and, from the beginning, guided this work with skill and devotion, allowing me to express myself freely. You have been patient and understanding of my struggles and always there when I needed to talk. It is a blessing to have you in my life.

PREFACE

I have often watched artists paint and observed that they always move from one spot to another, seldom lingering in one place too long. Yet, slowly, as I watched, I could see glimpses of what the overall picture was going to be like, and these glimpses gradually expanded as the artist moved to completion of the work. It is with this in mind that I have written this book, maintaining a sequential time-line as much as possible, but taking liberties with chronology within each chapter, thereby enabling events to flow into one another in what I hope will form an interesting whole. I take my cue from growing up on the Prairies, where distinct seasons melted into each other, creating a beautiful tapestry. At least that's the way it comes to me as I look back on those days in Saskatchewan, growing up in that rich, exquisitely barren place I still call home.

As it has been many years since the events in this account occurred, I would ask the reader's forgiveness for errors in the spelling of names and for occasional minor inaccuracies on things such as dates and names. I trust these are few and far between.

INTRODUCTION

The story you are about to read is a spiritual journey. There are, however, times when spirituality seems to be the furthest thing from my mind, as I delve into the ordinary, the mundane, the dangerous, and the humourous. Yet these too are part of my spiritual path, part of what has contributed to my becoming who I am today — all the virtues and faults, the strengths and weaknesses, the peaks and valleys. (A colleague of mine recently suggested that to know the essence of a person, one needs to pay attention to biography and that even seemingly innocuous details count.) I do not presume to be more spiritual than anyone else, nor do I lay claim to a heritage that has more truth than other traditions. What I do say is that all human beings have within them a vast repository of spiritual potential — a repository that, when tapped, brings to bloom the finest and most lofty human qualities and experiences found in both religious and non-religious literature. In other words, saint, sinner, and all degrees in between harbour an enormous spiritual energy, of which only a small fraction has yet manifested in the mere few thousand years of recorded history. It is, I believe, this untapped spiritual power that is the future of mankind as well as its salvation, whether considered in the context of organized religion or not.

When I speak of spirituality, I am not only speaking about lofty values, which can be, in my view, a product of the spiritual process. Nor am I speaking about a kind of "goodness" often associated with individuals deemed to be spiritual. My concept is very basic and simple. Spirituality for me is about *spirit*, that intangible force that is connected to our physical bodies but which can also exist independent of it. This dualism is the essence of spirit, for it presumes that in every human being there is an element that is eternal, that is beyond matter, and that continues beyond death with an integrity both unique and common. The term most often used in referring to this spiritual element is *soul*.

The words in this book are an attempt to share with the reader the unusual journey of one soul given the name Jerry and belonging to the family of Steinberg. It is a journey not unlike that of anyone else, except for certain aspects that reflect the dimension of spirit referred to above and that point to the mostly hidden potential that lies dormant in every soul, waiting to emerge for the benefit of the individual and society.

I am compelled to write this book not only as a legacy for my children, however important that is to me, but also to share with the reader my hopes and optimism for the future in spite of the difficulties that are every day brought before us by the news media and that, no doubt, all of us experience to some extent in our personal lives.

Since roughly the middle of the nineteenth century, through the confluence of the Industrial Revolution and the birth of modern scientific research and discovery, the promise has been held out for a better world. There is no doubt that this promise has been fulfilled, but only in part. While medicine and technology have made significant contributions, I have not discerned that people are happier today than they were before the beginning of this epoch. In fact, one does not have to look far afield to see poverty, sickness, brutality, and social unrest on a scale unprecedented in human history. While technological progress races ahead at an exponential rate, man's inner life, by comparison, appears arrested. The questions, Who am I? Why am I here? and What is life all about? remain as unanswered today as at any previous time. And it does not seem likely that the best of science and the best of technology will provide answers to these questions that satisfy at a deep inner level. Nor, for the most part, are these questions answered by traditional religion. No doubt, faith and dogma have their place, and for the few bring a modicum of inner peace and joy. But in general, at least from my observations as a rabbi and psychotherapist, the *peace that passes understanding* is as elusive as ever. If I may extrapolate from this statement, I would add that without inner peace, there can be no outer peace. I say this not only about individuals, but also in the context of world affairs and within the social structures of individual nations.

So where does this leave us? In one of the stories that follow, I had the unusual and profound experience of knowing inner peace for ten days. This was not just an inner peace along the lines of "I feel great," or "All is well in my life." It was a peace where nothing and no one could disturb or anger me, no matter what they did. It was, so to speak, a state of sublime grace, in which wholeness, compassion, and love wove in and throughout me a fabric of rich hues, unlike anything I had ever felt before in my life. Since that time I have had numerous other similar experiences, but none that lasted that long in one continuous stretch. Do I think that this experience was unique to me alone?

Not at all. I sometimes read about it in the mystical literature of different cultures and, on rare occasions, hear about it from people I meet. I bring this to the reader's attention not as a panacea for what troubles the world, but as one essential ingredient among others (like justice, social action, and benevolent government) that will contribute to mankind's well-being and, beyond even this, to the survival of our planet. Without the cultivation of the inner life, we will continue to race toward better means of transportation, a better means of communication, and better means for preserving our physical health — all at the cost of never questioning where we are going, what we are saying, or why we are here in the first place.

Many years ago, when I was studying to become a rabbi, one of my professors made it quite clear that all of our knowledge comes from the mind and that there is nothing beyond cognitive processes, although he did acknowledge there was something called *feelings*, which he couldn't quite define or categorize. This whole area of how we know anything at all he termed *epistemology*, a fancy word that, I much later realized, did not preclude forms of knowing beyond cognition. This realization was important for me because it validated, at least in my mind, non-cognitive experiences that I had been having from the time I was a child. It further validated my intuitive faith in revelation, which I discovered in abundance in the Hebrew Scriptures and later in the mystical traditions of other religions and among individuals with no formal religious associations. Additional reinforcement came to me during a two-year sojourn at an ashram, where cognition was the least of the modalities practised. By the time I reached the age of thirty-two, I was convinced of the existence of other dimensions of reality as sources of knowledge. To put it simply, my epistemological horizons had expanded.

While it is one thing to broaden one's sources of knowledge, it is something else to use these newfound sources for practical purposes. Coming down from the "ivory tower" and putting one's learning to use does, at the very least, prove that a lofty and rarified atmosphere does have some value. In the coming pages I try to give the reader an idea of what this all means, from my personal experiences and from experiences of others who have trodden a similar path.

While I have expressed my disagreement with those who espouse a cognitive epistemology as the *summum bonum* of human knowledge, at the same time I hold in high regard, even awe, the accomplishments of those many thousands and even millions of individuals who represent what the mind has given us over the centuries, in particular the past century. I have no quarrel with narrow empiricism (heavy reliance on sense data), that philosophical perspective that has birthed modern science. Like the rest of humanity, I benefit from its theories and products, aware at the same time of its downsides, such as the creation of destructive forces that may be unleashed at the touch of a finger. Narrow empiricism must always have a respected place as part of the process of acquiring knowledge. At the same time, I suggest that, when it is harmonized with a recognition of realities beyond the mind, narrow empiricism becomes a force for incalculable good. Blending the best of science and the best of religion produces a comprehensive epistemology that allows the mind to expand and the soul to soar.

In addition to the theme of spirituality, the reader will discern a thread of healing weaving itself throughout this work. Healing has been a strong force in my life, beginning at a tender age, when I saw my first blind person and made a pact with God that one day I would become a doctor and find a cure for blindness. Instead, I became a rabbi, but not without a brief foray in medical school. Someone once suggested to me that in my work as a rabbi and psychotherapist, I may have helped some to see better. I like to think that this is the case. At the very least, I know that because of my specialties in psychotherapy (past-life regression, dreams, and psychogenic illness) I have been a last resort for certain clients referred to me by psychiatrists, G.P. psychotherapists, and other health professionals. I have written a manuscript about some of the cases I have worked with over more than forty years of practise, and a few of these stories are presented here. Throughout this book I mention some of my own personal encounters with illness and how, through dreams, I have been able to focus on the health problems of others and bring information from other dimensions to help people in their healing process.

Having over the years encountered such a variety of manifestations of psychic phenomena in myself and others, I have come to the conclusion that, contrary to the conventional wisdom of mainstream Judaism, psychic phenomena are an asset and not a liability in one's spiritual development. In fact, I encourage their development, and suggest to people who have intentionally or inadvertently developed psychic abilities to continue working with them, and not to fear them, as many people seem to do. The enemy is fear, not the psychic phenomenon itself. As a prime directive, I suggest that everyone wishing to develop or expand psychic experiences do so with the firm determination that no matter what they experience, they will not do harm to themselves or anyone else. I emphasize, as well, that it is critical for one to be grounded in values that promote life and well-being.

Another thread that runs implicitly through this work is my belief that we need to abandon the anthropomorphic concept of God (the view that God is similar to a human being, but greater: a being who is omnipotent, omniscient, and omnipresent) in favour of a view of God as unlimited realms of consciousness or unlimited dimensions of reality. Such a concept would change our ideas of good and evil, blessing and tragedy, and well-being and illness. I am not suggesting that this is a new concept — on the contrary, it has been part of Judaism almost from its inception and is clearly seen in the literature of Kabbalah, that mystical stream of the Jewish faith that has recently been in vogue thanks to certain celebrities. I have written in detail about this concept and its implications for Judaism and beyond in another manuscript, "The Unlikely Nature of God — A Kabbalistic Perspective." As the book you're reading now is a memoir and not a theological treatise, I mention the subject only briefly, toward the end. However, this concept of God underlies all I have written here.

One more point regarding the need for a different God concept. The past few years have seen a plethora of writings by four individuals, sometimes referred to as "the four horsemen," bent on undermining monotheism as conventionally understood and practised by the world's great religions. They are particularly critical of theodicy (the attempt by theologians and clergy to reconcile a loving God with suffering in the world), and in this regard I can understand their point. I find these criticisms difficult to counter only as long as one buys into the conventional God concept described above — the only God concept they deal with. It is my hope that in these memoirs, the reader will find some evidence for an understanding of God that goes beyond the conventional and contributes to a different perception of the world and the universe in which we live. It is, of course, also my hope that the reader will simply enjoy the story of my life and the many stories that make up that life.

For me, the past seventy-five years seem to have been filled with a series of synchronistic events. I can't explain it clearly, but I feel that every time I met a barrier, something helped me through it, and every time I stumbled, someone helped me get up again and move on. Sometimes help came from a person or event in this reality, and sometimes from another place — an experience of expanded consciousness, a dream, or a strong intuitive sense. Even in my moments of deepest despair, there was always a feeling that I was being guided by forces unseen, from realms beyond conventional understanding. I call these forces my guides, and every now and then one or more come to me in the flesh. On both levels, these are my *malachim*, my messengers, and I am always grateful for their presence and influence.

GROWING UP JEWISH ON THE FLATLAND

Regina 1935–1954

This is my birth moment
        the coming of my soul
                into humanity
        the God moment
          kissed by the angels
             delivered to my task
This is the moment of my earthing
        When I breathe my first
     and ask not to forget
            my holy guides
This is the moment of greeting
        my new keepers
     who shall harvest
         and sift me
            from the chaff
This is the moment
        when God and I
             smile at each other
         wish one another well
              and promise to write

I was born at the General Hospital in Regina, Saskatchewan on June 8, 1935 at 7:10 a.m. central standard time. It wasn't pretty. According to reports from my mother, my father, and my father's older brother, Israel, I was very wrinkled, very red, somewhat misshapen, and crying bitter tears. My dad told me many years later that as they viewed me through the maternity ward window, his brother suggested I be given a return ticket. My dad also told me that both my mother and I almost died; I was a breech birth — I came out feet first, wanting to test the waters before wading in (or out).

The first weeks of my new life were not much different from the first minutes. I continued to struggle for survival, as my mother (pre-La Leche League) was unable to provide me with natural nutrients, and I refused all attempts at substitutions. I was literally starving to death. My pediatrician and parents were beside themselves, bringing to my lips a variety of liquids, trying to encourage me to eat (or drink). I can imagine their panic, intermingled with cooing and tears and probably some well-intentioned stuffing. All to no avail. I was wasting away and, from lack of strength, crying with less enthusiasm. Finally, someone suggested Carnation milk. I drank like there was no tomorrow (as there almost wasn't). I am eternally grateful to the Carnation milk company (I have no shares) and to the unknown angel who made the suggestion. To this day, seventy-five years later, I always have Carnation milk in my fridge and use it instead of cream. Sometimes I just stare at the can with gratitude.

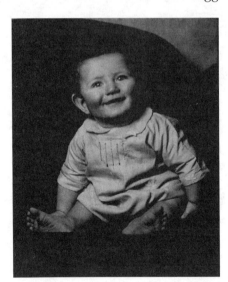

Jerry high on Carnation milk

My earliest memory dates from when I was about two or three. At the time, we lived at 1838 Ottawa Street (no longer there) in a side-by-side duplex, which we referred to as a "double house." A half block away, on the other side of the street, at 1819 Ottawa (also no longer there), lived my maternal grandparents. I was still wearing sleepers and sleeping in a bed with an adjustable side. It was probably a crib, either because I was too young to have a regular bed, or more likely because my parents were unable to afford one at the time.

One sunny summer morning, I awoke from a nap and called for my mother. There was no reply. I called again and again. Still no answer. I began to panic, and when shrill screaming brought no response, I took matters into my own hands and climbed over the railing. I don't know how I accomplished this, especially since I had never done it before. I presume it was one of those moments I've heard about, where extraordinary feats of strength and daring come to the fore at a time of perceived crisis. At any rate, there I was, all thirty or so pounds of me, running out the front door in my sleepers and heading to my grandparents' house. Now, in those days, sleepers had a bum flap, and I realized as I was running that my flap was fully open and my derriere exposed for all to see (not that there was anyone around). I was too anxious to get to my grandparents to stop and try to button it up, which I doubt I could

Jerry in front of 1819 Ottawa Street (circa 1970)

have done anyway, since I had never buttoned anything before, let alone something that was behind me. So, with one hand trying unsuccessfully to hold up the flap (I guess modesty is innate), I burst through my grandparents' side door into the kitchen, where I found my mother talking to her mother. I recall yelling and screaming at her for abandoning me. Of course I didn't use that term, but I do remember the sentiment. She never did that again, and thereafter always took me with her on frequent visits to my grandmother. When I asked my mother about the incident many years later, she told me that, upon leaving me alone, she would always ask the woman who lived next door in the double house to listen for me and check up on me periodically, but the neighbour had failed to do so on this occasion. In fairness, some years later the woman next door saved my life.

> Since the little boy
> > left uncovered his bottom
> much has occurred
> > to uncover his top

I was born in the middle of the Great Depression. My parents both had to work hard to make ends meet, and my father, despite a somewhat withered leg from polio, never complained or turned down a job, even when it meant walking a lot or carrying heavy weights. I was left during the day with a part-time nanny. The first nanny's tenure came to an abrupt end one evening when my parents decided to go out to a movie, a rare occurrence for them. They had gotten no farther than the end of the block when my mother had an uneasy feeling and said she wanted to return to the house. They came onto the porch quietly and, upon looking through the door window, saw the nanny dumping my food into the sink and then spanking me. She was dismissed on the spot. What else she might have done to me during the days when my parents were at work is not known. It's possible that my stuttering and an unusual nervous illness, which several years later required me to miss a year of school, may have had their roots in what happened with that nanny.

After that I had other nannies, all of them competent and caring, but my favourite was Suzy. She was a great fan of the country singer Wilf Carter and would sing his songs and listen to him on the radio for hours. I trace my love of country music back to Suzy, who was also a good sport and very kind.

One day when I was about six, as I watched Suzy ironing clothes in the living room at 1838 Ottawa Street, I developed a burning curiosity to look under her skirt. It had occurred to me that women were different from men, and I thought that if I looked under Suzy's skirt, I might find out exactly what the difference was, as I had heard that this was where it lay. I crept up near her, pretending I was playing, and when the opportune moment presented itself, placed my head between her feet and looked up. This was my introduction to bloomers. Suzy caught me in the act, and I made her promise she wouldn't tell my parents. She kept her word.

On another occasion, I decided to play a joke on her. I had a sled with runners, as did most boys in the neighbourhood. I would run with the sled and then jump on it, skating along the snowbound sidewalk and coasting for maybe ten or fifteen yards. On this particular day Suzy was out walking, so I decided to run at her from behind and knock her feet out from under her with the sled. I was successful, but what I hadn't counted on was Suzy falling on my head. She was fine, my head and neck having cushioned her fall. But I was bruised and very dizzy. She never told my parents about that one, either. To this day, I cherish her memory.

Another memory, which I'm sure accounts for my fondness for almost every kind of vegetable, occurred in the alley behind my home, which was in the middle of the block on the west side. On the other side of the common wall of our double house at 1840 Ottawa Street lived the Lymans and their son Earl, my first best friend. The neighbourhood in general was middle class or a notch below (maybe two notches). No one seemed to have much money, yet the homes (at least the ones I had access to) were for the most part neat and clean. Gardens were big in those days, and many backyards were filled with assorted vegetables, especially carrots, radishes, cucumbers, tomatoes, dill, and cabbages. I was intimately familiar with many of the gardens, because one of our pastimes, as rebellious and hungry young gentlemen, was to raid these treasures of the earth and later compare the loot. The strategy for these daring military-style excursions was for a group of us, usually two to four guys, to await darkness and a bright moon, and then, under cover of night, sneak up, often on our bellies, through the spaces between the rows of vegetables, to inspect and collect the choicest of the day. We had a code to keep each other informed if danger lurked — usually in the form of a suspicious homeowner hearing a noise or seeing a form or shadow, or at times police patrolling the alleyways. The designated raider guard would make a sound such as a cat's meow — one meow meant "stay still," two meows, "get the hell out of there fast." If an owner discovered us, he would of course make chase, but we had the advantage; we were young, we had a head start, and we could usually run faster and farther. The slowest of the group was always designated the raider guard, and would therefore be more distant from the action and in a better position to escape. I don't recall anyone ever actually getting caught, as we would quickly disappear into the night. After a successful raid, we would gather at a safe haven and divvy up the spoils, complimenting those who had managed to procure extra-succulent produce. Then, after cleaning as much dirt from the vegetables as possible (sometimes with a hose), we would have a banquet.

The Second World War happened during the early years of my life, and the military was heavily on our minds, which might in part account for our commando-like vegetable sorties. My buddies and I must have seen every war movie of the time, from *Sergeant York* to *The Halls of Montezuma*. Earl's brother Harvey was in the army, and I was always in awe of his uniform and shiny black boots. I remember seeing him once on Eleventh Avenue, saluting an officer as he passed him in front of the Army and Navy Store. "Awesome!" I thought to myself.

Earl and I would play war games, at his place or mine, pretending to be characters from one of the war movies we had seen and acting out scenarios that we made up as we went along. For example, I might be Sergeant York and he Colonel McGuire. The situation was grim; the enemy outnumbered us, yet we had to make a stand:

York: Keep your head down, Colonel. The shells are coming in thick and fast. Watch out on your right! I see someone coming.

Earl on left and Jerry (circa 1952)

McGuire: I got him in my sights, Sergeant. Don't worry. Bang! Pow! One less Hun!

York: Good shooting, Colonel.

McGuire: Thanks, York. Look out. Here comes a Stuka. Boom!

York: Colonel, are you okay? Colonel, answer me! (McGuire is motionless on the bed.) The dirty Huns. They killed the colonel. I'll get them. Ratta tat tat! Ratta tat tat! Take that you slimy bastards!

And so on, through many battles on the mattress behind pillows, in a fort of large wooden boxes, or some other structure that fit our imaginations. Sometimes we were pilots or sailors or commandos. More often than not, someone died. For some reason there was glory in death and pride in avenging the death. Sometimes both Earl and I were killed, which would finish that scenario, but always with vindication at the end. Then we'd go out and have a milkshake.

I was, and still am, fascinated by guns. Just before Harvey enlisted in the army, he made a Luger out of wood and painted it black. I loved that gun and was grateful whenever he let me handle it, at which time I would make sound effects as I shot at an imaginary enemy: "*kshh, kshh, bukch, bukch,*" and "*kerch, kerch.*" (They sounded better than they look in print.)

I wasn't alone in my love of guns. Most of my friends and I had this in common, and we expressed our predatory feelings by buying or making a variety of toy weapons, from cap guns to water pistols to elastic guns. The last was a working device that consisted of a wooden rudimentary gun-like shape with a clothespin attached at the end of the butt. We procured tire tubes (tubeless tires weren't around yet) from gas stations that no longer had a use for them and cut them into rings. These elastics were knotted in one or two places, then stretched from the tip of the gun to the other end and attached to the clothespin. The elastic would be released by pressing down on the bottom of the clothespin. At close range, these missiles could do damage, especially if someone was hit in the eye. So, whenever we took to the back lanes for a fight, we had to agree on simple terms of engagement — no shooting at close range and no aiming at the head. This seemed to work, as I recall no injuries worse than a small welt. It was a lot of fun, running and hiding and shooting and ducking and surrendering when surprise-attacked. At the end of the game, each player reclaimed his elastics, identifying it by the grade or colour of the rubber, although most elastics were black or red. Later, someone invented a wooden rifle using the same clothespin-and-elastic design, but with a slot on top running the length of the barrel, which held an arrow made from a shingle. It was too dangerous to use in our back-alley battles, but we competed to see who could shoot the farthest.

Another small weapon we made ourselves was a bean shooter. This gun-like device was made from two clothespins — one intact, the other disassembled for parts, its spring used as a trigger. The end product would shoot a bean about thirty feet. For bean shooters, we used the same terms of engagement as with elastic guns.

Our back-alley excursions, though occasionally about military battles, were mainly about our other passion, cowboy movies — good guys and bad guys. Each of us had a favourite; my hero was Wild Bill Hickok. He carried one gun on each hip and could draw fast and shoot both guns at the same time with deadly accuracy. Also, he was a good guy. Others we revered were Gene Autry, Roy Rogers, Hopalong Cassidy, and comic-book heroes like Red Ryder. No one wanted to be a bad guy, especially since in the movies and comics the bad guys always lost. (Darth Vader was not yet born.)

Just after the war, army surplus became a big business. In Regina, the major outlet was the Army and Navy Store. Several members of my family worked there — my mother in ladies' coats and my father in menswear, the latter an occupation he and my mother would eventually take up on their own. My dad's oldest brother, the uncle who was present just after my birth, was a manager at the store. With all these connections, it was inevitable that I too would someday work there, which happened one summer when I was about sixteen. For two months I worked in the basement, in a section that sold military products left over from the war. I was particularly excited to find a large collection of .303 rifles, which were mine to sell. This gave me the opportunity to handle the rifles, or more accurately, to caress them. Each had its own personality, whether it was the colour and grain of the butt or the way light glinted off the barrel. To say I was an enthusiastic salesman would be an understatement. Yet there was a sad element to all of this, because I couldn't help wondering about the history of each rifle. Was its original owner still alive, or maimed? Who, or how many, had he left behind to grieve? I was grateful my father never had to go into the army since his childhood bout with polio had left him with a thin leg and a lifetime limp.

Sketch of Army and Navy Store with United Cigar Store on corner, where I bought most of my comic books (circa 1940; sketch courtesy of William Argan)

The Army and Navy Store had an in-house detective whose name was Mr. Spiers. I naively asked him one day if he carried a gun. He told me he had a handgun at home but didn't usually carry it when he was at work. I asked him if he could bring it sometime and show it to me. He said he would but never did, until I pestered him so much that finally one day he brought it in and, in a secluded corner of the store, showed it to me. I was very excited and wanted to hold it, but he refused to let me touch it. My disappointment was palpable.

Many years later I did finally get to not only touch a gun but actually fire it, a story that I'll relate further on.

Let me mention another item pertaining to guns. We were always proud to think of Regina as the home of the Royal Canadian Mounted Police (sometimes referred to as the Force), since all their training was done there. Their barracks were located on West Dewdney Avenue, and on many occasions, I went there to visit their museum, which displayed a vast array of weapons, including a Gatling gun. I would spend hours poring over every piece of military equipment, each of which had some kind of history pertinent to the development of Canada. There were other artifacts of interest, such as the nooses with which certain individuals were hung, including Louis Riel, and the Mountie hat of a constable killed in the Regina riots of 1935, with the crease where he was struck still intact. Each time I went to the museum, I discovered something new. Although I never seriously considered it, the thought of becoming a member of the Force always had a certain romantic appeal, perhaps in part because when the Mountie band came to play annually at my high school, the female students went wild.

Although my gunplay was confined to my imagination, there were real, if subtle, battles to be fought in Regina. The east end of the city was, in a sense, a small Jewish ghetto, and as Jews we were often easily identified. Our neighbourhood was unlike many of the ghettos of Europe, in that we were not secluded or confined within a particular section of the city, nor were there walls to enclose our activities. Officially, there were no restrictions on where we could work or study, but I was not aware of any Jewish politicians or bankers in Regina at that time, or of any Jewish teachers in the public school system. We lived among non-Jews, many of them our neighbours and our friends (my dad's best friend, Frank Schmidt, was Catholic) and some our enemies, singling us out for derision and physical attacks. On my street there were several Jewish families, and the same applied to the surrounding streets, extending for several blocks in all directions. We had one synagogue for the entire community, originally located in the twentieth block of Ottawa Street. It was called Beth Jacob (House of Jacob), and it existed until about 1943, when the property was sold and everything moved over to the Hebrew School building on

Top: Royal Canadian Mounted Police Barracks, museum in building on left (courtesy Saskatchewan Archives Board)
Above: Back view of the original Beth Jacob Synagogue on twentieth block of Ottawa Street, west side (circa 1930; courtesy Saskatchewan Archives Board and Beth Jacob Synagogue)

Halifax Street. This was where I had my *bar mitzvah* in 1948. The death of my grandfather a few months earlier cast a shadow over this event; I was his first grandchild, and he had very much looked forward to being present. Two years later, a new synagogue was completed and stood until about 1990, when a donor gave a large sum of money toward the purchase of another property for the community's religious needs.

My bond with Judaism was deepened at an early age by the synagogue and Hebrew school and by my membership in the Jewish youth movement known as Young Judaea. One of the projects of Young Judaea in Regina was to collect money from Jewish residents to fund tree-planting and other activities in Israel; the goal was to reclaim that arid land and make the desert bloom. The vehicle through which this was done was known as the Jewish National Fund (JNF). Almost every home in the community had a small blue and white tin box called a *pishke*, designed like a piggy bank with a slot at one end and a locked opening at the other. It was expected, and considered a *mitzvah* (good deed), that every household would put spare change in the box regularly, and the boxes were often full when we arrived. As collectors, we were each provided with a key, and approximately once a month, in rain, shine, blizzard, or gale, a team of Young Judaeans spread out across the city to collect the money and send it to Israel. We looked upon this as a sacred task, one undertaken by Jews all over the world decades before Israel was declared a nation in 1948. Today there are JNF forests and other projects throughout Israel, bought and sustained by money collected not only from *pishkas* but through a variety of other programs.

As evidence of our dedication to Israel and the Jewish National Fund, I include the following excerpt from our Judaean news bulletin, *Din V'Chashban* (Judgment and Accountability). It's an editorial from around 1953:

J.N.F. CHAIRMAN — STAN SUNSHINE

The last collection, which was partial, brought in $79.58, and also the checking at the Yom Kippur dance netted $17.60. We quote Stan Sunshine [a good friend of mine]: "If Regina can get out enough collection and really put our hearts into the job, we've got a great chance of winning the J.N.F. award for Western Canada. Fort William won the award last year and it would be a feather in our hat if we won it this year."

As I perused old papers and keepsakes for these memoirs, I was taken aback by the draft of an article I wrote around 1951, when I was sixteen, addressed to Beth Jacob's congregation and intended for the monthly newsletter. I had to sit for a while and try to decide if I wanted to include it here, as I felt embarrassed reading it, but then I thought, "I didn't realize my passion for Judaism was that strong at such an early age." I would ask the reader to forgive my youthful exuberance and unmitigated chutzpah. In retrospect, I can recognize the seeds of a rabbi in the making—fire, brimstone, and all. And perhaps I was an angry young man.

DON'T READ THIS

You saw the title. It said, "Don't Read This"—unless you want to be ashamed of yourself.

I walked into the synagogue the other night, a bit late for the *Oneg Shabbat* [celebration of the Sabbath] and expected to see a multitude of people there, attentively listening to the rabbi. Why a multitude of people? Well, it was the last night of Chanukah and a large turnout is naturally expected. Before entering the *shul* [synagogue] from the Memorial Chamber, I happened to look through the small window in the door and I could see the rabbi on the platform and beside him eight Chanukah lights proudly radiating the spirit of Chanukah. It was indeed a beautiful and meaningful sight.

I opened the door and walked in. My heart sank! I couldn't believe what I saw. The *shul* was almost empty. You couldn't count the people twice on your fingers and toes. There sat 37 members of our community. Thirty-seven people at an Oneg Shabbat commemorating the final day of Chanukah? "Surely," I thought, "this must be some joke. Perhaps everyone else is a little late. Certainly they will be here shortly." But, no one came. The doors at the back of the *shul* did not open until the people opened them to leave.

The rabbi preached his sermon to 37 people. There were twice as many rows of seats in the *shul* as there were people. I couldn't understand it.

I left the *shul* feeling thoroughly ashamed of myself and of my Jewish community, a community I was so proud of, a community I boasted about to my friends when I went on my summer vacations. I told them of the magnificent synagogue we had built and of how proud we all were of it and ourselves. Proud of ourselves? We should be ashamed of ourselves! We aren't worthy of such a synagogue! We don't do it justice! Better we should sell it! At least we'll know then that those who buy it will make better use of it no matter what they use it for. It would be highly impossible to make any less use of it.

A few weeks ago, a group of gentiles from one of the churches here in Regina asked me if they could come down some Friday night and watch our Sabbath services. I told them that as far as I could see, it would be perfectly all right. I'm sorry I said that! I hope they never come! If they do, I'll never be able to look one of them straight in the eyes again, because I know that if they come, there will be more Christians in our synagogue than there will be Jews. I'm sure they would laugh to themselves when they heard us sing *Shabbat Shalom* [Sabbath Peace]. The tiny tots we all heard sing at the Chanukah concert could more than drown out the meek congregation present on December 19th. Those that don't know the song don't sing; not that I blame them. But, why not hum? Is the tune so difficult? And those of you who do know the words, are you afraid of making fools of yourselves by raising your voices? Surely they're not that bad!

In closing I would just like to pose one question. Answer it to yourselves!

Is it too much to ask that you devote one hour a week to your religion?

A member of your humble community

A few days after submitting this article for publication to the secretary at the synagogue, I received a call that the rabbi wanted to see me. Our rabbi at that time was Avraham Hartstein, a conservatively dressed, somewhat dour-looking man whom I liked very much. Rabbi Hartstein began by telling me that he appreciated the sentiments expressed in my article, but he felt it was a little too strong and harsh. Would I consider either rewriting it in a different tone or withdrawing it from publication? He also told me that an article published in the congregational bulletin could not be published anonymously. My name would have to be there. I don't recall everything he said, but I do remember that he was very respectful of me and spoke softly. Nor do I recall whether the article ever got published in any form. I don't think so. But I do remember clearly our interaction that day, and how a wise and gentle man assuaged my angry feelings with skill and sensitivity, giving me perspective. The qualities he displayed that day are ones I try to emulate in my own rabbinate, and I hope that at times I am successful.

At this time in my life, about five years after the end of the Second World War, the early photos of the Holocaust began to appear. I recall staring at them in disbelief, not able to comprehend the inhumanity they portrayed. Over the succeeding years, as more evidence of the Nazi scourge emerged and survivors began coming to Regina, the reality of what had happened set in. The impact of the Holocaust on me has been profound. Although I occasionally attend Holocaust remembrance events, more often I stay away, as I have difficulty coping with the pain they bring me. I believe strongly that to forget the Holocaust is to invite it to happen again.

In 1951, my involvement in Young Judaea brought me the opportunity to attend a camp on Otty Lake near Perth, Ontario. It was the first training institute for Young Judaean leaders in Canada and was called Biluim, after a group of Jewish pioneers from Russia who went to Palestine (now Israel) in 1881. I was sent to the camp for two months, with the hopes that when I returned to Regina I would organize and breathe new life into our then-moribund Young Judaean group. It was a task I found daunting, but I was excited at the chance to do something for a movement that had given me so much. With the help of friends back in Regina, I believe I made a positive contribution, as this excerpt from our national Judaean paper attests:

REGINA DESIGNATED AS BEST *MACHANEH* [GROUP] OF THE MONTH

Two years ago, the National Executive, in its discussion of Western Yehuda Hatzair [Western Young Judaea] was gravely concerned with the state of affairs in Regina Young Judaea. What was once a flourishing *machaneh* now lacked even the barest resemblance of the once proud centre. Regina was, to tell the truth, a *machaneh* which had disintegrated. It lacked leadership, activity and *chaverim* [members]. No wonder, then, that things seemed quite hopeless. In fact, Regina was about given up until a great event in Canadian Yehuda Hatzair occurred. This was the advent of the National Leadership Training Institute.

To the first Institute came one *chaver* [friend, member] — Jerry Steinberg. He participated enthusiastically in the program and was determined to do something about Regina's inactivity upon his return to that *machaneh*. To say that Jerry did something is to say the least. For last year, Regina became one of the foremost *machanot* [groups] in the west. Recognizing the importance of good leadership for the future, four Regina *chaverim* attended the Leadership Institute this past summer [1952]. They too have returned with a great deal of enthusiasm, and today Regina is a hotbed of Judaean activities. Its membership today is near 100...It is because of all these factors that we have chosen Regina Yehuda Hatzair as the outstanding *machaneh* of this month.

In those days being a Jew in Regina had its difficulties. I went to Thomson Public School from kindergarten to grade eight; between Thomson and Wetmore schools, there were about seventeen Jewish boys my age and in my grade (and one Jewish girl, whom we all thought of as "one of the guys," although she later married one of the guys). When it came to defending our faith in the face of anti-Semitism, most of us were not much for fighting. The terms "Dirty Jew" and "Christ Killer" were sometimes hurled at us by peers who were eager to beat us up, and often did. I was the only one in our group who would fight, and I received and gave more than one bloody nose. Say the words "Dirty Jew," and I was all over you. My grandparents and parents were

Jerry on the front step of Thomson School (circa 1970)

beside themselves trying to keep me from fighting, yet secretly, I knew my dad was proud that I wouldn't let anyone, especially an anti-Semite, push me around. My mother went along with my dad but didn't say much.

Anti-Semitism wasn't limited to the students who attended Thomson School; it was also prevalent among the teachers. When I was in grade three, the Jewish High Holidays fell mid-week, which meant that all the Jewish kids were absent and attending religious services. It so happened that our teacher scheduled an exam for the day after the holidays, knowing full well we wouldn't be able to prepare for it. When we walked into class and found out we were about to have an exam, we complained that it wasn't fair, whereupon she took two of the Jewish boys out in the hall and strapped them. I was third in line. When she raised the strap and told me to stick out my hand, I did, but I quickly withdrew it just before she struck, so that she hit her own thigh. Enraged, she took me to the principal, Mr. Howe, who, to his credit, listened patiently to my story and did nothing to punish me. Later, the Jewish community raised the issue with the school board, and there were no further instances of this kind at Thomson School, at least not while I was there. I presume something was said to my teacher, as thereafter she was very careful in her manner toward her Jewish students.

The Catholics, like the Jews, were to a certain extent marginalized in Regina. Their elementary school, St. Joseph's, was directly across the street from ours, but very seldom was there any interaction between the two. In those days, interfaith activities were for the most part unheard of, except in a negative sense. So it was that the Jews and the Protestants (everyone at Thomson who was not Jewish) fought together side by side against the Catholics in what became an annual event. Every winter, on a day when the snow was abundant and sticky, a snowball fight broke out between our two schools. It raged on for maybe a half hour, with snowballs flying in both directions and occasional forays across the street by both sides to get a better shot at their opponents. No one was ever hurt, and both schools always claimed victory. The fight only ended when the principal or teachers from one school or the other, sometimes both at the same time, came out and laid down the law. Then, full of joy and camaraderie, Jew and Protestant marched back to class, there being no longer any religious distinction. Those who fight together, unite together.

A development at Thomson initiated a broader religious rapprochement, which included the Catholic students. A student traffic-control program was implemented on an experimental basis by the school board and the city. Older students were trained to help younger students safely cross at traffic-heavy street corners on their way to and from school. I volunteered for the program and, after some simple but careful instruction, was given a white belt and diagonal shoulder strap and told to monitor the southeast corner of Victoria Avenue and Toronto Street. My fellow traffic controllers and I had to arrive early in the morning; then, as students came to school, we would stop cars and usher the students across the street. Once a group had crossed, we would give the proper hand signal to wave the autos on. We were back on duty at the beginning and end of each lunch hour, and once more when school was out for the day. I recall that I and the other volunteers were very proud to have been selected. The white belt and shoulder strap gave us a feeling of authority. "Wow," some of us thought, "to actually be able to stop cars, and then feel good about contributing to the safety of our fellow students!" But it went beyond this. Since St. Joseph's was so close by, its students also had to cross the streets we patrolled. The common good did not differentiate between religions. A subtle, unrecognized act of interfaith co-operation played out between our two schools, making it obvious that even with religious trappings, kids were still kids. I don't recall, but it's possible that St. Joseph's kids were also patrollers and ushered Thomson students across the streets closer to their school.

Even at Christmas, there was a blending of the faiths at Thomson. Beginning in early December, when the bell rang at 9:00 a.m., everyone gathered in the hall to say the Lord's Prayer (we thought it was from the Old Testament) and sing Christmas carols. Even though this was a dubious activity for Jews, and certainly not encouraged by our parents and Hebrew teachers, there we were, a minority among a very large majority, engulfed by these wonderful melodies and joyous words, caught up in their fervour and rhythm;

how could we be expected to abstain? So we figured out a way to participate in the singsong and at the same time be true to Judaism. First, we would sing in full all those carols where the word "Jesus" was not mentioned, such as "Jingle Bells" or "Good King Wenceslas." When it came to a carol with Jesus' name in it or a reference to him, we would sing the carol but remain silent when that part occurred, exchanging knowing glances with each other. I always wondered what it must have looked or sounded like to a non-Jewish student watching us and listening in — "Hark the herald angels sing [silence]. Peace on earth and mercy mild, God and sinners reconciled" (that part could be Jewish).

In the autumn of 1947, my parents moved from 1819 Ottawa Street, where we had been living with my grandparents, to the Elgin Apartments in the west end of the city. The building was owned by my father's employer, Charlie Glassman of Ideal Men's Wear on South Railway Street. Mr. Glassman must have given my dad a very generous deal, as the men liked one another and got along well in the business. So the move was economically a good one for my parents, although it put them at a considerably longer distance from work. (From 1819 Ottawa Street, both my parents could walk to work.) From the Elgin Apartments they had to get a ride with someone, drive, or take the streetcar. That problem they were able to deal with. The difficult part for me was that I had to change schools. I couldn't see my friends or have lunch at my grandmother's and I was very lonely. My mother would frequently, during her lunch break at the Army and Navy Store, come home to make me lunch or take me out somewhere for a bite. This helped, and seemed to work fine for a while, until a more serious problem arose.

I was enrolled at Victoria School, about a ten-minute walk from our apartment. It was a very old school and had a round, fully enclosed chute down which one would slide in the event of a fire. I remember almost wishing for a fire, or at least a fire drill, so I could go for a ride. Otherwise, the building was pretty normal, but not as new and elegant as I remember Thomson to be.

My classmates at first seemed pretty average, although I did from time to time receive odd stares from some of the boys. I didn't think much of it, although it made me a bit uncomfortable. Then one day, during recess, a classmate walked up to me, all the while looking straight into my eyes, and with great force lifted his knee into my testicles. I collapsed onto the pavement, writhing in unbearable agony. He casually walked away, muttering something about me being Jewish. When I eventually recovered and went to the boys' room to inspect my privates, I found I was bleeding. That evening I told my father and showed him the damage, whereupon I was taken to our family doctor, Sam Kraminsky. My father spoke to the principal, Mr.

Wilkinson, who tried to discipline the student, but to no avail, as a few weeks later the incident was repeated by the same boy. Then another of my classmates, a friend of the first boy, did the same thing to me. After repeated talks with the principal, who seemed unable to effect any change in the perpetrators' behaviour, my parents decided that my well-being, if not my life, was in danger, and moved back to 1819 Ottawa Street.

> You hurt me
> badly
> when you kicked me
> in the balls
> lifting your knee
> like an anvil
> crushing me
> in more ways
> than you could ever imagine
> locking rage
> into my groin
> that remains
> like bullets
> on a frozen hair-trigger
> and all because
> I'm a Jew
> no other reason
> one day
> should we ever meet again
> I may kill you

As I later learned, I was the only Jewish kid ever to attend Victoria School. The odd looks I received were from students who had never knowingly seen a Jew and who, at home, had been brainwashed into believing that we were physically different and, more important, we had killed Christ. It seemed that perceiving one who had slain their Lord justified reprisal, even if it was 2,000 years later. To this day I relive those beatings, wondering what I could have done to protect myself and how I could have fought back—if not at the moment, when I was caught by surprise, then later in retaliation. The truth is I was afraid. The boy in question was the school bully. He was older, bigger, meaner, and tougher than anyone else. To boot, he led a gang that did his bidding. I don't think I would have stood a chance against him, and somehow I knew it. Still, I chide myself for not trying, even if it would have meant getting beaten up. In my imagination, through the years, I have won many victories over my assailant, but the soul scars remain. My grandfather bore similar scars; on a number of occasions I woke to his screams, caused by nightmares about his anti-Semitic encounters in Romania.

Moving back to Thomson School was a blessing in more ways than I could have imagined. I was reunited with my friends, anti-Semitism was light, I could handle my adversaries, the teachers treated me well, and I liked the new principal, Mr. Drury. I also, by the way, liked the former principal, Mr. Howe, a very gentle and fair man. And I was back with my grandparents, who showered me with love and little favors.

But one blessing emerged that took me by surprise.

It was the tradition at Thomson, like other schools in Regina, to have a field day every spring. This consisted of various competitive events such as baseball, track and field, novelty races like jumping in a sack, three-legged races, and everyone's favourite, the wheelbarrow race. I entered many of the events and achieved only moderate success. Then came the hundred-yard dash. There were two runners favoured to win, as they had shown their prowess in former years. I hoped to come in a distant third, if I placed at all. About two-thirds of the way through the race, I found myself neck and neck with the favourites and still felt I had speed in reserve. So I turned it on and won the race. This was a pivotal point in my life: I had dug down deep into myself, and against the prevailing odds, succeeded in doing something I didn't think was possible. At that moment an athlete was born. In the ensuing years, I won many races and played many sports with distinction, including hockey, football, soccer, and of course track and field; in my last two years at Central Collegiate Institute, I won the overall track and field championships. But more than this, by accomplishing what I previously thought was impossible, I unknowingly laid the foundation for unusual spiritual experiences in later years that I would never have thought possible or even imaginable.

Also, as a young man, I took up boxing at the Regina police gym and wrestling at the YMCA. I was once slated to wrestle on a preliminary card before a professional wrestling match, but my opponent didn't show up. I was allowed to stay and watch Earl McCready and Whipper Billy Watson, in my opinion two of the best world-class wrestlers of their time, though Lou Thesz was touted as the world champion and had a fancy belt to prove it. This was when wrestling was real, not the Hollywood production it is today (except in the Olympics).

I found hockey a most exciting and rewarding sport. Not being a very good skater (I never seemed to be able to tie my laces tight enough), I ended up in goal. I had a good sense of where to be between the pipes when someone took a shot at me and was adept at poke-checking any player who came near my crease. Still, I let in my share of pucks and always marvelled at the skill of certain forwards who could pick a corner when I was sure I had it covered.

Initially, I played on outdoor rinks in school leagues. The games always took place either right after school or in the early evening. Our motto was "the show must go on," and go on it did, even when to a non-player's eye it should have been cancelled. I refer here to the weather. In Regina, the temperature dips in the winter to what some consider unbelievable lows. As hockey players, we were expected to show up no matter how cold it was. However, there was a point of cancellation — when the Fahrenheit thermometer dropped to thirty degrees below. But at minus twenty-nine degrees we still played, and once the game started there was no turning back, no matter how much colder it became. These numbers don't include the wind-chill factor, which in my hockey days we had never even heard of. Many a night after a game my feet were completely frozen, and I walked home not feeling anything below my ankles. This was a scary experience, not because I minded having frozen feet, but the anticipation of the thawing process was daunting. Once home and in bare feet, I awaited the inevitable slow thaw that, at its peak, felt like a million needles going through my flesh and bones.

It will come, then, as no surprise that when I graduated to the bantam level of hockey, which was conducted as a league across the province, I breathed a sigh of relief — these games were played indoors, where the controlled temperature rarely dipped below a balmy minus ten degrees Fahrenheit. Also, for the first time I had quality goalie pads, which I loved. They protected me well, they looked good, they covered the five-hole properly, and they were made of real leather. I used to smell them before each game, and sometimes after as well. (I have a keen sense of smell, which would come into play in a spiritual context much later.) For a while I thought I was on track for the NHL, given my success and the men who came to watch us play. Their comments were encouraging, and I presumed that among them were scouts for the professional teams, although I never knew this for sure. However, fate intervened.

Although I was playing regularly indoors, I still occasionally played outdoors in the school league. Once, while playing at night in the northwest end of the city, I got hit in the eye with a puck. The outdoor rinks were illuminated by several strings of lights suspended overhead, but above the lights nothing could be seen except the black night. An opposing player lifted the puck above the lights, where it disappeared. I was without a mask — these weren't fully accepted, and you were considered a chicken if you wore one. Also, those were the days before the slapshot. The puck descended and caught me below the left eye. I don't remember the impact, only that I found myself on my knees with a pool of blood on the ice in front of me. I was taken to the emergency ward at the Grey Nuns hospital. While the intern was stitching me up, a nurse came in and told me there was a phone call from my parents. They insisted on speaking to me, and I had to get off the table and answer the phone at the nursing station. One of my teammates, Laurie Schmidt, feeling quite correctly that my parents should know what had occurred, had dropped by our house and told them, "Jerry got hit in the eye with a puck and is in the hospital." I went to the phone, needle and thread dangling from my upper cheekbone, and assured my parents I hadn't lost an eye or suffered a concussion. Returning to school the next day with my eye well bandaged, I was some kind of hero, but not to my parents. I never played hockey again. (Besides, as my grandparents would say, "It's not for a Jewish boy!")

At Thomson there were days of awakening in other respects besides sports, as I found myself developing one crush after another on a variety of girls. However, in spite of lavish romantic notions, I never got beyond the crush stage, not daring to express my feelings to any of the girls, and not even knowing what I would say if the opportunity arose, which never happened. The closest I ever came was at birthday parties where we would play post office and spin the bottle, games involving hugs and kisses, under parental supervision (more or less).

Although, as mentioned, there were seventeen Jewish boys my age in Thompson School and only one Jewish girl (although there were other Jewish girls both younger and older, and later, in high school, a difference of a year or two wouldn't matter as much), it was frowned upon for us to spend time — especially alone — with non-Jewish girls. So we were pleasantly surprised when an influx of young Jewish women suddenly came our way with the Winnipeg flood of 1950. Winnipeg had the third-largest Jewish community in Canada, so when the flood inundated a good part of the city, many Jewish families came to Regina and stayed with relatives or friends until they could return home. As a result, for a brief time we had Jewish girls to talk to and spend time with, but alas, not for long.

The other way in which we socialized with the opposite sex within the Jewish realm was through Young Judaea. Judaean centres existed in every major city across the country and in some of the larger towns. When I was a little older, there was an annual regional convention, and in my last two years of high school, I was president of the western region, which stretched from Manitoba to British Columbia. At the conventions, besides dealing with pertinent issues involving the organization, Israel, and Jewish history, we socialized into the wee hours — folk dancing and slow dancing, singing Jewish songs, and, where and when it was possible, necking. It was always difficult when the conventions came to an end after three or four days, and we had to return to our homes and, in Regina's case, the near-total absence of age-appropriate Jewish females.

Our other social outlet was the Jewish camp. There were several such camps scattered across the country. In Saskatchewan we met at Camp Kevutza, which I believe was near a place called Sandy Beach. We lived in sparse, even crude, conditions but didn't really care, because we had such a good time for the two weeks we were there. My aunt Molly, who lived near us in Regina, was the camp cook, and we never lacked for tasty victuals.

It was at camp that I learned a new word — "spirit." Our counsellors would always be saying "That's the spirit!" whenever anyone did something with determination and enthusiasm. This puzzled me. I kept looking around for something called a "spirit" to appear, not knowing exactly what that might be. When I inquired about the word, it was defined by words I thought I understood but really didn't. For years I struggled with the term, but for some reason I couldn't grasp the concept; I was always looking for an entity to appear. Not until my mid-teens did I get it. And little did I know then that the word, according to my original understanding, was to play a major role in my later thinking and views on spirituality, religion, and reality.

There was another word I had just as much trouble understanding. My dad's brother, Jay, had a small rubber toy ambulance that I used to play with whenever we visited him in his home at 914 15th Avenue. I became very attached to it and one day asked him if I could have it. He replied in a soft and gentle manner that he couldn't give it to me because it had sentiment. I looked all over and under the car but could see nothing unusual. I asked him where the sentiment was. He tried to explain it to me, but I never understood. Whenever I played with the car after that, I would ask him to show me the sentiment. He always got a big kick out of this and would wink at my father. In later years, both men smiled whenever we reminisced over this topic.

One evening, I was with my father at my uncle Jay's home. Jay's daughter, Lynn, was there, asleep, but his wife, my aunt Ida, was out. He heard a noise coming from the cellar. Very quickly and quietly, he went to the bedroom and returned a moment later, carrying a revolver and several bullets.

Interior of Army and Navy Store. From left to right, my uncle Jay, Harry Gold, and Lou Lazarus

He loaded the bullets into the gun chamber and went to the door leading to the cellar, with my dad and I right behind him. He opened the door slowly, crouched, pointed the gun downwards, and said in a firm, strong voice, "I know you're there. Come out with your hands up!" He repeated this two or three times while my father and I strained to see what was going to happen, almost climbing onto his back. No one appeared, and nothing happened. We never did hear the story of how he came to possess a handgun, nor would he let me touch it as I stood mesmerized by its presence.

At Thomson School, two more events were to have an impact on my life.

In grade two, I became very ill with a nervous disorder that was never clearly diagnosed but that put me in bed for a few months and made me miss much of my school year. As a result, I had to repeat grade two, which meant I was in a class full of students who were new to me, a few of whom became lifelong friends. It also meant I was always a year older than most of my classmates. This bothered me at first but later it didn't seem to matter at all. The nervous disorder affected my speech, and throughout elementary school, I had a pronounced stutter, traces of which stayed with me into high school and university. Eventually I overcame it, although even today I sometimes catch myself repeating words when repetition is not called for.

The other significant event occurred in grade four. My favourite teacher at Thomson School was Dorothy Graham. She was Scottish, and with her began my lifelong romance with Scottish people that endures to the present day. (For some reason, I always get along well with Scots, and I attribute this in part to Miss Graham's presence in my life.) She had a beautiful voice and was in charge of the school choir, which met regularly to sing and rehearse for various events. Because everyone in our class had to participate, I made it into this august group despite the fact that I sang off-key and threw everyone around me off-key. Miss Graham was patient with me, but finally saw that she had to do something about the situation or the choir would never be ready for its performance. She asked me to please not sing, only move my lips so it would appear I was singing. This way, I would look like a fully participating choir member without affecting the others. To a certain extent this hurt my ego, but my voice was my voice, and for the good of the majority, I had to remain silent. So, why did I like Miss Graham so much? Well, she was always positive about everything I did and would compliment me at every opportunity. Once, when we were singing in class together, Miss Graham, bending her ear to hear each student as she walked the aisles between the desks, drew near me, listened, and exclaimed, "Gerald, that's wonderful!" She had caught me on key. That was such a boost to my ego that I couldn't stop singing wherever I went and nearly drove everyone at home crazy. Eventually I settled down. To this day, I sing "Comin' Thru the Rye" (Miss Graham's favourite song) with a Scottish brogue. About thirty years later, when visiting Regina, I looked up Miss Graham and took her to lunch, where I thanked her for the care and support she gave me as a child.

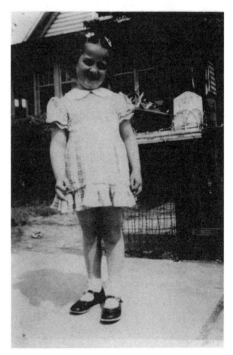

Most of the time I still sing off-key, but in November of 2009, I attended the biennial conference of the Union for Reform Judaism in Toronto, and after a singsong, someone came up to me and asked me if I was a cantor. I almost fell off of my chair. This was the highest compliment I could ever receive regarding my singing. I guess it was one of those rare occasions when, again, I was on key. Miss Graham would have been proud of me.

Around the time that I was in Miss Graham's choir, I acquired a sister. She was actually my first cousin. When her father suddenly died, she and her mother (my mother's sister) moved in with us at 1819 Ottawa Street. We lived together for ten years, went through

Linda at about five years of age, in front of 1819 Ottawa Street

all the machinations that befuddle young siblings, and developed a close relationship that remains so to this day. Linda is now a lawyer practising in Roswell, Georgia, near Atlanta. We see each other every few years and speak frequently on the phone. Her passion is Toronto cheese bagels, which are unknown in Georgia, so I bring some down to her whenever I visit. This is not a criticism of Georgia; grits are foreign to Ontario.

In Regina, Central Collegiate Institute was the high school you attended if you wanted to pursue a profession; Balfour Technical School was where you went to learn a trade. I never knew of any Jewish boy or girl who wanted to learn a trade, although I did give passing thought to attending Balfour, since to me there was something appealing about knowing how to work with your hands. However, I had my sights on medicine, and Central Collegiate was at that time the ticket for getting into pre-med at university.

I don't think my high school was much different from most other high schools. I know we had a good reputation for academics and for some sports, although I don't recall much fame in the latter category, despite the fact that we had some fine athletes, like the Montgomery brothers, Jerry and Skip. I was not at their level, though I enjoyed some prowess in track and field. I also played football, baseball, and basketball and rounded out my athletic career by being a weekly sports reporter for the Regina high schools on radio station CKRM. My other involvements at Central Collegiate were drama, musicals, and oratorical contests, where I won a regional championship on the topic, "This Atomic Age." I never made it to the nationals.

My children, Meher and Dahlia, in front of Central Collegiate (circa 1988)

There were many good teachers at Central Collegiate, and in particular I enjoyed Mr. Smith, who taught English. He was an unflappable gentleman who knew how to deal with rebels and quickly extract their sting by talking to them as if they were small children. Something I didn't discover until later was his inability to understand religions other than Christianity. In a conversation with him at his home, where he invited me one day (I probably engineered the invitation), he said he couldn't comprehend why somebody wouldn't accept Jesus as his saviour. He argued his case, and I argued mine, but in the end neither of us got through to the other. This encounter left me perplexed, as it was beyond me how anyone, especially a highly intelligent and sensitive man like Mr. Smith, could expect a Jew to see Jesus as anything other than a fellow religionist who rebelled against the status quo of his time, as did almost all of the biblical prophets. This was not the last time I was to debate this issue with Christians, often with the same result. However, my talk with Mr. Smith did stimulate my interest in Christianity, so I endeavoured to learn more. Over the ensuing years I met with evangelists, Baptists, and Catholic priests, and visited several churches and monasteries.

Also during my high school years, I made a vow that each night, before going to sleep, I would read (in English) one chapter from the Hebrew Scriptures until I had covered the entire work. This is the inscription I wrote on the flyleaf:

> On this day, May 8, 1953, I, Jerry Steinberg, did begin this book, and each day until I have completed it will I read at least one chapter.
>
> I only pray to God, that from this book may I receive wisdom, foresight and strength in my convictions. Amen.

I, of course, did not realize at the time that was a prophetic prayer, and that one day I would not only read the bible again many times, but study it in depth and in Hebrew.

Regina seemed to me to be a haven for evangelists. Hardly a week passed when there weren't flyers posted announcing an upcoming visit from a preacher, usually from south of the border. I decided one day to go to one of these and hear what the preacher had to say. The event took place in a packed hall downtown, and after the talk I introduced myself to the speaker, letting him know I was Jewish. We then spent the next couple of hours talking over coffee in a restaurant. This scenario, with different preachers, was repeated several times over the next two or three years. They always wanted to talk to me. I realized later that the attraction was probably because I was Jewish, and if they could convince me to become a Christian, it would be a real coup. A few tried, but for the most part they were respectful and didn't push their case. Years later, when reflecting upon why I was attracted to evangelical meetings, I realized that I was fascinated by the strength of their convictions. For these men, there was no doubt that God existed, and they knew this from personal experience. "Personal experience?" I wanted to know God from personal experience too, not Jesus, just God. They inspired me. What was more, they weren't afraid to talk about God, something Jews seldom did, except at religious services where everything was rote. But to actually speak of God as part of a conversation or sermon, without anyone wondering if you were going over the deep end, was new for me, and kindled a desire to find God in my own personal way. The journey since then has been exciting — at times frustrating, at times joyous, but always, at the end of the day, rewarding.

At Central Collegiate, a very special young man came into my life. His name was Hervey Segall. As the name denotes, he was Jewish, and had moved to Regina with his parents and sister from one of the smaller Saskatchewan towns. His mother was a teacher, so in his family there was a healthy respect for education. Hervey and I hit it off right away. In a sense, I was his bigger brother — not older, only bigger, as Hervey was short. He had a great sense of humour and was mischievous, which appealed to me and which at times tickled me to no end. But Hervey had one big problem: he wouldn't study. His parents were beside themselves because Hervey wasn't getting the grades they felt he was capable of. And they were right. The kid was brilliant but lazy. Jerry to the rescue: I had nowhere near Hervey's grey matter, but I did know how to study. So, with the agreement of his parents, I became Hervey's study buddy, and I was free to pursue by any means the goal of putting Hervey into the upper echelons of academia. My method was simple: Hervey, in spite of his small stature, had a voracious appetite. So the deal was that Hervey couldn't eat dinner until he had completed to my satisfaction (I tested him) a designated amount of material on a particular subject, be it English or biology, etc. Then he couldn't have dessert until another designated section was mastered, and so on with in-between snacks. It worked. He far exceeded me in his grades, becoming a straight-A student while I lingered in the middle and high Bs with an occasional A. His parents were delighted and grateful.

As I've said, Hervey was also mischievous.

Scotty Fife was our grade 12 English teacher. In his own right, he was a character, a delightful one, with a good eye for the unusual along with a healthy Scottish brogue with which he taught us Chaucer. (Ask me some day to recite the first few lines from the "Prologue.") Now, for some reason, he took to Hervey, which leads me to the other side of my friend.

The classrooms at Central were all equipped with desks that had tops you could lift open. Inside we stored our books, lunches, etc. Each desktop had an opening to hold a small bottle of writing ink. (Ballpoint pens were just making an appearance, but were not yet standard. Also, some teachers did not appreciate the way ballpoints wrote, and insisted on pen and ink.) I sat at the desk immediately behind Hervey. One day, while Mr. Fife was waxing eloquent on Wordsworth or Shelley, I noticed that smoke was beginning to rise through the empty inkwell hole on Hervey's desk. Gradually more and thicker smoke escaped and, as it came out, Hervey passed a handkerchief through it at quick intervals. He was sending smoke signals from a fire smouldering in his desk. Mr. Fife, upon noticing the spectacle, turned red and unceremoniously ushered Hervey out of the room, leaving him standing in the hall until the class was over. I don't recall any serious repercussions to my friend, and Mr. Fife seemed to get over the incident rather quickly. I can't say the same for the desk.

But this is not the end of the story. While visiting Regina many years later, I decided to look up Mr. Fife in the telephone directory. I called, told him I was a former student, and he invited me over. As hard as he tried, he couldn't place me, but when I mentioned the name "Hervey," his eyes lit up, and for the rest of our visit we discussed the "rascal," as he put it.

My time at Central Collegiate was a time of raging hormones, and I can't think of one student, male or female, for whom this was not the case. Going steady, wearing a pin or a ring, or, for the girls, walking around in a boyfriend's jacket, was the norm. While high school brought many new feminine faces, the Jewish quota remained steady, except for one new girl from out of town. So we started dating non-Jewish girls, with or without our parents' approval. The big event, whether at school or at someone's house, was slow dancing. Here everyone had sanction to get close and actually feel, touch, and smell the opposite sex. It was ecstasy when there was a mutual liking, and torture when there wasn't, since not every dance involved a choice. For example, during a bingo dance, the master of ceremonies would call out "Bingo!" every minute or so, whereupon each couple had to split up and form new pairs.

The other venue for getting to know the opposite sex on a more personal basis was the family car, especially the back seat. When a good buddy was driving, and you were with a girl in the back, and she refused to budge away from the door, a small code word — "C.O.D." ("Come Over, Dearie") — would alert the driver to the situation. He would then make a fast, sharp turn, leaving centrifugal force to do the rest. Problem solved. Sometimes.

Graduation at Central Collegiate was a gala affair. My date, Betty-Anne Pressman from Weyburn, was stunning, and I was proud to have her on my arm. The occasion was bittersweet, however, as we were all going off in different directions, and nobody knew when they would see their friends again. And so it was.

Much later, on a roots trip (to be discussed more fully further on), I took my children, Meher and Dahlia, to visit Thomson School and Central Collegiate. By that time, my alma mater was being torn down to make way for some kind of construction project. We snuck past barriers, ignored the demolition danger signs, and again I walked the halls. It was sad to see the grand old lady being laid to rest.

One other fond but strange memory comes to mind. The field next to the southeast corner of the eighteen-block Ottawa Street, where I lived and which I often crossed to get to Thomson School on the other side, was called Earl Grey Park, though it was hardly a park. At the far end, bordering Victoria Avenue, was a row of houses. The rest was empty space, where in the winter we had a skating rink, when the city got around to making ice. It was also used as a place to dump snow, so for months we had huge mounds of snow where often I and others played. But these are the secondary memories of Earl Grey Park. The primary one is of Willie.

I've heard it said that every village has its idiot. At first glance, this seemed to be Willie's role. I first encountered him when I was a young boy, walking diagonally through Earl Grey Park on my way to school. Coming toward me was a tall, slim and lanky man, perhaps in his twenties, though no one ever knew for sure his age. He walked briskly, taking long strides, and he sang and yodelled as he walked. I tried to say hello a few times when we passed, but he just smiled and kept on walking. I often turned and watched him as he continued on his way, never missing a note or a yodel. In the ensuing years, this happened many times — me walking to school, him walking toward me, and always the song and the yodel. I never did figure out what he was singing about, but it always was cheery and upbeat. When people talked about him they scratched their heads and laughed, pointing a finger toward their temples and turning it around several times to indicate "crazy." When I left Thomson School for Central Collegiate, I walked a different route, so I did not encounter him again. Yet I have never forgotten Willie. There was a simplicity and purity about the man that I have rarely since encountered. He touched me, and I carry clearly his imprint to this day. As I look around the world in this, the twenty-first century, I often wish there were more Willies to gladden the landscape, more such "idiots" rejoicing in life every minute of every day, who seem to have more going for them than most people perceived as normal whom I see struggling to make sense out of life.

Speaking of what might be considered normal or not, the backyards of Ottawa Street were a world in themselves, utterly abnormal by today's urban standards. Many times I'd go for a walk, peering to my left and right, just to take in the sights: from broken-down cars, to broken-down garages, to assorted laundry lines with everything on them including the unmentionables, to animals of various sorts (mostly cats and dogs, sometimes a pig or two), to rusted implements (and some good ones), to chairs and sofas (we called them chesterfields), to assorted garbage, tin cans, lumber, firewood for winter, hoses, sleighs, hockey sticks, and of course, vegetable gardens. In some ways the backyard was more important than the house. When a garage window faced the alley, I tried to peek in, but usually the window was so covered by dust or other things that not much was visible. On occasion the backyard and garage was a business where we could bring small appliances for repair or, in one case, even have a tire changed and the car fixed. In those days, everyone parked behind their homes and entered the alley from either end of the block.

Our backyard at 1819 Ottawa was as discolourful as any on the street. Immediately behind the house was a small patch of earth where, every spring, we tried to grow flowers or vegetables. Alas, our efforts were never rewarded, no matter how much fertilizer or rich earth we mixed into the stubborn soil. Meanwhile, just on the other side of the flimsy wire fence, our neighbour was selling his surplus of vegetables. Go figure!

Behind the small patch of infertile soil was a shack and then the chicken coop: an open-air part in front and an enclosed shed at the back, where the chickens went for protection from the elements and to roost and lay eggs. I don't recall ever going to the grocery store to buy eggs as long as we lived at that house. And the yolks were bright yellow, at times almost orange, not the pale colour I find today (unless the eggs are organic — which in my youth they always were, without having to be labelled as such). I remember eating breakfast at a restaurant in the interior of B.C. in the late sixties and seeing tourists refusing to eat the eggs served them because the yellow in the yolks was too bright.

Of course, every chicken coop had its rooster, and ours had two or three, the number varying from year to year and sometimes from month to month. One of them I designated my pet; I named him Quiet, because I never heard him crow. I was, however, awakened every morning by the sound of one or more roosters crowing and eventually learned to imitate the sound, which I do fairly well to the present day. I used to try crowing in Quiet's presence in the hope of getting a response. He never went for it. I told my *zaida* (grandfather) that Quiet was my special pet and must never be taken to market. He honoured my request for several months, but one day, when I went out to say hello to Quiet, he wasn't there. That night we had chicken for supper, and I railed at my *zaida* and cried some as I made my pet part of me.

Just past the chicken coop and seemingly attached to it was the truck garage, to be distinguished from the car garage, where we stored our supply of winter wood for the kitchen stove and which never saw a car. (My father parked his car behind the car garage, next to the truck garage.) The truck garage was much larger and housed a blue Chevrolet, which was used by my grandfather to transport cattle that he bought from farmers in various parts of the province. He would go out in the morning with his driver (he never learned to drive) and return that evening, or the next day, or the day after that, with a truckload of cattle (one to four or five, depending on the size of the animals). If he got back late in the day and the abattoir was closed, the animals remained on the truck overnight and could be heard lowing on and off until morning. The driver was either a hired hand, like our next-door neighbour Pete or his son Louis, or my dad. On occasion I accompanied them into the countryside on their buying excursions. We never ate any of the meat from these or other cattle killed in the local abattoir, which I believe was called Prairie Packers. Our meat came from Winnipeg, where the animals were slaughtered according to Jewish law and then shipped to Regina. Our local kosher butcher carved the meat into different cuts and sold it to the Jewish residents. Some of my friends and I, to augment our weekly allowances, used to deliver the packaged meat in the carriers of our bicycles every

Backyard at 1819 Ottawa Street many years after my family left. To the right is the garage where the cattle truck was kept. The car garage is gone, as is the chicken coop. In the distance is the back of our house (circa 1970)

Friday afternoon before sundown unless there was severely inclement weather, and sometimes even then. We seldom collected money directly from the customers, as most of them had running tabs with the butcher and would come in periodically to settle up.

There was no lock on the truck garage, and as the truck was often not there, I sometimes played there with my friends. It had a dirt floor, with two wide, long wooden planks onto which the truck would be driven. These planks were necessary because the back lanes were also dirt, and in wet or slushy weather, they became a quagmire. At times the moisture would seep under the garage doors, and without the planks, the truck would have gotten stuck. How it got down the alley and to the garage in these circumstances is another story. (It required a lot of help from friendly neighbours, not to mention chains on the tires, shovels, sand, and expert driving. Well, I guess that is the story.)

The truck garage served one other, rather unseemly purpose. In the winter, going inside the house to pee was a lengthy production. First you had to leave your galoshes or moccasins on the porch, which meant having to undo the buckles or laces or both. Once inside the house, you had to remove your outer clothes — hat, usually a toque, scarf, perhaps earmuffs, parka, gloves — and then go to the bathroom, where after unbuttoning your fly (zippers weren't common on winter pants) and fumbling through one or more layers of underwear, you'd finally find what you were looking for, and bliss would follow. Then you had to put all those clothes back on, go onto the porch, affix your galoshes or mocca- sins, tie the laces, snap the buckles into place, and carry on with your day. So I'm sure the reader can understand why an empty truck garage with a dirt floor was a blessing in the winter — nothing had to be taken off. We even used it for summer emergencies, but my grandfather would usually know if I or my friends had been peeing in the garage because of the stench that greeted him when he returned from his trips. He would say to me in clear and certain Yiddish, "Yona [my Yiddish name], stop *pishing* in the garage." So for the most part we relegated our clandestine activities to the winter, since anything that turns to ice doesn't usually smell (until it melts).

On the other side of the lane, almost directly across from our truck garage, was the Bronstein truck garage. Mr. Bronstein was also a cattle buyer, making that section of the alley almost a ranch. I was close friends with Mr. Bronstein's son Joey and with Morley Beiser, who lived across the street from the Bronsteins. We formed a trio and, among other things, walked together to school almost every day. I would cut through my backyard into Joey's, pick him up, and together we would cross the street to collect Morley. On the ten-minute walk to school, we'd solve the neighbourhood's problems, including some of our own. Our route always led us past the *shteibl*, a narrow structure that served as the Jewish funeral home. In this building the body was washed

Top: Boba (circa early 1900s)
Above: Zaida (circa early 1900s)

according to Jewish custom and prepared for burial. It was also where, in most cases, the funeral service was held. I remember, many years later, returning to Regina as a rabbi to help conduct the service for my uncle Israel (my dad's brother, who had counselled him at my birth).

My buddies, a couple of girls, and I would on occasion play "strip poker." We called it that, but it was actually rummy or blackjack, since none of us knew how to play poker. If you lost a hand you had to take off a piece of cloth- ing, so everyone usually came well layered. It was always an exciting time, as none of us, as far as I knew, had ever seen the private parts of the opposite sex. As it turned out, whenever someone got down to underpants or bras, he or she quit the game, got dressed, and made a hurried exit, to cries of "Chicken!" or "Poor sport!" Of course, the critics, when they approached the nitty-gritty, also defaulted and headed for the door. Still, the game was fun, even though the hoped-for benefits never materialized.

I adored both of my grandparents, whom I knew as *boba* and *zaida*. Being their first grandchild, I think I occupied a special place in their hearts. My *boba* used to rock me on her lap and sing Yiddish lullabies; one in particular, "*Rozshinkes mit Mandlen*" (raisins and almonds), I requested again and again. Being of Romanian extraction, my grandmother had a good bit of the Gypsy in her. Many times I would watch her *varf coorten* (throw cards). She shuffled regular playing cards, spread them on the table, and then determined from the way they came up what events, good and bad, were in the future for her and the family. She was also adept at a ceremony called *shlogen kapporis*, literally "hitting the scapegoat." For this, she would take a slaughtered chicken to the basement, pluck out its feathers, and then singe the remaining prickles with a torch made from tightly rolled newspaper, creating a smell that filled the house. Then she would swing the chicken around over her head several times, chanting some kind of incantation to protect her loved ones from the "evil eye" or any other kind of possible harm. She was also a phenomenal cook, so much so that there are tastes and textures I still recall from her dishes that I have never been able to find or duplicate. She died in 1950.

In the spring of 1966, while I was living with my wife, Shula, in an ashram in the interior of B.C., my *boba* came to me in a dream and diagnosed a long-standing medical condition in Shula, which had eluded various specialists. The treatment following this diagnosis was successful and long-lasting. The full story about my *boba*'s diagnosis is in a later chapter.

My grandfather, who like my grandmother spoke a broken English, was a simple and practical man with a big heart. When we walked to synagogue together, he would always take my hand to cross streets and often hold onto it until we reached home. The feeling of warmth and security from those moments still occupies a fond place in my memory. My grandparents spoke Yiddish to each other at home, unless they didn't want me to know what they were talking about, in which case they switched to Romanian. Both languages were common in the Regina Jewish community, in particular among the early settlers, and this was not unusual elsewhere in the province where Jews lived. My recollection, however, is that Yiddish predominated, and this could certainly be heard in gatherings at the synagogue.

The Beth Jacob Synagogue, two and a half blocks south of where we lived, served the community for many years. You entered the building from the back and proceeded up a flight of stairs and through two large doors. Inside, the decor was mostly dark wood, with a balcony for the women that wrapped around the entire wall except for the front. Upon entering, the women would climb a set of stairs that led up to the balcony while the men prayed on the lower level. This was in keeping with the Jewish tradition of separating men and women during prayer, ostensibly so neither, especially the men, would be distracted. It seemed to work, as the men could sit and stand for hours without looking up unless there was a disturbance in the upper realm, such as a child crying or the women talking too loudly. On the occasion of a *bar mitzvah* (the celebration when a boy turns thirteen and takes on religious duties, such as counting in a quorum of ten men, called a *minyon*) the women had an important role to fill. At the end of the boy's recitation of the blessing, after he read from the *Haftarah* (Prophets), the women would rain down candies upon him as a symbol of a sweet life. The rest of us kids would wait for that moment, crouching in the aisles, ready to be the first to run up and collect as many candies as possible, to earn bragging rights with the other kids. Usually, once a boy had his *bar mitzvah*, he wasn't supposed to go candy-gathering, but this stricture was often observed more in the breach than in the practice. It was too much fun.

When the service for a *bar mitzvah* ended, there was always a celebration, either in the basement of the synagogue or in the *Talmud Torah*, a building where religious school was held. The synagogue basement was quite ordinary, except for a door over in one corner that no one ever entered. Among us kids this was a cause for speculation, and we had many lively discussions about what was behind that door, never reaching consensus but always enjoying the element of mystery. It never occurred to us to ask an adult. Finally, one day, when no one was around, a few of us decided to finally solve the mystery. With great stealth, and with a guard to warn us if anyone was coming, we tried to open the door. It was stuck. However, after several minutes of pulling and prodding, we pried the door back. It was dark inside, and we stood in the entrance trying to find a light switch, to no avail. Too nervous to move farther in, we tried peering through the darkness to see if we could discern anything from the available light coming through the entrance. All we could determine was that the room was quite large and mostly empty, with some kind of structure on the floor. No one suggested additional forays, even with a flashlight. We closed the door and that was the end of it.

In later years, it occurred to me that there was probably a *mikveh* in the room (a special pool of rainwater where ritual ablutions take place, such as for women after menstruation, and for conversions), since every orthodox Jewish community is required to have one. But this conclusion raises a question: Since it was obvious — from the cobwebs near the door, the unoiled hinges, and the musty smell that greeted us — that this room was rarely entered, had the rabbi and elders abandoned this requirement, thus abrogating the law? Or was there a *mikveh* hidden away in another place that none of us kids knew about? To this day, I don't know the answers.

The *Talmud Torah* was Regina's Jewish community centre, where I went every weekday after school to study Hebrew and prepare for my *bar mitzvah*. I was a less-than-stellar student, reluctant to attend class, always wishing I could play hockey or football instead, or just goof off. But tradition is tradition. So, along with some friends, including Earl Lyman and Boris Kreel (the butcher's son), I went religiously, if one will pardon the expression. I fought with my teachers, challenged my parents and grandparents about having to go, and in the end went on to become a rabbi. At the time of this writing and to the best of my knowledge, I'm one of only two rabbis born and raised in Regina, the other being Saul Hyman.

My main Hebrew teacher was Louis Gold, who liked to throw chalk at anyone who wasn't paying attention. He also liked Buckley's Mixture, the cough syrup that today is advertised on TV with the slogan, "It tastes awful. And it works." Whenever Mr. Gold had a cold, he took a spoonful or two of Buckley's and then held out the spoon to the class and asked if anyone wanted some. There were never any takers, but because of Mr. Gold's influence, I did try Buckley's myself at home. I actually liked the brew but could never figure out if it worked, as I was usually taking other things at the same time to help my cold or sore throat. My grandmother's recipe was hot milk with butter and honey, which I loved and drank often, even when I didn't have a sore throat.

I visited Mr. Gold many years later in Toronto. He was very proud that one of his students had become a rabbi, although in his mind, I was probably one of the least likely to do so. I dreamed of his death one night when I was living at the ashram; I saw him lying on the street in a pool of blood, with people all around. Two weeks later I received in the mail a Jewish newspaper (probably the *Winnipeg Jewish Post*) announcing his death. Some years later, I was informed that he died as a result of being struck by a car as he stepped off the curb.

Speaking of rabbis, to be one in Regina in those days you had to have many talents. First, of course, was ordination. Then you had to be a *mohel* (ritual circumciser), *chazan* (religious singer), and *shochet* (ritual slaughterer). You could get away with not being a *chazan* because we had Charlie Friedman, who elevated our souls with his sweet voice during the High Holidays. You might even get away with not being a *mohel*, since the circumcision could be done by a doctor—alone if he knew the proper prayers, with a rabbi present if he did not. You could even get away with not being a *shochet* (for fowl) if you were prepared to pay the extra amount to have the killing done in Winnipeg and then shipped. I guess the bottom line here was ordination, referred to in Judaism as *Semichah*. However, we did have one man who fulfilled all the requirements. Haskell Wachsmann arrived in Regina around 1947 and was our rabbi for many years. I remember him fondly, but nearly gave him apoplexy when I told him, during a visit to Regina many years after I left, that I was going to be a Reform rabbi. Reform Judaism was anathema to him, as it was to all orthodox rabbis. He felt I would be lost to Judaism. If he is still alive and reads this book, I can assure him Judaism is very strong in me and continues to grow. I also thank him for his teaching, direction, and inspiration.

Rabbi Haskell A. Wachsmann (circa 1960; courtesy Beth Jacob Synagogue)

I would see Rabbi Wachsmann often in his capacity as *shochet*, as my grandfather frequently took me along when he brought chickens to be slaughtered. I always felt sorry for the poor creatures as I watched the process. First the rabbi would bend the chicken's head back, then pluck a few feathers from its neck, and then slit the throat with a razor-sharp blade, after which the chicken would be placed head down in an opening on a metal counter through which the blood could drain out completely. (The bible forbids Jews to eat blood, so all kosher slaughtering must obey this commandment, whether it be a chicken, cow, or any other permitted animal.)

Next to the *Talmud Torah* was the Regina Curling Club. Many times after Hebrew school, my friends and I would watch the curlers, and I gradually developed a love for the game. We were not allowed on the ice at that time because of our age, so we improvised at Thomson School. With the assistance of our janitor, Mr. Walton, we made our own curling rinks. To do this, we took empty jam pails and filled them three-quarters full with cement. Then we used some kind of dye or paint to make the circles on the ice, and brought old brooms from home to sweep the rocks as they slid toward the circles. We would play during recess and hurry back from lunch to get in a game before afternoon classes resumed. When we were a bit older, we were allowed to throw a few rocks at the curling club and eventually play full games.

The Regina Curling Club was the home for periodic Jewish bonspiels, when curlers from across Saskatchewan, Manitoba, and Alberta would come into town. I believe it was sponsored by the B'nai Brith (Sons of the Covenant), a Jewish fraternal organization. Those of us teenagers who had driver's licences were loaned cars by Regina's Jewish families and asked to pick up the out-of-town curlers at the airport or train station and chauffeur them around during their stay. As ersatz taxi drivers, we had the opportunity to drive many different vehicles in the course of a bonspiel and were always eager to try different cars and discuss their merits with our fellow drivers. I had a love of cars then, and it has not diminished.

Our house was the first house south of Eleventh Avenue, on the east side of Ottawa Street. Immediately north of us, on the southeast corner of the intersection, was a small apartment complex where my best non-Jewish friend lived, Beverly Dinnon. Bev was about two years older than me — a tough kid with a soft heart. In terms of street smarts and sexual maturity, he was probably ten years ahead of me, at a conservative estimate. He knew about a lot of things and educated me in a few of them, like girls for example. My first insights into the working relationships of male and female came from Bev, as he would describe to me some of his sexual activities. I listened with fascination as he talked about things I knew nothing about and hardly understood. In a sense he took me under his wing and tutored me, innocent and naive as I was. I'm not sure why there was such a kinship between us, but it lasted a few years, until he moved away. I never saw him again.

The building that Beverly lived in, called the Tozaka Apartments, was full of mystery, somewhat like that room in the basement of the synagogue. I was told by my grandparents never to go in there, as if there was some danger lurking in the hallways and apartments, giving me the feeling that people in the building were diseased and I might catch something. Finally one day when I was older, I went in to give one of the residents something. The place was dark and filled with the smells of cooking, but otherwise I couldn't see what all the fuss was about.

My grandfather's driver at one time lived in that building and later opened a car repair shop in the garage attached to it, about eighteen inches from our house. I know it was about eighteen inches because occasionally I squeezed into the narrow space to retrieve a ball or other lost object. The car repair shop was an unmitigated nuisance to my grandparents, especially in the summer when everything was open and the noise of pounding and clanking and buzzing and whirring filled the air, often accompanied by smoke and fumes. In the winter, with doors everywhere closed tightly, it was tolerable.

Directly across the street from us lived my grandfather's best friend, Mike Yankovitch. Mike had incredible eyebrows. They were so big and bushy that I could see them distinctly from our front porch. Mike's other endearing quality was that he smoked a Sherlock Holmes–style pipe with the most delicious-smelling tobacco. It was from Mike Yankovitch that I acquired the desire to one day try a pipe. When, as a university student, I finally did, I encountered two recurring problems—I could never keep the damn thing lit, and after a few bowls, I developed a sore throat. I must have quit the pipe and then decided to try again a dozen times, trying all kinds of mild tobaccos, some costing three to four dollars an ounce. Between that and the fact that I was practically supporting the Eddy Match Company, I finally gave up. Until recently, I had three pipes on my desk to remind me of the bowl or two that I so enjoyed before I got frustrated. Also, I loved feeling the wood the pipes were made of and admiring the elegant designs and grains. From time to time, I used to glance in their direction and think of Mike Yankovitch sitting with my *zaida*, puffing away as they solved the problems of the day.

Around the corner from Mike Yankovitch on Eleventh Avenue was Ben Finkelstein's grocery store. That's where

My father and me in front of 1819 Ottawa with the Tozaka Apartments in the near background and, behind that, partially in view, the Windsor Apartments, where my cousin Eddie David and family lived.

I developed my taste for Greek olives. Mr. Finkelstein had a huge barrel of black olives and my grandfather would always be bringing some home. I think it was a Romanian thing. At first I found them too bitter, until one day I liked the bitter taste and there was no turning back. In the back of Finkelstein's store was a small space with a round table where Mr. Finkelstein and his friends would play cards when there were no customers in the store. I think they played pinochle, although it may at times have been poker. If the game was in a critical phase when I entered the store, it took a lot of coughing and shuffling of my feet to get Ben away from the table. At such moments, first things came first.

The other grocery store, which was around the corner from us and also on Eleventh Avenue, belonged to Joe Beiser, Morley's dad. I shopped there about as often as at Ben Finkelstein's store. If one store didn't have what I was sent for, I went to the other. If both were out of the product, there were always several other stores within a five-minute walk. Joe Beiser's store was in a building with an upstairs suite that, from around 1950, he rented out to the Golubs, a Jewish family recently arrived in Canada from Poland. The family's son, Alex, became a good friend of mine. His father had been an obstetrician and gynecologist in Europe and was interning in Regina to obtain his Canadian medical licence. There was also a girl, I believe a cousin or niece, who came over with them, whose name was Amelia. They had escaped the horrors of the Holocaust and were beginning a new life. If I remember correctly, Alex's mother was a nurse. Later, after Dr. Golub received his licence, the family moved to Lampman, Saskatchewan, where for many years he practised medicine and delivered most of the area's babies. I stayed with them one summer for about two weeks; Alex and I worked on dismantling old tractors.

The two "geniuses." Alex is on the left (circa 1952).

While they were still living above Joe Beiser's grocery store, across from our house, Alex and I decided one day we wanted to have better communication. We had heard that if you took two empty tin cans, punched a small hole in the bottom of each, and attached them by the holes to each end of a length of uncovered copper wire, you could make a telephone—well, a sort of telephone. The theory was that if you spoke into one can, your voice would be transmitted along the wire to the other can, and vice versa. We bought a large coil of copper wire and strung it from his bedroom to my bathroom, the windows of which faced each other across a distance of about a hundred feet. Then we initiated our first trans-backyard conversation. I could hear something coming through, but it wasn't very clear, so I shouted to Alex through the window to speak louder. He tried, but there was no improvement. Then Alex shouted to me through his window to try speaking so he could see if it worked better in the other direction. Then I heard Alex calling me again from his window to speak louder. I tried, but he shouted back that he couldn't hear me. Next ensued a brief conversation between the windows about what we might do to fix the situation. We decided to have a meeting, at which time, after some deliberation, we both realized, since we were talking to each other from our respective windows without using the ersatz phones, that we didn't need the tin can telephone system in the first place. Not bad for two geniuses, one of whom went on to university and five years' post-graduate studies to become a rabbi, the other of whom studied nine years to become a physician and then another four or five to follow his father's specialty.

One of the foremost Jewish philosophers of the twentieth century was Martin Buber. He wrote, among other things, a thin book entitled *I and Thou*. It was a book about relationships and became well known in and out of Jewish circles. The book states that there are two kinds of relationships: the "I—Thou" relationship and the "I—It" relationship. The latter is a superficial, at-arm's-length relationship, neither intimate nor genuine. The "I—Thou" relationship, on the other hand, whether with a person or with an object, is totally genuine and very personal. Buber says, for example, that one could even have an "I—Thou" relationship with a tree. When I read this during my rabbinic studies, I was relieved, because I had a very special relationship with a tree in the front yard of 1838 Ottawa Street when I was between four and eight. I would hug it, and nuzzle my back against it, and talk to

My tree

it. It was my tree, and I found comfort in relating to it in times of difficulty. Even after we moved to 1819 Ottawa Street I would continue to visit it, and years later, when I visited Regina, I would come by to say hello to my old friend. The last time I was in Regina, the tree was still there, though, as mentioned earlier, the house no longer exists.

During the early years of my life at 1838 Ottawa Street, I contracted a nasty chest and throat condition called the croup, and one night I awoke in the middle of the night, barely able to breathe. My parents began to panic as I struggled for air, fearing I was going to asphyxiate, which is exactly how it felt to me. Time seemed of the essence — by the time a doctor arrived, it might be too late. Desperate and knowing that Earl's mother had trained as a practical nurse, they began pounding on the wall that separated our residence from the Lymans. Before long, Bertha Lyman came running to our door and within a few minutes had calmed everyone down, especially me. As I began to relax, my breathing eased up. I don't remember what else Mrs. Lyman did, but I was grateful to her on that occasion, and on two others when the croup again attacked me.

Bertha Lyman was an interesting woman. She had enormous energy and was constantly on the move. Her trademark was that she always wore a hat, even when in her home. As a young man I didn't particularly notice this or care much, though comments about her hat came from others, who thought it odd that anyone would spend the entire day at home with a hat on. I liked Mrs. Lyman. She was always very upfront, spoke her mind, and had a good heart. One time she had some ladies over for tea, and while they were sitting in her living room talking, I wandered in, probably looking for Earl. As soon as she saw me, she drew her company's attention to my head and exclaimed, "Look at the ears! Look at the ears!" It was true, I was born with large ears; they stuck out while the rest of my body grew, until eventually everything evened out and I looked normal. Bertha always got a kick out of my ears, and I chuckle now as I think back on that day and know that there wasn't an ounce of meanness in her. Bertha was Bertha.

In the middle of the nineteenth block of Ottawa Street, on the west side, was a Lutheran church. The pastor was the father of my classmate Randolf Holfeld. I liked Randolf but never got to know him very well. On our way back from synagogue, which was one block to the south, we would pass the church. Some of my friends would always look the other way as we went by, or put a hand over their eyes, so as not to see it. These were usually kids from more strict religious homes whose parents wanted their children to have as little as possible to do with Christianity. Not looking at the church was a gesture to indicate this and to make the point that a lot of Jews over the centuries died at Christian hands. For me, the church was an object of fascination and mystery. I tried to imagine what it looked like inside and what happened during a service. I once even climbed the front steps to peer in, but everything was locked up. One day I saw that the doors were open, so I went up and stood near the doorway and even ventured to take a few steps inside. A man came to meet me and see what I wanted. I told him my name, and that Randolf Holfeld was my friend and his father was in charge of this church. He told me he was Randolf's father. I was not invited in, and after a brief exchange of words I left, feeling that I was not welcome. My friendship with Randolf continued, and later I heard that he, like his father, had become a minister, though I don't know this for sure.

Before leaving Regina in 1954, I became good friends with a Baptist minister, Richard Grabke. I don't recall how it began, but I do remember that we took to each other right away and stayed in contact over the years. The last time I saw Richard was when I visited Regina after being ordained. I let him know in advance that I was coming, and he invited me to dinner at his home. A young nephew of Richard's was visiting at the time and joined us for the meal. It was a pleasant evening, both of us happy to see each other again. Later, as I was putting on my coat, about to leave, I noticed that the young boy was staring at my forehead. Richard asked him what he was doing. He replied, "Where are his horns?" Richard flushed and began to sputter something. I quickly interjected, and in a soft voice told the young man that Jews don't have horns. I went on to explain, in as simple terms as I could, that this myth began with a misinterpretation by Michelangelo of a biblical text on Moses. The word *"Karnayim,"* meaning, in context, "beams," appears in Michelangelo's bible as "horns." So the great sculptor affixed horns to the forehead of his famous statue of Moses. The line, I explained, should have been translated "beams of light" rather than "horns of light." I think the lad understood.

Then Richard said, "Jerry, before you go, can I ask you when the Jewish Holidays begin this fall?" I told him and then asked why he wanted to know. He was a little embarrassed and replied that his father, who was a farmer in Saskatchewan, told him that it always rains at the time of the Jewish holy days, and he wanted to be sure to get his crops in before that happened. I remarked that coincidence sometimes does strange things.

I would at times find myself walking or standing in the crops in Saskatchewan when I would accompany my father and grandfather on cattle-buying excursions, and I would always find this exciting, even when there was nothing apparent to be excited about. For me, just the smells of the land and the clover and the wheat were in themselves wonderful, and even manure had its moments. When my dad wasn't working for my grandfather, he was selling small wares across the province from his panel truck, and now and then he took my mother and me along. I loved these trips, as it meant that I would be able to stand in the middle of a field and see the horizon in all four directions, which gave me a sense of space and freedom that was intoxicating. At night I could see the stars, clear and bright, almost within reach. To this day, from time to time, I feel the call of the Prairies and the desire to return for the kind of natural spiritual nourishment I find in few other places. Many years later, the impact of growing up on the flatland found its way into many of my writings, even those of a romantic nature.

> I want to walk with you
> through the fields
> naked to the sky
> our feet in the rich black earth
> I want to feel the wind
> on our nipples
> and the sun
> between our legs
> I want to look through you
> at the rippling wheat
> and blend your hair
> into the sweet clover

In Saskatchewan, even in the city, sunrises and sunsets can only be compared to what one witnesses in the desert or on the ocean. To view the panorama of the sky across the entire horizon, without obstruction, is an unforgettable experience. Even after my nineteen years in Saskatchewan, having witnessed countless risings and settings of the sun, I have never taken a single sunrise or sunset for granted. This is not to say that each and every one is spectacular, but even the ordinary on the flatland is not so ordinary.

Rainstorms on the Prairies are usually short-lived but extremely intense and dramatic. During such storms, my grandmother, my aunt Marion, my cousin Linda, and I would hide under the dining room table. Occasionally, after the rain, we could see a rainbow spreading across the horizon and, if we were lucky, a double rainbow — a smaller rainbow under and seemingly cradled by the main one; if we were even luckier, a triple rainbow, the third one smaller yet and tucked under its older brother, the second. A triple rainbow was rare, but once seen, never forgotten. The same could be said about the northern lights, which on the Prairies are magnificent, dancing across the night sky in multiple colours, as if choreographed. I always felt I was watching a celestial performance of unusual magnitude and poetic brilliance. Once, when my son was about ten years old and we were on a camping trip, I awakened him and dragged him, protesting, out of our tent, so he could see his first display of aurora borealis. We still, from time to time, reminisce fondly about this.

> The prairie sky
>   stretches my soul
> and leaves me no room
>   to be small
> I connect with the infinite stars
>   that draw me upwards
>   out of my bony husk
>   and spread me
>   into distant galaxies

On one trip to the country with my dad and grandfather, I was given the opportunity to ride a horse for the first time in my life. The farmer had no saddle to provide me with, only a pair of reins. I was helped onto the horse and told to tug on the right rein if I wanted to go right, on the left rein if I wanted to go left, and on both reins at the same time if I wanted the horse to stop. Everything went well until we were out of sight of the farmer, at which point the horse, as if he knew he wasn't being watched, took off at a fast gallop, something I was totally unprepared for. Remembering what the farmer told me about pulling on both reins, I pulled mightily, only to be ignored by the horse while I held onto the reins for dear life. Then, for no reason I could discern, the horse abruptly and without warning stopped dead in its tracks, sending me head over heels over its neck and into a pile of freshly dropped cow dung. I landed on my rear, which was fortunate, and in retrospect it was probably good the pile of dung was there to cushion my fall. Nevertheless, I had two problems: I was a long distance from the farm, and every time I tried to get on the horse, the dung acted like grease, and I quickly slid off. As the horse refused to budge, I began the long trek back without him, and arrived — to the dismay of the farmer and my grandfather — not only sans horse, but smelling to high heaven. It was a hot day on the Prairies; the ride back, even with the car windows wide open, was unpleasant, and my grandfather was less than pleased. I had the sense, however, that my dad was trying to suppress a smirk.

Summer holidays in July and August were always a treat, and I looked forward to them with eagerness and anticipation. One or more of three things happened during this time: I went fishing, I went to camp, or I went to Watrous.

Like most fishermen, I have my tales. Suffice to say I love to fish, I love fish fries, and I love being on the water. From fishing I learned an important lesson—patience. And when patience did not produce fish, my demeanour did not change nor my mood diminish. After all, I had the camaraderie of my father, my uncle Jay, and others, not to mention great sandwiches. As for a tale, well, the really big one got away—but you should have seen it! Actually, the biggest fish I ever caught was a thirteen-and-a-half-pound northern pike. I was very proud of myself and eagerly took in the praise from my father and uncle.

At Camp Kevutza, the Jewish camp I attended in Saskatchewan, I learned other lessons. Things were rough, the beds were hard, there was no waterfront, and our days were completely filled with programming, which consisted of lectures, discussions, and some sporting activities. Bonfires at night were a big attraction, as we sang songs (many in Hebrew), roasted hot dogs or marshmallows, and told stories. At the end of the evening, the women would leave, and the men would stand around the bonfire in a circle, putting it out with private hoses. With my aunt Molly cooking, the food was excellent and abundant, although for growing youngsters, there was never enough. Drinking water was carefully consumed, as we had to carry it by pail from a hand pump a quarter mile away. (Camp lesson one: Never take drinking water for granted.)

It was at camp that I discarded any feelings of false modesty I might have had. We had only outhouses and these were built for groups. So we would sit, five at a time, beside each other, and do what we had to do. At first it was embarrassing, but after a while it seemed perfectly natural and no big deal. (Camp lesson two: Unpleasantness happens in life, no matter how hard we try to avoid it. But how I react to unpleasantness is up to me.) The only big deal came when one of the fellows accidentally dropped his wristwatch into the mire below. We lowered him with a heavy rope attached to his feet and a clothespin clipped to his nose, down to where the watch lay, and he retrieved it. Such were the joys of Camp Kevutza. (Camp lesson three: If I value something, there's no length to which I won't go to find it or keep it.)

Watrous, Saskatchewan is a small town located about an hour's drive southeast of Saskatoon, the province's other large city. A few miles from Watrous is Manitou Lake, which is where my parents and I holidayed most summers for two weeks, renting a room in a large cottage where other vacationers also stayed. There was a communal kitchen where each family did their own cooking, and occasionally the owner's wife would bake a pie from fresh Saskatoon berries that some of us had picked that day. This was always one of the highlights of our stay.

Another highlight was the very large dance hall, not because we liked to dance — in fact, we didn't know how to — but for another, completely unrelated reason. Manitou Lake was a gathering place for Jewish families from all over the province. This meant that Jewish girls our age would be present and available for semi-dates. Sometimes we would go on walks, or talk near Lollie's potato-chip stand, where we munched the best French fries in the world. But what we really relished was buying a girl a milkshake, going behind the dance hall where nobody could see us, and drinking the milkshake forehead to forehead, with two straws. For me this meant sleepless nights and days of anticipation.

One might think that Manitou Lake is a lake like any other. Not so! The only other body of water in the world that I am aware of that is similar to Manitou Lake is the Dead Sea in Israel. Only Manitou Lake has an even denser mineral content than that famous sea, so dense that the water at times appears black and it's virtually impossible for anyone to sink in it, let alone drown. I remember floating one day in the lake while reading a comic book, attested to by this photo.

Circa 1950

One of the reasons Jewish families came to Manitou Lake to vacation was for the healing properties of the water's mineral content, which gave relief to the many who suffered from arthritis of one form or another. The main treatment consisted of caking oneself from head to foot (literally) with the rich, black mud that lined the shore, and then lying in the sun for hours at a time, while the mud baked on one's body and soothed the bones and joints. At the end of the day, the mud bathers would take a fresh-water shower to clear the salt and mud, returning the following day to repeat this unconventional medical procedure. It must have been of considerable help to their arthritic pain, as the same people returned year after year.

I learned many years later that a study of the mud revealed, at least from a scientific perspective, that it had no actual healing properties, and for some decades this stopped the flow of people to the lake. Then I heard that things had changed once more, and vacationers were returning, as the study had apparently been called into question. I have not received a report on the current status.

There was also a large indoor pool with the same black water, so in poor weather everyone went inside to swim and float. In the shallow end of the pool, a narrow pipe with holes spanned the width. Hot water spouted out of these holes in an arch that came down on the backs of a row of usually elderly bathers who would periodically exclaim with delight in Yiddish, "Oy, it's a *mechiah*!" (Oh, it's wonderful!). My *boba* was one of those bathers.

I had the pleasure, while living in Regina, to hear Premier Tommy Douglas speak. Not only was he the father of medicare, which gave universal health care to all Canadians, he was also perhaps the finest orator I have ever heard. He spoke one day in our synagogue on Victoria Avenue, attracting to our large sanctuary a capacity crowd. Mr. Douglas spoke for well over an hour. I don't recall the content of his speech (many decades have passed), but what I do remember clearly is that for the entire duration of his talk, no one shuffled in their seat, no one left to go to the bathroom, and no one whispered to the person in the next seat. Except for the premier's voice, there was complete silence. That scene still rings clearly in my mind, and I feel honoured to have been in his presence. I went to Central Collegiate with his daughter Shirley (later married to actor Donald Sutherland), and we performed together in the operetta *Carmen*. Many years later, I introduced my daughter to her outside of her dressing room after a performance she gave at the O'Keefe Centre in Toronto.

My parents in front of the indoor pool at Watrous (circa 1950)

During my travels with my father and grandfather, I got to see many parts of Saskatchewan. Two places in particular remain strong in my memory—Lumsden Valley and the Qu'Appelle Valley. Perhaps this is because valleys on the plains are not common, everything being so flat. Also, both valleys, in different ways, held some kind of spiritual connection for me and continue to do so whenever I think of them, though the exact nature of the connection still eludes me.

Lumsden is about halfway between Regina and Regina Beach, so we had to pass through it on the way to our fishing outings. We would drive along

A small section of the Qu'Appelle Valley, NE of Regina

the road, which was straight, as roads on the Prairies tend to be, and then suddenly dip into this beautiful valley, at the bottom of which was the town of Lumsden. We passed through the small town quickly and then ascended the hill on the other side, once more onto the flatland. The whole trip in and out of the valley seemed to me like a passage through an oasis, traversed briefly during a desert voyage. I don't recall ever actually stopping in the town. About twenty-five years later, sometime after my ordination as a rabbi, I revisited Lumsden with my wife, where a transcendental meditation conference was taking place. We were invited to meet Maharishi Mahesh Yogi, who told me I was the first rabbi to make his acquaintance. (More on our meeting in a later chapter.)

The Qu'Appelle ("Who Calls?") Valley haunts me. It's a long valley with soft, low hills. I've always felt that I could sit and stare at those hills for hours, as if in some strange way this was once my home.

There is a beautiful poem by Pauline Johnson called "The Legend of the Qu'Appelle Valley," which seems to capture the mystery of these seemingly innocuous hills.

The Legend of Qu'Appelle Valley

I am the one who loved her as my life,
Had watched her grow to sweet young womanhood;
Won the dear privilege to call her wife,
And found the world, because of her, was good.
I am the one who heard the spirit voice,
Of which the paleface settlers love to tell;
From whose strange story they have made their choice
Of naming this fair valley the "Qu'Appelle."

The big yearly event in Regina was the Exhibition, which took place during the summer, preceded by a big parade. All the kids went, parents in tow until we were older. I liked the rides, the games, and the exhibits, but I was especially fond of the bumper cars—my introduction to driving. When I was fifteen and I first drove a real car, on a prairie side road with my father, I was proud to keep us from going into the ditch, a skill I attribute to my experience in dodging bumper cars.

But what interested me most at the Exhibition grounds were the Indians and their teepees. I always tried to look inside, wondering what it must be like to have such a home and how they kept warm in the winter. I was also fascinated by their dress and the ease with which they walked. However, there was a disconnect for me between these noble-looking men and women and the cowboy-and-Indian movies I saw regularly, where the Indians were usually, with the exception of Little Beaver and Tonto, the bad guys. I was pleased to see in recent years the movie *Dances with Wolves,* which corrects the image that was left with so many of my generation and puts our Native people in a light of elegance and respect. (When I was in my thirties, as I will explain further on, I had the opportunity to be of help to an Indian woman who was ill.)

My goal in life was to become a doctor; my reason was that whenever I saw a blind person I was very moved, which made me decide that one day I would discover a cure for blindness. I took all the science courses I needed in high school to be on track for a career in medicine. Also, I used to visit a small room at the General Hospital in Regina, where I was fascinated by a display of organs of the human body and unborn fetal babies, all preserved in jars of formaldehyde.

Rubber baby
    I remember you taken from the jar
Formaldehyde
    dripping from your Mongolian eyes

```
you were so perfect
        I wanted to hold you
                    and rock you
trembling
        I touched your skin
    almost afraid
        you might come alive
wondering
    if a soul was trapped
                    somewhere
        in your preserved flesh
wondering
        where you might be
    or if I might meet you
                as someone
                        again
```

Down the hall from this room was the mortuary, and it was in the hallway between the two rooms that one day I met Johnny Champagneure.

Johnny Champagneure was of French-Canadian descent. Short, with black hair and a dark complexion, he was affable and easygoing, and we quickly became friends. Johnny was second in charge of post-mortems, under a physician who was the head of pathology at the hospital. Johnny allowed me to watch him at work as he opened dead bodies and removed organs for examination by the pathologist. There were two autopsy tables in the morgue, and at times both he and the physician would work side by side, each at one of the tables. In a small adjoining room were more specimens in formaldehyde, in all likelihood the overflow from the room down the hall. In my senior year at high school, with permission from the pathologist, I was able to bring members of my biology club and give them a tour of the display rooms and the main autopsy room. This was done over two or three evenings (to keep the groups small) when no one was around and the day's work had been placed elsewhere.

It was in part because of my association with Johnny Champagneure that I never became a smoker. One day I visited him in the autopsy room and saw a body on each of the tables. Their chests had been opened and the lungs fully exposed. Johnny told me that the man with the pink lungs had been a farmer and non-smoker while the man with the grey lungs with black flecks was from the city and a heavy smoker. Now, granted, both men were dead, but the farmer did not die from a lung-related illness, whereas the city dwell-er's lungs were a contributing factor to his demise. I have never forgotten that scene, and any temptations to smoke were dispelled by that memory. (The exception, of course, was my short adventure with the pipe mentioned earlier. I recall convincing myself at that time that since people don't inhale pipe tobacco, my lungs were safe. Throat and mouth cancer were not on my radar.)

My friendship with Johnny Champagneure continued for some years, and I would look him up whenever I came back to Regina for visits. I also saw him often in the hospital when, during the summers of 1953 and 1954, I worked there as an orderly.

Being an orderly in the fifties was quite different from what I under-stand it is today, as we did minor medical procedures, such as testing urine samples and giving enemas. I was once asked by a doctor to clear out a patient's blocked stool by hand, which I did, much to the man's relief and gratitude. And when someone died, it was my job to prepare the body and take it to the morgue. This was particularly difficult for me when the person was young, as was the case once with a twelve-year-old girl. Her death left an indelible impression on my mind until one day, many years later, I expressed my feelings for her in a poem:

> I don't know why I think about you today
> when I was so young
> we never met
> And you were dead
> Oh, so young
> a call in the night
> and I went to pick you up
> and I wrapped you in a sheet
> with safety pins
> as I held back the tears
> such a small form
> and
> frail
> They never told me how you died
> and no one can ever tell me why
> I picked you up in my arms
> and rolled you to a steel drawer
> and closed you inside
> and some of me with you

it was so cold inside
I went upstairs
washed my hands
and wept into the night

It was also my job to change oxygen and nitrous oxide tanks when necessary. On one occasion, while working the night shift, I delivered an oxygen
tank to the obstetrics case room. Upon entering the room with the large tank
on my dolly, I encountered three nurses sitting around giggling and then
breaking out in peals of uproarious laughter. I said hello, which resulted in
more laughter, as they seemed unable to contain themselves. Every word that
came from my mouth, no matter how mundane, and every action I took, such
as walking, brought forth more laughter. Then I noticed that they were sniff-
ing nitrous oxide (laughing gas). I exclaimed, "What are you doing?" More
laughter. I gave up, collected an empty oxygen tank, and left, chuckling as I
made my way to the elevator.

As the reader may have gathered from the description of my hockey
days, winters in Regina could be brutal. Temperatures on occasion dropped to
fifty below Fahrenheit. And it was long. Snow that arrived in October often
didn't depart until April or even early May, and at times it was so high you
couldn't see cars or trucks pass on the other side of a boulevard. Once, on an
evening that was unusually cold even by Saskatchewan standards, I had to
pick up a prescription for a family member at the neighbourhood drug store
only two short blocks away. I knew things were bad outside so I took extra
precautions, bundling up with everything I had, including a scarf over my
face and my toque pulled well down over my head such that only my eyes
were visible. I left the house and ran all the way to the pharmacy, which took
me no more than five minutes. When I got there the pharmacist looked at me
and said that my earlobes were frozen. I had not pulled my toque far enough
down and about half of each lobe was white. I remained in the drug store until
both lobes had thawed, then made sure they were well covered and headed
home. Later I learned that it was fifty-two degrees below zero that night without wind-chill, and the wind was blowing hard.

The situation in winter at 1819 Ottawa Street was at times grim. Seven of
us lived in the small two-storey house — my grandparents (whose house it
was), my parents, Linda and her mother, Marion, and myself. The house was
heated by a coal furnace in the basement, with an adjoining coal shed. At
night, before going to bed, my father would make sure the furnace was loaded
with enough fuel to last for as long as possible. But "as long as possible" meant,

usually, that by sometime around 4 a.m., not much heat would be getting to us, and my father would need to get up, stoke the coals, reload the furnace, and then return to bed. I, of course, slept through all of this — until I was about fifteen, at which point the title of "Keeper of the Furnace" was turned over to me. It was then that I learned in more depth what this auspicious task entailed. First, I had to be sure to wake up before the fire went out, because rekindling a dead coal stove and getting it up to snuff could take the better part of an hour, especially for an amateur. An alarm clock wasn't a good idea because it would wake everybody up, since the bedrooms were at close quarters. The trick was to notice, while sleeping, that the temperature in the house had dropped and it was time to arise and feed the iron behemoth. To sleep through the drop in temperature was to invoke the wrath of the household when they awoke to a refrigerator-like ambience. I endured this several times, until even in my sleep I became sufficiently attuned to the household climate to notice when it changed, at which time I would sit bolt upright in bed and prepare to dismount. I say "prepare" because, by this time, the wooden floor felt like a block of ice and sent shock waves up through my body when my feet touched it. Eventually I remembered, upon going to bed, to place my house slippers immediately below where my legs hung down from the edge of the bed. Even they were cold by this time, but not like the floor. (A small carpet would have helped, but for some reason one wasn't available.)

The journey to the basement was usually accompanied by a flashlight, as turning on lights meant a higher electrical bill, although I did click on one small light near the furnace. When I opened the furnace door, I would find some small coals still burning, enough to ignite the larger pieces that I would then shovel in. But first, I had to shake the accumulated ash into a receiving bin at the bottom of the furnace, so there would be sufficient oxygen to allow the fire to burn. I also had to clear out the clinkers, which are the remains of pieces of coal when they have burned themselves out. A clinker is not unlike the skeleton that is left over after a person dies, but each clinker, like a piece of molten lava, is different and unique. Much later in life, when I was on a lecture tour in Iceland, I would come to appreciate the artistic possibilities of clinkers. (More on this later.)

With the clinkers out of the way and the ashes dropped, I entered the coal bin with my flashlight to select pieces of coal that were small enough to catch fire easily and large enough that they wouldn't burn too quickly. When I couldn't find pieces of the right size, which was often the case, I had to use an axe to chop up larger pieces. This I did by the dim light of the bulb nearby, which was hardly adequate, and with the help of my flashlight, which I had to position on a piece of coal. Once I had enough appropriately sized pieces, I put them on the shovel and arranged them carefully in the furnace. With time and patience, I got the fire going, but then had to wait around until I was sure it wouldn't go out. This in itself could take fifteen to twenty minutes and sometimes much longer. Finally, when I felt confident that all was well, I went back upstairs and washed the coal residue off my hands. (Later, I got gloves to wear while handling the coal.) Before going back to sleep, my final step was to look in the bathroom mirror to see if I had coal smudges on my face, as these would mean a dirty pillowcase by morning. Then I returned to bed, which by then no longer contained any warmth to comfort my body. In the morning, upon rising, I could tell immediately whether I had provided a good fire by the temperature of the floor and the presence or absence of complaints from my family. I'm sure the reader will be pleased to learn that an oil-burning furnace with a thermostat eventually replaced the coal monster, and nobody had to get up early to heat the house.

Heat in the wintertime in Regina was always a problem, for one reason or another. For example, at 1819 Ottawa, we never had enough hot water, probably due to an insufficiently sized hot water tank in the basement. When I took a bath (showers were luxuries, and few homes that I knew of had one), I was lucky to have six inches of hot — make that warm — water. Baths were taken quickly; such a small amount of water cooled down fast, and besides, with the only toilet in the house next to the bathtub, the bathroom was in constant demand. On those rare occasions when one was allowed to linger, a family member of the same gender would bring a kettle of boiling water up from the kitchen stove and add it to one end of the bathtub, once one's feet were drawn up. This would combat the rapid heat loss of the tub water and give the bather an additional five to ten minutes of bliss.

Hardships aside, for a kid, winter in Regina was a wonderland. Hockey, skating on a pond or rink, curling (a sport finally getting its due), sledding across the ice or down a snowbank, and wonderful, exhilarating snowball fights were all on the winter menu. Of course, there was also sucking icicles — which were always plentiful, especially as spring approached — not to mention making snow angels. This you did by standing next to a thick blanket of freshly fallen snow and falling straight backwards, landing softly, then waving arms and legs to leave an angel imprint. You would then get up, usually with someone's help so as not to spoil the angel shape, turn around, and admire what you had just created. (Only many years later did the concept of the angel come to play a significant role in my theology and in my life.)

However, as wonderful as winter could be, there were hazards. An emergency occurred once at Thomson School. At the boys' entrance, there was a long scraper for cleaning your boots in the winter. Several boys could use it at one time. About three feet above the scraper was an iron bar to hold onto while you scraped. On particularly cold days it was common practice, much to the chagrin of our teachers, for guys to place their lips very close to the iron bar and slowly drool onto it. The fun was in watching the spittle freeze in mid-air, sometimes before it even reached the bar. By the end of the day, gobs of frozen spittle covered the bar from end to end, requiring the janitor to clean it off with some special solution. One day a student's tongue came too close to the bar and touched it. Instantly his tongue adhered to the bar so firmly that he couldn't break away. At first, those of us who observed this began to laugh, but then, as the student panicked and began to scream, we tried to rescue him but found ourselves helpless to do anything. It seemed like his tongue was welded to the iron and he would have to remain there until spring. Finally Mr. Walton, our janitor, arrived. Somehow, perhaps with hot water or the above-mentioned special solution, he loosened the boy's tongue from the bar, but not without leaving a small piece of flesh that was later scraped off with a chisel. The kid spoke funny for weeks afterwards.

Regina's future construction engineers received their early training by building snow forts, huts, and ersatz igloos, while nascent sculptors cut their teeth on snowmen, often using small pieces of coal to represent facial features. The resident winter artist on the Prairies was Jack Frost, who used window-panes as his canvases for original and delightful designs, which changed with weather conditions and provided us with endless surprises when we awoke in the mornings. We prairie dwellers are indebted to him for many winters of artistic displays.

Driving in the winter could be hazardous, especially in the country. It wasn't so much the amount of snow, although this could present problems, but rather the wind blowing snow across the road, mile after mile, for long periods of time. This could make the driver dizzy and nauseous, even if the day was clear and the sun shining brightly. Add to this a heavy snowfall and you get what is commonly known as a whiteout, a situation in which it is impossible to see the road and at times even difficult to see the end of the car's hood. I recall once being in a whiteout on a good single-lane highway. I had to open the door and look down to see what little road was visible, all the while listening for a change in the sound of my wheels, which would mean I had gone off the road onto the shoulder and would find myself in the ditch if I didn't correct my direction. I also had to worry that a car coming up behind would see me too late or, if I was on the wrong side of the road, a car coming head-on would not brake in time. Stopping altogether was an option, but also dangerous — if the cars behind kept moving, I would become a target. The best thing was to try to find a side road and pull over until the whiteout ended. If a whiteout occurred while a person was driving at night, the best thing to do was pray. (Even in the daytime this wasn't a bad idea.)

In the spring the mud was awful, especially on the dirt roads — which were the only roads, except for a few blacktop main highways and some secondary roads covered with gravel. I remember once driving in the country with my uncle Lou in a rainstorm. The road was very slippery during the storm and for some time afterwards, until the sun came out. Fortunately my uncle Lou, a good driver, was able to navigate without sliding into the ditch. But the wet road wasn't the only problem. Whenever we got behind another car, our windshield was soon covered with mud. Those were the days before windshield washer systems were invented, so the wipers only smeared the mud across the glass, taking away all visibility. My uncle had to keep getting out of the car and wiping off the mud with a cloth, which periodically had to be shaken and wrung out. This only helped for a short time, as he soon caught up to the car ahead of us, which sprayed us again with mud from its rear wheels. He fell back to a safe distance, but that didn't entirely solve the problem either, because cars passing the other way threw up massive amounts of mud. Of course, all the other drivers were having the same problems. When eventually we got back to Regina, you couldn't tell what colour the car was. We were a blob of mobile mud.

In Regina and elsewhere on the Prairies, clothing was always an important consideration in winter. My mother worked for a time in the women's coat department on the second floor of the Army and Navy Store. I would often visit her there after school or on Saturdays, although the latter was usually discouraged because it was the store's busiest day of the week and she would rarely have time to spend with me. If she was with a customer when I came up, I would bide my time among the fur coats, which dangled from hangers on racks. Their texture attracted me, especially the very soft furs like Hudson seal and mouton. I would bury myself in their folds, letting them caress my face and hands. As spring approached, the stock became depleted, so often my visits were met with disappointment as the rougher pelts remained while my favourites found homes elsewhere.

Television was only just being introduced at the time, so my indoor entertainment consisted of comic books and the radio. The beauty of radio was that it left a lot to the imagination. In my mind I could see the Green

Hornet rushing to the rescue, or the Shadow describing the "evil that lurks in the minds of men," or the scene in the rink as Maurice Richard raced down the ice and scored, or Joe Louis knocking out Billy Conn. I knew how the real people actually looked from pictures in magazines or comic books, so it was easy to project them into the situations described on the radio.

Another curiosity of winters on the Prairies was milk. Store-bought milk was a rarity for my family. I don't recall seeing it in stores, although I'm sure it was there — somewhere. Milk was delivered daily to our home by a milkman, who arrived each morning very early in a horse-drawn carriage. (My cousin Linda, upon reading an earlier draft of this manuscript, reminded me, "We were always happy when the horse that drew the milk truck didn't take a dump in front of our house.") He left the bottles of milk in the front porch of our home, which was always left unlocked. His name was Johnny, and once a week he collected money for his product.

Milk in those days always came in glass bottles with round, flat cardboard tops, on which was indicated the breed of cow that had produced this particular bovine beverage. For example, my favourite milk came from a Jersey cow, and was so labelled. Harvey Lyman used to drink milk directly from the bottle. He drank with such gusto that I was inspired, and to this day I also drink my milk straight from the bottle or carton, when not in company. From a glass bottle, though, it somehow tastes better. (I also learned from Harvey the joy of open-faced ketchup sandwiches, especially on fresh white bread.)

Since the milk was delivered about two hours before anyone was awake and ready to bring it in, during the winter we always found it frozen. Upon entering the porch to retrieve the bottles, we'd see that the frozen milk had risen out of the neck of the bottle by one or two inches, with the cardboard cap sitting on top like a hat. As well, the milk would have separated, with the cream filling the upper quarter of the bottle and protruding out into the open air. (I have sometimes wondered if that wasn't the original inspiration for creating Popsicles and Creamsicles.) Once the milk thawed, one had the choice of skimming off the cream and using it separately for coffee or other purposes, leaving skim milk, or shaking the bottle (a process we today call "homogenization") until everything was blended, giving a rich-tasting beverage. In warm weather the milk and cream separated the same way, minus the added height.

In summer, perishables were stored in the basement, which was the coolest part of the house, but not cool enough to keep some items from spoiling after two or three days. We threw out a lot of stuff. Eventually we got an icebox, which meant twice-weekly deliveries from the iceman, and which was an improvement over the basement. Great excitement was aroused in our home when we finally got a refrigerator. As I loved really cold milk, I was in heaven.

Still on the topic of milk: At Thomson School, when lunch hour came, a select group of children were sent to one of the classrooms where, I eventually learned, they were given free milk to drink. I was envious of them and always wondered why I was being excluded. One day, after complaining to someone about not being one of the chosen, I was informed that these kids came from very poor families who couldn't afford to provide all the nutrition their children needed. The milk was a supplement, and, to the best of my knowledge, this program was in effect across the city, if not the entire province. I felt somewhat ashamed that I had been envious of those less fortunate than myself, as I always went home at lunchtime to a healthy and abundant meal, no matter what financial struggles my parents and grandparents were having. I think I can say the same for all the Jewish kids, who, it seemed, never lacked food, even though times were difficult. In a Jewish home in those days, the recurring expression by parents was *"ess mine kint"* (eat, my child), and it's the same today.

You may be curious about what we cooked on: It was a wood stove, with the wood delivered periodically by the woodman and housed in the car garage. My job was to chop it into sizeable pieces and bring it in. We never did get an electric stove.

In the spring, as everything melted, streams of water would hurry toward sewer grates, and we took advantage of this by racing matchsticks, twigs, or other make-believe boats down the waterways. The blood in our veins kept pace with the flowing water; we thawed and began removing layer after layer of clothing. On the Prairies, each season is clear and distinct — spring is spring, summer is summer, and so on. There are no grey seasons; each has its own personality that brings with it a bounty of magnificence as well as challenges. For example, one of the challenges of spring was the arrival of infestations of grasshoppers. On our trips into the country, when I walked through the wheat fields, as each step rustled the wheat, swarms of grasshoppers would jump up. They were a real menace to the farmers, destroying crops and bringing financial hardship.

Somewhere north of Regina, on a fishing trip with my dad and his friend Frank Schmidt, I fired my last shot at a living creature. (Prior to this, I had done some small-time hunting but rarely hit anything.) On a day that wasn't conducive to fishing, I took a .22-calibre rifle belonging to Frank and went out into the bush to hunt crows and gophers. My justification for wanting to kill these creatures was that they were a nuisance to farmers and, like the grasshoppers, damaged their crops. I didn't find any gophers, but I did spot some crows. For those not familiar with crows, they're big, black, and very smart. Every time I lifted the rifle and took aim, the crow flew off. It was uncanny, as if the crow had a sixth sense and was teasing me. Finally, one stood still long enough for me to get off a shot. The bullet grazed its chest; I saw a few feathers fly and watched the crow, merely startled, soar into the sky out of sight. I realized then that a .22-calibre bullet was useless against a crow, unless it was hit in the head at relatively close range. Later, I would learn that there are .22-calibre bullets, and there are .22-calibre bullets. Some are more powerful than others.

The next day my dad and I left to return home. I asked Frank if I could take the gun with me and return it to him in Regina, just in case along the way I saw something I wanted to shoot at. As it happened, we had driven only a few miles along the country road when I spotted a hawk sitting at a considerable distance on top of a telephone pole. I asked my father to stop the car so I could take a shot, explaining that hawks steal and kill farmers' chickens and therefore deserve to die. He reluctantly stopped the car, and I took the gun out of the trunk. It occurred to me, as I steadied my arm on a fence post, that if a crow was practically impervious to a .22 bullet, a hawk, which was bigger and stronger, was an impossible target. I also realized that my chances of hitting the bird at that distance were slim, if the bullet even made it that far. I pulled the trigger and, to my astonishment, watched the hawk, with only one wing flapping, fall slowly to the ground. I ran over to where it stood, unable to fly, and saw that the bullet had broken its wing. My dad came over as quickly as he could, limping on his polio-ravaged leg. It was the first time either of us had seen a hawk up close. It was a magnificent creature and glared at us with a ferocity I'll never forget. Then I realized that I couldn't leave it to starve or be attacked by other animals. This would have added to the cruelty I had already inflicted. I told my dad that I had to destroy the animal. I aimed at its head and again pulled the trigger. But it wouldn't die. I had to shoot it over and over again, until finally it fell over and was still. To this day that scene haunts me, and deep regrets remain embedded in my memory. I have never since pointed a gun at anything that lives.

As mentioned, I learned to drive when I was fifteen, one year below the legal driving age in Saskatchewan. My dad felt I was ready, and probably wanted to stop me from pestering him so much, so he took me outside the city onto a country road, switched places with me, explained how the clutch worked, and away I went in his black Pontiac. I guess I was a natural at driving; after just a few lessons I felt I had been behind the wheel for years. He would not, of course, let me drive in the city until I earned my licence. When that glorious day arrived, I couldn't have been more happy. The taste of freedom that the car offered was intoxicating, and thereafter I drove at every opportunity. Later on, when cars started showing up with automatic transmissions, I didn't trust them, and it was years before I felt comfortable in a clutchless auto. To this day I prefer a stick shift, but only in cars with a sportslike transmission such as a BMW, where my body can move in rhythm to the sound of the engine as it revs up on a quiet country road. In the city, I prefer an automatic, and since I live in the city and I can't afford two cars, that's what I drive. My current car has a feature that allows me to switch to manual, but I never use it because it doesn't sound or feel like the real thing. I have taught both my children to drive standard so that they will be able to cope with any type of vehicle, in any situation. My romance with the automobile has indeed been an ongoing affair.

A final note on the Army and Navy Store, where many members of my family worked. My uncle Israel, who had suggested the "return ticket" when I was born, was the manager of the ladies' wear department on the second floor. He had a wry and unusual sense of humour, and I've always considered the following story a family heirloom: One day he saw my mother struggling to persuade a customer to buy a coat. He came over, my mother stepped aside, and he took the sleeve of the coat in his hands. Looking straight at the customer, he said, "Madam, do you realize that this coat is made of one hundred percent pure imported *drek* [Yiddish for "crap"] from England?"

"Really!" she replied.

"Yes," he responded, "pure *drek*."

Israel Steinberg

She bought the coat. (According to my mother, it was actually a good coat, but my uncle couldn't let an opportunity pass to have some good-natured fun.)

There is an old song that begins, "The sky at night is clear and bright, deep in the heart of Texas." This, as alluded to earlier, is typical of the Prairies. For a period of time in the sixties, my father was a partner in the Dreamland Motel in Moose Jaw, which we used to visit frequently. Moose Jaw is forty miles west of Regina, and it takes about three-quarters of an hour to drive

Sign on outskirts of Regina:
  In the distance is the horizon.
  If one were to turn around in a circle,
  he would see the horizon in all four directions

from one city to the other. Often, when we left Moose Jaw at night, the air and sky were so clear that when we'd driven no more than a mile or two, we could already see the lights of Regina in the distance. At the time Regina had a population of only fifty or sixty thousand, so it gave off a small amount of light compared to other places. Even small towns and hamlets came into view when still a long way off, and even when only a few lights were on. This was especially important in the winter; if your car broke down, and you needed to walk to the nearest farmhouse, sometimes a single light made all the difference.

Speaking of lights, when I was around eight years old, I used to visit my mother's sister, Anne, in Assiniboia, about a hundred and twenty-five miles southwest of Regina. She and her family were good friends with a Catholic priest, Father Honoré Labrecque. He was a wise and kind man to whom people from all walks of life, whether Catholic or not, came for guidance and comfort. I visited him whenever I came to Assiniboia, and he always took time to talk with me. There was, however, one rather peculiar aspect to his taste in furniture that I never quite figured out. In his living room, next to his favourite chesterfield chair, was a bomb. It was white, about two feet high, obviously defused with explosives removed, and mounted so it would stand upright with the point facing the floor. But it was definitely a real bomb, very heavy and somehow procured by the good father, probably given to him as a gift from an admiring aviator during the war. Certain images from childhood never leave one's mind, and in my case, one of them is a white bomb in a priest's living room.

During one of my stays in Assiniboia, I developed a great aversion to snoring. My aunt's mother-in-law came to visit with a friend, and they were housed in the room directly below me. At night, both women snored so loudly that the sound came up through the heat transits and into my room. The snoring was continuous all through the night. They developed a rhythm; as soon as one finished her snore, the other began. Every now and then, in different keys, they snored in unison, making perfect counterpoint. By the fourth day, having not slept at all, I became ill, and my aunt Marion had to come from Regina by train to bring me home. I still can't sleep in or near a room with a snorer. This was negative conditioning at its best.

It seems to me that as a schoolboy, I was sexually very naive, at least compared to some of my friends, particularly those who were not Jewish. I've already mentioned my friend Bev Dinnon; he once told me, when talking about a girl, that he had "put it in her." I gave him a blank stare, wondering where he put what, although as he continued to talk, I began to get the drift of what he was saying. Still, it

Father Honoré Labrecque, circa 1920s (courtesy Archdiocese of Regina)

was all very fuzzy. For example, my friend Norm Rauhaus had a big dog named Blackie. One day he told me that Blackie was a "fucker." I pretended I knew what he meant, but I had never heard the word before and didn't have the foggiest notion what he was talking about. Then, some time later, we observed Blackie having intercourse with another dog. "See," said Norm, "I told you." Eventually I put two and two together, but thought the word only applied to dogs.

Another time, my newly married uncle Lou and aunt Madge returned from their honeymoon and visited with our family for a few days. We lodged them in my room upstairs, and I slept on the couch downstairs. One afternoon, Madge was sitting on the sofa chair, with Lou perched on the arm. He looked at Madge and indicated he wanted to go upstairs with her. Innocently,

Above left: My uncle Lou and auntie Madge not too long after their marriage, circa 1950
Above right: My cousin Sorrel Steinberg with my father, circa 1990
Right: My Zaida's gravestone in the Regina Jewish Cemetery. My son's middle name is "Isaac," after his great-grandfather

I asked him why they were going upstairs. It was, after all, the middle of the day. He replied, "We're going to the races!" Madge flushed, while Lou had a big grin on his face. As for me, I couldn't figure out how they were going to race upstairs, especially since the hallway was so narrow and short. It took me years to get that one.

I always look forward to visiting Regina, not only because my cousin Sorrel still lives there, although that is certainly a good reason in itself, but also because this is where my roots are. I love to wander the streets and reminisce, talk to the people and breathe the clean, fresh air. On each occasion that I return, I always spend some time in the Jewish cemetery. There I first say hello to my grandparents, Rebecca and Isaac David, and then walk slowly between the rows of gravestones, looking at the names and bringing to mind and heart a whole history of my childhood. Even the rabbi who circumcised me is buried there.

In the summer of 1988, my dad, my children, and I took a roots trip. My kids and I flew to Winnipeg from Toronto and from there drove Dad's maroon

'88 Oldsmobile to Saskatchewan. We visited Thomson School (some construction was being done inside, so the doors were open), and I showed my kids the rooms where I was a student and even where I sat. I introduced them to 1819 Ottawa Street and the back alleys where I used to play. We wandered around the Army and Navy Store, went to the cemetery so that Dahlia and Meher could meet their great-grandparents on my mother's side, and visited with other relatives. While in Regina, we stayed with my cousin Sorrel and his family.

What stands out most in my mind from that very special time is a moment on the way to Hirsch, where my father was born. We suddenly came upon a vast field of sunflowers, many the size of a dinner plate, stretching out to the horizon. I stopped the car at what I thought would be an opportune spot to take a good picture of my children among the sunflowers. They initially objected because there was a ditch with water in it between us and the field, but I coaxed them into jumping over it. We climbed the short but steep bank, and entered a sea of gold. The picture I took has been reproduced many times for different occasions, and for years commanded a prominent place in my living room.

We left the sunflower field (by the way, for those not in the know, sunflowers follow the sun, turning as the sun moves across the sky) and continued on into Hirsch, where there was one store, a few other structures, and not much else. Time has not been kind to this once thriving farming community. We tried to find the homestead where my

Top: My children, Meher and Dahlia, 1988
Above: Dahlia on the tractor, 1988

father was born and spent his early years, but were unable to locate it. We did, however, find one Jewish farmer, who welcomed our visit, showed us around his highly successful farming operation, and gave my children permission to climb up and sit in the seat of his massive tractor.

We left the farm and continued on for several miles until we arrived at the Hirsch Jewish cemetery. It's next to the road and seems to be in the middle of nowhere. My father's mother, Sarah Steinberg, is buried there, and it was a moving moment for my father and my kids, not to mention myself, to see the grave of my children's great-grandmother. Fortunately, the Hirsch cemetery has been designated a historical site, commemorating the arrival of Jewish settlers from eastern Europe under the auspices of Baron de Hirsch and the Canadian government. It is therefore looked after, more or less. From here we travelled a short distance to Estevan, where my father and his siblings lived and went to school for many years, and then on to Regina.

Full circle: my children, Meher and Dahlia, in front of 1819 Ottawa Street, 1988

Over the years I have visited Regina many times. On each occasion, I pay my respects to the Maple Leaf Bakery on Eleventh Avenue, just two blocks from where I used to live. In all my travels I have never tasted rye bread as good as that baked at this small, aromatic bakery. As a kid, I used to arrive there when I knew it was time for the bread to come out of the oven, and I could hardly wait to bring it home, where it would enhance any condiment. I was not alone in my praise of this bread; often, I would have to wait in a long line before acquiring a loaf, and more than once I was disappointed when it sold out before my turn came. Upon one visit to Regina, I learned that the bakery had burned down and been rebuilt, with new ovens. As usual, I went in and bought a loaf. It was good, but never again the same.

"IF YOU WILL IT, IT IS NOT A DREAM"

—THEODOR HERZL, FATHER OF THE JEWISH STATE
Israel, 1954–1955, 1998, 2005

1954–1955

I knew the welcome was canned
                    but it didn't matter
            passing over the shoreline
                        over corrugated roofs
            we touched down
                        on soil
                                aged with the wisdom
                    and struggle
                                of forty centuries
                It didn't matter
                        that peace was not yet
                                        in the land
                        that group rallied
                                        against group
                        that Isaiah's vision
                                        remained a vision
                in this moment
                                it didn't matter

On a late summer day in Regina in 1954, with the sun bright, the air clear and dry, and the temperature in the mid eighties, I boarded a train at the CNR station on South Railway Street. My parents saw me off, their eyes moist, their hearts reluctant to let me go. In my hands was a large brown paper bag filled almost to the brim with food, just to be sure I had enough to eat on the three-day journey to Montreal. Other relatives were also present, though I don't recall exactly who. I found my seat and looked out the window at my parents and well-wishers, waving as the train sounded its bell and began to move out of the station. I was on my way to Israel.

A program had been developed by the Israeli government in conjunction with the World Zionist Organization to bring Jewish students from around the world to Israel for one year of intensive training as youth leaders. It was expected that, following the training, the students would return to their respective countries and serve the cause of Judaism and Israel for at least two years. Funds were provided by the Zionist Organization to cover almost all costs for each student. Everyone was sponsored by one of the worldwide Jewish youth movements — in my case, Young Judaea.

In Montreal, I met with my fellow travellers, nine Young Judaeans in all, seven girls and two boys, some of whom I already knew from camps and conferences. For all of us, it would be our first time in Israel.

Our flight was aboard a four-engine aircraft with a refuelling stop in Gander, Newfoundland. The long flight itself was relatively uneventful, except when morning came. Just before breakfast, several men with black hats and *peyos* (sidelocks) stood up in the aisles, put on *tefillin* (phylacteries — small black boxes containing parchment with scriptural readings attached to black leather straps) over their heads and around uncovered arms, and began to pray aloud. It was time for *Shachrit*, the Jewish morning prayers.

A few hours later, the captain's voice informed us that we were beginning our descent to Lydda airport near Tel Aviv. Those of us with window seats strained to get our first glimpse of the coastline. The air was electric, and we broke out with Hebrew songs that we had learned over the years, our spirits soaring as the plane brought us closer. Finally the coastline came into view, and our voices responded with fervour. Upon touching down there were shouts and tears, and when we disembarked, I don't think there was a dry eye among our group. Upon setting foot on Israeli soil, I and a few others bent down and kissed the tarmac. I was overwhelmed.

We boarded a small bus waiting for us outside the airport and began a ninety-minute journey to Jerusalem, which was to be our home for the next five months. En route, we passed burned-out military vehicles, left by the roadside as memorials and reminders of the price paid by Jewish soldiers who gave their lives so that we and others might come to this ancient land in peace, to visit, to live, or to find sanctuary.

The Institute for Training Youth Leaders from Abroad, called for short the Machon, was situated in the Katamon district of Jerusalem, not far from what is known as the German Colony. The residences for the students, about 120 of us from all over the world, were divided into two locations. The main residence was in the heart of Katamon at 15 Rechov Melachim (Street of the Kings). The other residence, which is where I lived, was a fifteen-minute walk across a barren field and, before Israel became a state six years earlier, had been a brothel. Upon entering the front door of this three-story heavy stone building, one was greeted by a long, narrow set of stairs, at the top of which was a small room with an open window facing the stairs. This is where the brothel's madam would sit during business hours, and one wouldn't have been able to get farther into the building without passing her and paying the appropriate fee. Outside each room was a balcony where I was told the women would stand and, in various ways, try to attract interested customers on the street below. In my overactive imagination I tried to picture what that scene must have been like.

> This brothel
> where once I lived
> now houses decent folk
> no more
> do illicit ladies
> adorn the balconies
> no more
> the soldiers in heat
> straining their necks
> for a glimpse

of a naked calf
an uncovered thigh
a silhouetted breast

no more
cash flow
through the narrow window
past the guardian
of stolen delights

now
only stone memories
ghosts of passion
and grey floors

The furnishings in my room were simple: a bed, more like a cot, a small table and chair, and not much else. In the winter, the heating system was poor — I had to wear layers to keep warm — and the walk to the main resi-dence, which also housed classrooms and offices, was often cold and windy, not at all matching my vision of Israel as a place with a warm climate. However, an hour's drive south of Jerusalem brought one to the desert where, except at night, it was always warm.

After settling in, everyone was required to register with the Machon secretary, a man I can only recall by the name of Carmeli. I entered his office and introduced myself. He asked me a number of questions in English, such as where I was from and what my background was regarding the Hebrew language. Then he asked for my Hebrew name. I told him it was Yoina.

"Yoina?" he responded. "There is no such name."

"But," I protested, "Yoina is what I've been called all of my life."

"No such name!" he repeated.

"I don't understand," I replied, trying to push my case further. He was adamant that the name Yoina did not exist. Then, ignoring my protests, he went on: "I can give you a choice of two names — Yoel or Yuval" (often spelled Jubal in English). Realizing that I was not going to win this contest, I decided on Yuval, which in Hebrew means Jubilee, referring in the bible to the Jubilee year when land was returned to its original owner. There is also a Yuval, in the book of Genesis, who is associated with music. I soon regretted my choice, as once my friends learned of my new name they often called me "Jewballs."

The irony of all this is that not only is one of the books of the Hebrew Scriptures called by my name, Yona, but one of my teachers at the Machon, and many Israelis, had the same name. So what was Mr. Carmeli thinking? I can only surmise that he didn't like the name Yoina, with an "i" in it, as opposed to Yona, without the "i," because the former has an Ashkenazi pronunciation and the latter a Sephardi pronunciation. He probably associated the Ashkenazi pronunciation with old eastern European Jewry, as opposed to modern Israeli Jewry, who have always followed the Sephardi pronunciation. Pronunciation aside, the names are exactly the same. He was no doubt saying to me, "Mr. Steinberg, you are now in Israel, this is a Jewish state, so get used to how we speak around here." Of course, he never explained any of this to me. He just insisted that there was no such name as Yoina. To this day, those who knew me in Israel call me Yuval, and sometimes, with a smile, Jewballs.

The program at the Machon was intensive and consisted, among other things, of studies in the Hebrew language, Jewish history, literature, philosophy, geography, song and dance, and the development of the Zionist movement leading to the establishment of the State of Israel. It also involved extended hikes or tours across the country. Our first, lasting five days, was

Machon photo of all those associated with Young Judaea from different countries. I'm standing in the middle at the back. Jerusalem 1955

to the southern part of Israel known as the Negev. Army trucks picked us up in Jerusalem and, accompanied by three soldiers, we started out on our excursion. Two of the soldiers sat in the front, one driving, and the third joined us in the back. All three were armed. The soldier sitting at the back of the covered truck held between his legs a 50-calibre machine gun.

About two hours into our journey, we approached a section of the road called Ma'a'ley Akravim (Scorpion's Pass), where a year or so earlier a convoy of army vehicles had been ambushed by the Arabs and several soldiers killed. A minute before entering the pass, the soldier sitting with us positioned his machine gun so that the barrel protruded from the end of the truck and could be clearly seen by any enemy who might be awaiting us. He primed the gun, as we waited anxiously to get through the pass. Fortunately, nothing happened. A few miles down the road we stopped to stretch our legs, and the soldier, along with his machine gun, accompanied us. At one point, near a valley, he set the gun on the ground and fired several rounds over to the other side. We could see the puffs of dust fly up as each bullet landed. Of course, being a lover of guns, I was fascinated and would gladly have taken command of the gun myself had the soldier offered. This didn't happen, and the soldier was careful not to let anyone near the weapon. It was the first and only time in my life that I was present when a machine gun was fired.

Later that night, we slept in the desert, where I learned just how cold deserts can be when the sun goes down. Aside from this, however, I found the desert to be a magnificent place. Somehow, it spoke to my soul, perhaps because I'm from the Prairies, where the expanse of land and sky is very much the same. I remember lying on the sand and looking up through the crystal-clear air at the stars, feeling that if I just extended my arm a little, I could touch one.

The following morning we stopped at the Dead Sea, took a swim — or more accurately, a float atop the water (just like Manitou Lake) — and moved from there to Kibbutz Ein Hashloshah. There was discussion among our leaders about visiting Masada, but they decided we didn't have time. I was disappointed, having very much wanted to see the place where the Jews had held off the Romans 1,900 years earlier and where, in modern Israel, we were told, the paratroopers received their final initiation.

At Ein Hashloshah, I had a brush with death. The first night there, I went to sleep on a very lumpy bed. At about two a.m., I got up to relieve myself and headed for the outhouse. The first thing I noticed as I emerged from my cabin was a string of very bright lights surrounding the kibbutz. I knew we were near the Gaza Strip and that there was danger, but I couldn't figure out why they would want to light up the kibbutz. Wasn't this an invitation to anyone who wanted to find this settlement and do it harm? Then, below the lights, I saw the movement of a guard. He was dressed all in white, and if not for his movement, I would not have seen him at all. He was fully camouflaged. Also, because the lights illuminated a considerable distance, he would be able to see anyone approach without them seeing him.

I continued on, but somehow wandered off the path to the outhouse. As I tried to find my way back, I suddenly heard a loud voice shout *"Mi zeh sham?"* (Who goes there?) I froze in my tracks and, looking up, saw the barrel of a .303 rifle aimed at my head. I quickly sputtered *"Ani — Yuval, min ha Machon"* (Me, Yuval, from the Machon). To my relief, I saw the barrel lowered, and the voice, much softer, said *"B'seder!"* (Okay). I caught my breath, asked for directions to the outhouse, and stumbled on with trembling legs the rest of the way.

The next morning, after a rough night's sleep, I decided to look under the mattress to see why it was so lumpy. I discovered several clips of live rifle ammunition, stored there in case of an emergency.

The following day we left Ein Hashloshah and headed for the well-known kibbutz of S'dey Boker, where David Ben Gurion resided. (At that time, he was taking a two-year break from the position of Prime Minister of Israel.) He came to greet us, and we conversed for about half an hour. I was honoured to be in the presence of such a great man, one whom I had read about many times but never expected to actually meet in person. I recall that as I listened to his every word, the image of him standing on his head kept creeping into my mind. I had heard that he was a practitioner of yoga, of which at the time I knew nothing, except that it taught that standing on one's head was healthy and invigorating. So, here was this great man sharing with us his wisdom, while I kept seeing him inverted, his tufts of white side-hair drooping toward the ground. (Many years later in Cincinnati, I went to hear a lecture by the renowned violinist Yehudi Menuhin. I had read somewhere that he too was a student of yoga and the headstand, so while he spoke, I envisioned him balancing on his head, violin in hand, playing away, and I thought of Ben Gurion.)

Also on that trip, I recall that one day our group was approached by a Bedouin boy, perhaps fifteen years of age, with a submachine gun in his hands. Apparently the soldiers with us knew him, so they were not concerned. The boy spoke to us briefly in Arabic, his words translated by one of the soldiers. For me, this encounter presented a disconnect. Back in Canada, the thought of a fifteen-year-old with a machine gun would be beyond comprehension; a BB gun, yes, or even a .22-calibre rifle, but anything beyond this would never have crossed my mind.

My memory of the desert is profound for two reasons. First, it is exquisitely beautiful and powerful. And second, each kibbutz we visited had performed what the world had thought impossible — they made the desert bloom. Trees, flowers, gardens, and crops of various kinds — all were there for me to see, and everywhere else, sand. It was a modern miracle, and this agricultural know-how has since been exported by Israel to many countries. I also felt proud that in some small way, back in Regina, I had contributed to all of this by collecting money for the Jewish National Fund in order to reclaim the land in what was then Palestine and now Israel.

The desert bloomed as the result of human effort, but it also presented its own natural vegetation. The best example of this that I recall seeing was in the area around Ein Gedi, in the northeastern part of the desert. We hiked for about an hour into the hills and gorges of this remarkable landscape, ending up at a pool fed by a waterfall. We all went in, some in bathing suits and others in their clothes. It was glorious, especially after a hike in the desert heat. Today, near Ein Gedi, a kibbutz by the same name sports an array of flora that is breathtaking.

I was well into my studies and had been progressing with the language, but the day after we returned to Jerusalem from our five-day tour and hike, my life was rudely and painfully interrupted. As I was walking from my residence to classes at the main building, I noticed that I had a slight crick in my right knee. Thinking I must have strained my leg while on the tour, I thought nothing of it, expecting it to disappear after a day or two of rest. Instead, things continued to get worse, until I was forced into bed. My knee swelled up to at least double its normal size, accompanied by intense discomfort. Within two weeks I was in the Machon infirmary, in such excruciating pain that I was unable to shave myself and could take very little food. I was fortunately blessed to have a wonderful nurse, Dahlia, and two of my friends from Canada — Richy Soberman and Henny Lowy — were nothing short of angels, helping and attending to my every need.

A week later I was in Hadassah Hospital, where I remained for the next two weeks. The doctors there were unable to diagnose my condition, which seemed to deteriorate with each passing day. They kept sticking a very large needle into my knee and drawing out fluid, which was then sent to the lab. This procedure was so painful that before they began, the nurses would close all the doors on the floor, so the other patients wouldn't hear my screams. The doctors, Macki and Weinberg, decided that surgery would be called for unless there was some improvement. Either that or I would have to be sent home to Canada, as it appeared there was nothing more they could do. My body, or my psyche, or my unconscious, didn't like either option, and within two days I began to respond to treatment. A week later I was returned to the Machon infirmary, and eventually back to my residence. I had lost twenty-seven pounds, was walking with a cane, and was very much behind in my studies. I returned to my classes at a lower level and did the best I could for the next two months before leaving the Machon for Kibbutz Tel Yitzchak.

To this day, my knee has never been the same, although it did recover well enough that I could walk normally, and I eventually learned to downhill ski. From time to time it still acts up, and at present I have substituted curling for skiing because the latter requires two good knees.

Like everyone else at the Machon, we went to live on one or more kibbutzim (plural) for the next five months. This was built into our program and was an essential part of our Israel experience. All the Canadians stayed together for the kibbutz sojourns; we spent three months at Tel Yitzchak, and later two months at Hasolelim. Tel Yitzchak, a kibbutz affiliated with Canadian Young *Judaea*, was located between Tel Aviv and Haifa.

Like my companions, I did whatever work was required of me. One day I would be out in the fields, the next day in the kitchen, and then back to the fields or elsewhere. The routine was to arise at five a.m. and go to work. If we were heading to the fields, we would take supplies for breakfast with us, as the distance was too great to come back for breakfast or lunch in the communal dining hall. Usually we worked until eight a.m., then broke for breakfast. I found that working hard for three hours before eating resulted in a hunger the likes of which I had never experienced. It was, therefore, with good reason that the supplies we brought with us were abundant, my appetite being matched by my fellow workers. On occasion, a local Arab, a friend of the kibbutz, would join us for breakfast, and he would ply us with thick, delicious black Turkish coffee. After breakfast all I wanted to do was sleep, but the day was demanding and there was no time to be idle. One of my main tasks in the fields was to rotate pipes so that the crops could be evenly watered. This meant detaching each pipe and moving it to another location. By the time I had detached a long series of pipes and placed them elsewhere, it was time to start over again from the beginning. Usually it took two of us to work a pipe, as they were long and heavy.

Perhaps the easiest and most enjoyable job at Tel Yitzchak was working in the orchard, where the trees were heavy with oranges and grapefruit. I would begin by placing a ladder up against a tree, the ladder's top in the branches. Then I would climb as high as I could and begin picking oranges or grapefruit and placing them in a sack that I had slung over one shoulder. When the sack was filled I would climb down and empty it into a cart, which, when full, would be attached to a tractor and taken away. It was my responsibility to stay with the same tree until all the ripe fruits were picked and then move on to the next one.

My first day on the ladder did not end well. Israeli oranges, often called Jaffas, are particularly sweet and juicy with an irresistible fragrance, especially when your head is planted in their midst. So, every fifteen or twenty minutes I would eat an orange, letting the peels drop to the ground. Averaging three to four oranges an hour, by early afternoon I had downed over a dozen. As I was about to indulge in my fourteenth or fifteenth orange, I suddenly didn't feel too well. I spent the next two days in bed within close range of the toilet. I had a severe case of what the Israelis call *shilshul*, or, as we call it back in Canada, the runs.

By the third day I was well enough to return to the orchard, this time very wary of the enemy. I would not go beyond inhaling the fragrance — and actually, having had my fill, was not even tempted. Instead, remembering that not long ago I had pitched fastball in high school and had aspirations to be a big-league pitcher, I decided to exercise my arm. Every now and then, spotting the perfect-sized orange, I would throw it as far as I could while standing on the ladder. The orange would whistle through distant branches, sometimes dislodging other oranges and sometimes hitting one of my fellow workers. Being high up in the tree, I figured I was well hidden and no one would know who was throwing. Before long, however, the man in charge of the orchard saw the direction from which each orange was coming, put two and two together, and asked me not to throw any more oranges, as each orange that I dislodged became bruised when it hit the ground and was then not fit for market. Besides, he said, I might hurt someone. The first reason made more sense to me than the second, as I couldn't imagine that an orange, thrown from a distance, could harm anyone. So I resisted the ongoing temptation to throw — unless I believed no one was around to catch me. I was careless, however, and my next few missiles drew a shout from my boss: "*Yuval, al tizrok tapuzim.*" (Yuval, don't throw oranges.) Finally, his patience was exhausted and, before long, I was assigned to other, less enjoyable work.

One day, in the early evening, I went for a walk with one of my female friends from Canada. We ended up on the outskirts of the kibbutz, where we sat down on the ground to talk. About an hour later, deep in conversation, we did not hear approaching footsteps. Suddenly, a firm and sharp voice called out to us, asking us who we were and what we were doing here. We looked up to see a man with a rifle pointed at us (shades of Ein Hashloshah). We identified ourselves and then were raked over the coals for not informing anyone at the kibbutz where we were going. Apparently, an alert had gone out that two people, unknown to anyone, were on the ground near the end of the kibbutz. From the perspective of the kibbutz, there were two unwelcome possibilities: we might be Arabs bent on attacking the kibbutz, or we might be visitors to the kibbutz, in which case our lives could be in danger. It was a lesson to all of us from the Machon, and thereafter the rules were carefully observed.

When I left Jerusalem for Tel Yitzchak, I had decided that I was not going to let my knee stand in the way of doing what was expected of me on the kibbutz. As it turned out, this was a good decision. By the two-month point of our stay at Tel Yitzchak my health was fully restored, and by the time I left the kibbutz I was not only healthy, but also stronger than I had ever been in my life. In fact, instead of my normal weight of 172 pounds, I was now 185 pounds, all muscle and without an ounce of fat on me. I felt I could lift a horse and was more than ready for whatever awaited me at my next residence.

Just before departing from Tel Yitzchak, I had an interesting side adventure in the world of medicine. As I've mentioned, I had always wanted to be a doctor ever since I was a very young man. While at Tel Yitzchak I learned that only a few miles away was a very good hospital by the name of Beilinson. Somehow I managed to get permission from the kibbutz to explore the possibility of working there for a short time. Given my orderly experience, the hospital was happy to have me, and I agreed to work in return for room and board but without any other compensation. I was assigned to a senior orderly and followed him around for the first few days, doing whatever needed to be done.

I don't recall the senior orderly's name, but I do recall something he said that left its mark on me. We received a call one day to pick up the body of a young child who had just died. Upon entering the ward, we passed through a small waiting room where the parents of the child were sitting, apparently waiting to complete the paperwork that is required in such situations. My senior colleague somehow knew that these were the child's parents and, once we had passed through the waiting room, mentioned this fact to me. We entered the room where the child's body lay, whereupon my colleague took a small sheet, placed the body on it, and tied the sheet in such a way that it looked like he was carrying a bag of laundry. We then walked back through the waiting room, past the unsuspecting parents, and out of the building. Though my colleague seemed cavalier about this act, it must have had some effect on him, as he turned to me while we were walking and said, *"Mah zeh ben adom? Kloom!"* ("What is man? Nothing!") Perhaps he was echoing words from the Book of Ecclesiastes — "All is vanity" — or similar sentiments from other Jewish sources. Whatever the case, I pondered his words off and on for many years, always in the end denying their meaning and then questioning my denial. Only much later, as my understanding of spirituality broadened, particularly with regard to the existence of the soul, did I feel confident in asserting the unquestionable worth of a human being.

I had made it known that I was going to enter pre-med in university when I returned to Canada, so when there was no work for me to do as an orderly, I was given free rein to explore the hospital. I was even permitted to enter any operating room and watch surgical procedures. (I don't know how I pulled this one off. I suspect that in Israel, or at least in this particular hospital, regulations were much less stringent than they would have been back in Canada.) So, dressed in full gown and mask, I wandered the halls of the operating floor, visiting one operating theatre after another, talking with the surgeons and asking questions while they worked. In one operating room, a man lay with his legs in stirrups while an instrument protruded from his penis. At the end of the instrument was what appeared to be an eyepiece of some kind, and one of the doctors was looking through it, making some remarks about how interesting this case was. I was invited to look also (they most likely thought I was an intern). Upon doing so, in order not to expose my complete ignorance, I said something neutral but mildly enthusiastic, like, "Hmmm!"

The most exciting part of my entire stay at Beilinson Hospital was the hour I spent watching brain surgery by the acclaimed neurosurgeon Dr. Ashkenazi. I remember waiting for him to enter the operating room while other doctors prepared the patient by removing the top part of his skull. When Dr. Ashkenazi came in, they stepped aside while he looked at the brain tissue and did some kind of procedure. After about twenty minutes, he concluded his work, walked out of the room, and left the other doctors to close up the opening. As I recall, the entire operation took several hours, all of it used for preparation and closure, except for those few minutes with Dr. Ashkenazi. To say I was impressed would be a gross understatement. I remember asking about the doctor as we awaited his presence and being told of the near-miraculous surgeries he had performed on many soldiers with head wounds during and after the 1948 War of Independence. When I left Beilinson Hospital a few days later, I felt that I had been very privileged to be in this great man's presence and was further inspired to pursue medicine as a career.

MY NEXT RESIDENCE was at Kibbutz Hasolelim, which was somewhat smaller than Tel Yitzchak and not as well developed. It was about twenty miles from Nazareth, the largest Arab community in Israel. As best I can recall, Hasolelim was populated mostly by North Americans, with some others from Israel and Europe. My stay there was as interesting and eventful as my Tel Yitzchak experience.

What first comes to mind is my first day stooking hay. The day began like any other, warm and bright. My job was to take hay lying on the ground and, with my pitchfork, toss it onto a lorry. This work reminded me of shovelling snow in Regina, as it had to be done with many breaks so I could catch my breath. Even with the Regina experience under my belt, five or ten minutes of stooking was all I could do in one stretch. Then I would lean against my pitchfork or sit on the ground until I was breathing normally again. By noon I was exhausted and welcomed the one-hour lunch break.

After lunch, and revived, I returned to my task. About an hour later, I noticed that the air began to feel heavy, and a soft, very warm wind started to blow. Over the ensuing minutes I found myself getting weaker and weaker, until finally I could barely lift my pitchfork. I thought initially that there must be something wrong with me, until I noticed that even the hardened kibbutzniks were slowing down. Then I heard someone say, *"Hamsin!"* I asked for an explanation and was told that a *Hamsin*, or desert wind, had arrived, and that our workday would probably be shortened. Before long, I couldn't lift my pitchfork, even though I was in the best shape of my life. It was as though every bit of vital energy in me had been sapped. I packed it in, and everyone else followed a short time later. In talking about this to long-standing kibbutz members, I was assured that my reaction was normal and that a *Hamsin* made everyone feel debilitated. No exceptions. It was the only time while in Israel that I had this experience. The next day, everything was back to normal.

On another day, I was assigned to work in the *refet* (cow barn). The cows were lined up one beside the other, with their rear ends perched over a trough in the cement floor. This design allowed the animals to defecate directly into the trough, making it easier to clean up. My job was to shovel the droppings into a wheelbarrow and take it out to a dumping spot. Again, I was reminded of shovelling snow, only now I had to be careful not to get the stuff all over me as, unlike snow, it doesn't come off easily. Of course, I didn't succeed, which is why, when lunchtime came, I and the others working in the *refet* were made to wait until everyone else had left the dining room before we could enter. Once inside, with the smell all over my fellow workers and me, it was difficult to enjoy the food, no matter how hungry I was.

Two other events remain embedded in my memory from my stay at Hasolelim.

One morning, a member of the kibbutz came to our group and informed us that we would be having lunch in a Bedouin's home. When we arrived at the home, which turned out to be a tent, we were greeted by a young man, perhaps in his mid-twenties. He invited us into his tent, which was divided into two sections: one for dining and sleeping, the other a kitchen. We were told that he had been recently married and that his wife was busy preparing lunch for us on the other side of the divide.

We sat in a circle on the floor, which consisted of earth and a few mats. He spoke neither English nor Hebrew, only Arabic, so our guide acted as interpreter. Our conversation with him was nothing out of the ordinary, mainly about how he passed his day, when he got married, and so on. In return, we answered his questions about where we came from and how we liked Israel.

After some chitchat, a plate was passed through an opening in the partition that separated the kitchen from where we were sitting. On the plate was a stack of pita bread, each piece about the size of a large dinner plate. We were told that these were our napkins and we should use them as such. Some of us placed them on our laps while others tried, with only moderate success, to stuff them bib-style into their shirts or blouses.

Eventually, the food began to arrive, one dish at a time, always almost surreptitiously passed through the opening in the partition. Only one time did we get a glimpse of our host's wife, and she was stunning. I hoped that at some point her husband would bring her out and introduce her to us, just so we could enjoy her beauty. That never happened. I was reminded of the line from Thomas Grey's poem "Elegy in a Country Churchyard" — "Many a flower is born to blush unseen and waste its sweetness in the desert air."

The dishes were tasty and mostly cooked in oil, meaning that we often had recourse to our napkins, which by the end of the meal (we ate with our hands) were well coated in grease spots. The main course was chicken, accompanied by an assortment of vegetables, some fried and some not. The meal was completed with a cake-like dessert, also very oily, and dark coffee. All went well until, after about two hours, we felt it was time to leave. We indicated to our guide that we should be going. Having received some instructions from our host, he informed us that we had to eat our napkins. "Astonishment" would be too mild a word to describe the look on our faces. We turned to him and almost with one voice exclaimed, "You've got to be kidding!" He assured us he wasn't; such was the etiquette in this Bedouin's home. Over the next twenty minutes or so, haltingly and with groans and grimaces, we downed our napkins, every last bit. (I felt I might throw up.) Finally, it was time to leave. Our guide then informed us that we couldn't leave until everyone had burped. "This," he exclaimed, "is the custom in a Bedouin's tent, a way of saying 'thank you.' It would be impolite, if not dangerous, to not comply." For the guys this was not a problem, but for the girls it was embarrassing. We (the guys) expressed our appreciation with gusto, whereas for the girls, it was sheer agony. One by one, over a period of a half hour, they squeaked out small sounds that seemed to satisfy our host. Finally, with forced smiles on our faces, we said goodbye and returned to the kibbutz.

On another day, I was asked to be a cowboy. A member of the kibbutz picked me up on his horse, and we rode out to a very wide field on the shores of Lake Kinneret. We dismounted from his steed near a large herd of motley cows, and he introduced me to the cowherder, an Arab who, like the Bedouin, didn't speak or understand a word of Hebrew or English. The kibbutznik told me to help the man out and said that he was my boss — I should do whatever he asked of me. When I asked how I was to do this when we had no common language with which to communicate, he simply said, "Work it out!" and rode away, promising to come back and pick me up at the end of the day. The Arab looked me up and down, turned toward the cattle, and walked away. I awaited instructions, even though I didn't know how they would be presented. After a while the herd began to move. I took a step to follow, which seemed the natural thing to do, but was motioned by the Arab to stay where I was. About an hour later, the herd started moving again, and once more I started to move with them. Again, with his arms and hands, he told me to sit down. This sequence of the herd moving, me trying to move with them, and the Arab telling me to stay where I was happened several more times, until I could barely see the Arab or the herd. I never moved from that spot for the whole day, sitting on the ground in the hot sun until I heard the pounding of hooves at about four p.m. The kibbutznik rode up and asked me what I was doing. When I explained to him what had happened, he gave me a look of disgust and told me to get on the horse behind him, and we rode back to the kibbutz. I was not asked again to tend to that or any other herd. Over the next few days, as I thought about things, it finally dawned on me what was really going on; at least this is my theory. The Arab probably thought that I was to be trained by him to do his job, which would then make him dispensable. So he decided to make me look useless — and succeeded. I trust the herd found its way back.

Fifty years later, almost to the day, I revisited Hasolelim and was not able to recognize the kibbutz. In fact, I was hard-pressed to even see it as a kibbutz, so much had changed.

Originally, the kibbutz was an experiment in living together. In the early days, before Israel became a state, there was no army to protect the settlers; by uniting together in small farming communities, people found physical and economic security in numbers. Some members would guard the kibbutz while others worked the land, looked after the children, and performed other duties such as cooking and building. The children did not live with their parents but stayed in special quarters designed for them. When the parents returned from work each day, they would be with their children until bedtime. On days when there was no school and no work, such as on the Sabbath and other holidays, the family came together, and often the children stayed overnight with their parents. This experiment in communal living was very successful for many decades. Eventually it began to break down, as many of the children left the kibbutz for purposes of higher education and to pursue social and employment opportunities. Today, the kibbutz, with few exceptions, is a shadow of its former self. The original project, rooted in ideologies of equal sharing and looking after one another, has been transformed into a more commercial, privatized enterprise.

I feel a certain sadness in seeing the demise of this great social experiment, one that has been written about extensively and has served as an international model for communal living. This is not the place, nor am I qualified to give an in-depth analysis of the rise and fall of the kibbutz movement. This has been done by others, and the subject continues to be written about by Israeli scholars and by academics around the world. Suffice to say, an era has passed into history, leaving us with much yet to learn about social and communal systems.

When our stay at Hasolelim ended, we returned to Jerusalem for six weeks to complete our program. Back in the city, after five months on kibbutzim, we were assigned to the same residences as before, though not necessarily the same rooms.

On a chilly day in the late spring of 1955, I was in my reassigned room, and I decided I wanted a hot drink. I had water, a tea bag, and a glass, but nothing with which to heat up the water. Some time earlier, one of my friends had told me how to make a simple heating device that could quickly bring water to a boil. Remembering his instructions, I was easily able to put the device together using the plastic moulding from a light switch, two size-D flashlight batteries, and a cord with a plug at the end. I stripped the carbon rods from the batteries, mounted them through the two holes in the moulding, about an inch apart, and attached their ends to the wires of the cord. Voilà! A water heater (if memory serves me, it was called a *koom-koom*). To use it, the plug had to be inserted into an electric wall outlet and the rods placed in a glass of water. I was excited to test my creation. I filled a glass with water and then, while holding the rods in my left hand, I put the plug into the outlet. Oops! The 220 volts threw me across the room and almost out the window and over the balcony. My error, of course, was in holding the live rods in my hand instead of putting them into the water. When I recovered and realized my mistake, I couldn't stop ruminating over my stupidity. But in the end, I did get my glass of hot tea (and many more afterwards).

At the Machon there were many students who belonged to one or another religious movement, the men always recognizable by the skullcaps, or *yarmulkes*, that they wore. One day I came into our main residence building and saw a lineup of five or six students, three of them with *yarmulkes* on, at the door to one of the bedrooms. I asked what they were waiting for, and they answered with some evasive words and one or two covert smiles. Then I saw the bedroom door open and one of the students emerge. A quick glance inside revealed a woman who did not belong to the Machon group. The next student in line entered the room and came out about fifteen minutes later, motioning to the next in line to go in. I got the idea. But what didn't make sense to me was that the line included religious boys. Not only that, but they kept their *yarmulkes* on until just before entering the room. Then, quickly, the hand went up and the *yarmulke* disappeared into a pocket. For me, there was something incongruent about all of this. My image of orthodoxy was one of purity and sexual self-denial until marriage. Yet here were these overtly religious young men satisfying their lust in public. I concluded that either these particular men were exceptions to the rule or more was going on in the orthodox community than met the naked eye (pardon the pun).

Tsedakah (charity) has always been one of the pillars of Judaism. It expresses itself in so many ways that I doubt there is any place with more charitable foundations per capita than the Jewish world. One hot summer's day, I received an unexpected lesson on the lengths some will go to in order to solicit a donation. I was on an Egged bus in Jerusalem, and the windows were open. The bus stopped to pick up passengers, and an old blind woman dressed in black rags approached the open windows with her arms outstretched. Various passengers, including myself, were moved by her condition and gave her money. When the bus pulled away, I commented to the person next to me how sad it was to see such a sight in Jerusalem. He explained that her condition was of her own choosing; begging in the Middle East was a profession, and some beggars purposely mutilated themselves to evoke an onlooker's pity. He told me that it would not surprise him to learn that this woman had intentionally blinded herself for this purpose. In the end, he said, not only were we doing a *mitzvah* (good deed) by giving her money, but she was also doing a *mitzvah* by being a beggar and giving us the opportunity to fulfill this most important of requirements for being a good Jew. I was dumbfounded by this, though later I slowly began to accept that there was some sense in his take on the subject, though it may have been specific to the culture of that place. Whatever the case, I reasoned that it always felt good to give, no matter what the circumstances.

Another incident with an Egged bus occurred one day while I was walking the streets in Jerusalem. As I turned a corner, I encountered an ice-cream seller shouting from his stand, *"Glidah, Glidah!"* ("Ice cream, ice cream!"). Then, a little farther on, I saw a bus near the entrance to a building with a group of people standing nearby. The driver's seat was empty, and there was an eerie stillness in the air. I walked over and asked a woman for an explanation, and she pointed to the underside of the bus, where I saw a small figure lying. A little boy had just run out from the building and into the path of the bus. The driver and others were waiting for the ambulance and police to arrive. As I waited with them, a woman came out of the building and began wailing as she recognized the dead boy under the bus as her son. With tears in my eyes I left, turned the corner and again heard the sounds of *"Glidah, Glidah!"* The juxtaposition of *"glidah"* and a dead boy, somehow, in a strange way, portrayed for me the whole history of Judaism over the past two thousand years: joy and tragedy. And here in modern Israel, that story continues.

Before 1967, the old city of Jerusalem was not accessible to Israelis. Between it and the new city stood a wall and a piece of property frequently referred to as "no man's land." The wall, of course, was the Wailing Wall or Western Wall, symbol of what was left of the Second Temple. One day during my stay, we visited the Israeli side of "no man's land," where we were given a history lesson about the temple and the wall. I could see quite clearly the Jordanian legionnaires walking back and forth on top of the wall, rifles in hand. I asked our tour guide if I could take a picture, and he said, "Definitely not." He went on to explain that to a legionnaire, the sun reflecting off a camera lens could be mistaken for the reflection of a rifle barrel, leading the legionnaire to shoot at the photographer. The explanation was plausible—but I still wanted a picture. So, as the group moved on, I lingered, hid behind a bush, and, from between the branches, took a picture, which I have in my collection to the present day.

At the Machon, one of the classes we took was in drama. Our teacher was Yehuda, a somewhat delicate-looking man who clearly had an artistic flair about him. One evening he and his wife invited members of the drama group to their home for coffee. We talked about many things: drama in general, the upcoming plays that we were going to perform, the situation with the theatre arts in Israel, and so on. Then, as we went on to other topics, he casually said, within the context of the conversation, "When my wife and I were living together before we were married…" My ears perked up at his statement. I had never heard of this before. Living together before being married! I couldn't get over it. No one else in the group had any discernable reaction to his words, and I wondered if I was the only one to be astonished. Apparently, I later learned, this was not uncommon in Israel in the early days. But back in Canada, at least the part I came from, this would have been considered living in sin. I found myself with a moral dilemma. On the one hand, the idea went against everything I had been taught—namely, that it was wrong for unmarried people to live together. On the other hand, there was something in it that I found appealing. After all, I thought, a trial period before settling down made some sense. But what about societal mores? Didn't these count for something? Not to mention the teachings and practices of my religion. Little did I know that Yehuda and his wife were among the vanguard of what many years later became the norm, not only in Israel but around the world. Today, when I interview couples who come to me to marry them, I find that almost all are living together and have been doing so for many months or years. In fact, I'm quite surprised when I discover, on a rare occasion, that this is not the case.

Those attending the Machon adhered to many different ideologies, and some of these, such as Hashomer Hatzair and B'nai Akiba (both Jewish youth movements), were on opposite ends of the spectrum, but there was one common denominator that overrode ideological considerations — and that was *love*. During our time together during the first five months in Jerusalem, I saw many manifestations of this. For example, one member of our small Young Judaean group fell in love with a girl from another contingent with very different views, and this did not please leaders in either group. Nevertheless, there was no stopping it, human nature being what it is. An additional problem presented itself for the couple, however, when it was time to leave Jerusalem and go to their respective movements' kibbutzim. In fact, there were two problems. First, it was hard for them to part; and second, how was it going to be when, after five months on two different kibbutzim, they returned to Jerusalem for the final six weeks? And even if they still wanted to be together for the final few weeks, what would happen after that? Everyone was returning to his or her country of origin, and some countries were continents away from each other. To the best of my knowledge, although these relationships undoubtedly led to a great deal of initially intense letter-writing, very few of them remained intact for long after the people left Israel. Certainly, none of the Young Judaeans I knew ended up with partners from other movements whom they had met on the Machon.

Ever since my year in Israel, I have been puzzled by the Arab mind. While I have experienced wonderful hospitality, generosity, and intelligence from Arabs, I have also seen the results of their incredible cruelty and brutality. An example of the latter is the attack on the Etzion Bloc, a group of settlements not far from Jerusalem. During the 1948 war, the settlements stood in the path of Arab armies marching toward the holy city. The settlers comported themselves with courage and dignity in the face of overwhelming odds but eventually succumbed to defeat, with the loss of many lives. After overrunning the settlements, the Arabs stopped their march to dismember all the Jewish bodies. When Israelis came to bury the bodies, it was not possible to put them together; they had to collect the pieces and place them in a mass grave. As Uzi Narkiss, commander of a group of soldiers known as the Palmach, commented, "You kill your enemy, okay; but why do you have to dismember him?" I stood before that grave on one of our tours and read the names on the stones over the large mound of earth that is their resting place.

Such indiscriminate killing did not end in 1948; in the years since, there has been dancing and singing in the streets of Gaza, the West Bank, and elsewhere in the Arab world when Israeli women and children are blown to pieces by suicide bombers. I can understand war and the targeting of soldiers, but rejoicing in the deaths of innocent civilians? Something here doesn't fit, and the few Arabs I have spoken to about this over the years have not been able to give me an explanation that makes any sense. A Palestinian psychiatrist with whom I discussed this matter a few years ago said he agreed with me that it was cruel and unwarranted behaviour, which he believed could be attributed to the frustration felt by the Palestinian people. I responded that frustration is not a justification for killing.

About three weeks before my sojourn at Hasolelim came to an end, I began divesting myself of unnecessary possessions. I wished to bring many gifts back to family and friends, but money was scarce and the solution was to barter. I put together all the things I wanted to get rid of and headed for Nazareth, where I knew there were many Arab gift shops. I also knew that the Arabs understood bartering and were good at it. I chose a shop I had visited before, because I had enjoyed my conversation with the owner and he had expressed interest in the items I told him about. Fully loaded, I entered his shop. He greeted me warmly but refused to discuss business. Instead, he invited me to his home, where we chatted while he served me coffee and sweets. This went on for close to an hour before he was ready to deal with the matter at hand. By this time we were both in a good mood, and I appreciated the approach he was taking. Simply put, he had softened me up and, to tell the truth, I didn't mind a bit. He was particularly interested in my nylon sleeping bag, which at that time seemed to be a premium item in Israel, at least among the Arab shopkeepers. The bartering went well, and we both got what we wanted. I left Nazareth with two bags full of gifts and with the problem of how I was going to drag them around for three weeks, as I planned to tour Europe with a few of my Canadian friends. I have never forgotten this bartering transaction and still see it as a model for doing business. It also felt good leaving a commercial exchange having made a new friend. And I know — there is a disconnect between this paragraph and the previous one.

The final weeks in Jerusalem were crammed with classes, as the Machon faculty wanted to get in as much as they could before we left. It was also a sad time as we said goodbye to people we had become close to, knowing we might never see them again. It was, as I've mentioned, especially difficult for those with romantic attachments.

The trip through Europe was enjoyable. We visited Italy, Switzerland, and France. My best memory of Italy is of going to La Scala Opera House in Milan and seeing *Aida* in the huge amphitheatre. Also I loved the Vespas and Lambrettas that filled the streets, and I vowed to one day own one. (The Vespa is now gaining popularity in Toronto, so who knows?) Switzerland was a blur. We were only in Geneva, and all I can recall is one jewellery store after another. By the time we reached Paris, my finances were exhausted, and when American Express botched a money order sent to me by my parents, I had to borrow money from my friends. Nevertheless, I loved Paris and did the usual touristy things like visiting the Louvre and the Rodin Gallery — again, courtesy of my friends. We stayed in a Jewish youth hostel where breakfast was included in the price, so I stuffed myself in the mornings, knowing supper was iffy. Also, I had saved a can of salmon from one of several food packages sent from home over the year, and with the equivalent of twenty-five cents and high-school French, I managed to buy an apple, a bun, and a tomato, which I combined into a delicious dinner (salt and pepper were free at the hostel). Wine for dinner was H_2O, compliments of the Parisian waterworks.

1998

FORTY-THREE YEARS LATER (too long) I returned to Israel. I remember clearly passing through intense Israeli security at Pearson International Airport in Toronto and then entering the waiting lounge where, for the first time in my life, I saw in the distance the Star of David on the tail of a very large Israeli El Al airplane. (Up to this time I had only seen the symbol in magazines and on television.) I was profoundly moved, and as I walked closer to the window nearest the airplane my eyes filled with tears.

The occasion for this trip was to teach Jewish Russian immigrants to Israel how to speak or improve upon their English. The program was called *Yad B'Yad* (Hand in Hand). My plan was to teach for two weeks and then tour the land for two weeks with my partner, Susan Wehle, who was studying Hebrew at the Hebrew University. I taught an advanced class of about fifteen students, two of them Israelis. Almost all were in high-tech fields where English is the international language. In preparation for this venture, I took some instruction in Toronto in teaching English as a second language, then put together a songbook on my own to use as a teaching tool. The class's favourite song was "Michael, Row the Boat Ashore," and on our last day together they sang it in my honour with great gusto, led by Susan, who was a cantor and had a magnificent voice.

The return visit was three decades after the 1967 war, in which the old city of Jerusalem was recaptured by Israel. After arriving in Jerusalem and settling in, I couldn't wait to visit the wall for the first time. At the earlier time, 1954–1955, as mentioned, Jews did not have access to the wall as it was in Jordanian hands. That is why I had to hide behind a bush on the far side of "no man's land" away from the wall at a considerable distance to take my picture. Susan came with me but had to go to the women's section. I put my head against the wall and began to pray, my heart full of emotion and gratitude. About five minutes into my prayers I heard a voice: *"Adoni, adoni."* ("Sir, sir"). It was an intrusion, and I did not want to be disturbed, this being the moment I had been waiting for and dreaming about for many years. But the voice persisted. Finally, I opened my eyes and looked up. There stood an orthodox Jew, black hat, *tzitsis* (fringes) protruding from beneath his black waistcoat, and of course a beard. "A contribution for the rebuilding of the temple!" I was extremely annoyed. First, how dare he interrupt my prayers? Shouldn't he know better? Second, rebuilding the temple is not part of my theology. I wanted to cut this interaction short so I could get back to my prayers. I quickly reasoned that if I didn't give him some money, he would argue with me and pester me; I would become more agitated, and my mood for prayer would evaporate. So I reached into my pocket and gave him the equivalent of about five dollars. He took the money, looked at it, gave me a condescending look and said, "Is that all?" I had to restrain myself from slugging the guy, and if he hadn't quickly shoved the money into his pocket, I would have grabbed it back. He went away, and I concluded, "I'm in Israel. This is not a normal country." I returned to my prayers, but it took some time to calm down and connect once more with the wall and God.

> These stones
> lick at my heart
>   like psalms with eyes
> These stones
>   imprinted
>   by fingers of dust
>   beckon me
>   into silent places
>   where ghosts rest
>   and stir
>   only at night

These stones
    scrape my skin
        where lies blood
            ready to spill
                should they call

The incident that remains burned into my memory from that sojourn is a frightening one. Susan and I had rented a car and were returning from the Negev to Jerusalem. Instead of going by way of the Dead Sea, which is how we drove to the Negev, we decided to take a more direct route that took us near Hebron. After passing a heavily armed Israeli security checkpoint, we came into an Arab village. We were at first astonished to see that the main street was lined with garbage and junk of various kinds, piled several feet high. We noticed, too, that only Arabs were walking about, and no one in western dress could be seen. Our immediate reaction was to conclude that we had taken a wrong turn and were in a Palestinian village, having imperceptibly crossed the border. We believed we were driving farther into Palestinian territory, and it would be only a matter of time before someone spotted us, identified us as Jews, and took us as hostages, or worse. We were both frightened, which led to some verbal exchanges that were less than pleasant but could perhaps be accounted for by the disconcerting circumstances in which we found ourselves. To make matters worse, the air conditioning in the car stopped working, and it was over a hundred degrees Fahrenheit outside. A few minutes later we left the village, still not knowing where we were going and sweating profusely, when suddenly an Israeli army truck with soldiers in the back pulled in front of us. This was good news. At least we felt we had some protection, and we followed the army truck most of the way to Jerusalem. That night, still rattled from the experience, Susan and I had a major fight, cleared our minds and souls, and reconnected.

The most emotional experience for me on the visit, even surpassing the wall, was our day at Yad V'Shem, the Holocaust memorial in Jerusalem. I don't believe that anyone can adequately describe the impact Yad V'Shem can have on a person. I can only say that I was shaken to my roots, even though I had seen photos and read and heard accounts of the Holocaust most of my life. The most piercing moment for me was when I stood before a photo of a father trying to protect his young daughter from a Nazi's bullet. I broke down and couldn't stop weeping. As painful as this visit can be, I feel every Jew and non-Jew has an obligation to see what evil can overtake the human soul and then to vow, as do Jews everywhere today, that it will never happen to us again. And more than this, that it will never happen to any people again.

I want to see the ovens
so the bricks
can see my tears
and the spirits
carry my protests
to the un-hearing God
that I pray to
each day

Two dear friends whom I had known back in Canada, Hillel and Debby Millgram, invited Susan and me to their home for dinner one evening. Hillel is a Conservative rabbi who had held a pulpit in London, Ontario, which is where I met him and his wife, but by the time of our visit they had been living in Israel for many years. I asked Hillel what it meant for him to be living in Israel. He considered his answer for a few moments and then replied: "It means, among other things, that if an emergency occurred and I needed help, no matter where I was in Israel, there would be someone there to help and who knew what to do. That's what it means to be a Jew living in a Jewish state."

I have thought about his answer many times over the years. It touched something deep within and made me wonder why I had never seriously considered making *aliyah* (moving to Israel) myself. I can only come up with the following: I love Israel and I love Canada—both are my homes. The difference is that all of Israel moves me spiritually; no matter what part of the country I'm in, I feel I'm standing on holy ground, ground that is the cradle for the moral and ethical teachings of western civilization. In Canada, the landscapes take my breath away, and the freedoms and rights I have here are a blessing. But only one place always moves me in a profoundly spiritual manner, and that is the province of Saskatchewan. There is something about the endless fields and the endless sky, the smell of a wheat field, and the warm and gracious people who populate this simple and elegant province. My roots are in Saskatchewan, and each time I return to visit I feel renewed. When I'm in the desert in Israel, I'm in Saskatchewan, and when I'm in Saskatchewan, I'm in the desert in Israel. I also have a sense that were I to visit the far north in Canada, I would find there, too, a spiritual home.

So, at times I find myself torn. Since I can't be in two places at the same time, the best solution I can think of is to divide my time between the two countries. This, however, would require the means to do so, which I do not possess. Also, my children and close friends are all here, and the work I do as a rabbi calls me in a very special way; Israel has more than enough rabbis, and

I'm not sure what I would do there. Realistically, what I try to do is visit Israel as often as possible and stay for as long as I'm able. Which brings me to my third visit, just a few years ago.

2005

> The air
>> which flows
>>> past my nostrils
>> is the air
>>> breathed by Abraham
>>>> when he greeted
>>>>> the holy messengers
>> it is the air
>>> of Moses
>>>> giving life
>>>>> to the desert bush
>>>> that burned
>>>>> with holy power
>> it is the air
>>> of Elijah
>>>> which he breathed
>>>>> into a dead child
>>>>>> and restored
>> it is the air
>>> with which
>>>> David caressed Bathsheba
>>>>> as he nuzzled her
>>>>>> in the night
>> it is my air

My partner this time was Shelley, and it was her first visit. Again, I flew El Al. Somehow, it seems to me that if I'm flying to a Jewish state, I should fly on a Jewish airplane, even though there are many alternatives.

We stayed in a lovely section of Jerusalem, not far from the city's main market and within a twenty-five-minute walk of the wall. Our residence at 51 Usishkin Street was a wonderful two-bedroom flat with a living room, a kitchen, and a balcony, on the second of three floors of an old stone house. We seemed to be situated among a plethora of small synagogues; early each Shabbat morning, we could hear the sounds of prayers wafting in through our windows. It was delightful. The market, which we visited frequently, was colourful and teeming with produce of various kinds, most familiar but some with exotic names that I was hearing for the first time.

Shortly after arriving in Israel we had the pleasure of experiencing the holiday of *Shavuot* (literally "weeks"), which commemorates the giving of the Commandments to Moses atop Mt. Sinai and is a time for studying Torah into the wee hours of the morning. We began the evening by visiting the Jerusalem branch of my alma mater, the Hebrew Union College—Jewish Institute of Religion, where we were treated to wonderful lectures and sweets and from which we did not depart until almost 2:00 a.m. We then slowly wound our way home, enjoying along the way the vitality of the people walking the streets, and stopping in at an orthodox synagogue, where we took in another lecture. Everywhere the city was alive, and time stood still. Some people we met were planning to study all night and then go to the wall at sunrise for prayers.

Making our base in Jerusalem, we set out by auto, first to the south and later to the north. Our plan was to leave on a Sunday and return in time for the following Sabbath, leaving again on Sunday, which worked well for us.

The highlight of our southern trip was a visit to the ancient city of Petra, deep in the Jordanian hills. We were picked up by a jeep-like vehicle at a hotel in Eilat and, along with several others, taken to the border between Israel and Jordan. Here we disembarked and walked a kilometre or so across a "no man's land" to the border of Jordan, where we were met by a Jordanian guide, Ali. He helped us process our papers, after which we boarded a small bus and made the four-hour trek to Petra, stopping along the way for refreshments at a large gift shop.

Petra was the chief city of the Nabatean civilization, which existed from about the fourth century BCE. to the first century CE. The entire city is carved out of rock—nothing was built, only carved. It covers many acres of land, and on our tour we only got to see a part of it. The Nabateans were an ingenious people, creating systems of water troughs and dwellings that, for their time, were marvels of engineering and, in the eyes of many, still are. It was also of interest to me that perhaps the foremost Nabatean scholar of the twentieth century was Nelson Glueck, former president of the Hebrew Union College—Jewish Institute of Religion and the man who ordained me in 1965. We were treated to a wonderful lunch and later treated ourselves to a camel ride, in itself an experience. Before we left Petra, Ali disappeared for about twenty minutes and then returned with a large tray of freshly baked baklava. Without question, it was the best baklava I have ever tasted, gently sweetened and mouthwatering. I had three pieces, two more than I would have eaten anywhere else.

In Israel, synchronicity is commonplace. While we were waiting to be picked up at the hotel in Eilat for our trip to Petra, I entered into a conversation with the hotel guard. I mentioned to him that the following week, Shelley and I were going to the Gallil, which is the northern part of Israel, and I asked if he knew of a nice place where we could stay. He replied that his mother ran a bed and breakfast at a place called Amirim. He then took out his cell phone, called his mother, and we had a reservation. Simple!

While in the Negev we visited Kibbutz Yahel and Kibbutz Lotun, both associated with Judaism's Reform Movement. The latter was fascinating, as almost everything built on the kibbutz was made from recycled materials. One could probably refer to it as a recycled village. Our overnight lodging, however, was at Yahel, where we were received warmly.

Our northern trip had several highlights. Our stay with the hotel guard's mother was delightful, our room cozy, with fresh flower petals strewn across the bed, a small bottle of wine in a basket, some sweets, and some fruit. We ate out of doors on a patio with a view of Lake Kinneret in the distance.

In Tiberius we visited the tombs of Rambam (an outstanding medieval rabbi, philosopher, codifier of Jewish law, and physician) and Rabbi Akiva, perhaps the greatest of the Talmudic rabbis. As I read the description on Akiva's grave, familiarizing myself once more with his tragic life, I was filled with emotion.

In Safed, Judaism's mystical city, I revisited the synagogue of the Ari, one of the foremost Kabbalists in Jewish history. At a gift shop I bought a *tof* (Middle Eastern hand drum) for my musician son and a lovely necklace for my daughter.

The next day we went to Kibbutz Na'ot, where they make sandals by that name. I exchanged the Na'ots I had been wearing for several years for a new pair of exactly the same style. In addition, I bought a very comfortable and unique pair of shoes.

While in the Gallil we visited Capernum where, the New Testament tells us, Jesus walked on water. I felt this to be a holy place and wanted to experience the feel of the water on my feet, so I took off my sandals and waded in a short distance. In a small way, by doing this, I felt I was honouring another rabbi and teacher.

Our visit to Israel, as usual, was too short and went by too quickly. Once again it was difficult to leave, but my heart was full of memories that would have to sustain me until the next time.

Our flight back to Toronto was normal except for one thing. Between meals, the galley at the back of the airplane remained open. Any passenger, at any time, who felt like a nosh (snack) could wander back and help him or herself to a sandwich, a drink, a pastry — maybe a pickle. I realized then and there that the "Jewish mother" was alive and well on El Al Airlines.

CHANGING DREAMS
Winnipeg 1955–1958

The compass that guides me
                points in directions
                        I do not wish to look
      insisting
        that I turn my head
                my heart
                     my soul
           and peer
                beyond the shadows
                  upon vistas
          I have visited
              In forgotten dreams

I had expected to return from the Machon to Regina and from there make preparations to move to Saskatoon and attend university, eventually entering the faculty of medicine. However, as the saying goes, "Man makes plans and God laughs." While I was in Israel in 1955, my parents bought a small men's clothing store in St. Boniface, a community adjacent to Winnipeg. So one year after leaving Regina, I got off the bus in Winnipeg (350 miles to the east) and went to live in my new home at 503 Queenston Street in River Heights, which is in Winnipeg proper and about a twenty minute drive from St. Boniface. Initially I was disappointed with the move because it was not part of the scenario I had in mind. However, once I settled into my new home, I came to realize that Winnipeg was a great place for me to live.

The day of my return was significant for two reasons: I was beginning a new life, and my grandfather on my father's side, Shmuel, passed away before I was able to get to the hospital to say goodbye. I had brought him a *yarmulka* as a gift from Israel and was faced with the decision of whether to have it buried with him, or keep it and use it occasionally as a tribute to his memory and the affection I held for him. I decided on the latter.

My cousin Lynn (my father's brother's daughter) told me recently that our grandfather Shmuel once built a still and used it to produce his own liquor. The story goes like this: in his latter years, he lived in the Sharon Home, a very good Jewish seniors' residence in the north end of Winnipeg that is still in existence, though I was recently told it has moved to the south end. The policy of the home at that time was not to allow the residents any alcoholic beverages, and visitors were prohibited from bringing such in. To get around this, our grandfather slowly and methodically snuck in the implements necessary to put together a still and began producing his own whisky. When it was discovered that he was drinking, a search was made, and the whisky that was found was taken away and disposed of. His family was contacted and asked not to bring such "gifts" when visiting. The family, of course, was puzzled, since no one had supplied him with anything resembling alcohol. Several more times, alcohol was discovered in his room, and meetings with family members could not solve the mystery, nor was the still discovered — since it seems that after each run, my grandfather dismantled it so it couldn't be recognized as such. This went on for some time until one day the still was found intact. Word went out and finally his son-in-law, Jack, had to go into his room and forcibly remove the still components. I can imagine that was quite a blow to my *zaida's* (grandfather's) lifestyle, and took away one of the significant pleasures that remained in his life. He was eighty-nine when he died.

I realize that seniors' residences, like all institutions, have to have policies in place for the benefit and protection of their residents, but maybe a page could be taken from Maimonides Hospital and Home for the Aged in Montreal. There, many years ago, a gerontologist physician endorsed my children's other grandfather's desire for vodka and cigarettes, which he indulged in up to the time of his death at 101 years of age. Perhaps, had such a benevolent physician been around, and more lenient policies the order of the day, I would not have missed saying goodbye to my grandfather and might have had a few more months, even years, of his company.

Winnipeg is the gateway to the eastern Prairies. There is a small stretch of prairie land just before you arrive in the city, after which the flatland cuts a swath through the rest of Manitoba and into the provinces of Saskatchewan and Alberta.

My move to Winnipeg was a turning point in my life for a number of reasons. First, the University of Manitoba was my introduction to higher education. Second, Winnipeg at that time had the third-largest Jewish population in the country, after Montreal and Toronto respectively.

Top: My parents at their store, Charles Men's Wear, in Norwood, Manitoba, a suburb of St. Boniface.
Above: My grandfather Shmuel, the still maker, with my grandmother Sarah

This meant, among other things, that there were roughly equal numbers of Jewish girls and boys. For me, this engendered a social renaissance. Third, I was the student of a man who played a major role in my becoming a rabbi, my Hillel director, Rabbi Zalman Schachter, later to be founder of the Jewish Renewal Movement. As a member of Hillel, I held the position of cultural chairman and was responsible for promoting and organizing lectures, weekend retreats, and debates.

I found winters in Winnipeg to be just as cold as in Regina, but for some reason Winnipeg seemed to be more windy. The famous (or infamous) intersection of Portage and Main was at times hell on ice, as it seemed to funnel and concentrate the north wind that swept down Main Street. Many an individual nearly became an ice statue at this crossroads while waiting for a bus to appear or a light to change. It was, at times, so cold that it took your breath away. This happened one day to a close friend and classmate of mine from Connecticut, Ron Goff, whom I met in Cincinnati when I was studying there to become a rabbi and who came with me on one of my trips home to Winnipeg. It was his first experience of a prairie winter. We arrived around midnight after a thirty-hour car trip and immediately went to sleep. In the morning, after breakfast, not knowing that during the night the temperature had plummeted, we ventured outside. As we stepped out of the front door of my parents' home, my friend, delighted to get some fresh air, took a deep breath. There was a startled look on his face as he turned to me, somewhat panic-stricken, and tried to speak, without success. The hairs in his nostrils had frozen upon contact with the air, and he felt a sharp pain in his lungs. For the next week he nursed a bad chest cold, taking comfort in an occasional sip of Scotch and the company of a good woman. I had forgotten to warn him—one doesn't take deep breaths outside in prairie winters.

One also doesn't forget to plug in the car. Prairie cars are equipped with block heaters, devices that are mounted under the hood and have a power cord protruding outside. When you put your car into the garage at night, you plug in the heater. This keeps the oil from freezing or getting so thick that starting the car is difficult, if you can get it to start at all. Failure to plug in the vehicle often means that, in the morning, you will either wear out the battery trying to start the engine or need to call a tow truck for a boost. Sometimes a kind neighbour or stranger will give you a boost, provided one of you has the proper cables, a wise item to keep in the trunk. Even parking lots in Regina and Winnipeg have electrical outlets, as did the lot at the University of Manitoba. So, if you're not from the Prairies and you see a car with something dangling out the front grill, you'll know where it comes from.

During my second winter in Winnipeg, I was introduced to tobogganing. About ten miles outside of Winnipeg, there was a hill going down onto the Red River where my buddies and I would bring our dates and show off — piling onto the toboggan one on top of the other, four or five deep, spilling off as we descended onto the frozen river. Or — even more impressive — we'd go down standing backwards, either alone or with one or two fellow daredevils. I like to think that our dates must have been impressed, we guys being so brave, so reckless, and so carefree. They did laugh a lot.

My first day on campus at the University of Manitoba was both exciting and bewildering. To begin with, I didn't know anyone, as none of my friends from Regina came to Winnipeg. Between registration, getting a fix on where everything was, being rushed by fraternities, and just saying hello to equally overwhelmed and confused fellow students, there was much to do. To begin with, the university held a "freshie day" shortly after registration. This meant that students in their senior year could ask freshmen to do their bidding, sometimes skirting the boundaries of propriety. I managed to escape this hazing by virtue of the fact that I was technically not a freshman. Grade twelve in Saskatchewan was considered the equivalent of first-year university. Having graduated from Central Collegiate, I was in second year, and I would be able to receive my Bachelor of Arts degree in three years rather than four. Besides, I was twenty years old and too proud to suffer the indignities that might be placed upon me by an only slightly older senior student.

In the centre of the campus was the administration building, the university's oldest building, and its only one when it was just an agricultural college. I learned that the agriculture department had a fine reputation across the country and was at the forefront of experimentation and innovation. I also learned that the dairy section of "Aggie Row" had an outlet where one could buy fresh "home-made" ice cream in three flavours: chocolate, vanilla, and strawberry. I became a frequent visitor, not only because the price was right — pennies, compared to what was available elsewhere in Winnipeg — but also because it was superior in quality and taste.

Each faculty on campus had its own building, which meant walking from one building to another to take classes in different subjects. In the fall and spring this posed no difficulty, but in the winter it meant constantly getting dressed and undressed, not to mention facing the elements. However, to put a positive spin on this, we arrived at class in the winter wide awake, jolted by our brief journey through the cold air. On the other hand, the buildings were well heated, which had me, and probably others, dozing on and off through lectures.

If I had not noticed it in Regina at Central Collegiate, I certainly did in Winnipeg: in the spring, on campus, the female world revealed itself. The multiple layers of heavy clothing that hid the young students' bodies in the winter were shed in growing stages as the weather warmed. Like spring flowers, the women came into bloom. This was both intoxicating and distracting, because spring was exam time. Somehow we managed, and were finally released into the beautiful summers for which the Prairies are so well known.

My summers in Winnipeg were mostly times to make money. One summer I worked as a Fuller Brush salesman. This entailed, first of all, a few days of intensive training, where we role-played various scenarios to help us overcome any resistance from customers. We were also given a manual to memorize. Between the role-playing and the manual, there was hardly a situation we might encounter that wasn't covered. Every detail was orchestrated, even the words we were to use upon taking leave of the customer, such as "Toodle-doo, Mrs. Brown." However, I did encounter one situation for which neither the role-playing nor the manual had prepared me at all.

Upon knocking at the door of a house in a quiet neighbourhood near Osborne Street, I was invited in by a woman in her early thirties. I promptly opened my small black suitcase and began my pitch on the various products I was carrying. As I was demonstrating the magical properties of a cloth that polished furniture without furniture polish, I noticed a birdcage with a parakeet or some other kind of bird inside. This in itself was not unusual. But then I saw that the door on the cage was open, and the bird had the freedom to come and go as it pleased. I made a passing comment to the customer about how lucky the bird was to have a home where it could fly around wherever and whenever it wanted. Then I sat down to further extol the properties of my magic cloth and the other wonders I carried in my black bag. Midway through my talk the bird exited the cage, flew a few times around the room, and landed on top of my head. Not wanting to show disrespect to the animal, and not wanting to lose a sale, I made light of the landing and continued to sell while the bird perched. Then I felt something warm on my head, and the bird flew off. It had pooped in my hair. Not knowing what to do, I made some comment about the properties of a good fertilizer and how it might aid in the growth of my hair, perhaps lead to the development of a new formula. She smiled, seeming to appreciate my humour, while in the back of my mind I figured my patience and forbearance were also good for the sale. But, in the end, she didn't buy anything. Upon leaving, after my "toodle-doo," I pulled one of the brushes out of my case and put it to work on my head.

My most satisfying summer job came when I was hired by the Victoria General Hospital administrator to work as an orderly. As was the case with the hospital authority in Israel, this man was impressed with my orderly experience in Regina and realized that I would fit in right away, without the usual training period. Three events in particular that occurred during the four months that I worked at his hospital stand out in my mind.

One day, while I was eating a dinner of lamb chops at the hospital cafeteria, a nurse approached me and, though she was apologetic about interrupting my meal, told me that she had a task she needed me to do immediately. A man had had his leg surgically amputated, she said, and his son had arrived and was waiting to pick up the leg. I looked at her blankly and then asked if this could wait until after my dinner. She said it was rather urgent, as the son had already pulled his car up to the back door of the hospital and wanted to get this over with as quickly as possible. She further explained that the man who had the surgery was Jewish, and that it was the custom in Judaism for severed parts of the body to be buried with the owner when he or she died. The leg would therefore be kept frozen in cold storage until such a time. I went to the morgue, found the leg wrapped in multiple sheets of newspaper, and delivered it to the waiting son, placing it in the open trunk of his vehicle. He thanked me and drove off. I returned to the cafeteria but, upon seeing my cold lamb chops, quickly lost my appetite.

On another day I was again approached by a nurse, who this time needed me to perform a routine procedure — a pubic shave, which was done for male patients by the orderlies and for female patients by the nurses. I asked the nurse what the prescribed surgery was for, and she replied, "A broken penis!" I looked at her with surprise and asked, "How is that possible? Breaks only occur with bones." She replied that she didn't know, but "broken penis" was what was in his chart. I put together my pubic shave package and went to the designated private room. Upon entering, I saw a young man of about twenty-eight, in bed, with a woman sitting next to the bed holding his hand. They were engaged in animated conversation and chortling between sentences. I asked the woman to leave until I had completed my work. When I took back the covers and lifted the man's hospital gown, I saw a strange sight. The top half of the man's penis was sideways almost at right angles to the bottom half. Trying to be as delicate as I could, I asked the man what happened. He was very forthright and didn't hesitate for a moment to explain how he broke his penis. As close as I can recall, these were his words: "I just recently got married, and my wife and I, the lady you saw sitting beside me and comforting me, were on our honeymoon. Well, one night we were fooling around and I was being playful, and, with a full hard-on, I took a leap toward her on the bed — and missed."

"Missed?" I responded inquisitively.

"Yeah," he said. "I came down on the bed the wrong way."

"Ouch!" I said in my mind as a quiver ran through my body. "Double ouch!"

"So," he went on, "the docs are going to fix it."

I proceeded with the shave, wondering how one goes about fixing a broken penis. I then helped him onto a gurney and rolled him up to another floor and into an operating theatre. About a half hour later, a request came from the surgeon to bring up two tongue depressors — the thin pieces of wood that a doctor places over your tongue when he asks you to say "ah." This I couldn't figure out — why tongue depressors for surgery on a broken penis? The next day, when I was asked to help the patient get out of bed to go to the bathroom, I entered the room to find his wife there and the two of them once more talking and chortling. Obviously, this whole affair had tickled their mutual funny bone, and to their credit, they were taking things quite well. Later that day, while helping the patient bathe, I discovered that the two tongue depressors were affixed to his penis as splints, one on either side, to hold it straight while it healed.

I don't have a lot to say at this point about the third event, yet it had a profound and lasting impact on me. Working in a hospital often brings one into contact with death or near-death experiences. One day, a man in his sixties was admitted and underwent surgery. I don't recall what his illness was, only that it was serious. The surgery apparently didn't go as well as hoped, and over the following days the man's condition deteriorated. Subtle comments from the nurses indicated that he wasn't expected to survive. Each time I went into his room and looked at him, I could see that he was losing weight, his skin becoming paler, his breathing more laboured, and his conscious moments fewer. On one particular day, when I left my shift, the consensus seemed to be that he would not last the night, and the family was accordingly notified. Yet when I returned the next morning, he was still hanging on and continued to do so for the next two days, apparently against all odds. Then, a day later, something unusual and unexpected occurred: he began to rally. Over the next several days, his condition continued to improve. He started taking food, began to speak, and about two weeks later was released from the hospital, to the amazement of doctors, nurses, family, and myself. This was the first instance where I encountered someone given up for death who recovered — but it would not be the last. I will speak more about this further on, and expand on why and how this event and others like it have shaped my approach to life-threatening illnesses.

To fulfill my pre-med requirements, my selection of courses at the university for the next two years focused on the sciences. I took two courses in zoology — vertebrate and invertebrate — with a greater penchant for the former. Microbiology was different from anything I had encountered in high school, and I enjoyed it. Inorganic chemistry, on the other hand, was boring, except for the lab in qualitative analysis. This brought out the sleuth in me, as I had to determine what elements were in an undetermined given compound, and I was reasonably good at it. This was fun, and I felt a sense of accomplishment whenever I made a correct determination.

An incident in my inorganic lab brought home to me the importance of diligently proofreading laboratory manuals. I was working back to back with a dear friend, Clarence Guenter, in an experiment involving potassium permanganate, a deep purple solution. All of a sudden I heard a small explosion behind me and turned around to see Clarence's face covered with purple spots. The lab instructor rushed over to see what had happened and to check on Clarence's well-being. He was shaken, but other than a purple face he was fine as, fortunately, none of the solution had gotten into his eyes. An immediate investigation was initiated by the lab instructor to find the cause of the explosion. He couldn't figure it out until he looked at the instructions in the manual. There was a line about putting a rubber stopper into the test tube at a certain point, and the instructions were to stopper the tube *tightly*. It should have read, "Stopper the tube *lightly*." The experiment involved a vigorous chemical reaction in the test tube, which, if the stopper had been inserted lightly, would have resulted in the stopper being gently pushed out, rather than the volcano-like eruption that spattered my friend's face. We were fortunate that the stopper had come out before the glass tube broke — or the damage could have been much more serious than a few purple spots. It took close to two months for the spots on Clarence's face to finally disappear.

I was told before going to university that it was a place where myths were exploded and favoured traditions undermined. While this was not generally the case for me, there was one instance where one of my favourite foods was brought into question. Professor Stuart-Hay taught zoology and one day described to us the parasites that inhabit the flesh of the fish used in the making of a Jewish delicacy — gefilte fish. It took months, if not years, before I could again enjoy this delicacy, which my grandmother and thousands, if not millions, of other grandmothers fed (and continue to feed) their families. Today, I rationalize that with more stringent health requirements, those parasites no longer exist, or if they do, they are well cooked.

Organic chemistry was my favourite science subject, although at first I found it daunting, mainly because I couldn't understand a thing my chemistry professor said. He talked in a way that went right over my head, which frustrated me to the point that I was afraid I would not get through the course. I had heard from friends that the head of the chemistry department, Dr. Charlesworth, was an excellent teacher of organic chemistry. So, as it was still early in the term, I contacted him, expressed my concern, and asked him if I could please attend his lectures instead of my current professor's. He said it would be difficult for him to transfer me, but if I wanted, I could also attend his classes. I took him up on his offer and found his lectures clear and exciting. Eventually he let me stay in his class for the year and made my transfer official. This experience taught me two things: university professors don't have to be good teachers, and a university professor who is a good teacher is a joy to behold.

I found Dr. Charlesworth to be a rare gem, as a human being and as a man with broad interests who could relate these interests to the subject of chemistry. For example, in explaining for us the development of TNT and its chemical composition, he included some historical background about one of the foremost chemists who was active in its discovery, Chaim Weizmann, who later became the first president of the State of Israel. He brought to class a stamp he had collected with Weizmann's picture on it. Of course, I knew about Weizmann from my Young Judaean days, so to say that I was won over by Dr. Charlesworth would be an understatement. Throughout the year he kept bringing to his lectures other tidbits of history that enhanced the subject of chemistry, much to my delight and that of my classmates. I did well on my final exam.

On the other hand, I took a course in sociology that was by far the worst university course I ever encountered. On our first day of class, which took place in a large theatre that was two-thirds filled with students, the professor walked in with his arms laden with books. He put the books down on a table, looked at a girl sitting in the front row, and asked, "What size shoe do you take?" The girl, flustered by the suddenness and personal nature of the question, replied, "A six and a half." To which the professor rejoined, "Is it a perfect six and a half?" (His emphasis was on the word *perfect*.) She answered hesitantly, "I don't know." He looked at her with an air of disgust and commented, "That just goes to show how little you know about yourself." The poor girl flushed and didn't know quite what to do with herself. He then generalized about how little people know about themselves, after which he proceeded to read from his books for the rest of the hour. Subsequent classes took the form of him reading aloud, his nose buried in a book, with an occasional glance at the class and a rare comment on what he was reading. The class numbers dwindled as we realized that we could read as well as he, and on our own time. I vowed after that never to take another sociology course, and I never broke my vow. In later years, I heard that sociology could actually be interesting and even important. Regrettably, I missed out.

The subject I found most difficult at university was physics. Not that my professor was a poor teacher; actually, I thought he was probably good, but I couldn't get my head around the subject, in the class or in the lab. I ended up with a final mark of fifty-two per cent and was grateful for that, as a failure would probably have prevented me from getting into medicine.

Outside of science, my favourite subjects were English and psychology. What I didn't realize at the time was that I had a natural ability in these areas, certainly more so than in the sciences. I particularly enjoyed English and was blessed with good teachers. In one case, I sat in on a class on *Gulliver's Travels* by Professor Broeder, who was not my assigned teacher, but who had the reputation of being an expert on Jonathan Swift. His class was magical, and I was entranced by his exposition. "So this is what teaching English can be like," I said to myself.

The other subject I intuitively felt I would enjoy was philosophy, but for some reason I never took a course in it. In graduate school I paid for this omission and had to make up for a lot of lost ground with a professor who gave me a hard time and didn't like me, but from whom I learned a great deal. More on this further on.

In general, from high school through graduate school, I was never better than a B student. Not that I didn't, at times, receive As, but this was not my norm. On the other hand, most of my friends were straight A students, and brilliant to boot. Many of them went on to become physicians, mathematicians, economists, and professors of various sorts. Later, in rabbinical school, it was more of the same. My classmates and others at the school were graduates of universities like Harvard, Yale, Cornell, Johns Hopkins, Columbia, MIT, and so on. I could not match them, and it took me many years to come to terms with my average intellect and to realize I had other qualities to compensate. At times over the years I have been called an "intellectual" but have always denied this compliment, not out of false modesty but because, as I point out to the complimenter, I know many real intellectuals, and I'm not one of them.

In Winnipeg, I came into my own as a man, or perhaps more correctly one aspiring to be a man. My self-image, in terms of Eros, took off. There was no longer any need to date non-Jewish girls, as females of my faith were abundant and beautiful. I felt I had arrived at an oasis after a twenty-year trek in the desert. So, for the next three years I dated profusely, explored my sexuality, and began to realize I was reasonably attractive to women. However, whereas some of the guys found steady girlfriends, this did not happen to me until I was at my yeshiva (rabbinic school), where the woman I became involved with wasn't Jewish. Go figure!

A small cafeteria called Little Israel, in the basement of the main residence on campus, was the lunchtime gathering place for the Jewish students. Here we blustered, flirted, boasted, and made plans. Some of the students brought their own lunches, either because this was cheaper or because the cafeteria wasn't kosher. It was a fun place to be and a microcosm of the larger Jewish world in Winnipeg.

Like most campuses I've visited over the years, the University of Manitoba had religious centres for students. Included among these, as at many universities worldwide, was a Hillel centre for Jewish students — named after a famous Jewish sage of the first century. Then, as now, most Hillel centres had rabbis as their directors, as was the case in Winnipeg.

The rabbi who acted as Hillel director during my first year at the University of Manitoba was not a very impressive man. As I look back upon it, I don't think he really liked his job. I recall one day going to see him at his campus office (the actual Hillel House was downtown, at 67 Edmonton Street). He was busy at his desk reading some papers and making notes, and did not look up at me the entire time I was in his office, though he continued to talk to me, as if this was the normal way of counselling a student. I was not impressed and never went back to see him. He left his post at the end of the year, which cleared the way for a new Hillel director — one, referred to earlier, who was to have a great impact on my life.

Rabbi Zalman Schachter took the Winnipeg Jewish community by storm. He was dynamic, energetic, charismatic, and sported a short black beard and a somewhat portly frame. Born in Austria, he came to the United States at an early age and received a solid secular and rabbinic education. His *s'micha* (ordination) was from the Lubavitch Yeshiva in Brooklyn, and his *rebbe* (spiritual guru) was Rabbi Menachem Schneerson. Zalman was as talented as he was brilliant. He played six or seven musical instruments, sang with a pleasant voice, was mechanically gifted, and knew how to connect with the students.

The Jewish students at the University of Manitoba, and a few from United College (now the University of Winnipeg), flocked to Zalman as Hillel director, and by the time I left in 1958, Winnipeg Hillel was possibly the most active on the continent.

Not only was Hillel House always open to us; so too was Zalman's home on Inkster Boulevard in the north end of the city. His basement was a scene from another world, with mechanical and electronic devices of various kinds, some of his own invention. In his basement, one could experience a light show, a sound show, or an art show. He was one of the first persons I knew to have a lava lamp, that unusual lamp with coloured illuminated blobs of liquid floating up. It was also in his basement that unusual events took place.

One day I was invited to his home, where there were gathered several men I did not know. Zalman explained to me that everyone was about to go down to the basement and have a *latihan*. "What," I asked, "is a *latihan*?"

He told me it was a powerful expression of feelings where there were no restrictions. One removed his inner censor and let the emotions flow. It was the focal point of a religious group called *Subud* and was intended to give one a feeling of liberation, and perhaps even enlightenment. So I went with him and his guests to the basement where, before long, everyone was howling, crying, and, as the expression goes, "letting it all hang out." Everyone, that is, except me. I was a good observer but a poor participant.

Zalman had a prodigious appetite. It wasn't just that he could eat a lot; he ate with great fervour, gusto, and relish. The experience of watching him eat defies description. What I remember most clearly is that one day after a huge dinner at my parents' home, I went to see Zalman at Hillel House. He was working on a printing press, which he had salvaged and fixed up, and I arrived just as he was taking his dinner break. He took out a sandwich and began to eat. I sat there captivated and before long felt myself begin to salivate. Zalman saw me looking at him, transfixed, and offered me part of his sandwich. I accepted, and deprived the poor man of half his meal.

(Speaking of sandwiches, Oscar's Deli on Winnipeg's Main Street North had the best corned beef and pastrami I have ever tasted, surpassing, in my view, the finest that Montreal or even New York had to offer. I think it was their combination of just-out-of-the-oven rye bread with a crispy crust and tender melt-in-your-mouth thinly sliced meat, piled high and combined with fresh sliced tomato and hot mustard. Add a cold Coke, and it felt like the Messiah had arrived.)

On at least three occasions, I was invited to Passover *Seders* at Zalman's place. These were wonderful festive events celebrating the Jewish people's exodus from Egypt under Moses' guidance. He always had a large table surrounded by his family, Hillel students, and other interesting people. On one occasion, there were two United Church ministers present; they were professors at United College. About midway through the *Seder*, two of my friends from Hillel came in. Glancing at the ministers, who were easily identified by their collars, one of them exclaimed jokingly in Hebrew, "*Matai Nishchatam?*" ("When do we kill them?") — a reference to the blood libel accusations in the Middle Ages levelled against Jews who were suspected of slaughtering Christian children and using their blood in the baking of *matzah* (unleavened bread). What my friend didn't know was that the two Christian ministers taught Hebrew at the college and knew exactly what was being said. Zalman had to quickly do something, and began to laugh, looking upon all this as very funny. It was the right thing to do, and immediately relieved the tension. Later, when the ministers had left and my friend learned what he had done, he was very apologetic.

One of the best innovations Zalman brought to Hillel was retreats. These consisted of taking a group of fifteen to twenty Hillel students to a location, usually out of the city, where we would spend a weekend together studying Jewish topics, often with a guest scholar from another city. It began on Friday afternoon, led into the celebration of Shabbat, and ended some time on Sunday. These were always wonderful spiritual experiences.

It was through one of these retreats that I made my first acquaintance with a Canadian Jewish farmer. This both surprised and delighted me, although I had known that in the early years in Saskatchewan there were Jewish farmers.

This particular retreat with Zalman took us to a spot about forty miles from Winnipeg. While I don't remember the details of what we studied, I do recall that on this occasion I discovered the true meaning of coffee. There were about twenty of us, and the farmer and his wife, Mr. and Mrs. Maslovsky, invited us all to breakfast. Mrs. Maslovsky ground and brewed fresh coffee, and Mr. Maslovsky brought in fresh cream from the barn. By fresh, I mean he had just milked a cow and skimmed off the cream. It was light yellow in colour, moderately thick, and together with the coffee made one of the most delicious beverages I have ever tasted.

One may wonder how Mr. Maslovsky could serve us a milk product without first pasteurizing it. In those days on the Prairies, the regulations about pasteurization, while in place, were not as stringent as was the case in later years. Farms were carefully inspected and, to the best of my knowledge, there were never any problems. In fact, ten years later, when I returned to Winnipeg to work as a rabbi, I was able to obtain fresh unpasteurized milk for everyday use from one dairy on the outskirts of the city. There were two advantages to such milk: it tasted good, far superior to anything store-bought, and from it you could make cottage cheese. This was done by placing a bowl of milk, covered with cheesecloth, in a warm spot on top of the fridge for a few days, then inverting it and tying the bundle to a sink faucet so the remaining liquid drained out. Voilà! Delicious cottage cheese! Try this with pasteurized milk and all you get is a sour product that must be disposed of.

One other bit of information comes to mind as I write about our farm retreat. Sleeping arrangements had to be carefully orchestrated, as ours was a mixed group. Prior to arriving at the farm, a few buddies and myself thought everyone would sleep in the hayloft. We liked the idea of a co-ed loft and even fantasized about some of the possibilities. Zalman, however, had other thoughts. The arrangement turned out to be that the girls slept in the hayloft and the guys in the farmhouse, wherever there was space, even if it meant on the floor, while Zalman and our guest scholar (possibly Rabbi Everet Gendler or Rabbi Max Tikton) slept at the foot of the ladder leading to the loft. "Aww!" we exclaimed. Zalman smiled.

At another retreat in a different location, several of us decided to play a practical joke on Zalman. He was staying with others at one cottage, and we were at another. The plan was to pour water through some openings in the ceiling (which we had noticed earlier) onto Zalman and those with him, and then run like crazy. It was nighttime, and all were asleep at Zalman's cottage. We snuck up and poured the water. We missed most of those sleeping but woke some, including Zalman, who, in his long nightshirt, started yelling and began to chase us — but we were faster and easily outran him. At a distance, we stopped to watch Zalman run and saw him hit a very low fence. He fell over the fence, face down, into a mud puddle. He then stood up — fortunately uninjured, though his nightshirt was a mess — and, with the steam knocked out of him, told us to go away. We returned to our cottage and spent the rest of night debating whether we should feel bad and guilty for what we did to him. As in most discussions among Jews, there were two sides — in this case, one thinking that it was really a good prank and the other lamenting that it was not right to do what we did to a rabbi, especially our rabbi. The debate continued until dawn, without consensus. To his credit, Zalman was a good sport, and the next day made light of the whole incident, even laughing at himself for how he must have looked, standing in his nightshirt in the moonlight besmirched by water and mud.

Zalman's mind and interests were far-reaching. He had a curiosity about other religions and did not hesitate to explore beyond the academic level. When he could, he would take those of us who were willing along with him. So it happened one day that he managed to get an invitation for a group of us to visit a Trappist monastery in St. Norbert, on the outskirts of Winnipeg. Perhaps it was my early fascination with evangelical Christianity that prompted me to accept this rare and unusual opportunity, although certainly monastic life is far different from what evangelism offers, the former being secluded and introspective, while the latter is proactive in the public domain.

About a dozen of us showed up at Hillel House to take in the visit. We had to meet at one a.m. and then be at the monastery by one forty-five. At two a.m. a bell rang, and the monks awoke to begin the day with prayers, which we were privileged to witness. It was at this outing that I began to develop my love for Gregorian chants. We left the monastery around six a.m., accompanied by one of the senior monks, who had received permission to talk, although the order observes a continuing vow of silence. A second monk accompanied him but was not permitted to speak. When we said goodbye, the second monk smiled at us, as if to say, "Godspeed, many blessings—it was good to have you here." One of our group commented later on the beauty and simplicity of his smile, to which Zalman replied, "Yes, and it took a lot of work to come to the point where he could smile like that."

Over the ensuing years I visited other Trappist monasteries, including Gethsemani in Kentucky, where my roommate at my yeshiva, Ron Goff, and I spent several rich and inspiring days with Father Thomas Merton and his colleague Father Gerard. (I will speak more of this in the next part of this work.)

In the lounge area of the library at the University of Manitoba, my friends and I would often gather to chat, go over material from the last class, or talk with the women. At times we would challenge each other to contests of various sorts, such as who could hold their breath the longest. In this regard I was the champion, having on one occasion gone without breathing for three minutes and fifteen seconds. I would usually build up to it by hyperventilating several times and then take a deep breath. However, I was put to shame one day when, visiting Regina, I met up with an old schoolmate, Bill Peart, whose father owned Peart's Hardware on the south side of Eleventh Avenue, just east of Broad Street. Bill had been travelling around the world for several years and had spent some time as a pearl diver—without oxygen tanks. He told me he had reached the point where he could hold his breath while swimming underwater for up to five minutes. This both fascinated and amazed me. When I commented on how tall he had grown since I last saw him, he replied that this related to his diving; the expansion of his lung capacity had stimulated his growth. I don't know what the medical explanation for this is, but I know what I saw, and Bill had grown at least two inches since our last meeting, when he was eighteen years old and supposedly full-grown.

At the end of my second year of pre-med, I was accepted into the Faculty of Medicine at the University of Manitoba. Receiving my acceptance letter in the mail was a glorious moment. My lifelong ambition to become a doctor had taken a critical step, and in September of 1957, along with one of my closest friends, Donny Silverberg, I became a medical student.

The first few weeks were exciting. Even just buying the required textbooks, like *Gray's Anatomy*, excited me. And entering the cadaver room to learn anatomy from a dead body said to me, "This is the real thing." I remember one day between classes, as Donny and I stood in front of adjacent urinals going about our business, I said to him, "And how are you today Dr. Silverberg?" To which he responded, "Just fine. And how about you Dr. Steinberg?" Just hearing the honorific "doctor" in front of my name brought home to me just how significant this moment was in my life.

I have never seen anywhere a description of what it is like in the room where one dissects bodies in a medical school. Nor have I ever heard anyone describe it. So let me take a few moments to give the reader a sense of this unusual experience, which only medical students are privileged to have. As it has now been more than fifty years since these events took place, my description in general will be accurate but some of the finer details may be forgotten or blurred. Also, as I did not complete the first year, I can't describe anything beyond the first few months.

The cadaver room was large and well-lit. Upon entering for the first time, I could see perhaps fifteen or twenty tables, each with a corpse covered by a sheet. Every table had a number, and usually four students were assigned to each table. We were instructed to remove the coverings and found each cadaver wrapped in some kind of tape, somewhat like a mummy. We were told by our anatomy instructors (some of whom were surgeons) to only remove the tape from those sections we were working on. Papers were handed to each team with our first assignment, and we proceeded with the requisite tools, of which perhaps the most important were a scalpel and a pair of tweezers. We took turns with different tasks — cutting, identifying, reading the instructions, and so on. Upon removing the first pieces of tape, I was surprised to see that our cadaver was covered in a thick coating of something that resembled Vaseline. For some reason I had expected the bodies to be preserved in formaldehyde, as were the various animals I had dissected in my zoology classes. Such, however, was clearly not the case. So, the first thing to do was scrape away the coating to expose the area to be worked on. At the end of the class, the exposed part was covered with tape and left for another day. The idea was that as the dissection of one area was completed, another area would be uncovered, and so on until the students had learned basic anatomy.

When we opened the bodies, things were certainly not the way they looked in the anatomy books, where arteries were coloured red, veins a solid blue, and muscles a lighter blue, with everything else some other colour. Instead, everything was grey, and often one of our instructors had to come and distinguish one part from another. Some of us gave our cadavers names, as we were not told their real names. One of us asked where the cadavers came from, and was told that some were individuals who had indicated before dying that they wished to donate their bodies, and others were unclaimed bodies, perhaps from the local prisons. As to what happened to the bodies afterwards, we were told that they were given proper burials and, where possible, we could attend if there was a service. As mentioned, I never got far enough in the class to see what happened at the end of the year. I do recall, however, that we were told on the first day that the bodies were to be treated respectfully, and except for the occasional bit of humour, usually to relieve tension, no one stepped out of line.

I realized by the end of the first month that I was in over my head. I had difficulty absorbing and remembering all the material we had to cover, and when it came to physiology, I was a lost cause. At about the sixth week we had our first physiology exam, which was multiple choice. I looked at the questions, answered a few, and after twenty minutes left the exam room. I was in great turmoil and sweating profusely, so much so that when I went outside, where it was about fifteen below zero, I didn't feel the cold at all. Two weeks later, in a state of despair, I went to see the dean and told him I was leaving medicine. I knew that it was either leave on my own or, before long, be asked to leave. This was one of the worst moments of my life. In the ensuing days and weeks I was in a state of intense consternation, having just abandoned my dream of becoming a doctor and not knowing what I was going to do with my life.

My decision to leave medical school had a profound impact on my parents. The end of my dream was also the end of their dream. I felt bad, as they had done everything they could to support me in my quest, and I had let them down. I suspected that in their minds, especially my mother's, there could be no greater accomplishment for their son than to be a doctor. On a number of occasions over the ensuing years, my mother would introduce me to people with the phrase, "This is my son, Jerry, who almost became a doctor." One day, I sat down with my parents and told them that when I was introduced or referred to in that manner, it hurt. They heard me, and it was never spoken of again.

As I reflected upon my decision, I came to realize that in addition to not having the head to deal with all the material, I was less interested in medicine as a science than I was in being a healer. At the time, it didn't occur to me that there were other paths to being a healer, and it was many years before I became aware of this. Also, at the time, I had to try to come to terms with the powerful healing instinct in my soul, which began when I was a child and now had no apparent outlet. As I've mentioned, when I was young something stirred in me whenever I saw a blind person, prompting me to want to find a surgical procedure that would restore sight, a goal I took with me into medical school. What I had to learn was that blindness has aspects other than the physical, that blessings sometimes come in painful disguises, and that some-times angels come in human form. My angel turned out to be Zalman.

I met with Zalman at his office at 67 Edmonton Street and told him what had happened. He listened carefully, letting me express the full range of my feelings, and then quietly asked me what other professions I might be inter-ested in. I told him I was considering getting a Ph.D. in one of three fields: English, psychology, or philosophy (the last of which, as mentioned, I knew nothing about but for some reason appealed to me). We explored each of these paths, and then Zalman asked, "Have you ever considered becoming a rabbi?"

I almost fell out of my chair. "No," I told him unequivocally. "It's not a field I have any interest in. Besides, even if I was interested, I could never be an orthodox rabbi because I simply don't believe in all the things the orthodox believe. Conservative Judaism also has no appeal for me, since I've heard that to become a Conservative rabbi you have to sign a document stating that you're going to keep kosher and observe the laws of Shabbat. I would never make that kind of commitment in writing."

He looked at me, took a gentle breath, and continued, "What about Reform?"

"Reform," I almost choked, "no way. I don't want to be a *goy* [gentile]." (The reader will recall that my upbringing was orthodox; in Regina, that was all I had known. Conservative Judaism was acceptable, but still not the real thing. Reform Judaism was anathema — no self-respecting Jew would want to have anything to do with those people.)

Zalman patiently took all this in and then asked me one more question: "What do you know about Reform Judaism?" I gave him a blank stare and knew, in that moment, that he had me.

"Nothing," I replied.

At which point he opened his filing cabinet, withdrew a thick folder, and handed it to me. "Take this home and read. When you're finished, let me know what you think, and if you're interested we'll take the next step."

Two things happened in that moment. First, I humbly took the folder, and second, I was perplexed that an orthodox rabbi — no, a *very* orthodox rabbi — not only knew something about Reform Judaism, but had a folder of material on the subject in his possession. "I guess," I thought cautiously, "I'll have a look at the material."

That evening, I lay on my bed with the folder next to me and began to read. As I absorbed page after page of articles, pamphlets, and photographs, I could feel a subtle excitement beginning to rise in my chest. Almost every-thing I read spoke to some part of me, and I began to see Judaism in a new light. In particular, I was impressed by how much freedom Reform Judaism embraced in thought and practice. I also appreciated that Reform did not make a religious distinction between men and women. (About twenty years later the first female Reform rabbi was ordained, followed much later by the Conservative movement ordaining its first woman rabbi.) Moreover, it

Zalman on far right, next to my wife, Shula, and Ron Goff, my classmate and friend circa 1965

occurred to me that as a rabbi, I could bring the other disciplines I was interested in to bear on my profession; psychology, philosophy, and English were all grist for the mill. I went to sleep that night with some peace of mind, for the first time in days.

The next day I went back to see Zalman. I told him I was interested but still hesitant, and I asked him what he would suggest. He said that, if I liked, he would try to make arrangements for me to visit the Hebrew Union College — Jewish Institute of Religion in Cincinnati. He had a friend there on faculty, and he would see what his friend could arrange. About two weeks later, I was on a bus to Cincinnati.

Arrangements had been made for me to stay in the students' dormitory, and permission was granted to sit in on classes. Over the next seven days, I availed myself of all the privileges given to me. The classes were fascinating, the students warm and welcoming, and the dormitory food excellent. I spoke to many students about why they wanted to be rabbis and found that their answers, for the most part, resonated with me. Zalman's friend, Dr. Jakob Petuchowski, was professor of Talmud and very kind to me. He and his wife invited me to Shabbat dinner, a dinner more traditional than what I had experienced anywhere before. Charles Kroloff, a senior who was about to be ordained in the spring, and his wife, Teri, also had me to dinner at their home and were very generous in sharing their thoughts about Reform Judaism.

After a few days at the college, I had an interview with the provost, Dr. Samuel Sandmel, who instructed me on how to apply for admission to the yeshiva. There was, however, one small problem. To be a full student in the rabbinic program, one had to have a bachelor's degree from an accredited university. As I had been accepted into medicine after my third year, I did not have a degree of any kind. A fourth year at the University of Manitoba would have given me a B.A. Dr. Sandmel told me that I could choose either to return to Winnipeg and obtain my degree or to enroll at the University of Cincinnati for a year and obtain it there. If I did the year in Cincinnati, he told me, I could live in the college dormitory and take a class in Hebrew each semester, which would stand me in good stead when I finally entered the yeshiva full time. I chose the latter alternative and made arrangements with the University of Manitoba to transfer my credits. By the end of the week, I had decided to become a rabbi, and I returned to Winnipeg to begin the process of applying to two institutions. I was accepted to the University of Cincinnati as a fourth-year student, and as a pre-rabbinical student at the Hebrew Union College.

Back in Winnipeg, I told Zalman of my decision and he was delighted. My parents, however, were not thrilled, but supported me nonetheless. One of their concerns was whether I would be able to make a living as a rabbi. At that time, as today, rabbis were not generally in the higher echelons of wage earning, but I assured my parents I would do fine, as things had changed for the better in this regard, and in fact some rabbis did quite well. I don't think they were convinced, but they went along with it.

It was December of 1957, and I had the rest of the school year to do what I wanted. I took a Hebrew course at the University of Manitoba and remained active in Hillel. I read and dreamed. Life had taken a turn, and even with regrets about medicine, I looked forward to the new direction my future had taken.

During this last year at the University of Manitoba, an incident occurred that was to have a profound and elevating impact on my life. Years earlier, when I was a member of Young Judaea, I learned many Israeli dances. The learning in my head, however, did not translate well to my feet; I watched my peers dance and tried to emulate their grace without success. I finally had to accept that I was clumsy, or as the saying goes, I had "two left feet." But this never stopped me from dancing. During my year in Israel, folk dancing was a strong expression of our connection with everything Jewish. We had excellent teachers, and a performing group was formed. I tried out for the group, but I knew full well that my chances were slight, and I was not mistaken. Again, I sat on the sidelines and watched the others dance while wishing I could be one of them.

When I returned to Canada, I discovered that at the University of Manitoba, there was also a performing Israeli dance troupe. I, stubbornly refusing to give up, auditioned for the troupe and was asked by the teacher if I would be a backup. I accepted, but again had to sit on the sidelines and watch others dance. At least, I thought, this is progress. Nobody before had ever asked me to even be a backup. Then, one day, toward the end of my sojourn at the university and a few hours before a performance, the dance teacher informed me that one of the dancers was ill and asked if I would be willing to take his place. A rehearsal was called, and I was fitted in, quickly trying to polish my steps so as to seamlessly blend in. I performed with the group, but afterwards felt critical of myself. Then two individuals in the audience came up to me, independently of each other, and told me how much they had enjoyed watching me dance. (Echoes of Miss Graham back at Thomson School.) I hesitantly accepted their compliments, feeling somewhat embarrassed, and wondered if they were just saying this to make me feel good, or if they really meant it. Whatever the case, their words had a deep impact on me and changed the way I danced and perceived myself as a dancer. (This was to yield unexpected results four years later.) They also reminded me how just a few timely words, spoken to someone struggling with an issue, can alter that person's life for the better. It's a lesson I have never forgotten, and I apply it to others whenever the opportunity presents itself. In later years, in my psychotherapy practice, I often suggested to clients that at least once a day they find something, however seemingly small or insignificant, about each of their loved ones to compliment.

> the right word
> > the right time
> > > the right place
> > lifts the soul

My two closest friends in Winnipeg were Donny Silverberg (mentioned earlier) and Mark Schulman. Donny finished medical school and is a distinguished kidney specialist residing in Israel. Donny's father was a mathematics teacher and during the High Holidays served as a cantor in one of the local synagogues. Many times I ate at Donny's parents' home on Hartford Avenue in the north end, and many times Donny ate in my parents' home on Queenston Street in the south end. After I left for Cincinnati, Donny often came to our home to study since, with nobody home during the day, it was a very quiet place to focus. If I recall correctly, he would sometimes stay for dinner when my parents returned from work and then continue to study into the evening.

Mark was a quiet, somewhat introverted young man with a talent for playing jazz piano and an excellent arm for throwing a football. When we got together for a scrub game, Mark would always be our quarterback. He was also a brilliant chess player — at one time, Manitoba champion. I recall that at one point in his life he had to choose between chess and family life. Wisely, he chose the latter. Mark and I were very close, often spending time together and sharing the day-to-day happenings in our lives. I was always a welcome guest in his home, and on more than one occasion his mother told me that I was a good influence on her son and instrumental in bringing him out of his shell. Mark was also a fairly observant Jew and enjoyed most things having to do with his religion. His father had a well-established law practice in Winnipeg, and often Mark and his brother, Perry, would help their dad out in the office. As far as I could tell, the expectation of his parents was that both he and his brother would become lawyers and go into the family business.

In the third year of our friendship, after I returned from my visit to Cincinnati, I was excited and enthusiastic about becoming a rabbi, and I shared my enthusiasm with Mark. This triggered something in him, and he began to talk to me about his interest in furthering his Jewish studies. I suggested that maybe he, too, should consider the rabbinate as a profession, although it would probably be in the Conservative movement. He gave this some serious thought and began to shift his interest from law to becoming a rabbi. He talked to his parents about this. One day, when I came to his home for a routine visit, his mother answered the door and told me I was no longer welcome in their home. To say I was shocked would be an understatement. I tried to ask for an explanation, but the door quickly closed. I walked away in turmoil and then turned around and looked up to Mark's window on the second floor. I could see him pacing, and when he spotted me, he sort of waved. An hour later I received a call from him, asking me to meet him. We got together at a neutral spot, and he told me that his parents were very unhappy with his thoughts about becoming a rabbi and blamed his thinking on my influence. He said he had to reconsider his future but that no matter what happened, he wanted our friendship to remain intact. It did, although our meetings were never again in his parents' home.

In thinking back to that time in my life, I have a better understanding of his parents' position. Like my parents, I believe Mark's were concerned with his ability to make a living as a rabbi, which in those days could be difficult. Law was no doubt a safer haven as a profession. Also, his parents had a dream: that father and sons would work together and the firm of Schulman, Schulman, and Schulman would be a highly respected establishment in the Winnipeg community. In fact, this is what happened, although I don't recall if that was the exact name of their firm. Mark's brother, Perry, later became a professor of law at the university, and later still a judge in the Manitoba Court of Queens Bench, where he remains at the time of this writing. Mark continued on as a successful lawyer, highly regarded in the city, and a member of an orthodox synagogue where, at one point, he was president. Our friendship through the years always remained strong and loving. When I would visit Winnipeg years later, after moving to Ontario, he and his wife and children would get together with my parents and me (and my kids, if they were in town) for a penny-ante poker game at his place or mine. The only ones who came out behind at these meetings were the hosts, who always provided excellent food, which often was more the focus of the evening than the game itself, and certainly cost a lot more than anyone ever lost. (A dollar and a half down after three hours of playing was considered a big loss.) We had a lot of fun, and I look back on those days fondly.

In 2006 I received a call from Mark's son David, informing me that his father was dying and asking me if I could I come to Winnipeg. I had known Mark was seriously ill but thought he still had time. I caught the next available flight, and a few hours later was in his room at the new Victoria General Hospital on south Pembina Avenue. He rallied briefly from his drug-induced sleep and said, "Hi!" A few days later I kissed him goodbye, and two weeks after that he was gone.

> A good friend
> is like a sweet apple
> nourishing
> delicious
> and when it is no more
> the seeds spawn new blossoms

During my visit to Winnipeg, I got to know Mark's brother, Perry, better. I believe if we lived in the same city, we would be good friends. From time to time we e-mail each other.

Satisfaction comes in strange ways. During the three years that I lived with my parents in Winnipeg while I attended university, I had to constantly shovel snow from the sidewalk in front of and to the side of our house. For some reason, this gave me a lot of pleasure. It was hard work, but in the end, the sidewalk was clear and clean, whereas before it had been impassable, often to the point where the mailman would not deliver mail because he couldn't get through. Of course, shovelling after a fresh snowfall was different from shovelling after the snow had compacted and become hard or turned to ice, which required a lot of chopping with the end of the shovel or a special tool with a blade at the end. Whatever the case, each square foot of cement that came into view gave me a feeling of accomplishment. When it was all done, my father would come out and compliment me on a fine job. That was the best part of all.

THE GROOMING OF A RABBI

Cincinnati 1958–1961
Montreal 1961–1962
Cincinnati 1962–1965

Little did I know
the seeds of my youth
would blossom
in such a way

Little did I know
the joys and wounds
of serving
would sculpt me
in such a way

Little did I know
that knowledge
would never define me
nor words describe
who I am

Upon my arrival in Cincinnati in the fall of 1958, I was assigned a room in the dormitory at my yeshiva (seminary), the Hebrew Union College—Jewish Institute of Religion (hereafter referred to as HUC), and settled in. My room was not large, but it was comfortable and had all the amenities a student needed, with bathrooms and showers down the hall. On the main floor of the dormitory were the kitchen, dining room, a few meeting rooms, and the "bumming room," where a television was located and where we gathered, much as one would in one's own living room. Basketball and the evening news with Chet Huntley and David Brinkley were among the main attractions, and it was here that I received an education on the importance of basketball—a game I had played in high school with little aplomb—to the American sports public. At one end of the building there was a suite of rooms where our dorm mother, Haddie Schiff, resided. Haddie was a warm and caring woman who gave counsel and support to many students over many years. Her home in the dormitory always had its doors open, if needed. Next to Haddie's suite were guest rooms where visitors to the college could stay for a short time.

Our dormitory food, prepared and served by an excellent staff, was wholesome and delicious, with special meals on Shabbat (Sabbath). For a small fee a student could bring a guest to dinner, and many a girlfriend or fiancée graced our tables. At the conclusion of every meal, perhaps with the exception of breakfast, we *benched* (said a blessing of gratitude for our food), led by different students, depending upon who was volunteering. Birthdays and other occasions were also celebrated in the dining room. Often on Shabbat, after dinner, we would sing songs appropriate to our day of rest.

As good as the dormitory food was, every now and then, budget permitting, my friends and I would go out to one of the local restaurants, like Frisch's Big Boy. My first visit to Frisch's almost landed me in jail. When it came time to pay, I took out my Canadian currency and the cashier thought I was handing her Monopoly money. I tried to argue that Canadian money was worth more than American money (which it was at that time), and that international relations were on the line—but to no avail. After that, my coloured money remained in my wallet until it was time to go back home to Canada.

Located a half-minute walk from the dormitory was the building that housed our classrooms, various offices for faculty and staff, and the chapel. The chapel was a warm and intimate space, with an upper level where the choir sang on Shabbat and other special occasions. The pews, able to accommodate about 200 worshipers, were made of wood and were not particularly comfortable. As part of the *bima* (the area at the front where the service is conducted), there was an organ that was played during some of the services. Coming from an orthodox background, organ music in a synagogue was something I struggled with, having always associated it with the church. About midway through my five-year program, I finally got used to it, and by the time I was ordained, I actually enjoyed hearing it played.

Another aspect of chapel life at HUC that I had to come to terms with was the fact that, in those days, most of the students and faculty did not wear any head coverings during services. I, of course, always wore my *kippah* (skullcap), as did a few other students. As there was no hard and fast rule in this regard, every student had the option of wearing a *kippah* or not. However, I never did get used to being at a Jewish service where others prayed bare-headed. I have been told that there were temples where one would be asked not to wear a *kippah*, but although I myself have attended services in a few temples across the United States at which I was virtually the only person with a *kippah*, I was never asked to remove it. Later, as a congregational rabbi, I never objected if someone came to my service and opted not to wear anything on his head, but while I bought into the concept of freedom of choice in ritual matters, I also encouraged my congregation to observe certain rituals and traditions, among them the wearing of a *kippah*. To the present day I always wear a *kippah* at services, whether I'm conducting the service or not. As for the *talit* (prayer shawl), I always wore mine in the chapel on Shabbat. Toward the end of my studies, when ordination approached, wearing a *kippah* and *talit* became an issue for me, as I was told that no student had ever been ordained wearing these.

At one point during my student days, my yeshiva hosted a renowned personality, Rabbi Mordecai Kaplan, who was a professor at the Conservative-based Jewish Theological Seminary and the founder of the Reconstructionist movement in Judaism. A portly and affable-looking gentleman, he entered our chapel wearing a small *kippah*, was introduced by one of our faculty, took his place at the podium, slowly looked over his audience, and began with the following statement: "Gentlemen, the difference between Reform and Conservative Judaism is really nothing more than the drop of a hat!" We all stood up and enthusiastically applauded. After that opening remark, he had us in the palm of his hand.

In general I found the services at HUC, conducted mostly by students, to be warm and uplifting. They were certainly shorter than what I was used to in Regina, and contained an element I had not before encountered: silent meditation. As time went on, this became one of my favourite parts of the service. The only part I liked better was when the choir, directed by Joe Topel, would sing—especially when our two student soloists, Laszlo Berkowits and Howard Greenstein, offered liturgical renderings with their beautiful voices.

My first year in Cincinnati was very full, as I was completing my final year of undergraduate studies at the University of Cincinnati (UC) and also taking classes at HUC. Fortunately, my credits from the University of Manitoba were accepted at UC, and I was able to devote myself solely to the subject of psychology, one of my loves. For the most part, I had good teachers and only one area where I struggled—statistics. This was not the fault of the professor; math in general has never been my forte. The only text, recommended as supplementary reading, that I was able to get my head around was titled *How to Lie with Statistics*. If everything in the course had been as clear as this concise book, I would have been fine. For example, I never knew there were three different kinds of averages—mean, median, and mode. This told me that if someone wishing to make a point found it to his advantage to choose median or mode instead of mean, which is what most people think of as average, he could easily mislead his audience without lying. Or, as the author maintained, this was one way of "lying with statistics" without technically lying. The book continued in this vein and for me was an eye-opener.

At every other university that I knew of, in the undergraduate program in psychology, one was only required to take written exams; but in the psychology department at the University of Cincinnati, the graduating student had to take written exams and oral exams, and write a dissertation. So I had my work cut out for me. My dissertation topic was "The Effects of Schizophrenia on Bi-Lateral Transfer of Training." I won't bore the reader with the details of what this entailed, except to say that I had to do part of my research at the Longview State Mental Hospital. I used schizophrenic patients there as my subjects, while my control group consisted of my fellow students at HUC. I can't say the results of my research made any significant contribution to the field, but I enjoyed the process and learned something about schizophrenia, not to mention the chi square method of statistical application.

One patient I met at Longview Hospital taught me that some schizophrenics are very clever and can easily fool a neophyte like myself. A gentleman working in the office at the hospital engaged me in a protracted conversation about psychology and schizophrenic conditions. He was very knowledgeable, and thinking he was one of the clinical Ph.D.s on staff, I spent about an hour or so discussing and learning about schizophrenia. Only later did I find out that he was a patient. Not once during our discussion did he declare his status, nor did I twig to his illness, as he displayed no erratic or incoherent behaviour. He seemed to be in command of the subject, and in the final analysis this was all that really mattered to me. Still, I get a chuckle when I imagine how much he must have enjoyed letting me think he was a doctor or professor. (As I reflect on this, I suppose he could have been a doctor or professor with a schizophrenic condition.)

My access to Longview Hospital was made possible by my clinical psychology professor, Dr. George Kisker, an expert in hypnosis. He was the most interesting and colourful of all my teachers at UC, and under him I did some graduate work in psychology after I received my B.A. As a teenager, I had dabbled in hypnosis and found I was pretty good at it, experimenting on friends and having fun with harmless post-hypnotic suggestions. What I learned from Dr. Kisker was how to do group hypnosis. One day, he hypnotized almost the entire class of thirty or so students, all at the same time. I found this fascinating, and in subsequent years tried it myself with considerable success. From this, I came to understand how professional stage hypnotists manage to be so successful. In essence, they do group hypnosis, knowing that approximately ten per cent of the audience will be good subjects. These they select and invite onto the stage, and then continue with their show, to the amazement of the less susceptible remainder of those present. It works every time. I also learned that children roughly between the ages of eight and sixteen are a good target audience, with a higher degree of receptivity than what is generally found in a normal adult population.

Dr. Kisker defined hypnosis as "a state of heightened receptivity." I have yet to find a better definition. By now he is probably in the great beyond, but I remember him fondly as a good professor, a good man, as well as a connoisseur of fine automobiles. In my mind's eye I can still see him driving around in his yellow Corvette with the top down, his full head of grey-streaked hair waving in the wind.

The walk between the University of Cincinnati and the Hebrew Union College, both located on Clifton Avenue, was about twelve minutes. Between these institutions was Burnett Woods, a lovely park where other students and

I would go when the need to be close to nature arose, or when the pressures of too much study encroached upon us. The other escape, although it was a far cry from the woods, was our local watering hole, the Busy Bee, a ten-minute walk from HUC and a great gathering place with a piano bar and entertainer. Here I was introduced to apple pie with melted Cheddar cheese on top, a delicacy I have continued to savour over the years. It was there, too, that one day we put one of my classmates to a test. He was boasting that he could drink more beer faster than anyone else. The other four of us accepted his challenge, and told him that if he could drink ten beers in thirty minutes and keep them down for at least a half hour, we would cover the cost — but if he failed, he had to pay. Without hesitation, he began ordering the beers, one at a time, while I watched the clock. He downed the first three or four quickly, then began to slow down. By the sixth beer, he was faltering, but still chugging away. Then, at about the twenty-minute mark, on his eighth beer, something very strange and unexpected occurred. He started to shiver, and a few minutes later his lips turned blue. He couldn't finish beer number eight, and upon leaving the Busy Bee (having paid for the eight beers), proceeded to throw up on the sidewalk. We had to drag and carry him to the dormitory while he ranted and raved about this and that and said that for sure on another occasion he would take us on again and prove his mettle.

When I thought back on this incident, it occurred to me that his mistake was in ordering the beers one by one. As such, each beer came to him cold, so as he continued to drink, his body temperature became hypothermic, and before long he couldn't go on. Had he ordered all ten beers at once, they would have warmed up as he drank, and possibly he could have downed all ten and kept them inside for the prescribed time. He never did repeat the challenge.

Another delicacy I discovered in Cincinnati was German chocolate cake. With a strong Germanic contingent in the city, it was easy to find and always delicious. What distinguished German chocolate cake from other cakes of the same genre was the addition of coconut or macaroon in one of the layers or in the icing. I am a great fan of chocolate cake in general, but since leaving Cincinnati I have rarely been able to find a cake to match what I had there, although I'm sure they exist somewhere (besides Germany).

While Cincinnati is a very attractive city, built on seven hills, it is also the home of Procter and Gamble. Not that I had any issue with their products, but I did take issue with the preparation of their products. When the wind was coming from the wrong direction, the heating and processing of animal fat for soap would send a foul smell, which could linger for days, over the city. I suppose those native to the city got used to it, but I never could, and would always be sure to leave the city during the summer months when the odour was at its worst. Furthermore, like many others, I had allergies — Cincinnati may well have been the allergy capital of America and had a reputation for having the largest number of allergy specialists per capita of any U.S. city. For these reasons, I wasn't interested in remaining in the city any longer than I had to.

I was never much of a basketball fan, but in Cincinnati one could not help but be drawn into the basketball culture, which was dominated by one figure in particular: Oscar "The Cat" Robertson, also known as the "Big O." I was at UC at the same time as Oscar and from time to time saw him on campus, always accompanied by a contingent of friends and admirers. Finally, one day, I went to watch him play. It was an experience I'll not soon forget. The man was rightly nicknamed; he did move like a cat — quickly, deliberately, and ferociously. Pity any opposing player in his way! I had never seen basketball played this way, and it wasn't only Oscar; one or two of his teammates, like Jerry Lucas, were close to him in skill. Those were the heady days of college basketball at UC, and, I don't know if the university ever again reached that level in the sport. Oscar, of course, went on to be a star in the NBA.

The university bookstore, called Dubois, was across the street from the main campus and privately owned. When I first asked someone for directions to get to the store, using the French pronunciation of Dubois — "Doobwah" — I received a blank stare followed by the Cincinnati word for "pardon," which is "Please?" (as one would say in German, where the word is *bitte*). I asked my question again. Once more a blank stare, and "Please?" This went back and forth for a minute or so, until finally the individual got a glint in her eye and said, "You mean, *Dubois*" (she pronounced it "*Dooboys*").

"Isn't it pronounced *Doobwah*?" I countered.

"No," she replied, "it's *Dooboys*!"

I went to the store, bought some books, and checked with a clerk on the correct pronunciation of the name. I was assured it was "Dooboys," and not the French pronunciation, which I felt it must originally have been. "Strange people, these Cincinnatians," I thought.

Internships, assigned in order of seniority, were an important part of the five-year training program for rabbis at HUC. From the time a student entered the yeshiva, he became eligible to go out into the field and accumulate experience. Beginning in the first year, a student would take on a small congregation without a rabbi somewhere in the United States or Canada, provided one was available. On a monthly or bi-weekly basis, he would visit his congregation to conduct services, supervise the religious school, and attend to whatever other duties were called for. Usually, he would fly in on a Friday afternoon and return Sunday evening. His congregations would usually change each year, so over the course of his studies, he could be the student rabbi at five postings. The postings always began with the High Holidays of Rosh Hashanah (New Year) and Yom Kippur (Day of Atonement), usually in mid to late September or early October. Postings would end when classes ended, around the end of April. The experience of these internships was invaluable and gave us a feel for what would be out there in the field when we graduated.

Sometimes, for various reasons such as financial constraints, a congregation would request that a student come only for the High Holidays. Because of such a situation I was asked, upon arriving in Cincinnati in the fall of 1958, to go to Petersburg, Virginia, and conduct High Holiday services, though I wasn't yet a rabbinical student. There was a shortage of students available for the High Holidays. I was asked because of my background and fluency in reading Hebrew. Knowing that I would be expected to chant a good portion of the liturgy, I spent many hours listening to a tape of High Holiday melodies chanted by Zalman (who had prepared the tape especially for me), practising and trying to memorize the music. Those who knew me might have wondered why I even bothered to learn how to sing the prayers, since carrying a tune was not one of my strengths. However, not to be deterred, I gave it my best shot.

I boarded a four-engine prop airplane at the Cincinnati Airport, which was located in Kentucky (I never did figure that one out), and took off for Petersburg. Halfway to Petersburg, we encountered the tail end of a hurricane. The plane was tossed around like a kite, and I began to panic until the stewardess, nonchalantly and in a soft, calm voice, asked me if I would like a beverage. How she was able to remain standing and negotiate the aisle is another mystery I've never been able to solve. But her manner and demeanour calmed me, and then the captain's voice came on to tell us that he was going to climb and go over the disturbance. To my great relief, we landed in one piece in Richmond, where I was picked up and driven to Petersburg. The plan was for me to stay for ten days in Petersburg, as the two holidays are ten days apart, and then return to Cincinnati.

All in all, my first experience in the pulpit was a good one. I conducted my first Rosh Hashanah service without comment from anyone about my singing. They were probably being polite. I gave my first sermon, which was on respecting the aged, and in general seemed to acquit myself quite well. However, when I went to the back of the sanctuary after the service to greet the members and wish them a *Shanah Tovah* (Happy New Year), I encountered an unexpected problem. I couldn't understand what several of them were saying to me. For example, one man came over, wished me what was no doubt a happy new year, and introduced himself. His southern drawl was so pronounced that I couldn't make out a word. I said, "Pardon?" In retrospect this was the wrong thing to say, but he was gracious and repeated himself. His greeting sounded something like "*Gityontrabuymahnamssamung*," which didn't help and took several seconds to articulate, as his drawl drew the words out. Finally, not knowing what to do, I simply wished him a happy new year and moved on to the next person. (Later on, I tried to put together what he said, and came up with, "*Gut Yomtov* [Happy holiday], Rabbi. My name is Sam Unger.")

Then a small ten-year-old girl, as beautiful as they come, walked up to greet me and stretched out her drawl even more than Mr. Unger. Her words were expressed in a singsong manner with highs and lows, and she charmed me right out of my shoes, though I think all she said was, "*Shanah Tova* [Happy New Year], Rabbi." Eventually I got better at making out what people were saying. "Welcome to the not-so-deep-south, Jerry," I thought. "I can't imagine what it must be like in Mississippi."

It is the custom on Rosh Hashanah to blow the *shofar* (ram's horn). For many, this is a daunting task; I well recall, back in Regina, how the *shofar* blower always had difficulty getting sound out of this hollow instrument. Fortunately, it seems I was born with *shofar* lips and have never encountered a *shofar* I couldn't blow on my first try. One of the members of the Petersburg congregation was an elderly woman who was too frail to come to services but wanted to hear the *shofar*. So, after one of the services, I went to her home and accommodated her request. She was very grateful, and we spent a warm and meaningful hour together. If I remember correctly, her name was Maddy. Before leaving, she said she wanted to tell me something. I listened. She said she had been married over sixty years, her husband was deceased, and she wanted to share with me what she believed was the secret to a successful marriage. I waited eagerly to hear her words. "On our wedding night," she said, "my husband and I promised that we would never go to bed angry with one another. And we never did. It wasn't always easy, but we stuck to it and it took us through a number of difficult moments." I thanked her for her wisdom and wished her many more years of fruitful living. I tried to apply her advice some years later in my own marriage and found that, indeed, sometimes it's not at all easy. Unfortunately, my wife and I were not as adept at it as Maddy and her husband.

As I had several free days between Rosh Hashanah and Yom Kippur in Petersburg, I decided to visit Duke University in Durham, North Carolina. At that time, Duke had a department for psychic research, headed by J.B. Rhine, who was probably the world's most notable name in this field and would be for many years. To get to Duke I had to hitchhike, as I couldn't afford the transportation costs. It took me the better part of a day. I was picked up by three cars, all driven by Christian ministers—two Baptists, and the other I don't recall. They all asked who I was and where was I going. I told them I was a rabbinic student on his way to talk to someone at Duke University. While our talks touched on religion, none of these men tried to convince me to accept Jesus. They were amiable, pleasant, and wished me well. I was impressed and thanked each for his kindness in picking me up.

At Duke I was received cordially by Dr. Rhine, who showed me around his department. As I recall, a grant had been given to the university some years earlier by a tobacco tycoon for the express purpose of establishing a department of psychic research. Dr. Rhine's work was fascinating, ranging from experiments in telepathy, clairvoyance, and telekinesis to the phenomenon of clocks stopping at the time of their owner's death. The good doctor gave me a deck of ESP cards, a small but very appropriate gift, which I still have. Many years later, I was privileged to sit on a panel with him in Montreal, where we were both speakers at a conference sponsored by the International Institute of Integrated Human Sciences.

Shortly after my return to Petersburg, I was invited to a congregant's home for barbecued steak dinner. My host was a medical doctor, and, while tending the fire and turning the steaks, he waxed eloquent about the scientific evidence which showed that anatomically, physiologically, and mentally, black people were inferior to white people. I was taken aback by his words, particularly since one of my best friends in Winnipeg at the University of Manitoba was a very black Trinidadian, and there certainly wasn't anything inferior about him. I challenged the doctor on his statements, but he was certain that the evidence was solid and would soon become universally recognized. "Shades of Aryan purity," I thought, as images of Jews, Gypsies, and others being herded into gas chambers passed through my mind; they were slaughtered because the Nazis believed the same thing about their superiority. My comments to my host along these lines were simply ignored and the parallel not acknowledged.

This was not my first taste of colour prejudice, as there had been an incident in Winnipeg two years earlier involving my black friend. He and a Jewish girl had fallen in love, much to the chagrin of her family. My friend didn't have a car, so when I took him to pick her up in my father's car, I had to pretend she was my date, while he hid, crouched down in the back seat. Their romance blossomed and held solid for a considerable period of time. Eventually he returned to Trinidad, but without her.

In Cincinnati, I met someone who was to become one of my closest and dearest friends. The beginning of our friendship, however, was less than auspicious. Brahms Silver was also in the pre-rabbinic program, but at an earlier stage than myself. As he was one of the few other Canadians there, we quickly bonded, only to see the bond severed after a few weeks because of a bout of stupidity on my part. He confided something in me over a meal at a restaurant, and being a psychology major I proceeded to give him what I thought was sound advice, presented with the latest professional jargon, which I thought would impress him. My immature evaluation of his situation turned him off completely, and after that he stayed away from me. From that incident I learned two things: first, I didn't know it all; and second, no matter how much knowledge I might acquire in the future, there are times when it's best to shut up and just plain listen. Fortunately, about three weeks later I got the chance to redeem myself and be forgiven. Brahms's car went dead while parked in Burnett Woods, and he needed several guys to give him a push to get it started. I volunteered, and he appreciated my effort (and probably my contrition) and, transcending pettiness, put the earlier matter behind him. As I write, we have been "brothers" for over fifty years. After Cincinnati, Brahms and I would soon be together again in his city of Montreal for a year, where each of us played a significant role in the other's life. And we've done so many more times since.

In my first year of rabbinic school, I was to meet another individual who to this day is a close and dear friend: Saul Joel. Saul arrived at HUC from Bombay, India, to study in the pre-rabbinic program, with the intention of entering the full program and becoming a rabbi. As with Brahms, for various reasons this didn't work out. Both men pursued other careers, Brahms in business and Saul as a professor of social work. In recent years, Saul has retired from his position as department head at York University, where he made a major contribution in building a fine program, and Brahms has become a social worker in the oncology department at the Jewish General Hospital in Montreal, where he is loved by both patients and staff.

In the late spring of 1959 I graduated from UC with my B.A., which meant I could enter the full rabbinic program. However, as my interest in clinical psychology had been kindled by Dr. Kisker, I decided to pursue an M.A. in psychology at the same time. By the end of the following year I realized that trying to do two graduate programs at the same time was too much. Regrettably, I relinquished the program in clinical psychology and turned my full attention to my rabbinic studies, which turned out to be a wise choice. However, my love for clinical psychology never left me and some years later came to be a major part of my life.

My parents flew in from Winnipeg to attend my graduation at UC. I went to the airport to pick them up in my '52 Plymouth, which I had purchased for $135 earlier in the year. As we drove on the highway, they noticed that there was a hole in the floor below my feet that was large enough to allow them to easily see the highway passing beneath. This, and the condition of the car in general, did not please them, especially from a safety perspective. A few months later they bought me a brand-new 1961 Nash Rambler, which served me well for the next several years. There was, however, one small problem with the car. Unless I went alone, I could not get into any of the outdoor drive-in movie establishments. This was because Cincinnati was a very conservative community, and the Rambler's front seats could fold back all the way and make a reasonably comfortable bed for two. The movie places apparently knew this and were not about to encourage any hanky-panky during the show. On numerous occasions, my date, a lovely young brunette from New York, and I were turned away in spite of protests that we would behave. I encountered the same thing in Wisconsin, with another female companion, when I worked there one summer at a Jewish children's camp. Somehow, interstate communications had announced that Steinberg and his gal were on the prowl in a '61 Rambler and attendants should be on their guard. If he's alone, be sure to search the trunk.

The rabbinical program was divided into two parts. The first two years were directed toward obtaining a Bachelor of Hebrew Letters Degree (B.A.H.L.). It was a sort of test period to see if a student had the stuff to warrant continuing on for the next three years to ordination. Failure to obtain the B.A.H.L. meant a person would have to leave the program and seek another profession. Therefore, writing the B.A.H.L. exams was a very tense and intense time for me. It was, however, uncommon for a student not to make it through.

The academic level at HUC was high, and our professors were experts in their fields. As in all my previous studies, I was not an academic standout, fitting somewhere in the middle of the pack. Some of my classmates were nothing short of brilliant, which left me wondering what it must be like to have minds like theirs and be able to grasp things so easily and clearly. Still, I held my own and made it through the B.A.H.L. exams, which covered numerous aspects of biblical and rabbinic Hebrew, including Talmud, Midrash, Codes, and Aramaic.

At some point during my first two years in the rabbinic program, Richard Levy, Morty Pomerantz, and I founded a student journal, which we called *Variant*. The three of us were the editors, and the purpose of the journal was to give students at HUC a voice in the form of articles, poetry, and anything else of a creative and relevant nature. As editors, we didn't always agree on what was appropriate to print, and from time to time we clashed. In retrospect I see our differences as growing experiences, in particular because we were always able to work things out and come to some agreement. For example, there was the time I wrote a poem that I wanted to be in the journal. The other editors thought it was too strong, perhaps brazen, and felt it would not be a suitable contribution to *Variant*. We argued back and forth; I made a case for freedom of creative expression, and they countered with the right of editors to discern what was acceptable for publication and what was not. As it was two to one, I was on the short end of the stick. However, after further consideration, Richard and Morty, to their credit, agreed to print the poem on the grounds that poetic taste is very personal and should be left up to the audience. And they were right; some students liked the poem and others did not. Most simply did not comment.

A Note To You

Your chocolate face is bittersweet
Not a bit like snow,
Yet far beneath the surface reef
Cool waters lie, I know
Cool waters black and rippled through,
Blinking the light of night.
Upon the crest, baring your breast,
Soft reeds of coral blush and glow.

Variant remained in existence for several years, continuing, to the best of my knowledge, after we were ordained — Morty and Richard in 1964 and myself in 1965. Then it ceased. I'm not sure about the reason, but I presume no one wanted to take it on and put in the effort it took to sustain its existence.

In my second year of studies at HUC, two things happened involving Saul, who was still working on his B.A. at UC in the joint program. The first was rather funny in retrospect, but certainly not at the time. Saul wanted to learn how to drive and elected me to be his teacher. I had at that time my trusty 1952 blue Plymouth and one day took it on the street with Saul at the wheel.

Everything was going well until we approached the corner of Clifton and Ludlow, where I asked Saul to turn right. He misunderstood my instruction and continued to go straight, while I urged him again to go right. This time he understood and tried at the last second to make the turn. It was too late. He lost control of the car and sheared off a lamppost, which fell onto the sidewalk while pedestrians scattered in all directions. Finally, he brought the car to a stop, well onto the sidewalk. We got out, looked around, and breathed a sigh of relief at discovering that nobody was hurt, including ourselves, although the lamppost lay shattered on the cement. A short time later, the police arrived and took a statement. Saul had to appear in court but got off as a first offender, although I believe he had to pay the cost of replacing the lamppost. My Plymouth, being built like a tank, sustained only a dented fender.

Little did I realize that before long I would be in court to face my own charges. One night, at about 2:00 a.m., I stopped for a red light on a deserted street. I waited for it to change but nothing happened. I sat at the corner for almost ten minutes, no other cars to be seen. Finally, I figured that the light was stuck and went through. Sure enough, flashing lights were immediately behind me, and I was pulled over. I explained to the officer that I had waited a good ten minutes before deciding that the light was broken. He was very polite and understanding. In fact, he told me that the light was controlled by traffic, and if there wasn't any traffic flowing, it wouldn't change. He was very sympathetic as he wrote out the ticket. In fact, he apologized for having to give me the ticket and said that if I chose to challenge it in court, there was a good chance I would get off. He wished me well and moved on into the empty night.

A couple of months later my court date came up. When I checked in at the police station, the first thing required of me was to have my fingerprints taken. I looked at the policeman and softly protested, "For a traffic ticket?" He assured me this was the protocol. I began to have visions of time behind bars and dreaded entering the courtroom. Once inside, I had to wait about two hours while the judge dealt with several other cases. Men were being sentenced to three months in jail, a year in jail, substantial fines, and so on. I was sure I was either going to the slammer, or was going to be fined well beyond anything I could afford — maybe even deported.

Finally, my turn came. I had to surrender my driver's licence and registration and then stand before the judge, a slim gentleman with grey hair and a sombre demeanour. The policeman who gave me the ticket was present. The court clerk read out the charge, and the judge asked me how I pleaded.

"Guilty, your honour, but with an explanation." Someone had advised me that, given my situation, this was the best way to plead.

"And what is your explanation?" the judge asked. I told him the story. He asked the policeman to take the stand and give his version. He told the judge what he had told me about the light being controlled by traffic. The judge looked at me and in a deep, sonorous tone spoke as follows:

Judge: Mr. Steinberg.

Me: Yes, your honour.

Judge: What do you do?

Me: I'm a student studying to be a rabbi, your honour.

Judge: I see. (Pause) Mr. Steinberg.

Me: Yes, your honour.

Judge: You are a student.

Me: Yes, your honour.

Judge: As a student, you have certain goals.

Me. Yes, your honour.

Judge: And to achieve those goals you must travel along a certain path.

Me: Yes, your honour.

Judge: And while you are on that path, you must take care not to make mistakes.

Me: Yes, your honour.

(By this time I could hear snickers from those waiting behind me, as well as from the court clerk, and even the policeman was trying to hold himself back.)

Judge: And so it is with driving.

Me: Yes, your honour.

Judge: You have a destination, and slowly and carefully you must proceed to your destination. Do you understand what I'm saying to you, Mr. Steinberg?

Me: Yes, I do, your honour.

Judge: Case dismissed. Return the gentleman's licence and registration. Good luck, Mr. Steinberg.

Me: Thank you, your honour.

I left the courtroom with a big sigh of relief, although it took a while for my legs to stop trembling. I have always remembered the judge's words about moving slowly and carefully to my destination, and I try to heed them, though at times I do stray.

It was my habit, on occasion, to grow a beard. In the late spring of 1960, I returned to Winnipeg for the summer with a very full growth of red hair on my face. (The hair on my head is a light brown, but for some reason this does not carry over to my face). I arrived in Winnipeg around mid morning, and after settling in at my parents' home, I drove to their business in St. Boniface. After parking my car, I crossed the street to their store and saw a man, also with a beard, unloading sacks of potatoes nearby for delivery to the corner restaurant. I recognized him as a Mennonite, a member of a Christian sect, many of whom live communally in settlements in Manitoba. As I approached, he looked up, put down a sack, and after examining me carefully, asked, "Are you my brother?" Without giving the question much thought, I shook my head and replied, "No!" He smiled. I smiled. He went back to his potatoes, and I went in to say hello to my parents. Years later, thinking back on the incident, I regretted not saying yes to his question. It would, I feel, have been the right answer.

In early 1961, Saul told me he had a favour to ask, which prompted a visit to the Busy Bee for a drink and a talk. He told me that a woman had come from India to study for her Ph.D. in chemistry at UC, and that he was helping her get oriented to the city and, in general, to a new way of life. However, he had to go away for a couple of weeks and was wondering if I would be willing

Zarine (circa 1960)

to look out for her while he was gone. I said I would be happy to, so he gave me her phone number and told her about me. A few days later I called her, and we met for a coffee, again at the Busy Bee. To make a long story short, Zarine was beautiful, inwardly and outwardly, with a gentle sensuality that I found overpowering, and before long we fell in love. We saw each other at every opportunity and spent wonderful hours and days together. Zarine and I both belonged to the International Students Organization, so when they had functions such as parties or dances we would go together. I was the envy of the Indian men at these social occasions; they would often look in our direction, and I could see that any one of them would have liked to have Zarine on his arm. I was happy and proud to be with my elegant and gracious partner.

One day, as our relationship deepened, she asked me if I knew what her religion was. I guessed Hindu, but was wrong. She said she was Muslim. I wasn't familiar with the word, so she explained to me a little about what she believed. There seemed to be a number of similarities to Judaism, and we had an interesting discussion and then never broached the subject again. I'm not sure what I was thinking in those days, but probably something along the lines that if our relationship got more serious, she might consider converting to Judaism. We never had that talk, as circumstances dictated another direction for both of us.

In late spring, Zarine told me that she had been promised to an Indian man who was living in England. Her family in India was pressuring her to go to England and marry him. But she was involved with me and didn't know which way to turn. I felt strongly that if I said I wanted her to stay and told her we could work out a future together, she would have done so without hesitation. But I was also conflicted and not ready to make that kind of commitment. So, as the weeks went by, I tried to steel myself to her leaving for England to marry someone she hardly knew and had serious doubts about marrying. I let the moment slip by and said goodbye to Zarine as she left for London and I went off to work at a Jewish summer camp. I was emotionally in turmoil and, during my two months at the camp, thought about her every day. Also, I had another matter on my mind.

INTERLUDE—MONTREAL 1961–1962

SPIRITUALLY, HUC WAS not giving me what I needed. Most of what was being offered was head stuff: rationalism, empiricism, and a critical examination of the Hebrew scriptures. The mystical element was lacking, and for me nothing was more important. On two occasions, senior students challenged me about my view of God. Each, independently, came to me and said they had heard that I believed in a personal relationship with God. I replied that this was true. They then suggested that I see a psychiatrist. As it happens, every student applying to HUC had to undergo a screening by the college psychiatrist. At my screening, the man was very interested in my relationship with my parents but never once brought up anything about my relationship with God. The two senior students probably meant well, but they were the product of the zeitgeist at the college and no doubt heavily influenced by our professor of philosophy, about whom I will speak shortly. I mention all this to explain my decision to take a break from HUC for one year to go elsewhere and study Jewish mysticism. My question was, "Where do I go?"

A few of my classmates and I had made friends with a Lubavitcher rabbi in Cincinnati, Zev Scharfstein. We would go over to his home one evening a week and study Talmud with him. He was an excellent teacher, and between his scholarship and his wife Reena's cooking and baking, we honed our Talmudic skills. The Lubavitch movement is one of the mystical branches of Judaism, so I asked him for some direction. He suggested I go to Montreal and study at the Lubavitch yeshiva there, as he felt it would be a better place to learn than their headquarters in New York. So, once I had received permission to take a break from HUC, Rabbi Scharfstein made arrangements for me to become a student in Montreal. Some of my professors and fellow students were concerned that I would never return to HUC. I assured them that I would and that this year was merely an interlude. It was not only that I wanted to study Jewish mysticism; I needed a break. Period. I've never been one who could undertake long periods of intense study without getting away for a while to refresh and regenerate. This was one reason I did not go straight from high school to university, but took off to Israel for a year instead. And there was another reason. I was twenty-six years old, tired of dating and feeling lonely. As things with Zarine didn't seem likely to work out, I felt it was time to get married, and Montreal was an excellent city in which to find a Jewish wife. At that time I believed the two best cities in Canada to meet Jewish women were Montreal and Winnipeg, the former being the Jerusalem of the East and the latter the Jerusalem of the West.

So, in the autumn of 1961, I arrived in Montreal and took up residence in a basement apartment at 7400 Mountainsights Avenue, almost directly behind Ruby Foo's Restaurant, a Montreal landmark. Brahms and his family, especially his mother, were instrumental in helping me find a place to live. Often during that year, his mother either fed me at their home on Brighton Avenue or gave me large doggie bags of food to take back to my apartment. And it was good food — especially the produce, as the family ran a fruit and vegetable business, which Brahms later took over and developed to new levels.

I checked in at the Lubavitch Yeshiva on Park Avenue and was assigned a teacher. Naphtali Berg was about my age, had a well-developed beard and a slim frame, and was very bright and easy to get along with. There were, however, two problems with our arrangement. First, we weren't really studying Jewish mysticism, but rather a work known as *Tanya*, which consisted of the basic teachings of Rabbi Schneur Zalman of Liadi, the founder of Chabad Hassidism in Eastern Europe (1745–1812). It's not that the teachings weren't interesting; it's just that they weren't what I thought Jewish mysticism was all about. In other words, *Tanya* didn't speak about the *rebbe*'s personal spiritual experiences. (The term *rebbe* denotes a Jewish spiritual leader who has a number of disciples whom he guides in their spiritual quests, much like a guru in the Hindu tradition.) At times we studied Talmud instead of *Tanya*, but it was always one or the other. The other problem was that Naphtali liked to sleep. We would set up a meeting for 9:00 a.m., and instead of meeting at the yeshiva, I would have to go to where he lived and wake him up. Seldom would we get started before noon. His need to sleep in may have been because he stayed up late studying, perhaps into the wee hours.

The first time I went to wake him was an interesting experience. He slept in a large home on Park Avenue that had been slightly modified to serve as a small dormitory. The room in which he slept housed three other students, and on the morning I arrived, all were fast asleep. I quietly entered the room and awoke Naphtali. Eventually he responded to my voice and prodding, which apparently also woke the other young men, who all sounded groggy and a bit disoriented. Before Naphtali got out of bed, he said something to one of his roommates, who immediately reached over for a pitcher of water, a small basin, and a towel. This was passed from bed to bed until it reached Naphtali. He said a blessing and poured some water over his hands, after which he dried them and proceeded to pass the implements back to one of the other men. Then, wearing a long nightshirt, he swung his legs out from under the covers and stepped onto the floor. Curious about what had occurred, I later asked Naphtali for an explanation. He told me that this was the ritual upon awakening in the morning. The pouring of the water over his hands, along with the blessing, was a rite of purification and would cleanse any impurities that may have been encountered during the night. I wasn't clear about what kind of impurities he was talking about. He mumbled something about unclean spirits but did not elaborate. At a later point I learned that touching the genitals while asleep or having a seminal emission was considered impure. Therefore, upon awakening and before getting out of bed, it was incumbent upon a Jew to undergo a rite of purification. Running water over the fingertips along with a blessing constituted such a rite. The water was referred to as *nagel vasser* (fingernail water).

The bottom line is I was disappointed in what I was being taught, and I began to have second thoughts about having come to Montreal instead of New York. I'm not sure I would have been any better off there, but at least I would have been in the same community as the then-current *rebbe*, Menachem Schneerson. I suspect that would have been a treat, and perhaps — just perhaps — under his influence I would have stayed indefinitely with Lubavitch and become a Hassid (a member of the Hassidic movement, which began with the Baal Shem Tov in the eighteenth century and of which Lubavitch is a branch). In all fairness, there was one individual at the yeshiva in Montreal who was a true mystic, Rabbi Greenglass. He even looked like what I imagined a stereotypical Jewish mystic to look like: long beard, a faraway look in his eyes, an otherworldly ambiance about him. I never had the courage to talk to him, as he seemed so distant, and also I rationalized that I would be disturbing him. In retrospect, I regret my lack of courage. The students referred to him as "the *Mekublan*," the Kabbalist, and I'm sure had I gotten to know him, I would have learned a lot of things relevant to my mystical leanings.

One day, a couple of months after coming to Montreal, I was walking down St. Lawrence Boulevard on the west side when I passed a doorway with a sign outside that read "Yoga." I had heard this word once or twice before but knew absolutely nothing about what it meant. Having time on my hands, I decided to go in and check it out. I climbed a long staircase up to the second floor and entered a large room completely devoid of furniture, with a soft blue wall-to-wall carpet. There I was greeted by an East Indian man, lightly clad in a soft fabric wrap. He asked if he could be of help, and I told him that I had seen the sign downstairs and was curious. We sat down together on the carpet, and he patiently explained to me a little about yoga. It was interesting enough that I accepted his invitation to return the following day to watch or take part in a class.

The class had about eight students, with my host as the teacher. He demonstrated some poses and had the class follow. As the class went on and he showed more poses, I slowly began to realize that this was no ordinary man. He was not only in excellent physical shape, but as flexible as soft rubber. Later we talked some more, and I bought from him a book he had written, *The Complete Illustrated Book of Yoga* by Swami Vishnudevananda. I took the book home and pored over it that evening, examining picture after picture of the author in some of the most impossible poses I had ever seen or could ever have imagined. Needless to say, I became his student.

As Vishnu's yoga studio was only about a fifteen-minute walk from the yeshiva, I found myself jockeying back and forth between the two locations for most of the rest of the year. On many days my schedule was *Tanya* in the morning, Talmud in the afternoon, and yoga in the evening — or variations of this order. As the year went on, Vishnu and I became good friends, a friendship that was to last, with interesting twists, for many years.

While I was juggling these Western and Eastern philosophies and practices, the Zarine ball remained suspended in mid-air, and I still didn't know when it was going to drop or where it would land. We had kept in touch by mail, which is how I learned that the marriage situation in England was not going anywhere and she was in limbo. We finally spoke on the phone and mutually decided that she should come to Canada, live with me, and see where things would go from there. The only problems had to do with immigration and employment. To come to Canada she would need to have some kind of job lined up, as I was in no position to be financially responsible for her. It occurred to me that with her background in chemistry, it might be possible to find her a teaching position at one of the local high schools. "What high school," I said to her, "wouldn't want a Ph.D. candidate in chemistry on its faculty?" I believed she would be a shoo-in. I was excited at the prospect of seeing Zarine again, and having a chance to live with her and further explore and deepen our relationship.

After making some inquiries, I set up an appointment with the Catholic school board and went to see the appropriate hiring person. The first thing he asked me was whether Zarine was Catholic. His question threw me, as I couldn't understand what difference that would make as long as she was a qualified teacher. He told me that in the province of Quebec there were two school boards, one Catholic and one Protestant, and that to work for the Catholic school board you had to be Catholic. "Does this mean that the Protestant school board will only hire Protestants?" I asked.

"No!" I was told. "The Protestant school board also hires Jews."

"So," I thought, "it looks like the Protestant school board has more flexibility. Surely, if they hire Jews they will also hire people other than Jews." So I made an appointment with the Protestant school board.

The gentleman at the Protestant school board was very warm and also very interested in Zarine. Even without a teaching certificate, he was sure a place could be found for her, given her academic qualifications. I was beside myself with joy. Then he said that there was only one last question he needed to ask: "What is her religion?" I said she was Muslim. He took a deep breath. With what I perceived as genuine regret in his voice, he told me that she had to be either Protestant or Jewish, and that even atheists were not allowed to work for the Protestant school board. I couldn't believe my ears, and tried to give him arguments about civil rights and religious discrimination. He didn't disagree with my arguments but said his hands were tied. I left his office in great consternation.

Later in the day I called Zarine and told her the bad news. I could hear the deep disappointment in her voice and conveyed my own. We continued to write for a while. A short time later, she informed me that she had met another Indian man and they were going to get married. Not long after that we lost touch.

A final comment on Zarine. While we were together in Cincinnati, she told me one day that she had a premonition she would die prematurely. I found this disconcerting and tried to convince her to change her thinking. I don't know to this day (2010) what happened to her. In 1998, Brahms and I returned to Cincinnati for a visit to HUC. It was my first time back in more than thirty years. While there, I went to the University of Cincinnati office for international students and tried to get an address for Zarine, in the hopes that I might contact her and find her alive and well. They said they would have to retrieve old files from another building and would get back to me when they did. I never heard from them. To this day, fifty years after I met her, the memory of Zarine and the sweet fragrance of her skin remain with me. On occasion, she visits me in my dreams.

A DREAM

IT IS 6:29 a.m., May 1, 2011. I have just awoken from the following vivid dream:

Saul brought me to India for some reason. I see Zarine. We are in some kind of desert, and the air is warm and pleasant. There are many people around and Zarine is walking with them. She is aware of my presence but makes every effort not to be alone with me, always making sure to have other women around her. All the women, including Zarine, are wearing saris. Determined to speak to her, I follow wherever she goes, almost losing her at one point. Finally I shout to her from a distance that I have one thing that I have to tell her. She continues to try to get away. Finally I catch up with her, and we are standing alone. I am as taken with her beauty now as I was in Cincinnati. I place my hands gently on her arms and say to her, "I want you to know that I made a big mistake when I let you go." I feel her soften and can see she is moved. I look at her tenderly, but with some anxiety, as I say: "Also, I've written a book and it's almost finished — no, it *is* finished — and our story is in there. I'm telling the world about us." She looks a little concerned, but I'm relieved to see that her protest is mild. I awaken from the dream. There is a soft churning in my solar plexus. I look outside. The sun is rising.

I got up to do a Google search for Zarine and learned, much to my dismay, that Zarine and her husband, Gulgee, a renowned Pakistani artist, along with a maid, were murdered in 2008. The assailants, a former driver for the family and his accomplice, were on trial for the murder. Zarine and Gulgee are survived by two sons.

TO SUSTAIN MYSELF in Montreal, I had to find work. Rabbi Stern, an HUC alumnus at Temple Emanu-el, gave me a part-time teaching job, and the Zionist Organization of Canada gave me work as a folk-dance teacher. In terms of my prowess as a dancer, I felt vindicated. A kind word at the University of Manitoba had paved the way. As a dance teacher, I had two duties. One was to teach Israeli folk dancing to the general student population at McGill and Sir George Williams (now Concordia University), and the other was to prepare a performing dance troupe. For the general students, it was simply a matter of teaching what I knew, which was mostly Israeli or Yiddish dances with some international ones. The performing troupe, however, was more of a challenge. First, these were knowledgeable and good dancers, and second, if we were to perform for the public, which was our mandate, I would need to work out the appropriate choreography. To do so, I would take a piece of Yiddish or Israeli music, such as "Zemer Attik" or "Debka Gilboa" (both dances), and spend hours in my apartment listening to each part of the piece over and over again. I would let the music infuse me and allow my body to move in whatever way the music dictated. In this way, I was able to create new steps and develop choreographies for each dance. At times this meant taking a song for which there was no known corresponding dance and creating an entirely new dance. It was hard work, but in the end it paid off. We performed for different audiences, always to good applause and expressions of appreciation. Our "tour de force" came in the form of an invitation from McGill University to take part in their annual "Flying Carpet," an evening of dance with troupes from many different nationalities. Judging by the audience response, I believe we did very well. For one of our dances, I gave a solo performance. "Not bad," I thought, "for a guy with two left feet."

The next summer, I was asked by the Zionist Organization to spend July and August travelling from my home base in Montreal to various Jewish camps in the provinces of Quebec and Ontario, teaching dances and giving the camps' dance teachers tips on how to improve their teaching skills. By this time I had a repertoire of perhaps seventy or eighty dances, including several from other countries like Italy, Greece, and the Soviet Union. The dance teachers I encountered on my camp visits sometimes knew dances that I was not familiar with, and they taught their dances to me. It was an enjoyable summer.

I always looked forward to rehearsals with the performing troupe, because I enjoyed working with them, but also because I was romantically interested in one of the dancers. Shulamit (Shula, for short) was one of my two best female dancers. She moved with consummate grace and passion, and I always enjoyed watching her. Eventually, I asked her out, and this was the beginning of a courtship leading to marriage.

Shula was born in the town of Rovno in eastern Poland in 1941. Shortly after her birth, her parents fled to the Soviet Union to escape the Germans, and her father joined the army. He was never heard from again, and to this day no one knows what happened to him. Shula and her mother eventually left the Soviet Union and went to Belgium, where they lived for a few years and then moved on to Israel. Finally they immigrated to Canada and, after some time in Calgary, came to live in Montreal. Shula's mother had remarried, and her earlier married name of Lizak or Lisak was changed to Goldfinger. I mention these names in the hopes that a reader may recognize them and perhaps cast some light on what happened to Shula's biological father, Joseph Lizak.

Shula possessed the qualities I was looking for in a wife: she was beautiful, intelligent, sensitive, and intuitively spiritual. By February of 1962 she introduced me to her parents, and eventually I was invited for Shabbat dinners and, on occasion, other meals. I saw Shula frequently, at dance rehearsals and whenever we could find time together. Our relationship grew, and my feelings for her deepened.

In the early spring of 1962, I asked Shula if she would honour me by becoming my wife. She was hesitant at first, wanting to be sure I knew what I was doing. I assured her this was what I wanted, and she accepted. From then on, I was a regular guest in the Goldfinger home at 3245 Goyer Avenue, Apt. 11. Mrs. Goldfinger took over from Mrs. Silver in providing me with hot, nourishing meals, although I still sometimes ate at Brahms' parents' home. Shula's mother was a fine cook and welcomed me as a son. I, of course, saw Shula almost every day, and our relationship continued to blossom. As I recall, it was a pretty normal courtship for those times, by which I mean we did not live together before marriage, as do most couples I meet today. Still, since I had my own apartment, we were able to find time to be alone together, though Shula never stayed overnight, as she was always concerned that her mother would worry if she came home too late. I respected and admired Shula's devotion to her mother, even though at times I wished her mother felt more relaxed about her daughter's nocturnal whereabouts.

On September 9 of that year, 1962, we were married at the Chevra Kaddisha Synagogue in Montreal. Zalman came in from Winnipeg to assist the resident rabbi in performing the ceremony, and Brahms was my best man. It was a joyous occasion, but there was a damper on the event. A few months earlier, Shula's mother had been diagnosed with cancer, and the prognosis was not good. It was all she could do to get up from her bed and attend the ceremony, but she did it. Not only that, but, determined to be fully present at her only child's wedding, she and her husband walked Shula down the aisle, and she stood for the entire proceeding under the *chupah* (wedding canopy), even though a chair had been provided. Her physician, Dr. Ballon, was present as a guest and couldn't get over her will and determination.

Later, during the reception, Shula and I were presented with a wonderful surprise. Our entire dance troupe was there, and at a certain point in the celebration, they asked us to come up onto the small stage in the banquet room. One of the dances I had created for them, which we had performed a few times in public, was a Hassidic wedding dance, in which I played the rabbi and Shula had another role. At the wedding, the dance troupe, as a tribute to Shula and me, performed the entire work, only this time Shula and I were in the roles of bride and groom. It had the flavour of *Fiddler on the Roof*, with a courtship scene followed by a proposal and family celebration, and an ending under the *chupah*. This was followed by vigorous, joyous dancing, with Shula and me sitting on chairs side by side, and the dancers doing somersaults and *kezachkes* (a Russian dance where the men are in a sitting position and their legs kick out and back one at a time) in front of us. That moment holds a very special place in my heart.

Our honeymoon in the Eastern Townships of Quebec lasted only five days, as Shula needed to get back to Montreal to help care for her mother. Still, we had a good time, except for one unfortunate incident.

Shula (circa 1973)

As we were travelling back to Montreal, I was driving along peacefully, being careful not to exceed the speed limit, when I saw a large Buick come up behind me with two men in the front seat. The driver was in a hurry and became impatient with my "not going over the speed limit" driving style. In fact, I was travelling at exactly the speed limit. Coming right up to the back of my car, he decided to pass, not taking into account that we were on a long curve and his forward vision was limited. He gunned his engine and began to pass, coming up even with my car, when suddenly a small pickup truck appeared in his lane, heading straight for him. He jammed on his brakes, pulled back behind me, and then lost control of his vehicle. It shot out across the road and into the oncoming truck — a terrible collision, part of which I saw in my rear-view mirror.

I pulled over, got out, and ran down the highway to see what damage had been done, and whether I could help in some way. Shula followed a moment later. The pickup was overturned in the ditch with the driver stuck inside. He was conscious but appeared to have a broken arm. I told him help was on the way, while Shula ran down the road to find a telephone and call for the police and an ambulance. Then I turned my attention to the occupants of the Buick, who were both lying unconscious next to the road in the same ditch as the truck. One man, probably in his forties, was out cold but breathing normally. The other man, with blood on his face, was in respiratory distress and struggling to get air. I held his mouth open as much as possible so he could breathe, and this seemed to help.

The police arrived shortly, and then the ambulance. The police took a report from me, and I explained how the accident occurred. I asked them to please let me know how all the men made out, as I was concerned for their lives, especially the two men in the car. With everything out of my hands, I noticed that the Buick was sitting in the middle of the road, almost like nothing had happened, except that the hood was missing. Then I observed the car's engine resting in the ditch on the side of the road opposite from where the men were lying. It was as if someone had taken a saw, neatly severed the engine from its moorings in the car, and placed it upright in the ditch. The car had sustained no other noticeable damage.

I never heard from the police and can only assume that either the men recovered from their injuries and the police didn't bother to inform me, or they didn't make it and the police didn't want to give me bad news. Either way, I don't know what happened to the men in the car, although I'm sure the truck driver had a good recovery, given his less serious injury.

The car accident had a dampening effect on our joy and on the good feelings we had taken with us from our wedding. We were both shaken but also felt very close, as we had just encountered our first traumatic event as a couple and together had tried to help save lives. We returned to Montreal, and I prepared to return to Cincinnati to continue my studies while Shula would remain to look after her ailing mother. I knew she would be in good hands going through this most difficult time in her life, as she was well loved by family and friends. In addition, I felt confident that my own dear friend Brahms would be there for her in any way he could. I also knew that before long I would be returning to Montreal to attend my mother-in-law's funeral.

For Brahms, the greatest blessing of our year together in Montreal was Vivian. He met her in the library at Sir George Williams University and asked me what I thought about her. I advised him to go for it. Vivian was a vivacious woman who had come from Egypt around the time of the Suez Crisis, when continuing to live in Egypt was not healthy for Jews. They dated for a while; when things started to get serious, Vivian invited me to have dinner with her at La Crepe Bretonne, a student favourite within five minutes of the university. She wanted me to give her some deeper insights about Brahms.

I did what I could, but basically said he was a great guy. They got married a year after Shula and I, and several years ago I attended their fortieth wedding anniversary. Brahms and Vivian have three sons and four grandchildren at the time of this writing.

During the courting phase of my relationship with Shula, my friendship with Vishnu deepened. On one occasion he invited Shula and me to come and dance at an event he was sponsoring for a very gifted male Indian dancer. As part of the program, we performed two or three Israeli dances. The rest of the time, we watched the Indian dancer perform. It was the first time either of us had been exposed to this type of dance.

Another time, Vishnu, at my request, came to a smoke-filled home to try to help a man who was suffering from lung disease. He did his best, but the man was reluctant to change his ways — he was a heavy cigarette smoker — and the environment in the home was certainly not conducive to healing. I had met the man and his wife while working as an *Encyclopedia Britannica* salesman in Montreal. I was giving them my sales pitch when the man's wife told me that he was very ill, and she didn't think an encyclopedia would do him much good. In my best salesman-like style, I responded to her objection by pointing out that for an invalid like her husband, a set of encyclopedias was the perfect purchase, since he had so much time to read. The man, who was unable to speak due to his illness, wrote something on a piece of paper and gave it to me. It read, "I'm going to die soon." I stopped in my tracks. The woman told me that he had a fatal lung disease, and it was only a matter of time. I spent the next hour talking to them, trying to offer whatever help or comfort I could.

This is where Vishnu came in. I told him the story and asked if he would come and visit the couple, George and Ethel Ouimet, to see if there was anything he could do. He tried but, as I've said, to no avail. From this incident, two things resulted. I gave up selling encyclopedias, and I became friends with the Ouimets. George died not long after, and Shula and I maintained a long friendship with Ethel. When, many years later, she too passed on, we were informed that she had left something for our son, Meher, in her will.

I mention this last incident partly to try to counterbalance the view held by some, including his disciples, that Vishnu was cool and insensitive. I found him quite the contrary, despite his somewhat gruff exterior. Later in Vishnu's career, he invited me to his ashram in Val Morin, and on Friday evening he asked me and an Israeli woman to perform the rituals for Shabbat for all present, including many Jews. The woman lit the candles, and I said the blessings over the wine, then sang one or two Shabbat songs. Vishnu was always open to other perspectives, whether religious or secular.

Vishnu went on to establish ashrams in many parts of the world, and his following remains active today, although he has since passed on. He was a disciple of Swami Sivananda, a name that was later to come forcefully to my attention.

One day, about halfway through my stay in Montreal, I was asked if I wanted to observe Sh'chitah, which is the Jewish way of slaughtering animals. As a child, I had sometimes accompanied my grandfather to the small Sh'chitah house and seen our rabbi perform Sh'chitah on chickens. But I had never witnessed Sh'chitah for large animals like cows. With some hesitation, I accepted the invitation, not knowing what to expect.

We arrived at the abattoir around 9:00 a.m. on a Thursday. Upon entering the area where the animals were killed, I was overwhelmed by the smell of blood. This was not a good way to begin the day, but I was determined to stick it out, if for no other reason than to learn what Sh'chitah on this level was about. Also, since I was going to be a rabbi, I felt I should know more about Sh'chitah than what I'd picked up from hearsay or had read in books. The room was very large, with different stations for the processing of meat. At one end there was a small stall-like structure where the animals were directed for killing. The cows were assembled in an adjoining space and, one by one, led to the stall. They sensed that this was not going to be a pleasant experience; probably the smell of blood, along with their animal instincts, told them to resist the efforts of the men who were prodding and cajoling them to the stall and into position for slaughter. Once an animal was in the stall, a gate was closed behind it, restricting its movement in any direction. The animal's head protruded through an opening, and a small metal plate was immediately brought up under the jaws, slightly stretching the neck upwards. Then the shochet (ritual slaughterer), who wore a large rubber apron, tested his knife. At this point I feel it is important to pause for a moment and talk about the shochet and his knife.

It was explained to me that day, by one of the Hassidim in attendance, that the shochet had to undergo a long and protracted training, which included the study of anatomy, physiology, pathology, and all the various laws concerning Sh'chitah and Kashrut (the laws pertaining to kosher meat). In addition, the shochet had to take considerable training in how to sharpen the special knife used in Sh'chitah, and what kinds of tests to put the knife to before using it. For example, the blade had to be perfectly sharp and smooth; the shochet would run it lightly across his fingernail, and if he detected a rough spot, no matter how small, it had to be resharpened. Once the edge was completely smooth, the shochet would take a hair from his head, hold it up by one end, and bring the knife down upon it near the loose end. If the hair did not separate upon contact, the knife had to be resharpened and then tested all over again. The reason for all this sharpening was so that when the animal's throat was cut, there would be no pain. The best analogy I can make is to cutting oneself while shaving with a good razor; sometimes you can't even feel the cut and don't notice it until you see blood on the razor or in the mirror. The *shochet*'s efforts are intended to spare the animal any unnecessary suffering. The courses in anatomy, physiology, and pathology are taken so that the *shochet* has an intimate knowledge of the animal, allowing him to render it instantly unconscious with one cut and also to later identify any problems with its organs that might make the meat not kosher. If, for example, a suspicious spot is found on the lung, the animal is deemed unsuitable, all parts are rejected even if other parts look healthy, and it is passed on to the non-Jewish market. One non-Jewish government inspector at the abattoir told me that animals that undergo *Sh'chitah* are rarely inspected, since the kosher inspection process is much more stringent than the government-regulated non-kosher process.

The *shochet* must also be a pious man and an orthodox Jew, adhering to the moral and ethical injunctions prescribed in the Torah and interpreted by later generations of rabbis.

Once the cow is in the stall and the gate behind it is closed, a strong metal shackle is placed around one of its back legs, with the other end of the chain attached to a pulley near the ceiling. If it is the first animal of the day, the *shochet* then says a blessing over it; the blessing is intended for all the animals to be slaughtered that day. He positions himself next to the neck, with the long, wide blade in his hand. Then, with one cut in one direction only, he severs the animal's jugular veins and carotid arteries. Instantly, the cow's eyes roll up into its head, and the animal is unconscious. At the same time, the body is hoisted up by the shackle on its leg, so as to allow the blood to drain out quickly from its neck. All of this happens in seconds, and for all intents and purposes, the animal is dead at the cut of the knife. The carcass is then taken apart and the internal organs carefully examined.

I realize that this description may offend or even horrify some readers. But, if you are a meat eater, consider the alternatives. While at the abattoir, I also witnessed non-kosher methods of killing cows. One method used a gun-like apparatus with a metal spike attached to the end of the barrel. An explosive charge was placed in the gun, and the end of the barrel was placed on the cow's forehead between the eyes. The gun was discharged and the spike propelled into the animal's brain. However, sometimes the gun had to be loaded a second or even a third time. Meanwhile the cow was alive and suffering. Another method was for a man to stand on a platform with a sledgehammer and bring it down on the cow's head. This too was a hit-and-miss operation, which I witnessed once as a teenager in Regina. It's hard to forget the sight of an animal writhing on the floor after an unsuccessful attempt by its executioner.

Following my experience at the abattoir, I was not able to eat red meat for about two months. And it took longer than that for the stench of blood to evaporate from my memory. Today, I occasionally eat red meat, but never cooked rare. (Rare meat is also biblically forbidden.)

On two occasions, while in Montreal, Naphtali invited me to come to a *farbrengen* at the Lubavitch Yeshiva in Brooklyn, New York. A *farbrengen* is a "gathering," but not just any gathering. It's a gathering of Hassidim with their *rebbe*, and it happens two or three times a year. Naphtali said I might be able to get a personal audience with the *rebbe*.

So I went to the *farbrengen* with Naphtali and a couple of other yeshiva students. I was housed in the home of a Lubavitcher, within walking distance of the *rebbe*'s headquarters at 770 Eastern Parkway in Brooklyn. The *farbrengen* took place in a very large hall and was so packed with the *rebbe*'s followers that there was barely any standing room. If I was to estimate the number in attendance, I would say it was somewhere in the vicinity of several hundred men — all wearing black hats, black suits, and white shirts, with beards of various sizes and shapes, except for some of the younger men who had not yet reached that stage. We stood shoulder to shoulder with little, if any, wiggle room, awaiting the arrival of their spiritual leader and *rebbe*, Menachem Mendel Schneerson.

Soon the *rebbe* came in, sat at the head table with one or two of his closest disciples, and began to give a discourse on some aspect of Torah. The discourse continued on and off for the rest of the *farbrengen*. Every now and then the *rebbe* would raise his schnapps glass and toast Hassidim all over the room, one by one. Everyone wanted to get a *Lichayim* (to life) toast from the *rebbe*, so of course every Hassid also had a glass of schnapps (the word meaning, here, strong liquor — probably rye or vodka). Whoever was the provider of that alcohol did well by the *farbrengen*. On one of the two occasions, I did receive a *L'chayim* from the *rebbe* and felt good about it. As the evening went on, the Hassidim began to sing and dance on the floor and on the large, heavily reinforced, thick, and long wooden tables that were everywhere. There might be fifteen or more men on a table, all stomping and singing and drinking *L'chayims*. To a stranger walking in off the street, the scene would have seemed like bedlam. Yet no one got drunk or misbehaved or crossed any bounds of propriety. It was simply joyous and uplifting and went on until the wee hours of the morning.

On both of my visits I was scheduled to see the *rebbe,* and on both occasions, airplane loads of Hassidim from Israel came into town and got first dibs on him. So, regrettably, I never did meet the man.

On one of the two occasions, as I was waiting to be called in, I recall having a conversation with a Hassid on the front steps of 770 Eastern Parkway. It was about the coming of the Messiah, at which time peace and tranquility would reign in the world. I asked him when the Messiah was due to arrive and he replied, "Tomorrow!" The next day I came back to the same place, met the same Hassid, and asked him where the Messiah was. He replied, "He's coming tomorrow."

"But," I interjected, "you said yesterday that he was coming tomorrow, which is today."

He replied, "Sometimes he is delayed, but for sure he's coming tomorrow."

I did not return the following day. Nor was there any change in the world situation.

The purpose of my journey to Montreal was to study Jewish mysticism and, I hoped, to find a wife, if things with Zarine didn't work out. I was blessed to have both wishes realized: the first in meeting Shula, and the second in having a mystical experience I'll never forget.

Vishnu introduced me to various Hindu scriptures, such as the *Bhagavad Gita* and the *Upanishads.* One morning, I sat in my apartment and finished reading excerpts from the latter work, which I found quite lovely and spiritually satisfying. Then I noticed an unusual but pleasant fragrance. It was something I had never smelled before, and I thought it was probably coming from someone cooking in another apartment. The fragrance lingered for a considerable time, until finally I decided to trace it down. First, I wanted to make sure it was not originating in my own apartment, so I checked all the cupboards and all the rooms, even opening my refrigerator. Then I went out into the hall and walked by several apartments. The fragrance remained, but didn't seem to be coming from any of these locations. "It must be coming from outside," I thought. So I went out of the building, the fragrance continuing to linger with me all this time, but I still couldn't trace where it was coming from. I even went over to a tree and sniffed the bark. No luck. I returned to my apartment, closed the door, and sat down, bewildered. Finally, it began to dawn on me that the fragrance was part of me. Furthermore, I realized that it had nothing to do with my sense of smell, unless I wanted to visualize my entire being as a very large nose. I tried to think of how I could describe to someone else what the fragrance was like, but came up empty. As the day progressed and I went from place to place, the fragrance never left me. All this, in itself, was highly unusual and perplexing. But most remarkable of all, as the days passed and the fragrance remained ever present, was my discovery that no matter what normally disturbing or aggravating situation I found myself in, I could not get upset. I was totally at peace for ten days. Then, slowly, the fragrance began to diminish, until finally it was gone, carrying with it my deep state of tranquility. I felt something very precious had left, and I longed for its return.

As I later reflected on this experience, I realized that I had been in some kind of a state of grace. I figured that this state had been triggered by reading the *Upanishads*, so I went back to my book and read some more. But nothing happened. I was disappointed, so I tried reading other sacred literature, but again, nothing helped.

Since that time, I have over the years repeated that experience, but never for the same length of time. Usually, when it happens, it lasts for no more than a day or two. I have not been able to discern the trigger for any of these additional occurrences. They seem to come spontaneously and amidst varying circumstances and places. Also, the fragrance at times is different. I have on occasion been asked to describe the fragrance or compare it to something familiar to most people. I have not been able to do so, no matter how many fragrances I encounter in normal life. As William James might have said, "It's ineffable." Many years later I discovered, while reading some literature on mysticism, that fragrances of this nature have been described by other individuals and usually are indicative of a mystical state, which, generally speaking, is also ineffable. Recently, in the writings of Rabbi Nachman of Bratslav (great-grandson of the Baal Shem Tov), I came across a reference to this mystical fragrance: "For the Messiah will judge through the sense of smell…In the prayers which he receives, he will smell and sense every person as he is [in his essence]."

> Spirits touch me
>> without distinction they come
>> subtly invited
>> subtly intrusive
>> dispelling grey smoke
>> subtly lifting
>> subtly seeing
>>> I reach once more

It was early September 1962, and my interlude from HUC was over. It was time to return to Cincinnati. I had explored some aspects of mysticism, studied yoga, learned *Tanya* and *Talmud*, had an extraordinary mystical experience, and found a wife. Shula was not able to immediately return with me to Cincinnati, as her mother's condition was deteriorating rapidly. And in the middle of October 1962, Bronia Goldfinger passed away. I flew in and conducted the funeral — my first — and then returned with Shula to our new home in Cincinnati at 2242 City View Circle. A month or two later, Shula went back to Montreal to look after her mother's affairs and spend time with her father. Then she returned to Cincinnati and began studying at UC, where she became an honours student, excelling in French, philosophy, and the Greek classics.

CINCINNATI 1962–1965

ENTERING MY THIRD year of rabbinic studies after an absence of one year meant that my former classmates were a year ahead of me and a new class awaited. It was in this class that I forged close and long-lasting relationships. Ron Goff and Larry Kaplan were my day-to-day buddies, and in later years I became close friends with Steve Forstein. Somewhat on the periphery, but nevertheless important to me, were Don Berlin and Bob Seigel. In all, there were twenty-one class members in 1962, and all were ordained in 1965. At the time of this writing, three members of my class have passed on.

I was excited about the yoga skills I had learned from Vishnu and, upon my return from Montreal to Cincinnati, I was eager to impart them to anyone interested. I put the word out that I was going to give classes in yoga and arranged with Clarence Abrams, our HUC gym coach, to use a small area at the end of the gym and one level up. About a half dozen students showed up, and I continued with classes for a while, until a scheduling conflict developed with the gym, whereupon we switched to the basement of the dorm and continued there. Ron was among the more eager and agile students, and sometimes I would spend time with him alone, working on one or two *asanas* (postures). On a couple of occasions I remember professors passing by; seeing several students standing on their heads, they would scratch their own and move on.

The final three years of our program were intense and exciting. There was stress, humour, frustration, sadness, and growth. Here are some of my memories.

Two professors in particular had a lasting impact on me. One I loved and the other I hated.

Ellis Rivkin taught Jewish history. His keen and insightful mind brought me insights I could not find in texts. Although at that time the expression wasn't yet in vogue, he thought "out of the box." I always looked forward to his classes and the animated manner in which he delivered his lectures. I was, to say the least, never bored.

Dr. Rivkin's interests were broad and diverse. I discovered this one evening when he had our class over to his home to chat. The "chat" turned out to be one of the most profound and enlightening discourses of my entire stay at HUC. It would take a chapter in itself, if not a book, to present properly what he had to say, but here is the gist of his thinking in one area of his considerable expertise.

The topic pressing heavily on many people's minds in those days, and certainly on mine, was the race into space. The Soviet Union (from here on referred to as "Russia") had launched Sputnik, a 2,000-pound satellite, whereas the United States had only managed to put up a 13-pound satellite. Common thinking at the time was that the U.S. was falling behind Russia, and it would be only a matter of time before the space race, and the race for dominance in atomic power, would be won by the Soviets. Clearly, a 13-pound satellite could not be compared to a 2,000-pound satellite, and the latter certainly showed the superiority of the Russian engineers. "Not the case!" said Rivkin. He made two points. First, superiority was not in greater weight or size, but rather in miniaturization. The only reason the Russians put up a 2,000-pound satellite was because they weren't able to enclose all of their instrumentation in a smaller package. The United States, on the other hand, was able to accommodate more instruments and technology in a 13-pound vessel than the Russians could in their behemoth. This, he speculated, meant that U.S. technology was advanced far beyond anything the Russians were able to produce.

His second point, and this one I had to swallow hard on, was that the United States was actually helping the Russians in their efforts to conquer space. I could see my classmates' eyebrows go up, but Dr. Rivkin brought out clippings from the back pages of the *New York Times*, showing lists of materials being sent to Russia that were essential in the construction of satellites, such as advanced computer components. "But," he went on, "not nearly as advanced as what the United States has." In other words, the Russians were receiving outdated hardware from the U.S.

"Why would the United States want to help Russia," one of my classmates asked, "seeing that we're in a cold war with them?"

"Good question!" responded Rivkin. "The answer is *money*." Our ears, if they hadn't already perked up by this point, certainly came to attention at his statement. He went on to explain that in order for the United States to be able to provide their space program with the necessary funds, the people had to be convinced that such a program was needed. The best motivating factor to accomplish this was *fear*. In other words, if people were afraid that the Russians were getting ahead, they would want their government to do whatever was needed to counter this, and what was needed was the investment of vast amounts of money. *Fear* and *money* were the tickets to the domination of space.

As further evidence that the two governments were in collusion, he asked us to consider that the first and subsequent Sputniks were, for the most part, put up shortly before budgets were to be approved in the U.S. And a major element of each budget was funding for the space program. If they (whoever "they" were) had done their job, the citizens of this great country would be in a very fearful state and more than willing to support whatever measures their representatives decided were needed to catch up. So, without too much debate, the budgets were passed.

By this time my head was spinning, but at the same time, something inside me seemed to be settling down. There was, however, still one question that hadn't been answered, and several of us brought it up in different ways: "If all this is going on, why doesn't someone blow the whistle?" Rivkin's response to this question was, "Why would anyone want to blow a whistle on something that worked in their favour? Besides," he added, with a smile and a twinkle in his eyes, "who reads the back pages of the *New York Times*?"

I don't know for sure that Rivkin's theory was, if you will pardon the expression, "on the money," but I do know that I never again was concerned about the space race, or the possibility of the Russians dropping an atomic bomb on the United States or Canada, or, for that matter, about any kind of Russian superiority. I left his home with a feeling of peace in my heart. Later, it became quite clear that the Russians were far behind the United States in technological prowess.

The other professor who had a lasting effect, the man I hated, was Alvin Reines. He was our professor of philosophy. Having never taken a philosophy course in my life, I had to start from scratch. But "scratch" was not where he was starting from. He assumed, and with good reason, that anyone entering a graduate program in rabbinic studies would have had some kind of exposure to philosophy at the undergraduate level—at the very least, an introductory course. I was totally uninitiated. When he spoke about Plato or Socrates or Aristotle, these were only names I had heard over the years but knew nothing about. So, to understand what he was talking about, I had to educate myself on the side by consulting books that offered shortcuts to the works of the great philosophers. I soon learned that shortcuts made some of what Reines was saying even more unintelligible. Even basic concepts like *providence* and *predetermination* were confusing to me. To make matters worse, some of my classmates had been philosophy majors in university, and at times I even had difficulty following their questions. In short, it was a real struggle. So much so that for the first time in my life, I failed an exam, which was a shock.

Over time and many courses with Dr. Reines, I slowly began to understand what he was talking about, and eventually I discovered the fundamental difference between his thinking and mine. His epistemology (theory of the origins and nature of knowledge) was based strictly on reason, while mine incorporated intuition and personal revelation from sources beyond the mind. I did not dispute the importance of reason—I just felt it was not the whole picture. On one occasion in class I challenged Dr. Reines along these lines, and he quickly shot me down. At that point, my arguments in favour of an epistemology that went beyond reason were still in their infant stages, and I could not put up a strong defence. It was, however, a telling moment, in that it clearly defined our differences and, in fact, the difference between most of my classmates and myself—the former being, for the most part, in the Reines camp. I believe that the large majority of the professors and students at HUC, in those days and well beyond, were disciples of reason to the exclusion of the extraordinary avenues of knowledge, information, and wisdom, which were an intrinsic part of my spiritual outlook.

What I didn't know was that Dr. Reines didn't want me to graduate from HUC. I learned this only in 2008, in a discussion with a former classmate—one of the brightest in my class and someone whose views I hold in high regard. I had never realized that our differences had brought Dr. Reines to this point.

In 1998, when Brahms and I revisited HUC, I asked whether Dr. Reines was still teaching and was told that he held an occasional class for a few students, but only as an elective. I found out when his next class was and met him at the door, asking for his permission to sit in with Brahms. He welcomed me. After the class, when everyone except Brahms and I had left, I told Dr. Reines that I had something to say to him. He gave me his full attention.

"Dr. Reines," I began, "I want you to know that when I was your student many years ago, I hated your guts."

Without batting an eye, he responded, "I don't blame you."

I quickly went on, "But having said that, sir, I also want you to know that I learned more from you than almost anyone else in my entire education. And for that, Dr. Reines, I am indebted to you and with great respect, I want to thank you."

He looked at me kindly, wished me well, and left the room. A few years later, he passed away.

I meant every word of what I told him. If I were to sum up his gift to me in a few words, I would say that he taught me to think for myself. I can't imagine any finer gift one human being can give to another.

Jakob Petuchowski, one of our professors of Talmud and the man who watched out for me when I visited HUC for the first time, was, besides being a very good teacher, quite a character. He practised a tradition of his own creation whenever exam time rolled around. He would enter the classroom wearing a bright red tie, exams stashed under his arm, look at us, and in a deep, menacing voice, exclaim, "Gentlemen, today I am out for blood." We quaked (at least I did) as he distributed the exam questions and made sure that his tie was very visible.

I was to learn during my years at HUC that Dr. Petuchowski, in practice if not entirely in belief, was very committed to traditional rituals such as putting on *tephilin* each morning and keeping a kosher home. It was also, I was led to understand, his feeling that to become a rabbi, one should believe in a personal God. This apparently put him in a difficult position when it came time to sign the *s'micha* (ordination) documents of graduating students, since he felt that many or most of them did not accept his theological position and instead had an intellectual, non-personal concept of God. As he was on sabbatical the year we were ordained, his name is not on my *s'micha* nor on those of my classmates with, to the best of my knowledge, one exception. Steve Forstein told me that he went to see Petuchowski in his home a day or two after ordination and asked him to affix his name to the document. Dr. Petuchowski did so, but only after he was satisfied that Steve believed in the kind of God he felt all rabbis should believe in. Many years later, Dr. Petuchowski died during or shortly after surgery. His passing was a great loss, not only to his family but as well to his students and the Jewish world.

From time to time we would play pranks on our professors. I suppose this was partly to reduce pressure from the rigors of our program and also just to have some fun. Two incidents in particular come to mind.

One of our teachers was Norman Golb, a brilliant scholar. In some ways, he was your stereotypical absent-minded and quite oblivious professor. We decided one day to see just how oblivious he could be, and we weren't disappointed. At exactly the twenty-minute mark during one of his classes, every student—all twenty-one of us, including non-smokers—pulled out a cigarette, a cigar, or a pipe, lit up, and puffed hard for the next ten minutes. The room filled with smoke, to such density that my eyes, and I'm certain those of others, were beginning to sting. No reaction from the good professor. He carried on as if nothing was happening. Finally he commented that it seemed to be getting a little stuffy in the room. Five minutes later, unable to take it any longer, we burst out of the room into the hallway and then outside into the fresh air. He couldn't understand why we had left in such a hurry.

Another professor of Talmud, Alexander Guttmann, nicknamed "The Goose" by his students, was a mild-mannered and soft-spoken gentleman. In our senior year, on the last day we were to have classes with him, we purchased a live goose, put it in a box, and placed the box on top of his desk. He entered the room, saw the box, peered in, and began to laugh. To this day I don't know what he did with the goose. Probably took it home and had his wife cook it.

I mention these stories as a salute to a wonderful core of teachers who, for the most part, liked their students and could take a joke. After all, they were once students too, and I wonder what they did to amuse themselves and their teachers.

Speaking of excellent teachers, Shula also fit into this category, having earned a degree from the Hebrew Teacher's Seminary in Montreal. This stood us in good stead as, upon arriving in Cincinnati, she quickly found a part-time job at Feinberg Synagogue, where I also taught on weekends. Her background in Judaica, obtained in her studies at the seminary and from her involvement in a Jewish youth movement, was an asset to me and led to long discussions on topics I would bring home from my classes. When time permitted, Shula would sit in on my classes at HUC, in particular those of Dr. Rivkin, with whom she formed a special bond. Having lived in Israel for several years, Shula was more fluent than I in Hebrew, and I would consult with her on texts that were giving me problems. She was always patient and generous with her time.

Each year, Shula would take a week off and return to Montreal to visit her father and friends. On one of her visits, during the springtime, I was walking downtown with Ron Goff when we passed a pet shop. On display in the window were recently hatched ducklings. Ron and I looked at each other and realized we were thinking the same thing. We went in and bought three ducklings, two for Ron's fiancé, Tikvah, and the other for Shula. We named them Shadrach, Mishach, and Abednego, after a passage in the Book of Daniel: "Nebuchadnezer then approached the hatch of the burning, fiery furnace and called, 'Shadrach, Michach and Abednego, servants of the Most High God, come out of the fire'" (Daniel 3:26).

When Shula came home the next day, I had set up a large box in our study with the duckling in it and a sign reading "Welcome home, Shula. My name is Shadrach and I'm all yours." Shula, upon walking into the study, was surprised, delighted (with some hesitation), and perplexed. After all, it was a gift. "What do I do with it?" she asked. I didn't have a clear answer, other than for her to do what people generally do with pets.

Over the next few weeks, Shadrach fixated on Shula and would follow her all around our house, pooping along the way. House-training a duck was not an easy task. Then came the moment of initiation. We felt it was time Shadrach had his first swimming lesson. We put about an inch of water in the bathtub, set Shadrach in the water, and then slowly raised the water level until he was floating. Need I say he took to it like a... When Shadrach was almost full grown, we took him out of doors, and in a matter of minutes he was surrounded by neighbourhood children. He seemed to have little fear, having known only humans in his short life to date, and was always a hit with the kids when we gave him an airing.

One of the unusual aspects of HUC was that, in addition to rabbinic studies and a Ph.D. program for Jewish students, it offered a Ph.D. program for Christian clergy. We had several Christian ministers from various streams of Christianity, including priests, as our fellow students. They were known as Christian Fellows, and they took selected classes with us, like bible, Talmud, and Midrash, as well as studying subjects of their own interest with our professors, such as texts from early Christian and pre-Christian periods and languages specific to those texts. It was also an opportunity for these men to interact with future rabbis and learn from the inside something about Judaism. No doubt this program, which still exists, has spawned knowledge and goodwill in many Christian seminaries across the United States and elsewhere and in the many graduates of those seminaries. I sometimes wonder whether the relatively recent increase in support for Israel among Christians in the United States is due in some measure to the HUC Christian Fellows program.

Some time earlier, Zalman had told me that not far from Cincinnati was a monastery where lived the best-known monk in the country and perhaps in the entire world — Thomas Merton. As the monastery was only about a three-hour drive from Cincinnati, I wrote Father Merton a letter and asked him if Ron and I could come for a visit. He replied promptly and we set up a date. He told us to bring his letter, as this would make entrance into the monastery easier.

The following is an excerpt from my diary of November 16, 1960: *The letter from Thomas Merton arrived yesterday. It was a very warm letter and okayed our visit. We were both excited and went out and bought "The Secular Journal of Thomas Merton." I'm looking immensely forward to meeting him and being at the monastery.*

Months later, on a bright spring day, Ron and I drove across the bridge connecting Ohio to Kentucky and wended our way to the Abbey of Gethsemani. En route we got lost and had to ask someone for directions. The man we asked obliged us and said, "You go a piece down the road. Then you make a left turn and go a bit further. Take another left, go a few miles, and you're there." Ron and I looked at each other, thanked the man, and got lost again — four times. Finally we arrived, two hours late, at the gates of Gethsemani. It was 8:00 p.m. and everything was quiet. I rang a bell and waited. After five minutes I rang again. Finally, a sleepy monk came to the gate. (What we didn't realize was that bedtime at the monastery was 7:00 p.m.) We apologized for being late and showed him the letter. He took us to our rooms in the guest quarters.

Diary excerpt, November 23, 1960, 8:35 p.m.: *I must admit that Ron and I are taken aback by the guesthouse, which is really luxurious. We each have our own private room, small, but very clean and well equipped — sink, towels, soap, desk, bed, lamp, and holy water.*

The Guest Master told us that if we wished to attend services, they would begin at 2:15 a.m., and a bell would inform us that it was 2:00 a.m. and time to get ready.

At 2:00 a.m. the bell rocked us out of our beds, and we quickly got dressed and hurried to the upper level guest section of the sanctuary, where we remained for the next hour or more.

Diary excerpt, November 24, 2:10 a.m.: *First mass begins in five minutes. All night long bells were ringing — which in a way was good since they told time too. Ron is up. Tired. The bed was too soft.*

We watched the monks file in and take their places. Then the service began. It was one of the most beautiful and uplifting religious services I have ever attended. The sanctuary filled with Gregorian chants, and then a half-hour period of silence.

Diary excerpt, November 24, sometime in the wee hours: *We stayed up till 4 a.m. then went downstairs to read in the library…Ron went to lie down at about 5:15 while I remained in the library. I was met at about 5:30 by Father Francis of Assisi, the Guest Master. He told me to go lie down until just before breakfast at 7 a.m. I was woken up at 6:30 by an alarm lent me by Father Francis.*

Breakfasts were fairly ordinary but dinners were interesting. We ate with the monks at a long table, completely in silence. During the meal a tape would play with the abbot's voice giving a discourse on some aspect of scripture. When the tape ended, the meal ended. Everyone stood up and went their ways while Ron and I remained at the table, still finishing our food. Apparently, the protocol was to finish eating with the tape, but we were not aware of this for our first meal. At subsequent meals, we ate more quickly. It seemed that either the monks had a sense of how long a particular tape would be, or all the tapes were of the same length, and the monks therefore timed their meals accordingly. The food was simple and nourishing.

Diary excerpt, November 24, about 8:00 a.m.: *Ron and I put on tefillin* [phylacteries — two small black boxes with leather straps that go over one's head and on the left arm and fingers. Each box has scriptural writing in it. They are worn while saying morning prayers], *after which we went to breakfast: apple juice, bread, coffee, eggs, and hot cereal. Altogether delicious, especially the bread. At 7:30, while we were eating, a little push bell (like in a hotel) was tapped, whereupon everyone besides us suddenly arose, a priest (from outside) said a blessing and then all marched out. We at first didn't know what was happening* [this being our first breakfast in the monastery] *and were a bit taken aback.* [At the following breakfasts we were prepared for it.]

Diary excerpt, later that day: *We spoke for about an hour and a half with Father Francis and then took a walk to the gift shop where the lay brother in charge, a 50-year-old chap, quizzed us on what reasons the Jews had for not accepting Christ as the messiah. We gave him the usual answers.*

We then went to High Mass and at 11:30 ate lunch — turkey (it being Thanksgiving), fresh cranberries, potatoes, gravy, some kind of chopped-up garlic bread, vegetables, coffee, cheese and pumpkin pie... Delicious! Ron went wild over the cheese. It wasn't strong enough for me. After lunch we went out for a walk in the back — it's pretty, a bit rough — 14 stations where Christ fell, an artificial pond, and a lot of dead leaves.

At 12:30 Father Merton came to see us in our rooms. He was wearing his work clothes. He's a rather plain-looking fellow with a less-than-favourable complexion (although this may have been a temporary rash). He should have had braces on his teeth as a kid. We walked back and forth in front of the gate for about an hour, talking about politics, Rivkin, the Russians, the bible, his secular journal and so on. He's an astute person, very friendly and well read. He asked us about Heschel, whom he admires. Said he'd like to have him visit Gethsemani. He drew our attention to the warblers migrating and stopping to rest on the trees. I felt very much at ease in his presence. He told us that, if we wanted to (and we did), we should get ready for work in the woods with a saw. Twenty minutes later he appeared again at our rooms, dressed in jeans and a brown apron, and away we went, a distance of about a third of a mile, through mud and hills until finally we arrived at the spot. Along the way we talked about the four ways of biblical interpretation: p'shat *(the simple),* remez *(what it hints at),* drash *(imaginative conjecture), and* sod *(the mystical).*

At the spot was a sort of retreat house in the making, which he intends to use for small gatherings.

While we waited for the two men with the saws and axes to show up, I spoke to him about Zalman. He's interested in reading some of his works. I'll send him "The First Step." Somewhat ironic — "The First Step" for the Master of Novices at a Trappist monastery...Soon the other two monks arrived...It was tough work. The logs were thick. We got through one, started another and then took a five-minute rest that lasted about one and a half hours. Father Garrard was permitted to talk. [Trappist monks take vows of silence.] (While we were talking, Merton, who had been chopping wood, returned to the monastery.) We asked him [Father Garrard] about how a monk justifies his existence? His answer was that as he gets closer to God, he gets closer to all men, and therefore his prayers will help others, even though he doesn't know whom or where. This took a half hour.

[Father Garrard's explanation made sense to me from a Jewish perspective, except for the part about withdrawing from society, as is the practice of monks. For Jews, prayer also serves the purpose of sustaining the world, and focus, which we call "*kavanah,*" plays an important role.]

Next, what about Christ? "This is all very mystical," he said, and this too, took a half hour or more. We then headed back and on the way I asked him about sex. He replied that he thought sex was a very beautiful thing, and that renouncing it was a matter of loving God more and not wanting to be restricted in this love by a wife. As one gets closer to God, one needs less and less the company of a woman. He couldn't quite see how a woman might help a man achieve the same spiritual heights, although he admitted that love of another human being helped one to love God more.

We parted. Ron and I took showers in separate shower rooms. (They really want you to meditate here.) Ron went back to his room a bit before me. When I looked in on him about ten minutes later, he was dovening [praying] mincha and maariv [the Jewish afternoon and evening prayers]. I did the same... Supper was good — tuna fish casserole, a plate of groundnuts, fruit and small marshmallows, bread, coffee, cheese and toast, ice cream.

At 6:40, Father Garrard appeared at our rooms — now all dressed in white. We went to another room and he gave us a rundown of tomorrow's service, which we took notes on. Then we went to the final service, which was very beautiful. Ron was quite moved by it.

The fact that Ron and I were rabbinic students seemed to make a difference in the way we were treated. For example, through Father Merton's good graces, we were given privileges that were not forthcoming to most Catholics. He took us into the inner sanctum of the monastery, showed us where the monks slept, and invited us to attend a lecture he was giving to a class of new monks. He was the Master of Novitiates at Gethsemani, which meant that all new and aspiring monks were under his care. We visited the places where sandals were made and where the monastery's excellent cheese was produced.

Diary excerpt, November 25, 9:15 a.m.: *Service was interesting. Father Garrard gave us missals to follow but we got lost after a while. Now he's here waiting to take us on a tour before the novitiate class begins at 10:40. He's really very fine.*

4 p.m. The tour was very interesting.

Places seen:

New construction

Dormitory and cubicles for sleeping

Library. We found here…a bible in both Hebrew and English. And, wonder of wonders, a 1958 copy of the Hebrew Union College Annual. This really took us aback. Of all things, an huc *Annual in a Trappist monastery. There were on the walls many paintings by Chagall, a couple by Van Gogh and one or two by Picasso.*

Metal shop — where they make all their own metal products.

A baby pigpen.

The cheese factory.

Cow barns — very clean and very fat cows — electric milking.

Bakery — the baker gave us each a piece of oatmeal cake or cornbread or something. It was still hot — tasted awful…

Shoe shop — they make their own shoes here.

We then went to Father Merton's novitiate class. He was talking about the Egyptian monks of the 4th century. We were a few minutes late. He has a good sense of humour and the lecture was upbeat — the students were as well. One of them couldn't have been more than 16 years old. The class lasted a half hour after which we left. Father Louis waited at the door for us to leave, as did the others. He asked us how we were enjoying our stay. Our answer, of course, was obvious…

We visited the barbershop — two barbers at work — five men waiting, meditating and reading the bible…

Merton came up to see us. The three of us sat for a half hour in my room. He expressed his pleasure at our coming to Gethsemani and said that he would like more boys from huc *to come — as many as 15–20 at a time. He is allowed 12 such outside visits per year.*

I was anxious to ask him some serious questions and finally, with about 15 minutes left, I told him that certain questions were on my mind that I wanted to hear his views on:

Question: I am interested in mysticism and hope to go one day to India to study in an ashram. What literature would you suggest that I read, and what spiritual exercises can I now engage in to give me better contemplative powers?

Answer: I'm happy to hear you're going to India. Books: "Christian Yoga" by Dechanet (Harper's). It has a Christian slant but will give you fundamental exercises for postures and breathing...Also, "Zen and Japanese Culture" and any of the works of Gandhi.

Question: What is the criterion by which one knows that God has spoken to him?

Answer: If he becomes more humble as a result of God's message. Humility is the greatest attribute a man can possess.

Question: Do men of different faiths experience basically the same thing when having a mystical experience?

Answer: Yes! But retrospective interpretation of this experience is experienced within the framework of one's religious upbringing.

I told him more about Zalman and how I thought that his interest in Merton emanated from a feeling of common ground in higher-level spiritual matters. He said that Zalman and he were probably very close in their thinking, but before talking they would have to define their terms.

He said that mysticism is contact with God. I'll have to think about this as an adequate definition.

As Merton got up to leave, Ron asked him to bless a rosary for his friend [which he had purchased in the gift shop], *which he did with a special Indulgence Blessing. We also gave him a New Testament in Hebrew and English that we had brought along. We inscribed it "Yivrech'ch'chah Adonai B'Ahava Raba U'b'ahavat Olam" ("May God bless you with a great love and with an eternal love"), and then signed our names. He thanked us, commenting that now he would really have to learn Hebrew, and said that he would send us over a couple of his books. We bid each other adieu, and both Ron and I, at his repeated request, promised we would come again...*

Father Garrard came up with two of Merton's books. Both were inscribed. Mine is "The Sign of Jonas," Ron's is "No Man Is An Island"...

P.S. As we walked back from the cow barns, Ron said to me, "Steinberg, you said a very bad thing at breakfast this morning when you remarked to the guy beside you that the food was good. Tsk, tsk. Such material thoughts. You should be ashamed of yourself." He looked at me, a big grin spread over his face and then he added, "I would have burst out laughing — if it was permitted."

P.P.S. I miss Shabbat. So does Ron.

At our last service, before leaving, I prayed, "God, open my heart, that You may instruct me in the paths of humility, service and love. Amen."

About three years later, I took Shula to Gethsemani for a day. Father Merton was away at the time, but Father Garrard was there, and he and Shula got on famously. In noticing that Shula was very quiet and didn't speak a lot, Father Garrard nicknamed her "Shhh."

Many years later, in a tragic accident, Father Merton was electrocuted. His rich literary legacy continues to inspire Catholics and non-Catholics throughout the world.

BESIDES RON GOFF, Larry Kaplan was my other close friend and classmate. While my relationship with Ron was in general harmonious, with Larry it was frequently contentious. Larry was a very bright man, a former machinist who had decided he wanted to be a rabbi. He had the knack of being able to explain something complicated so that it seemed simple and clear. This is a talent, and it made him a fine teacher. Also, he had a quirky but great sense of humour. If something tickled him, he could laugh heartily for several minutes and make others laugh, even if they didn't know what they were laughing at. His temperament was mercurial, and it was this trait that caused friction between us more than anything else. I found him hard to read. But when we were on the same wavelength, it was a pleasure to be around him. Many years after our ordination, in a long-distance conversation, he told me that he had been doing some work on himself with a skilled therapist who had an outlook similar to mine, and that for the first time, he not only was beginning to understand me, but even to agree with some of my views. This was welcome news, and helped in our subsequent relationship. Of the five musketeers— Ron, Brahms, Saul, Larry, and myself—Larry was closest to Brahms, and their relationship grew and deepened over the years. Regrettably, Larry died in 1998. Perhaps with some irony, I was asked to conduct his funeral service and deliver the eulogy. It was my honour to do so, and I think I did him justice. In spite of our numerous disagreements and clashes, I miss him.

I spoke earlier about my first High Holiday pulpit in Petersburg, Virginia, and what I learned from Maddy about her secret for a successful marriage. In the ensuing years I had numerous other student pulpits (Bogalusa, Louisiana; Hutchinson, Kansas; Cortland State Teachers College in Cortland, New York; Hopkinsville, Kentucky; and the Miami of Ohio Hillel foundation), and from each one there was something to learn. In particular, an experience in Hopkinsville, Kentucky, in my fourth year reinforced my spiritual views on life-threatening illnesses.

Hopkinsville is several hours from Cincinnati by car. Usually, I took a train to Clarksville, Tennessee, and then went by taxi to Hopkinsville, which took about 45 minutes. The drive, at about the halfway point, passed the base of the 101st Airborne Division of the U.S. Military. (A Jewish dentist at the base was one of my congregants.) On one of my early trips, the taxi driver commented, somewhat disgruntledly, as we sped by the air base, that if God had wanted us to fly, He would have given us wings. I told him, in as nice a way as I could, that if God had wanted us to move at 60 miles per hour, He would have given us wheels. The rest of the way we rode in silence.

The first event in Hopkinsville that I remember clearly was an inter-faith exchange. When I met the minister of the Hopkinsville Presbyterian Church, we immediately took a liking to each other. He was open to some kind of inter-faith service and so was I, so we decided to do a pulpit exchange. This meant that at our Saturday morning Shabbat service, his congregation would be our guests and he would deliver the sermon. Then, on Sunday morning, my congregation would be their guests, with me delivering the sermon. We put the plan into action, and it was a big success. It was also the first inter-faith service I was ever a part of, and it has served as a model over the years.

The second event was more dramatic. One Shabbat evening, after services, I returned to the congregation's president's home, where I was staying, and became engaged in a conversation with the president's sister. She said, "Rabbi, can I tell you a story?" "Of course," I replied. She said that twenty years ago, she had been diagnosed with an aggressive form of cancer and was given little chance of surviving for more than a few months. She had a relative who was an oncologist in Nashville, and he made sure she had the best treatment available at the time. Everything was tried, yet she continued to deteriorate, to the point, she said, that she could no longer look after her most basic needs and was confined to bed. Her weight loss continued until she was barely more than skin and bones. Family members were beginning to make arrangements to come to Hopkinsville to attend her funeral, which appeared imminent as she was no longer taking food. "Then," she said, "all of a sudden something began to change. And it kept changing. I started feeling better and within a few months I was restored to good health." I asked her if she could in any way account for her seemingly miraculous healing. She said she had no answers, other than that maybe it wasn't her time. She was in her sixties and still in good health at the time of our meeting.

A year or two later I related this story to my good friend Donny Silverberg, who was doing postgraduate medical work at the Mayo Clinic, and asked him his thoughts. He replied that he had heard of similar cases, and that this phenomenon was know as *spontaneous remission of symptoms*. No one, he told me, had an explanation for it, including himself.

Because of this incident, and so many similar ones that have come to my attention, I always hold out hope when I'm counselling individuals, no matter how ill. And if they want to know why I'm hopeful when everyone else is so pessimistic, I tell them some of these stories, including the one from the Victoria General Hospital in Winnipeg (mentioned in an earlier chapter), and of my faith in the indomitable human spirit, and how little we know, relatively speaking, about the healing process. And, if they want to listen, I tell these stories to their families and friends as well.

There are other stories, not only about healing, that have influenced my rabbinate, my life, and my work as a therapist, a couple of which I'll tell now and others further on.

My classmate and friend Don Berlin got married. Several months after the wedding, Don and his lovely wife, Norma, invited three of us over to dinner. While Don and Norma were preparing something in the kitchen, one of us commented on how connected they appeared and how clear and loving was their communication. Later, after dinner, we asked them for the secret to their wonderful relationship. Don replied, "It's really no secret at all. We just decided right at the beginning that we would never take each other for granted and always work on our relationship."

Their words have continued to echo in my ears down through the years. I have told this story to many couples when standing with them under the *chupah*. And I have related to them the following epilogue:

About thirty years later, the annual meeting of the Central Conference of American Rabbis (the Reform rabbis' rabbinical organization) was held in Toronto. This gathering brings together about six hundred Reform rabbis, who often bring their spouses. As I was walking down a hallway in the hotel where the conference was taking place, I met Don, whom I hadn't seen in a long time. We were happy to see one another and chatted for a while. Then I reminded him of the above story. He smiled and asked me to come with him. We went to another floor, and he partly opened the door to his room and called out, "Are you decent, dear? I have a visitor." We went in, and I was warmly greeted by Norma, who still looked radiant. Then Don related to Norma the story I had just told him. A broad smile came across her face as she looked at me and said, "And we're still working on it."

No matter how much book learning I have, I have always found that experience is the best teacher. On some matters, I have held strong views that have changed over time, but rarely did such change come quickly. An exception was my once-held view that no matter how a woman looked, a man should love her just the way she was; physical changes should not be necessary, or even desirable. "After all," I thought, "if this is the way God made her, then that's the way she should remain. Anyway, looks are only skin deep." What I wasn't prepared to accept was that sometimes God makes mistakes.

My cousin Linda was a very pretty girl with a sweet disposition. The only problem was that she had too large a nose, and it definitely detracted from her appearance. As she entered her teens and had little success with boys, I kept reassuring her that one day, someone would see beyond her nose and appreciate her for the truly wonderful person she was. I don't think she took too much comfort in my words, and she continued to suffer socially. She left Canada and went to study at Ohio State University at the same time I was at HUC. Once or twice a year she would come down from Columbus to visit me.

On one of her last visits, we were sitting at the kitchen table and she commented that she still wasn't having much success socially and that she was quite miserable even though there were large numbers of eligible men at Ohio State. I felt very bad for her and didn't know any longer if there was anything I could say to give her comfort. Then something occurred to me.

Several months earlier, Dr. Peerless, a plastic surgeon who was also an ear, nose, and throat specialist, had corrected my deviated septum, which had given me breathing problems since I was a child. The result was remarkable. For the first time I could remember, I was able to breathe clearly through both nostrils at the same time. While I was on the operating table, he asked me if I would like him to flatten the small hill on my nose, just for cosmetic reasons. I thought about it for a moment, frozen and all, and said that I needed the bump to hold my glasses in place. He chuckled and left it alone.

I looked at Linda and said, "He's really an excellent surgeon. Would you like to see him?" She hesitated a moment and then agreed. It was late Saturday afternoon, so the chances of him being in his office, let alone willing to see her on such short notice, were minimal, but I put in the call and the doctor answered. I apprised him of the situation and told him that Linda had to leave the next day to return to school. He said he was working late, and I should bring her in right away. A few minutes after we arrived at his office, he examined Linda and told her that he could give her a beautiful nose, and about six weeks later she had the surgery.

When I went to pick her up at the hospital, her face was all bandaged, and the parts of her face that were not covered were black and blue. I brought her to my place for a few days of recuperation. About three weeks after that, she came back to Cincinnati to have her bandages removed. She couldn't get over her new nose and kept repeating, "It's so small." I again brought her to my place, but on the way had to stop at HUC to pick something up. I suggested she sit in the car, but she said she felt well enough to come in; apparently she didn't feel too self-conscious about being still somewhat swollen and discoloured. She sat in the bumming room until I was ready to leave, which was about fifteen minutes later. When we got in the car, she turned to me and said, "Jerry, two of the guys in the bumming room asked me out on a date." I was surprised. This I didn't expect to happen until well after the swelling and discolouration had gone. About a year later, Linda became engaged to a man at Ohio State. I performed the wedding ceremony for her and her fiancé, Ralph, at a small synagogue in Moose Jaw, Saskatchewan.

I had learned a valuable lesson. Appearance can matter, and there's no point in suffering when something can be done.

My last year at HUC was devoted mostly to writing my dissertation under the supervision of Dr. Sylvan Schwartzman, a kind and gentle man. The title was "Towards a Curriculum in Jewish Values Based on the Jewish Short Story." It was a course for junior and senior high-school students. Each lesson consisted of the class reading a Jewish short story, followed by a discussion based on a teacher's guide, and then handouts to the students, giving quotes from Jewish sources that supported the value being discussed. I tested the course out at Feinberg Synagogue, where I taught on weekends, with the support of their education director, Max Newman. The results were encouraging. Later, the manuscript was in line for publication by the Union of American Hebrew Congregations (UAHC), a major arm of the Reform Movement. Unfortunately, the man behind the project, Rabbi Jack Spiro, left his position, and his successor did not follow through on publication. The manuscript remains on my shelf.

In both the fourth and fifth years of the rabbinic programs, all students are required to give a Shabbat sermon based on the *parsha* (scriptural reading) of the week. This is worked on with great diligence under the tutorship of one of the professors; we were also coached by a full-time elocution teacher, a Christian minister named Lowell McCoy. I don't think I ever heard any student say an unkind word about this princely man. Not only was the preparation of our sermons a difficult and time-consuming task; we were all aware that we would be recorded on tape as we delivered them. On the Monday immediately following each sermon's delivery, a post-mortem was held. This consisted of a one-hour meeting to which all students and professors were invited, and where mimeographed copies of the sermon were handed out. The sermon was played back while those present made notes on their printed copies. After the tape ended, anyone who wished to could offer comments and criticisms. The author of the sermon was required to sit and listen without saying a word. The feedback could be brutal, but always there were positive remarks, and most of what was offered was of a constructive nature. Occasionally, a particularly good sermon received much praise and little criticism, although there was always something that could be improved upon. It was a good learning experience and has stood me — and, I'm sure, most of my colleagues — in good stead over the years. Dr. Petuchowski's view on sermons was that if you couldn't say what you wanted to say in twelve minutes, don't start.

One of my sermons — I believe it was the one I gave in my senior year — advocated that, in light of the loss of six million Jews in the Holocaust, it was incumbent upon us as rabbis to try to replace those numbers by gently proselytizing to those who do not belong to any faith and are seeking spiritual roots. I still hold to that view.

In the bumming room after lunch, there often would be a guest speaker. On one occasion, toward the end of my studies, Rabbi Maurice Davis addressed us. His topic was "When is a rabbi not a rabbi?" He went on at length, describing all the situations where a rabbi *is* a rabbi, such as at services, as a guest in a congregant's home, when representing the congregation in public, when teaching adults or children, at Jewish summer camps, and on and on until he had covered every circumstance that I — and, I'm sure, my fellow students — could think of. After a half hour or so of speaking, he concluded by saying, "So, gentlemen, when is a rabbi not a rabbi?" He paused and looked around. No one spoke. "Gentlemen, a rabbi is not a rabbi when he's with other rabbis. So, thank you for allowing me to let my hair down." Basically, I agree with Rabbi Davis. There are, however, in my view, two more exceptions: when one is with one's spouse or one's closest and most intimate friends. At least, this has been my experience and it has never backfired on me.

There was another professor with whom I had an interesting encounter. Dr. Abraham Cronbach was retired and no longer teaching. One day, however, Dr. Reines, who admired Dr. Cronbach, invited him to speak to our class. One of the opinions for which Dr. Cronbach was well known, though not the topic he spoke about on that particular day, was his firm stand in favour of pacifism. After hearing him speak, I wanted to have a conversation with him about his pacifistic views, since I had mixed feelings about the subject, and I felt he would be able to articulate his position clearly. By chance or providence, one day I passed him on campus, and I asked him if we could speak. He was very accommodating and gave me about a half hour of his time. As I expected, his position was simple and clear. He told me that pacifism means that, no matter what the situation, one does not resort to violence but rather to persuasion. As I tried to absorb the implications of his statement, I couldn't help thinking about the Holocaust. So I presented to him the following scenario: "Dr. Cronbach, if you were in Nazi Germany, and your daughter was about to be shot by a Nazi, and you had already seen that this particular Nazi had shot other women without giving it a second thought, and you had a gun and were in a position to prevent your daughter's death by shooting first and killing that Nazi, what would you do?"

He did not hesitate or equivocate in his answer: "I would talk to the Nazi and reason with him and try to persuade him not to shoot."

"But," I countered, "if he didn't want to talk or reason, and he was already aiming his gun, and his finger about to pull the trigger, what would you do?"

Again, he responded with the same answer: "I would ask him why he wanted to commit this act, and show him that it was not a good or reasonable thing to do."

I realized at this point that, no matter what I said, the man was not going to waver from his philosophy. I also realized that the pacifist position did not take into account the possibility that the party threatening violence might not be at all interested in talking, let alone reasoning, and that action to prevent the violent act, even if it meant another act of violence, was, in certain situations, warranted. And it became clear to me that unless everyone in the world was a pacifist, pacifism was a recipe for disaster. We shook hands and parted peacefully.

My exposure to philosophy and biblical criticism at the Hebrew Union College was a key element in how I came to think about *absolutism*. I do not accept that anything is absolute, although I certainly believe that some things, though relative, are fundamental to the human condition, particularly if that condition is to endure. I am talking here about moral precepts such as a reverence for life and fair play in human interactions.

My thinking in this regard got me into trouble one day when, upon the recommendation of a friend and colleague, Shula and I visited the Centre for Moral Re-Armament on Mackinac Island in northern Michigan. Moral Re-Armament (MRA) was a right-wing organization whose values revolved around four absolutes: absolute honesty, absolute purity, absolute unselfishness, and absolute love. On the surface, these appear to be praiseworthy values; however, a ride in a horse and buggy quickly revealed to me the ruthlessness with which these values were held by card-carrying members of MRA. Our tour guide, the buggy driver, launched into a sermon on absolute love. He told us that absolute love was so important that he would sacrifice another's life (in less eloquent terms: kill him) if he found that this person did not believe in absolute love and was trying to undermine this belief. In my naiveté I challenged the buggy driver, arguing that there were no such things as absolutes. He did not take kindly to my words. Thereafter, during our three-day stay with MRA, our presence was constantly monitored. For example, we were never left alone with any of the three hundred or so young people (mostly between the ages of eigh-

Walking Buffalo and me in front of his home (circa 1965)

teen and twenty-five) from around the world who were resident at the centre, and no matter how hard we tried to speak with one of them, a chaperone was always present. When Shula and I returned in the evening to our room, we spoke in whispers, fearing that the room might be bugged.

On the second day of our visit, we attended an assembly in a very large auditorium. At one point, the director of the assembly announced the entrance of Chief Walking Buffalo from Canada. A dignified Indian in full regalia marched down the aisle with a large walking stick. All present stood, shouted, and stomped their feet. I turned to Shula and said it reminded

me of what I had seen in news reports of Nazi rallies. To add to our discomfort, we attended a musical production that advocated the teachings of MRA, put on by their young people — a troupe called Up With People. It was a very sophisticated production and was put together using state-of-the-art technology, of which we were given a tour. It appeared that MRA had big money backing them, and their propaganda appealed to certain strains of the American mind. To make an understatement, both Shula and I were very happy to leave Mackinac Island. Apparently my colleague and his wife who suggested we visit MRA had a more positive experience than we did.

A footnote: A few weeks later, while we were travelling through Alberta, we passed a sign indicating an Indian reservation, which I recognized as the one where Walking Buffalo lived. Shula and I were both curious to see the man in his home setting and perhaps get a better picture of what he was all about. We were directed to his home and knocked on the door. Walking Buffalo answered wearing simple clothing and invited us in. He introduced us to his wife and told us she was quite ill. After about fifteen minutes, during which I explained to him about our visit to Moral Re-Armament, it seemed that we had run out of talk. The chief was pleasant and humble, very different from how we saw him at MRA. Seeing the distress his wife was in, I suggested that perhaps she should see a doctor. He told us that there was a clinic (or hospital) on the reservation, but he had no means of getting his wife there. I told him that we would be happy to take him and his wife there, as we had a car. The only problem was that our car, including the back seat, was fully loaded. I quickly discussed the situation with Shula, and she agreed to sit on top of some of the stuff in the back seat to make room for Walking Buffalo while his wife sat up front. We took them to the clinic and said our goodbyes. I was left with a soft spot in my heart for the chief and his wife, and was only sorry that he was involved with an organization that espoused views I felt were detrimental to society. This was the first of two experiences I had on an Indian reservation. The other one occurred about ten years later.

About two months before ordination, I awoke one Saturday morning and told Shula I wanted to bake cinnamon buns. She looked at me, her jaw dropped, and she asked, "Why?" I told her I didn't know why, that I just needed to do it. Seeing as I had never baked anything before in my life, I needed to ask Shula how to get started. She suggested a recipe book. "Logical. Why didn't I think of that?" So I consulted a recipe book, made a list of the needed ingredients, and went off to purchase them. I followed the recipe as closely as I could, and before long our home was filled with the smell of freshly baked cinnamon buns. They weren't great, but they weren't bad either. I mention this small incident because it was the beginning of a baking career that I'll talk about more in the next chapter. I've never figured out where the inspiration for baking came from — perhaps from a dream.

My dissertation was complete, and ordination day was fast approaching. I was, however, wrestling with a problem: I wanted to be ordained wearing my *kippah* and *talit*. This was not the protocol, and to the best of my knowledge and that of everyone I consulted, it had never been done. It seemed to me I had two choices. I could just appear with them on and hope for the best, or I could ask permission from the president of HUC, Nelson Glueck. But if I went to Dr. Glueck and he said no, then what was my position? I decided, upon advice from one of my close friends, to make an appointment to see Dr. Glueck, who at that time was one of the foremost biblical archaeologists in the world. He welcomed

Class ordination photo, Plum Street Temple, Cincinnati, May 29, 1965. I'm in the front row, third from the right (wearing my white socks — I always wore white socks on Shabbat). Next to me on my right is Steve Forstein, directly behind me is Larry Kaplan, and in the back row, second from the left, is Ron Goff

me into his office and asked me what was on my mind. I told him that I would like to wear a *kippah* and *talit* when he ordained me the following Saturday morning. He looked at me long and hard and exclaimed, "That's a *chidush!*" (innovation). I told him I agreed with him, that it was a *chidush*, but given my background and that I had always worn my *kippah* and *talit* on Shabbat in the chapel for services without objections from anyone, and that it was very important to me, I would appreciate having his blessing for this *chidush*. (I really wanted to say, "Dr. Glueck, Reform Judaism is a *chidush*," but felt this would be the wrong approach.) He said he wouldn't object. I was delighted.

On Shabbat morning, May 29, 1965, I was ordained. The ceremony took place at the historic and beautiful Plum Street Temple in Cincinnati. This was the temple where Isaac Meyer Wise, who founded the Hebrew Union College in 1875, served as rabbi for many years. It is built in a wonderful Gothic style and only used for special occasions like ordination, although recently I've been told that it is in regular use. I felt a sense of history all around me and couldn't imagine a more elegant setting for me to receive my *s'micha* (ordination scroll).

My parents were there, of course, along with many members of my family and some dear friends. The ceremony was moving, and when my name was called out, I went up and stood before the ark in front of Dr. Glueck with my *kippah* and *talit* on. He placed his hands on my shoulders, said some words to me, and gave me, in Hebrew, the Priestly Blessing: "May God bless you and keep you; May God cause His light to shine upon you and be gracious unto you; May God look favourably upon you and grant you peace." He congratulated me, gave me my *s'micha*, and I sat down. Almost thirty years from the day of my birth, I was a rabbi.

During the next few weeks, we sold our furniture and closed down our townhouse. Then, the day before leaving Cincinnati, we had the sad task of saying goodbye to Shadrach, who had become very much a member of the family and a favourite among the kids in the neighbourhood. For various reasons, taking him to Canada with us was not an option. We tried to find him a new home, but without success. Instead, we decided to try to find him a new family. We took him to a nearby woods that we had visited before, and where we knew there were families of ducks. We waited on the shore of a lake until we saw a mother duck come along with several ducklings in tow. Then we placed Shadrach in the water, where he could see and be easily seen by what we hoped would be his new family. The mother duck spotted him and came over, even though Shadrach was at least as big as she was. What we hadn't taken into account was that Shadrach had never seen another duck, except in the window at the pet shop. He was only familiar with humans. We didn't know what to do, as he wouldn't follow the mother duck. Finally, we decided that, with a whole summer ahead, we had to leave Shadrach to his own kind and pray (which we did) that he would be okay and eventually bond with his kin. We left the woods with mixed feelings.

As I look back upon my years in Cincinnati, I recognize that I learned a lot, grew a lot, and experienced a lot. They were hard years but good years. I forged friendships that have endured the tests of time and continue to enrich my life. However, from a spiritual perspective, I came up short. The college simply wasn't geared to provide the kind of spiritual leadership and nourishment I needed, although I have no doubt that many students left satisfied in this regard. In all fairness, HUC, being a liberal institution, did not take upon itself the mandate of trying to provide its students with a spiritual directive; it sought, rather, to provide them with tools that would help each one on his own spiritual search. For me, this search went beyond social action and the cultivation of values, although these elements were certainly an integral part of the picture. There was a part of me that needed to be watered, a part the college did not address, and it was because of this part that I still felt unprepared to go into the world, take a congregation, and be their spiritual leader. Academically, I was prepared. Spiritually, I was not.

I was wrestling with a number of questions at the time of my ordination. Some of them were clear to me, while others I was only dimly aware of; they were questions like: What is the nature of God? If God is all-powerful and loving, why is there suffering in the world? Who or what hears prayer? What is the nature of the soul? What does it mean to be chosen? Were the unusual and extraordinary phenomena expressed in the bible real events, or the product of someone's fantasy and imagination? Are rationalism and mysticism compatible? What is the relationship between spirituality and sexuality? And finally, could I find answers to these questions that would satisfy me, or at least sustain me?

My feeling of being unprepared, combined with my unusual experience of fragrance and peace in Montreal, propelled me into the next step of my journey. I wanted to go somewhere where the focus was on spirituality and where academics was not on the agenda. I was hungry for the experiential aspect of religion and, not finding it in Judaism, even at Lubavitch, I turned, like so many others at that time, to Eastern religions. This does not mean that I had any inclination to become a Buddhist or a Hindu. But my experience with Vishnu and the Upanishads indicated to me that there was something I needed to learn, which Judaism, up to this point in my life, had not provided.

I talked all this over with Shula, who was very supportive of my search, and we decided to try to find an ashram where we could immerse ourselves in the experiential dimensions of religion. Our first consideration was the Paramahansa Yogananda ashram in San Francisco, also know as the Self-Realization Fellowship. When this did not materialize, we did not know where to turn. I called Zalman in Winnipeg to ask if he had any ideas. He told me about a woman he had invited to one of his Passover *Seders* a couple of years earlier. Her name was Swami Sivananda Radha, and she had established an ashram in the interior of British Columbia. He suggested I contact her. I wrote to the swami and then spoke to her on the phone. She said she would be happy to have Shula and me come to live at her ashram for a year.

THE ASHRAM

1965–1967

There are moments
   when it doesn't matter
if it's Moses
   or Jesus
     or Buddha
who passes through one's soul
perhaps
  these are the most holy moments

Yasodhara Ashram is situated in the West Kootenay Mountains of British Columbia, about an hour and a half northeast of Nelson. You can get to it in the same time by driving through Creston and along the east side of Kootenay Lake, which is a faster route if you're coming from the east. However, Shula and I decided that we would approach the ashram from Nelson, on the other side of the lake, so we could take the ferry and arrive by water rather than the highway. It turned out to be a good decision, since going to Nelson from the east meant having the adventure of driving over the Nelson-Creston overpass, the highest in the country — so high that even though it was still summer, we encountered snow near the summit. The height played havoc with our car, which started bucking and gasping from lack of oxygen. I believe to this day that if we had not reached the summit, the engine would have conked out and sent us rolling backward. Fortunately, we just made it, then coasted most of the way down on the other side.

Nelson turned out to be an unusually pretty town, nestled in the heart of the Kootenays. Many years later it was the filming location of the movie *Roxanne* with Steve Martin and Daryl Hannah, based on the play *Cyrano de Bergerac* by Edmond Rostand. We wound our way through Nelson onto highway 3A and along Kootenay Lake to the ferry dock, forty-five minutes to the north at Balfour. A long line of cars awaited us, and we were not able to get on the ferry, but had to wait for the next one to come an hour later.

Two ferries operated between Balfour and Kootenay Bay, one large and one small. The former could carry about forty-five vehicles and the latter perhaps twenty. On the way from one port to the other, a journey of forty minutes or so, the ferries would pass each other halfway across the lake, sometimes sounding their horns in greeting. The amount of time it took to make the crossing would change depending on the weather, which could add fifteen or twenty minutes if the waves were high. In winter, only the larger ferry operated, which was a blessing, as it had a closed and heated space inside.

The smaller ferry had no such room, meaning that you either stood on the deck, weather permitting, or sat inside your car if it was raining or snowing. The ferries operated from 6:00 a.m. to 1:00 a.m. each day.

Our first crossing was magnificent. Guided by one of the ferry crew, I rolled our Rambler onto the deck, pulled the handbrake, and got out. We stood next to the railing near the bow for the entire crossing, taking in the exquisite scenery that surrounded us. Looking north we could see snow-capped mountains in the far distance, even though the temperature at ground level was in the eighties. I learned later that the water in Kootenay Lake was fed by glaciers, so pure and clear one could see many feet into the depths. In places you could drink the water straight, without danger, much like sipping from a flowing mountain stream. Being glacier-fed, it was of course always very cold, warming slightly by mid-August but swimmable only for the brave.

Swami Sivananda Radha (1967)

After docking we wound our way up a short hill, turned left onto a narrow road, and within five minutes saw a small sign to our left reading *Yasodhara Ashram*. We then began our descent, on a path so narrow it could barely be called a road and which wound around the side of the mountain. I kept my eyes glued to the dirt surface in front of us, afraid to look either to the left or the right for fear of going over the edge. There seemed to be no room for passing, and the thought flashed through my mind: "What if I meet a car coming up?" To my considerable relief, none came, and before long we arrived at the ashram office.

We parked, entered the office, and were greeted by a man in his late twenties who introduced himself as Swami Krishnananda — or Krishna, as we came to call him. He was one of Swami Radha's three original disciples and was in line to succeed her when the time came. The other two disciples were Swami Premananda (who went by "Prem") and Swami Turiananda ("Turi"). All three men were in the same age bracket: late twenties to early thirties. Krishna was a professional land surveyor; the room in which we were standing was where he did his in-house work, and was filled with drawings, blueprints, and various calculations. Prem and Turi worked with him in the field, which meant that they spent a good part of each week away from the ashram, doing jobs for various people in the area. Prem, who was born and raised in Germany, was a very skilled carpenter and all-around handyman. He had an impeccable eye for measurements and could spot at a distance, without a plumb line, whether a line on a structure was totally straight or not. He also had an insatiable appetite for chocolate and could easily eat a pound or more at a sitting. For some reason, no matter how many sweets he ate, his teeth were always white, well formed and strong. Turi was a man for all seasons, able to adapt himself to whatever the situation required. He was also a good athlete; more than once, when we played football together, he beat me, with post-game apologies.

One other swami lived at the ashram, having arrived just before Shula and I. Stan Hutchinson, who later took the name Swami Sivananda (after Swami Radha's guru), was initiated into the order of swami by Swami Radha during our second year there. Stan was a tall, slim young man with piercing eyes who had great mechanical skills, especially in the area of electronics. His expertise and personality were a considerable asset to the ashram and, from what I observed, he and Prem complemented each other well.

Krishna called Swami Radha on the phone, and she asked him to bring us to her cabin. We walked from the office down a path to another level, where the kitchen and work shed were located, and then down farther to Swami Radha's cabin on the lake, where she warmly greeted us. A vibrant woman in her forties, she was, like Prem, a native of Germany. As we learned later, she had lost two husbands in Germany during the war, one from illness and one who was executed for opposing the Nazis. The fact that Shula and I were Jewish, and I a rabbi, somehow had a special appeal for her. She was delighted to meet us, and after some tea and biscuits she showed us to our cabin, which overlooked the lake from a slight altitude. Though we were not right on the lake, we were close enough that at night (and often during the day) we could hear the waves lapping onto the shore, a sound I never tired of.

Our cabin was very old and consisted of two tiny bedrooms, a living room, and a tiny kitchenette with a sink, a small counter, and an electrical outlet. To one side was a wood stove for heating the cabin, which had to be fed often. During the winter, I had to get up two or three times during the night to stoke the coals and add wood so we wouldn't freeze. All in all, it was a cozy place, with a couch, a small table and chair near the window with a view of the lake, and a covered area just outside the door for storing wood. The bathroom facility was a nearby outhouse, which presented problems in the middle of winter, particularly if one had a sensitive butt. That being said, the advantage of the cold season, as I quickly discovered, was that everything froze, which meant there was no odour. In the summer it was a different story, and only generous doses of lime made the experience tolerable. I recall that there was one flush toilet in the ashram, located in the building that housed the main kitchen and the living quarters of our cook, Iris, and her two boys, John and Gregory. Iris was also an ashram member, and the boys attended a nearby school. I mention the indoor toilet because the entire building was heated, which made it a very attractive location, especially in winter. The toilet was supposed to be restricted to Iris and the boys because we were in the wild and the septic tank could only handle so much. However, when nature called and I thought no one was around or looking, I would sneak in, and at times I noticed others doing the same. Such are the joys of rural life.

Our cottage (1965)

We settled in, familiarized ourselves with the surroundings, and became quasi-members of the ashram. Full members made a lifetime commitment. Joining an ashram is not unlike joining a kibbutz in Israel, although one major difference is that the commitment is also to an individual — in our ashram, Swami Radha. She, too, had a commitment to someone: Swami Sivananda of Rishakesh, India, her mentor, who had initiated her into the order of swami when she lived in his ashram in India some years earlier. He was her guru, as she was guru to Krishna, Prem, Turi, and Stan. For those not familiar with the nature of the guru-disciple relationship, it means that the lives of guru and disciple are intertwined; the guru guides the life of the disciple, particularly in the spiritual domain, but often also in work, personal relationships, emotional issues, and day-to-day happenings. Most, if not all, swamis accept the concept of reincarnation and believe that the souls of guru and disciple may remain bound together over many lifetimes.

Although I accepted Swami Radha as my mentor, I never developed a guru-disciple relationship with her. However, I am and always will be grateful to her for her wisdom, insights, and guidance. Being her student was an honour, and what I learned during my stay at the ashram has stood me in good stead in many ways. But to be anyone's disciple in the context of a guru relationship has never appealed to me, even though at times it has been tempting. I say "tempting" because I find there is a certain attraction in having someone you trust guide and spiritually mould your life, particularly if you're moving into uncharted territory. However, the independent streak in me is very strong and prevented me from walking such a path. And there is another factor. I believe in an *inner guru*, an intelligence or force that, when I am in touch with it, guides me on paths that are sometimes straight and sometimes circuitous, but that, I always realize in retrospect, were necessary for my growth. It is this profound faith in my inner guru that has sustained and nourished me through turbulent and distracting times, a faith that has remained intact to the present moment. My inner guru, sometimes through dreams and sometimes in moments of intense clarity, has been the keel that has given my life balance and purpose.

Over the years since my stay at the ashram, I have met several gurus and for the most part have found them to be men and women of depth and integrity. However, I have always had difficulty with what I observe as guru worship. This difficulty began at the ashram, when I watched Swami Radha's disciples and visitors prostrate themselves before her. This was the tradition in which she was trained, and I respected it, but as a Jew who was brought up with the belief that one only bows down before God, this was not something I would ever participate in. Often Shula and I were the only ones not bowing; to the credit of Swami Radha and the others, we were not asked to participate nor criticized for not doing so.

Unlike another guru I met several years later (to be discussed in a later chapter), Swami Radha always encouraged questions and was up for a challenge whenever it came along. In this I did not disappoint her, and we had many a debate together. More than this, she encouraged Shula and me to share our Judaism with the members of the ashram, who like her were eager to learn. This took the form of having me conduct *satsang* (a spiritual assembly or service) every Friday evening (the Jewish Sabbath), while Shula conducted the closing of Shabbat at *satsang* on Saturday evenings.

At *Kabbalat Shabbat* (welcoming the Sabbath), Shula would light candles and say a prayer in Hebrew. I would then fill a glass with sweet kosher wine and make *Kiddush* (the blessing over the wine), after which the wine cup was passed around the room for everyone to sip. This was the only time Swami Radha permitted wine to be tasted at the ashram, and it was always a much-anticipated event. I would then tell Jewish stories or discuss the *parsha* (scriptural reading) of the week, answer questions about Judaism, and otherwise participate in dialogue with those present. I taught them Jewish songs and *nigunim* (melodies with or without words, somewhat like a mantra). We would also take time to meditate silently, ending each meditation with a *nigun*. *Havdalah* (closing the Sabbath) was always done by Shula and included again drinking wine, as well as lighting a braided candle, smelling spices like cinnamon or cloves or a mixture of both, chanting *nigunim*, and telling stories and meditation — everything done with her own personal touch. Both *Kabbalat Shabbat* and *Havdalah* were wonderful evenings for Shula and me and appeared to be enjoyed by all those present.

During our stay at the ashram, we also celebrated other Jewish holidays and festivals, especially Passover. (Rosh Hashanah and Yom Kippur found me conducting services, the first year in Vancouver and the next in Winnipeg). For Passover (which commemorates the exodus of the Jewish people from Egypt more than three thousand years ago), I conducted a *Seder* with guests (mostly not Jewish) invited by Swami Radha.

One such guest, and a friend of the ashram, was Father Joe Boyle, the local Catholic priest from Riondel, a nearby mining town. I mention him in particular because of an incident that occurred one Christmas during midnight mass at his Church of the Most Holy Redeemer. But first, a little background.

Swami Premananda, in addition to his many other talents, had a beautiful singing voice; it was always a joy for me to listen to him sing, at *satsang* or any other time. Prem had been brought up Catholic, and in addition to being a swami, he was a devout follower of his

Passover Seder (1966) Father Boyle is just behind me; Swami Premananda is in the foreground

Christian faith. Because of this combination of attributes — a good voice, a talent for music, and Catholicism — he was asked to become the choirmaster at the Riondel church. One evening, Shula and I were invited to attend the midnight service. Some time earlier, at one of our Shabbat evening *satsangs*, I taught a small portion of Psalm 135 as a *nigun*. The words in Hebrew are: *Halleluya, Halleluya, Hallelu et Shem Adonay* (Praise God, praise God, praise God's name). The *nigun* is quite lively and has a good beat. Keeping all of this in mind, we proceed to the following scene:

The church is packed, and Shula and I are sitting in the middle of the congregation, a bit toward the back, with the choir several rows behind us. When it comes time for communion, much to our surprise, the choir stands up and begins singing *"Halleluya, Halleluya, Hallelu et Shem Adonay."* They repeat the tune for the next ten or fifteen minutes while all present, except of course Shula and myself, march down the aisle and receive the communion wafer from Father Boyle. Apart from Prem, Shula, myself, and perhaps Father Boyle and members of the choir, I don't think anyone knew what was being sung. My best guess is that everyone thought it was Latin.

The small room where we did *satsang* every evening was directly across the hall from where Swami Radha lived. Like the swami's room, the *satsang* room overlooked the lake. On the wall facing the entrance was a large crucifix. At first I found this perplexing, but I came to understand that most people who came to the ashram were of a Christian upbringing, including Swami Radha. Also, Hinduism, which is the main influence at the ashram, accepts all faiths as aspects of the divine. So, in this sense, there is no contradiction. Still, for me, as a Jew, it took some adjusting, especially when I was conducting a Shabbat service, and I can't say I was ever completely comfortable with it. Yet I had had no problem with the Christian symbolism at the Abbey of Gethsemani in Kentucky, nor at the many monasteries and churches I have visited over the years. Probably the cross at the ashram bothered me because the ashram was my home, although others shared it with me, and because I was conducting Jewish services in that room.

Top: View from prayer room (circa 1965)
Above: View of prayer room from beach (circa 1967)

I also had the pleasure, while at the ashram, of becoming friends with Reverend Jim Hearne, a Protestant minister, a friendship that has lasted to the present day. Jim has a keen interest in Judaism, taking courses on the subject and calling or writing me whenever he has a question.

The ashram operated on a very low budget. The main day-to-day income came from surveying; other sources included donations, workshops, and guests like Shula and myself. (The only other guests while I was at the ashram were Joe and Stephanie Reuter, followers and teachers of the Rudolph Steiner school of thought. There was also a well-known mural painter, Douglas Riseborough, who rented an adjacent cabin from the ashram.) Swami Radha knew that I had very little money, except what I made by once a month servicing a new congregation in Vancouver called Temple Shalom. She therefore charged us only eighty dollars a month, which included room and board (and which, at the time, represented a good portion of my monthly income). I was touched by her generosity, and she never asked for more. I still wonder how we all survived.

When we arrived at the ashram, our intention was to stay for one year, after which I would take a congregation somewhere in either Canada or the United States. However, in the spring of 1966, when our year was coming to an end, Swami Radha met with us and encouraged us to stay on. Shula and I gave this serious consideration and concluded that neither of us felt complete about our ashram stay and another year was indeed needed. When we informed Swami Radha of our decision, she responded with delight.

During the first year at the ashram, I visited my parents in Winnipeg on one or two occasions. On one of these visits I met some people who wanted to start a congregation, which would consist of some thirty or so families, and they asked me if I would come and conduct services once a month during my second ashram year. I agreed to this, beginning my year with the High Holidays of Rosh Hashanah and Yom Kippur, just as I had done the previous year in Vancouver. The distance between the ashram and Winnipeg was some eight hundred to a thousand miles, and as the congregation lacked the money to fly me in, I took most of my trips by bus, a journey lasting almost thirty hours. I of course stayed with my parents on these visits, which saved the congregation a considerable amount on hotels and food. My parents were happy to see me on a regular basis, and that feeling was mutual.

AS SHULA AND I settled into ashram life, an issue emerged that challenged our relationship and even our concept of marriage — an issue that required an immediate and clear decision. Were Shula and I going to continue living as man and wife, in the usual sense of having sexual relations, or were we going to abstain? Swami Radha and her disciples had taken vows of celibacy, the theory being that abstinence from sexual activity enhanced spiritual growth and awareness. I had heard about this before coming to the ashram, in particular in my association with Vishnudevananda and in some of my readings. We discussed the matter at length with Swami Radha. While she encouraged us to abstain at the ashram, she never made this a requirement of our stay; she pointed out the benefits of such a choice, but left the final decision entirely up to us, with assurances that it would not affect our status. Shula and I had only been married for three years, with sexual relations a normal and enjoyable part of our relationship. To give this up would be a considerable sacrifice. Also, it did not seem natural to either Shula or me. We realized, however, that the opportunity to do this in a supportive environment did not arise often in a lifetime, and since our aim was to experience ashram life to the fullest, we decided that abstinence should be a part of our experience. So, with Swami Radha's blessing, we abstained from sex for two years.

Sexual abstinence was not easy for me (or Shula), especially since, in the Jewish tradition, sexual relations play a prominent role. Did Hinduism have something to say about sexuality and spirituality that Judaism had missed? Family life was a norm for most Hindus, and only much later in life did abstinence play a part. But for swamis, abstinence was crucial—one of the keys to achieving higher levels of spiritual fulfillment.

It came to my attention while at the ashram that there was a system—some refer to it as a science—where sexual energy can be directed by conscious effort to achieve spiritual enlightenment. This system is called Kundalini Yoga; Swami Radha had considerable knowledge of the subject and over the years had written extensively about it. Kundalini metaphorically envisions a snake curled up at the base of the spine, ready to ascend the spinal cord and enter the brain. This snake symbolizes spiritual energy and, given the right stimulus, will become activated and begin the journey. The energy begins at the base of the spine, in the region of the genitalia, but instead of being directed outward (resulting in the emission of seminal or vaginal fluids), it is directed inwards, allowing the essence of these fluids, in the form of a subtle but powerful energy, to climb the spiritual ladder of the spine and ignite seven spiritual centres along the way. Each centre has a name and each is responsible for certain physical, emotional, and psychic functions. The ultimate goal of the Kundalini system is to promote spiritual evolution.

My description is, of course, simplistic. Many books have been written on the subject, perhaps the best in my opinion being *Kundalini: The Evolutionary Energy in Man,* by Gopi Krishna. It is both readable and fascinating.

If abstinence meant that Shula and I would have a better chance of channelling our sexual drives upward rather than outward, and lighting up our chakras, then embracing it seemed like a good decision, I thought. I was therefore excited by what abstinence and Kundalini had to offer, but at the same time concerned about how Shula and I would fare without the satisfaction and closeness that physical intimacy always brought us.

So we slept together for two years and not once had sexual relations. This is not to say I didn't have sexual desires and nocturnal emissions. But I'm a stickler about commitments and was determined to see things through until we left the ashram.

At first, being abstinent was difficult, but gradually over the weeks and months my sexual desire waned. I wondered about this, and thought from time to time about the old aphorism, "If you don't use it, you lose it." As well, sometimes I wondered what would happen when we wanted to resume our sexual relationship: Would I be able to, or would it remain a distant memory? As to the waning of my desire, it occurred to me one day that sexual energy, in the carnal sense, was pretty much absent at the ashram. It was as if the entire atmosphere exuded sexual suppression, and at times I felt that to even have a sexual feeling or thought was wrong and would interfere with my spirituality. Yet, while celibacy and sexual denial seemed to be in the very air we breathed, every once in a while, when a sensuous woman visited the ashram, I would catch one of the swamis casting a fleeting and, I guessed, longing glance. I wondered what they were feeling and thinking, and at the same time I knew that my own glance was full of longing and not that fleeting. These moments of sexual awakening left me with mixed feelings. Was my spiritual development being hampered or set back by these awakenings, or should I be reassured that the carnal impulse in me was still alive and well, waiting for the opportunity to flower once more? I was comforted by the latter thought, which was periodically reinforced in bed with Shula, when the nearness of her body and the fragrance of her skin presented me with an erection.

Nocturnal emissions, however, presented me with a problem on two accounts. The first had to do with the fact that I was squandering my sexual energy by emitting seed that should have been contained and redirected, as spiritual energy, up the spinal cord to activate the chakras. The bottom line here was that expelling semen was a spiritual loss.

The second issue went back to my teenage years. I was brought up at a time when masturbation was considered just plain wrong. I read, or was told, that not only does the bible prohibit it, but that physically it is debilitating and can even lead to blindness. So what does one do with this information bearing down on raging hormones? What one does is masturbate, or have wet dreams, and feel guilty. And then the question arose for me: "How can something that feels so good be so bad?" So I had a physical and a moral dilemma, and both remained with me well after my teen years were over. The physical was easier to resolve, as studies eventually showed that masturbation was normal and healthy, and that myths of physical debilitation and blindness were just that — myths. The moral aspect was harder to deal with.

I needed to know the source of the prohibition against spilling one's seed. Where was it stated, and what were the events surrounding it? I had heard of the biblical story of "the sin of Onan," something about him pouring his seed onto the ground, but even in my rabbinical training, I'd never really examined this passage carefully. I decided it was time to do so, and to try to settle once and for all what this story was about, and why it has had such an impact on the post-biblical life of Jews and Christians. Here is the passage, as translated from the Hebrew in the Jewish Publication Society's presentation of the *Hebrew Scriptures*:

> Judah got a wife for Er his first-born; her name was Tamar. But Er, Judah's first born, was displeasing to the Lord, and the Lord took his life. Then Judah said to Onan, "Join with your brother's wife and do your duty by her as a brother-in-law, and provide offspring for your brother." But Onan, knowing the seed would not count as his, let it go to waste whenever he joined with his brother's wife, so as not to provide offspring for his brother. What he did was displeasing to the Lord, and He took his life also. (Genesis 38:6–11)

As the above passage states, if a man's wife died and there were no chil-dren, it was the duty of the man's brother to cohabit with his brother's wife and provide her with offspring. The child resulting from such a union would be solely that of the deceased brother's wife, with all consequent rights. In other words, in this instance, Onan would have no claim on these rights. Since he didn't much care for this idea, he avoided providing her with a baby by spilling his seed onto the ground whenever he was with her sexually. God didn't like what Onan did, and took his life.

Nowhere in this account does it say that God was displeased with Onan for releasing his seed in vain. The displeasure was for deliberately not provid-ing Tamar with a child. In other words, had Onan been off somewhere masturbating by himself, it is highly unlikely his act would have been men-tioned, let alone his life forfeited. Yet somehow, this passage was misconstrued centuries later by the rabbis to indicate a prohibition against a man spilling his seed without a woman to receive it. One would, in my view, have to stretch the text considerably to draw this conclusion.

Examining the text in this light eventually brought me relief from guilt and dispelled my conflict around spilling my seed nocturnally or deliberately. This didn't happen immediately upon re-examining the text, as years of baggage had accumulated around this issue. But it clearly was an important starting point, and the result was liberating.

Later, toward the end of our ashram stay, I tried to evaluate the effects of abstinence on my spiritual growth. Did I feel I had grown spiritually? Yes! Did I attribute any of this growth to sexual renunciation? I was unsure. Many factors contributed to my expanded spiritual awareness: meditation, chanting mantras, contact with Swami Radha and the other members of the ashram, reading in the ashram library, dream work, and being close to nature. It was difficult to discern the effect of the individual parts. However, as a whole, the impact was profound; my understanding of just how profound it was would unfold in stages over the ensuing years. My gut feeling about the contribution of abstinence? I don't feel it did much for me spiritually, if anything at all. Sometimes I think that non-abstinence would have done more for my spiritual development and, as wonderful as the ashram experience was for me, would have elevated it to a higher level. Of course I can't be certain of this, but in retrospect, this is what I sense. There was, however, one clear benefit of two years of holding back. It gave me greater patience when making love and greater patience when times were not conducive to lovemaking. For this gift I am grateful.

IN GENERAL, GRATITUDE was part of my everyday experience at the ashram. To be living in what Prem always described as "paradise" was something I never took for granted. The lake, the mountains, the sky, the exciting weather patterns, the fruit on the trees, the birds and animals, and the opportunity to spend two years in an ashram with gifted spiritual teachers all made me very appreciative of my good fortune. Many times I would go for a walk up one of the paths leading into the trees or down to a spot by the water, chanting a Hebrew *nigun* aloud — "*Mah Raboo Ma'asey Yadechah Adonay Eloheynu*" (How magnificent are the works of Your hands, O Lord our God). It's a *nigun* I still chant when I feel in awe of some aspect of creation.

As I'm writing these memoirs, it occurs to me that Chanukah and Christmas are but a short month away. This was always a warm and festive time at the ashram. The two holidays, because of their close proximity, were somehow blended into one big gift-giving venture. As I recall, a system was worked out so that everyone received one gift as a result of picking a name out of a hat. The gifts were simple and inexpensive, given with love. Also at this time of the year, the ashram celebrated the Hindu festival of Divali, which, like Chanukah, is a festival of lights. Everyone was given a small wooden boat with a candle attached. We then went down to the water's edge, lit our candles, made a wish, and set the boats onto the water. The boats would be carried out into the lake (provided the wind conditions were right) while we stood and watched.

Birthdays were also celebrated, with the celebrant being showered with gifts. In fact, at the ashram, if you could give a reason to celebrate, everyone would buy in. Yes, there was austerity and serious self-examination, but there was also balance, and to a large extent celebrations helped provide this.

Winter at the ashram was magical. Think of your favourite winter scene, worthy of a holiday greeting card; the ashram in winter could have been the model for all such cards. We were at the foot of a mountain, surrounded by pine, birch, and other trees, with open spaces in between, all covered with clean white snow, and nestled in this landscape were small wooden dwellings with lights on inside and smoke drifting up from the chimneys. If it was a clear night, the moon would be reflected in the lake. If there was a wind, the water could be heard lapping at the shore. To add to this: zero pollution. The air was crystal clear, smelling of earth and trees and firewood seasoning in the shed. And the silence! It seemed to me that the carol "Silent Night" must have been composed in a similar setting.

Food at the ashram was wholesome and simple. Iris would prepare the meals and we would do her the honour of making sure the plates were clean when we returned them for washing. The fare was often, but not strictly, vegetarian. At times there was chicken and, less frequently, a little red meat. What we ate had more to do with expense and availability than with any strict food regime. Occasionally we ate in silence, as Swami Radha wanted us to focus on every mouthful with awareness and appreciation. However, silence seldom worked, as mealtimes, especially dinner, were the only times we would come together and have the opportunity to share our day, something we all looked forward to.

Every now and then a group of us would go into Nelson for some good Chinese food. The others respected Shula's and my need to avoid shellfish and pork products, and always made sure there was adequate protein that we could consume. The restaurant we usually chose had a chef, Ken (possibly the owner), who knew we had little money. We ordered directly from him, telling him how much our group had to spend. If, for example, we said we had thirty-five dollars, he would bring us thirty-five dollars worth of food. The one condition was that Ken would select the menu, keeping in mind that there would be lots of chicken and perhaps some beef. He would bring us the dishes one by one, waiting for us to finish each dish before bringing the next one. Ken was very generous, and we always left the table with full bellies and good cheer.

After I had awoken in Cincinnati one morning with the strange desire to bake cinnamon buns, I perfected my technique and expanded my repertoire over the years to include bread and other baked goods. So when someone at the ashram asked me if I had any practical skills I could contribute, I said I could bake bread and some pastries. After that, every Monday morning I got up at five-thirty, went to the kitchen, and by six was in full swing. I worked until about five or six in the afternoon, by which time I had produced between fifteen and twenty loaves of various kinds of bread: white, rye, whole wheat, pumpernickel, rye with caraway seeds, and even herb bread. The loaves were frozen and consumed over the course of the week. I did all the kneading by hand, as the ashram didn't have a kneading machine. The job also involved a lot of running around. To produce twenty or so loaves, I needed two stoves. There was one in the kitchen and another partway up the mountain, in Krishna's trailer. Throughout the day I would run back and forth—or more correctly, up and down—checking the loaves, putting them in and taking them out of the ovens, laying them out for cooling, and getting the next batch ready. One of my greatest satisfactions at the ashram was watching the members enjoy the bread, especially on the first day, when it was still warm. During my ashram stay I also tried making other goods, such as doughnuts, and had fun experimenting. (Today, my specialty is pies, from the crust up. I've passed my knowledge along to my son, Meher, who so far has mastered blueberry and pumpkin, with apple, peach, banana cream, and lemon waiting to be discovered.)

ONE EVENING, TWO years before we went to the ashram, I was in Hopkinsville, Kentucky, sitting on the porch of a member of the congregation I was there to perform services for. In the course of our conversation, my host pointed out a small, innocuous house at the back of the property next to his. He told me some interesting and mysterious-sounding facts about the house, but beyond a passing curiosity, I thought no more about it.

One day, when I was in the ashram's small library, I picked up a book Swami Radha had recommended and began to read. The book was *There Is a River*, by Thomas Sugrue. It was a biography of Edgar Cayce, considered by some the most important American prophet of the twentieth century. Cayce's specialty was medical readings. He would enter a trance state, with his wife by his side and another woman ready with pen and pad. When his wife observed that he was deep enough in the trance, she would give Cayce the name and location of an ill person somewhere, usually in the U.S., someone totally unknown to Cayce. He would give a medical reading of the individual, consisting of a diagnosis, prescription, and prognosis. The reading would be forwarded to the ill person, who would usually act upon the information. Cayce did thousands of medical readings in his lifetime, with uncanny success. Often the sick person would take the relevant portion of the reading to a doctor, to get help in facilitating the prescription. The doctor, not knowing that Cayce was a layman with a grade-six education, no doubt thought the prescription was from a colleague. Cayce also did other kinds of readings, many of a theological, philosophical, or predictive nature. As I read, I learned that Edgar Cayce lived for many years in Hopkinsville, Kentucky. Suddenly it came to me: the house my congregant had pointed out to me was Cayce's home. I had come full circle.

At the ashram, Edgar Cayce's name was revered. Swami Radha spoke of him in glowing terms and supplied Shula and me with material she received regularly from the Cayce Foundation, known more fully as the Association for Research and Enlightenment (ARE), located at Virginia Beach, Virginia. Upon leaving the ashram, Shula and I became members of ARE and for several years had access to their files, enabling us to request information on readings Cayce had done in specific areas of health. When Shula experienced nausea during her pregnancy, we took advantage of our membership and asked for material relating to this problem. We knew that there were products on the market, both over the counter and by prescription, but we also knew that Shula had a highly sensitive constitution and would not easily tolerate any substance that was not natural. So we opted to follow Cayce's advice and discovered that in several readings on problems of nausea, he had prescribed decarbonated Coca-Cola blended with water in certain proportions. Decarbonated Coke was not readily available, and because it might not be suitable for this purpose to let a Coke go flat, I went on a search to find Coke syrup. After some unsuccessful attempts, I concluded that the only place I was going to find the product was at the local Coca-Cola plant. I went there, asked for the manager, and explained that my wife needed Coke syrup for a medical problem. He was very co-operative, and in a matter of minutes I had a jug of syrup to bring back to Shula. It did the trick, taking care of her nausea during her first trimester without any side effects. This incident also gave me the pleasure of buying carbonated water and mixing my Coke to taste.

I have remained a great admirer of Cayce for more than forty years and never cease to marvel at the wonders of the human soul as evidenced by his profound gift. I have, on occasion, tried to tap into the spiritual dimension of reality that so nourished Cayce. Swami Radha once experimented with me to see whether I could do health readings about people I had never met or heard of. She helped me move into an altered state of consciousness and then presented me with names and locations, as was done with Cayce. I would give her basic descriptions of the person, such as age, height, body shape, and complexion, and then tell her what I saw to be the medical problem and how it could be helped. She told me I was quite accurate in several of the cases, and she would pass on my diagnosis and prescription. I don't recall if there was any follow-up. There was, however, a very unusual and related incident that occurred in March of 1966, just six months after Shula and I went to the ashram.

Shortly after settling in at the ashram, we learned that Swami Radha was very interested in dreams. She encouraged us to keep a dream diary and work on our dreams every day. Since dreams had always been an important part of my life, I embraced her request and proceeded to write down everything I could remember upon awakening in the morning, or even during the night, if I woke up.

In early winter I had an unusual dream. Some background: My parents and I lived with my grandparents for many years when I was a young boy. My grandmother, whom I called *Boba* (the Yiddish word), was born in Romania and was something of a Gypsy, gifted at doing psychic readings with regular playing cards. Often, I watched her spread out the cards on the kitchen table and predict what was going to happen to her family in the year ahead. As I was her first grandchild, we were very close, and although she passed away in 1950, her influence remains strongly with me to this day. Sixteen years after her death, she appeared to me in a dream at the ashram. The scene was her grave in Regina; I saw her come up out of the ground, looking wonderful and healthy, and we had a conversation, most of which I do not recall. But I remember clearly her last words to me before the dream ended. She said, "A pain in the head connected to a nerve in the neck." With those words ringing in my mind, I started to emerge from the dream, my body experiencing a profound tingling, as if an electric current was going through it. I awoke with a start, took a few minutes to gather myself, got out of bed, and wrote down the dream, after which, it being the middle of the night, I returned to sleep.

In the morning, as had become our practice, Shula and I shared our dreams, and I was eager to tell her about my *boba*'s appearance. We discussed the dream for a while, searching for an interpretation that made sense to us. What seemed apparent was that my *boba* was trying to tell me something about a pain in my head. There was, however, a problem with this interpretation, namely: I never get headaches. Perhaps, we thought, the dream is forecasting a condition yet to develop. We played around with other possible meanings, but ended up in confusion, so I decided I would take the dream to Swami Radha and ask for her input. She pondered my *boba*'s words and, being unsure herself what they meant, suggested three or four possible interpretations. They all seemed plausible; I just didn't know which one was right. I did assume, however, that one of them was correct, given the swami's expertise in this area. The rest of that day passed without incident, and nothing was presented to me the next night while I was asleep.

The following morning, while we were sitting at breakfast, there was a knock at our cabin door. One of Swami Radha's disciples told me that the swami wanted to see me right away. Bear in mind that the swami and I had only known each other about four months, and I had never mentioned my *boba* to her until the previous morning. When I arrived at her cabin, she greeted me excitedly and quickly ushered me in.

"Jerry," she began, hardly able to contain herself, "your *boba* came to me in a dream last night."

I was taken aback. "Did she say anything?"

"Yes," Swami Radha replied. "She said we are not interpreting the dream correctly."

"And?" I asked, beside myself with anticipation. "What did she say it means?"

"She didn't say," Swami Radha responded, almost apologetically, sensing my disappointment. And we left it at that, each of us pondering the inscrutable.

Fast forward to about six weeks later. Shula and I had gone into Nelson to see the movie *Who's Afraid of Virginia Woolf?*, which has little or nothing to do with what followed, but I'll always remember it because of its proximity to what next unfolded. We were driving back to catch the 1:00 a.m. ferry; missing it would mean waiting on the dock until 6:00 a.m., when it resumed operations. We were about halfway to the ferry. I remember it clearly — the snow near the narrow highway, the hum of the car heater, and me lost in idle thought. Abruptly, Shula interrupted the silence. "Jerry, did you ever figure out your *boba*'s dream?"

My response to her question was that I was suddenly struck so powerfully by emotion that tears began running down my cheeks, blurring my vision such that I had to pull over onto the shoulder. I turned to Shula, and without knowing where the words were coming from, I said, "It's for you, Shula. The dream is for you."

Ever since she was a young woman, Shula had suffered with headaches. When she was attending the University of Cincinnati, she could never study or write papers for more than about forty minutes without taking a long break because of the onset of a headache. Visits over the years to specialists in everything from internal medicine to neurology to ophthalmology failed to yield either a diagnosis or a treatment. She was resigned to having to live her life with this painful malady. The dream made sense. But there were important questions: Was all of this just coincidence? Were we reading into my sudden emotional outburst something that really wasn't there? These and other questions were given their due, with no conclusion. But at least the possibility of a resolution to the puzzle of the dream about my *boba* was there. Another step had been taken (and we did catch the last ferry).

The final step came from an unexpected source. Three weeks before the incident on the way to the ferry, I had received a brief letter from a woman who lived in Cranbrook, about a hundred and fifty miles east of the ashram along Highway 3. The woman wrote that she wanted to come talk to me, and wondered if we could set up an appointment. She signed her name with the title of "doctor." About two weeks after the occurrence on the way to the ferry, she showed up, and we spent a few hours sitting and conversing on a very large boulder overlooking Kootenay Lake. She was interested in converting to Judaism, and since I was the only rabbi in a radius of approximately four hundred miles, she sought me out. After we had concluded this discussion, I asked her what kind of doctor she was. She replied she was a chiropractor. I had heard the word, but did not have any idea what chiropractors were or what exactly they did. She explained some things about the nervous system and the spine and used the word "adjustment." Without giving any background, I asked her if she would be willing to examine Shula. She said she would be happy to do so. We went to the cabin and I introduced the chiropractor to my wife, after which the woman explained her profession, and I asked Shula if she would like to be examined. Granted, a full examination was not possible away from the doctor's office, but she proceeded as best she could, and after a few minutes declared that there was something out of place in Shula's neck. She did a simple adjustment, and thereafter, up to the present, as long as Shula receives a periodic adjustment, her headaches have significantly diminished. I can even recall quite lengthy periods when she was headache free. My *boba* was right.

This incident also brought me face to face with a dilemma. Aside from being confronted — against all the wisdom and research of modern psychology, including the pronouncements of Sigmund Freud, that dreams were always about the dreamer — I had to conclude that while in most instances I agreed with the research, there were exceptions, and these exceptions pointed to limitations in twentieth-century dream theory. I surmised that at times dreams are not about the dreamer and are intended for others. Further, not only can a dream be about others, but the dream can also be an instrument of great benefit for others, especially in the area of physical well-being.

Let me give another example of dream healing. While at the ashram, I met a man in his late twenties who was suffering from some kind of rare illness for which there apparently was no cure. I was friends with his physician, Dr. Sam Bitnum, who did everything in his power to help the young man, but his help seemed to be of no avail. Based on my experience with Shula, I decided to try to have a dream that might be of help to the young man. When I went to sleep the next night, before closing my eyes, I said a prayer requesting information that might make a difference in his life. Shortly after falling asleep I found myself in a hospital, and in one of the hallways I met my family doctor, Sam Rusen, who lived in Winnipeg. I was aware that I was dreaming and also aware of what I had to do in this dream. I approached Dr. Rusen and asked, "What can be done to help Harry?" His reply was not clear, and what I could make out seemed to make no sense. It had something to do with eating grass.

I brought the dream to Swami Radha, and we tried to make heads or tails of it, but the best we could come up with was that perhaps there was some kind of remedy that sounds like the words "eating grass." Next, I decided to go into Nelson to a feed store and get a book that listed all kinds of grasses. Nothing on their long list sounded like "eating grass." So I gave up, returned to the ashram, and told Swami Radha that I couldn't find anything. She felt bad, but then she seemed to go into deep thought, as if she was searching for something. Suddenly, her face lit up and she said, "Just a minute." She proceeded to a latch on the floor and pulled on it, lifting a small door to reveal a space under the floorboards. She pulled up a box and began to rummage through it. Finally, she drew out a pamphlet and gave it to me. The cover page read: "Wheat Grass — God's Manna" by Ann Wigmore. I quickly read through the booklet and learned about a highly beneficial grass that was always preferred by cows and other grass-eating animals, when they were given a choice. In juice form, it was suitable for human consumption and had a high nutritional and medicinal value. The pamphlet gave instructions on extracting juice from the grass and the amounts to consume.

I checked with Dr. Bitnum to see if it would be okay to give this substance to Harry. He said it was fine. To his credit, Sam Bitnum had a soft spot for the ashram and the strange goings and comings that were part of the ashram way of life. He never laughed at what we came up with and was always open to considering different ways of looking at things. He was a great fan of Harvey's Bristol Cream sherry, which he did not hesitate to recommend as a tonic, and we made sure to always have some on hand when he visited.

So Swami Radha and I presented our findings to Harry and his wife. Harry was skeptical, even though Sam had endorsed the potential remedy as being non-harmful to his condition. Harry's wife was all for it and ready to start extracting juice from homegrown wheat grass. But Harry remained resistant and never did try it. Unfortunately, he died about a year later.

> Each of us
> is locked away
> in a mind cage
> trying desperately to be free
> not knowing
> we can only open our eyes
> so wide
> without becoming blind
> unless we first open them
> in our dreams

Being a rabbi in the wilds of the Kootenay Mountains had its humourous moments. About ten miles up the road from the ashram, heading towards Creston, there was a general store. This is where Iris would do most of her day-to-day shopping, the major shopping being left for excursions to Nelson. One day, Iris asked me if I would like to accompany her, and I was happy to do so, especially since general stores, for some reason, have always appealed to me. Sometimes, when travelling by car, if I come across a general store I'll stop and go in, even though there's nothing in particular that I need. I enjoy just walking the aisles and looking at the merchandise. More often than not, I'll find something that interests me and purchase it.

On this day an elderly woman was managing the store. She greeted Iris as I wandered off to begin my general store routine. I noticed out of the corner of my eye that the woman and Iris were engaged in conversation, and a moment later Iris motioned for me to come over. She introduced me to the woman as Rabbi Steinberg. There was a pause. The woman looked carefully at me and asked, "Are you Jewish?"

I smiled and replied, "Yes!"

She looked again. "From the top of your head to the bottom of your feet?"

I smiled again and was tempted to say "And all parts in between," but I didn't. Instead I simply repeated, "Yes!"

The conversation ended there; Iris pursued her shopping and I went back to examining the shelves. In the car on the way back to the ashram, we discussed the incident and concluded that the woman had probably never knowingly met a Jew before. In my own mind, I wondered whether she had been subjected to the myth of Jews having horns on their heads, much like Reverend Grabke's nephew back in Regina, since she did look rather intently at the top of my forehead.

ONE DAY I came across a book in the ashram library entitled *Fasting Can Save Your Life* by Herbert Shelton. It was a fascinating read and piqued my interest to try what the author was suggesting. In a nutshell, Shelton claimed that fasting while drinking only pure water for prolonged periods of time would cleanse one of all toxins and give the body a chance to heal from any illness. He also believed that even a healthy person would reap benefits from fasting. Being Jewish, I was no stranger to what it means to fast, as each year, on our holiest day, Yom Kippur (the Day of Atonement), I would fast from evening to evening—a full day, plus, usually, an additional few hours. Not even water passed my lips, unlike Shelton's practice. Shelton, however, was not talking about a one-day fast. He was talking about a prolonged fast, as long as six to eight weeks. He assured the reader that no harm would be incurred as long as the faster remained in a supportive environment, avoided physical exertion (unless their constitution could handle it), and drank copious amounts of pure water. He talked about what one could expect on such a fast, and when and how to end it. The ashram was certainly a supportive environment, and it occurred to me that if I could be excused from doing physical labour, this would be a most opportune time to experiment with fasting. Swami Radha approved, and I decided to fast for one week according to Shelton's instructions.

The first three days of the fast were very difficult because of my intense craving for food, so much so that I didn't think I would be able to continue. As Shelton had predicted, my tongue developed a thick, white coating, and I felt weak. I attempted to do physical work around the ashram but, as I had expected, found this exhausting. In retrospect, I believe that my weakness and exhaustion were more states of mind than states of body. Subconsciously, and to some degree even consciously, I expected that if I stopped eating, weakness and exhaustion would ensue, having been programmed with this attitude from the time I was a child. "Eat and you will be strong," I was told again and again, and I had bought into it.

By the end of the third day, I found my desire for food waning, and by the morning of the fourth day, my hunger had completely disappeared. Shelton had described this phenomenon, but reading about it was one thing—actually experiencing it was quite another.

From the beginning of the fast until the end, but particularly during the first three days, what I found very difficult was missing mealtimes. It wasn't so much the food I missed, but rather the time spent at the table and the camaraderie one enjoys while eating in the presence of friends and family. Three times a day, for a total of perhaps three hours, I was trying to pass the time alone. One may ask, "Well, why not read or do something useful?" This thought occurred to me, but for some reason, fasting had robbed me of the desire to do anything. Try as I might, I couldn't get myself out of this mental state. I discussed this with Swami Radha and Shula, but to no avail. I had to get through it and await the end of the fast.

Finally, day seven came. The plan was to break the fast at the evening meal. During the day, I took stock of myself. First, I had survived. Second, physically, I was feeling good. Third, I wasn't very hungry. Fourth, according to Shelton, I wasn't ready to break the fast; my tongue was still coated (only less so), my appetite hadn't fully returned, and the extra time to myself during the day was no longer so challenging. But I wanted to. This meant eating a small amount of food, mostly juices and soft foods, and gradually adding other items over the next few meals, until within two days I was back to a regular diet.

The experiment was over. I had lost twenty pounds, most of it in the first four days, and the rest gradually over the next three days. Strangely, I felt that I was at my optimum weight and if I didn't gain back a single pound, I would be just fine or better. I did gain back about ten pounds over the next several days, however, and have maintained this weight quite steadily until recently, four decades after my fast. During the year 2010, I altered my food consumption to two meals a day and finally achieved my long-sought-after goal of leaving the table with room still in my stomach. Well, most of the time.

Prem also read Shelton's book and he, along with a lady visitor from Quebec, started the water fast about two months later. Prem ended his fast after six weeks, and the young woman from Quebec after four weeks. Before beginning the fast, the woman was clearly on the heavy side, though not obese. She lost about thirty-five pounds and was the picture of health. I was astonished at the length of time she and Prem had fasted. But what amazed me even more was that both put in full days of manual labour for the entire duration of their fast. Some of the work would have taxed a normal person eating a regular regime. This served to confirm my belief that my own feelings of weakness and exhaustion had been states of mind, and that I needed to work on ridding myself of old programming from childhood that was obviously not serving me well.

While at the ashram I took upon myself another fast, but of a different nature and for a different reason. I had read a book called *The Coca Pulse Test* by Dr. Arthur Coca, founder of *The Journal of Immunology*. The premise of Dr. Coca's book was that there was a very simple way, without professional assistance, to determine which foods were compatible for your body and which were not. This involved first going on a short fast, as I recall two or three days, again drinking only water. Then, having compiled a list of foods to be tested, you re-introduced foods to your body one at a time, eating small portions of each and waiting a short time between each portion. For example, a bite of chocolate might be followed an hour or two later by a taste of red meat. Before taking a portion of food, you took your pulse and wrote down the rate of beats per minute. Then you ate the food, waited a few minutes, and took your pulse again. If the pulse was faster by a number of beats, it indicated that the food ingested was not suitable for you at this time in your life. (The exact details of how to go about this are presented in Dr. Coca's book. My description is only an approximation for purposes of illustration.)

I undertook the fast and then tested several foods, particularly the ones I ate most frequently. Sure enough, some accelerated my heart rate and others had no impact. For a while, I avoided the foods that caused a faster heartbeat, but some of them were favourites of mine; I gradually regressed and decided that sometimes pleasure takes precedence over virtue.

In the areas of fasting and food testing, I have experienced changes and developments over the years. My naturopath, for example, recommends a twice-a-year cleansing fast that lasts from five to fourteen days. On this fast, I drink different juices every two hours from 8:00 a.m. to 6:00 p.m. I visit his office twice a year, where he tests me for, among other things, food incompatibilities, using a system more sophisticated than the Coca test, but with some similarities. All this fasting and testing allows me to monitor which foods are serving me well at a particular time and which are not.

One more food-related event occurred at the ashram when a visitor came to give a lecture on this subject. His name, with apologies for a possible misspelling, was Arvo Tagapera. The essence of his thesis was that there is no food that is inherently bad for a person. Every food item, protein, fat, or carbohydrate, has its place and its time. In other words, even junk food, in certain limited situations, may be exactly what the system requires. For some reason, what Arvo had to say resonated with me and has since become part of my approach to what I eat. Every now and then (these being rare occasions), I will indulge in a Coke, sometimes just a sip and at other times a half can, and not feel guilty that I am contravening some sacred prohibition. The same applies to other normally undesirable and unhealthy foods in my otherwise very careful grocery selection.

AT THE ASHRAM, in return for the low amount we paid for board and room, Swami Radha asked Shula and me to put in two hours of work each day, doing whatever was needed. In other words, we were floaters, directed to the kitchen, or the work shed, or the office, and so on. I have already mentioned my weekly bread-baking; although I worked for twelve hours straight on those days, I was still available the rest of the week for daily tasks that sometimes took more than two hours, depending on what had to be done. Still, I had plenty of time for meditation and other introspective activities.

I found that the most difficult physical labour was in the spring, when wood had to be gathered for the following winter. I learned that trees had to be cut before the sap began to run, otherwise they were more difficult to portion out into firewood and would not dry as quickly or as well. Prem was my teacher, and we began by walking into the forest on ashram land with a chainsaw, selecting appropriate trees and cutting them down. This could mean thinning out a section where trees were crowding each other, or bringing down trees that were damaged or beginning to die. I came to appreciate the art of cutting down a tree with a chainsaw, learning from Prem, who was an expert and able to cut a tree so that it would fall in the direction he wanted. When Prem determined that we had felled enough trees to supply the coming winter's needs, including a hefty supply for our cabin's wood stove, we abandoned the chainsaw and brought in the tractor. This in itself was tricky, as the land was hilly, uneven, and full of ditches, holes, and obstacles like rocks and fallen branches. We took turns on the tractor, as we had done with the chainsaw. The task before us was to winch out the trees with a steel cord and drag them to a clearing, where they were piled to dry over the next six months.

In the fall, it was chainsaw time again, as we cut the trees into pieces that would fit our stoves. The chainsaw, a big Mccullough, was heavy and quickly became dull, which meant having to sharpen it at frequent intervals. Prem tried to teach me how to do this, but I could never get the hang of it, leaving him to do all the sharpening. I did eventually become quite adept at using the big saw, although in the beginning I came close a couple of times to cutting off my foot. (Thank God for thick, steel-reinforced work boots.) Eventually Prem set up a platform with a large circular blade attached to a motor, and this became the main implement for sawing the trees to size.

Preparing to cut logs for winter heating (1967)

But my work with the logs did not end there. They had to be piled onto a lorry, taken to the woodshed attached to our cabin, unloaded, and stacked. Then, before the first snowfall, I took an axe and chopped some of the logs into smaller pieces, a few for kindling and the rest large enough to fit the stove and last a long time. These logs were our only source of heat in the winter, and our well-being depended on them.

A short distance from our cabin was Swami Turiananda's residence. This was the size of a tool shed, so small that Turi had to crawl through an opening to enter. When he stretched out on his bed, both his head and feet were an inch or so from the walls. In the winter, for warmth, he had a small electric heater, the cord extending out of the shed and attached to an outlet on our cabin. I couldn't understand why he chose this kind of lodging when more comfortable accommodation was available to him. Only later did this become clear to me. The whole point of the shed was an exercise in austerity. In the coldest days of winter I would look at his "home" and feel bad, thinking about how he must be suffering. We had an extra room in our cabin where he could have slept comfortably, but I knew he was on some kind of mission to prove something to himself, and no amount of coaxing on my or Shula's part made any difference. I believe the other members of the ashram knew this and understood better than I the meaning of what he was doing. Certainly, extreme austerity is a part of most religions, but in mainstream Judaism it hardly exists unless forced upon one by extreme conditions. Perhaps my unfamiliarity with the concept of austerity contributed to my lack of under-standing or appreciation in this matter. My readings and conversations on the subject tell me that it has to do with denying the flesh, which, upon reflection, seems to me an aspect of abstinence, something that Shula and I were practis-ing ourselves at the time. As for the other swamis, they all stayed warm and comfortable in heated accommodations. Turi survived the winter but did not return to the shed in subsequent seasons.

At its inception in 1957, the ashram was located in Burnaby, B.C. The move to Kootenay Bay came several years later, and when we arrived, the new ashram location was only three years old. There was still much to do and many avenues of creative expression to follow, including one that came from Shula's love of plants; she decided she wanted to start a vegetable garden next to our cabin. Swami Radha was all for it. In a matter of days, the seeds were acquired and, it being spring, Shula began planting. Every day saw her tending the garden until finally, in the late summer and into the fall, fresh vegetables adorned our lunch and dinner plates. There was, however, one major obstacle she had to overcome. The garden attracted animals, mainly squirrels and deer. (The bears, fortunately, were mainly after the apple trees, and these were a distance away.) The only solution was to build a fence, which she did, and the produce was thereafter protected. Her garden remained intact after we left the ashram, attended by others. One summer a few years later, we returned to find the garden had been moved to the field where Prem and I had once cut logs. It was greatly expanded and a major source of food for ashram members and visitors.

Besides baking, my practical and creative contribution to the ashram was to build a coat and shoe rack for the entrance to the prayer room. I did this under Prem's guidance, although the design was my own. It had an Egyptian motif, in that the sides were shaped like Egyptian vases. I recall feeling proud of my accomplishment and have recently learned that it is still standing, in good shape and being used.

One item I had to learn about wood stoves is that the pipes collect creo-sote, and if they are not cleaned yearly, or if the fire is too hot, the creosote bursts into flames and causes what is commonly know as a "chimney fire." One day, while Shula and I were in our cabin, the big locomotive bell near the main house began to ring, alerting everyone that there was an emergency and all should gather there. Shula and I immediately left the cabin and headed for the bell. Halfway to our destination we encountered one of the visitors, Justin Stone, running the opposite way, that is, in our direction. We stopped Justin and asked him what the problem was. He said, "Turn around!" We did, and saw our cabin's chimney spouting flames. Within a few minutes, Prem and others arrived on the scene and brought the fire under control. After that, we carefully monitored our stove.

As for Justin Stone: He hailed from California, a tall, cultured gentleman with an intense interest in Zen Buddhism. His favourite expression whenever anyone engaged him in a metaphysical discussion was, "Gone, gone, gone to the other side." I sensed that there was something profound in his words, but never quite got to the bottom of it.

Justin introduced those at the ashram to a spiritual and martial art that he called tai chi. None of us had ever heard of it. We would meet in the parking lot in front of the office or near the work shed at a specified time each day, and he would teach us the various movements and the meaning behind each one. With time we became quite proficient. One day, as we were practising with Justin, a car came down the ashram road with a bunch of teenagers in it. They saw this group of people doing unfamiliar movements, which I'm sure seemed weird, perhaps even threatening, to them, and in seconds, they spun around and left in a cloud of dust. I can't say for certain, but it's possible that back in 1966 our little group might have been the first in Canada to learn tai chi, or at least the first among non-Asians.

MEDITATION FOR ME was always an elusive practice, even though it was part of my daily routine. At the ashram I was taught many different meditative techniques in four broad categories: breath, sound, visualization, and prayer. All four types were practised at the ashram. If I were to pick the one most characteristic of Swami Radha, I would say *sound*. By this I mean mantras, short phrases that are repeated over and over again, often with a melody. Two mantras were Swami Radha's favourites — *Om Nama Shivayah* and, in particular, *Hari Om*. Rarely a *satsang* passed without her or one of the other swamis playing the harmonium and leading us in either of these mantras. Sometimes the whole *satsang* (a Hindu-style spiritual gathering) lasting about an hour or longer, was devoted entirely to the mantra. (The exceptions were Friday and Saturday evenings, when Shula and I celebrated Shabbat.) According to Swami Radha, she never had a singing voice until she was introduced to mantras, and it seemed only mantras would allow her full vocal expression. If one listens to recordings of her voice chanting mantras, it is readily apparent that she is in her element, there being a richness of tone and timbre underscored by deep devotion and subtle passion. It was always a pleasure for me to sit in her company when she sang.

Visualization was the next most frequently practised form of meditation at the ashram. One such technique in particular, which Swami Radha called the Divine Light Invocation, was practised each evening at the conclusion of *satsang*. This technique, which was given to her in a vision one day while she meditated, consisted of charging oneself with spiritual light by repeating and visualizing the intention of the words, "I am created by Divine Light; I am sustained by Divine Light; I am surrounded and protected by Divine Light; I am ever growing into Divine Light." There are certain body movements that accompany the words, and a specific manner of breathing. Though it is primarily a visualization, I see the Divine Light Invocation as encompassing all four categories of meditation.

The technique was used for personal benefit and to benefit others. When *satsangs* ended, the group remained in the prayer room to form a healing circle. Names of people in ill health, sent to the ashram, were called out for healing, and the Divine Light Invocation was the medium for sending the people blessings. We charged ourselves with light by taking a deep breath and visualizing the light streaming from our outstretched hands toward those in need. We did the same for people suffering from natural disasters all over the world, and for the earth as a whole. Depending on the length of the list, the healing circle could last a half hour or more. Also, those present could add the names of people not on the list. When one of those forming the circle was in need of healing, that individual would step into the middle to receive the light. Periodically, during a healing session, we would recharge ourselves by repeating the Divine Light Invocation. We were aware from Swami Radha's instructions that not only were others benefiting from our efforts, but the light was also benefiting us as it coursed through our physical and spiritual bodies.

At one point during our ashram stay, I devoted a full week to intense meditation. This meant getting up at 4:00 a.m. and meditating most of the day until 10:00 in the evening. I confess, from time to time I would fall asleep, or be aroused from my meditative state by fish flies landing on me (it seemed to me there were at times hundreds in the cabin). It was also a week of silence; I was not permitted to speak except when Swami Radha came to see how I was doing. That week had a profound impact on my life. My meditations brought me into an awareness of other dimensions of reality, similar to my healing dream for Shula but in expanded form. The imagery and sensory impressions were such that there was little doubt that beings of intelligence and good will existed on other planes and were receptive to our efforts to contact them. And this was a reciprocal relationship. Only many years later did I come across this concept of spiritual reciprocity in a teaching of Kabbalah (Jewish mysticism), which stated that effort from below (the earth dimension) stimulates a response from above (other dimensions of reality). The effort begins with us, though at times it originates from the beings who inhabit those other dimensions. What I'm expressing here is the cumulative result of my experience during that transformational week. I was not allowed to make notes, as this would have put me into a cognitive mode and diminished my spiritual experience. It must also be said that deep spiritual impressions are difficult to translate because such personal experiences are substantially different in nature from thought processes. In other words, I don't remember the details, but the impressions have left a footprint on my soul. And this has been a blessing ever since.

That week gave me one more gift. In my rabbinical studies, the experiences of the great prophets of Israel, like Elijah, Isaiah, and Ezekiel, had been presented as flights of imagination or literary devices to impress an audience. They were not taken seriously as experiences of realities beyond imagination and literary technique. I saw clearly that that was wrong. What the prophets had were experiences of expanded consciousness, of forays into realms beyond conventional cognitive processes, holy realms where the human soul connects with God in one or more of perhaps an infinite number of dimensions. I saw that the prophets experienced *devekut* (connection to God, or as Swami Radha would say, "the Highest"). And this too was the meaning of the word *yoga* — "connection to God."

By the time I left the ashram, my view of the prophets had been transformed, this transformation being reinforced by my meditative experiences. I had always suspected there was more to the prophets than what I was being taught in my classes in Cincinnati. Once my suspicions were confirmed, I could speak with a conviction that was strong. And if the ashram experience gave me no more than that, then *dayeynu* ("it was enough").

Having said all this, I reformulate my earlier statement on meditation as a question: Why do I find the practice of meditation elusive? In a sense, meditation is like being in two places at the same time. For example, if one uses a meditative technique such as listening to one's breath to achieve another level of consciousness, the technique of listening to one's breath becomes in itself another level of consciousness. With the extended use of this technique (or any one of myriad other meditative techniques) one can reach a state of consciousness different from what one experienced earlier on in the breathing. In other words, the technique and the goal of the technique are one and the same — other levels of consciousness — only with variations as the meditation progresses. Another way of putting this would be to say that meditation, from its inception, is a dynamic process, even when it might seem that nothing is happening. Today, when I teach meditation, I encourage my students not to concern themselves about where they think the meditative technique might take them or what its contents are supposed to be, but simply to focus on practising the technique, which, I tell them, is in itself a state of meditation.

Besides learning about meditation from Swami Radha, we also learned Indian dancing. When she lived at Swami Sivananda's ashram in Rishakesh, Swami Radha had cultivated this art form, building on her background in dance. I was a particularly poor student of Indian dance, even though I loved to dance and had taught folk dancing. For some reason, I just couldn't get the hang of it. Others, particularly Monique Huchet, who lived with her family in Riondel, were much more adept.

Earlier I spoke about my relationship with Swami Vishnudevananda. Like Swami Radha, he was a mentor to me. From him I learned that there are many different kinds or paths of yoga. His main expertise was hatha yoga, which stresses body postures referred to as *asanas*. This is the form of yoga most familiar to people living in the West. That is not to say that Swami Vishnu, as he was affectionately called, was not adept in other forms of yoga; I have little doubt that he was. But this is not what was evident in his teaching, at least during the time I knew him best, which was from 1961 to 1962. I might also mention that he, like Swami Radha, had Swami Sivananda as his guru. So they knew each other but, at least on the surface, were miles apart both figuratively and geographically.

When I left Montreal I had some knowledge and skills in hatha yoga, thanks to Swami Vishnu. When I arrived at the ashram three years later, I was asked to teach visitors this form of yoga, since it seemed no one else at the ashram had the desire or training to take this on. So, for a short time, I was the ashram's hatha yoga teacher, imparting to the best of my ability the lessons learned in Montreal. It wasn't long, however, before people started arriving at the ashram who had more knowledge and training in this area than myself, at which point I gladly relinquished my position. There was, however, one *asana* I was particularly good at teaching, and that was the headstand. I was kept in reserve to help whenever someone had difficulty learning this posture. On the other hand, I was hopeless with the lotus position both as a student and a teacher. (If you ever want to know what a human pretzel looks like, open the pages of Swami Vishnu's book *The Complete Illustrated Book of Yoga*, referred to before, and you will see not only an excellent example of the lotus position, but of almost every other yoga *asana*.)

THE ONLY MEMBER of the ashram I have not yet mentioned was Nestor, a large, independent-minded collie. Nestor would disappear frequently, sometimes for days, but eventually turned up — until the day he didn't, and we never saw him again. His replacement, also a collie, was Shalom. I like to think Shula's and my presence at the ashram had something to do with his naming. Unlike Nestor, Shalom always seemed to be around, and had a sweet and peaceful disposition.

IN THE SPRING of 1967, as the end of our two-year stay at the ashram was approaching, I received a letter from Steve Forstein, who had been my class-mate and friend in Cincinnati. He was the rabbi at a congregation in Richmond, California, his first pulpit after ordination. In his letter he described what was occurring in San Francisco, just across the bay from Richmond. He told me about a generation of young people, many of them Jewish, who were rebelling against established religion — in fact, rebelling in general against what society was offering them. They were trying to bring to America a new vision, one of love and peace. He told me these young people were being referred to as "flower children" and "hippies." It was a time of great ferment on the west coast of the United States, and spiritual leadership was much needed. Would I, he asked, be interested in coming to San Francisco as a rabbi to the Jewish hippies?

In my reply to him, I expressed ignorance about the situation he described. Although I had heard the terms "hippie" and "flower child," I wasn't sure what they meant. I said I would be willing to come to San Francisco and have a look at what was going on, provided he could foot the expenses. His answer was that I should come and see for myself, and he would send the ticket. I spoke with Shula, and she encouraged me to go.

A few weeks later, my plane touched down in San Francisco and Steve was there to meet me. He had been one of the few of my classmates who, I felt, understood me. In some special way, our souls touched. It was good to see him again.

Steve took me to his car, and I got in, but when he turned on the ignition, I nearly jumped out of my seat. He had forgotten to turn his car stereo off, and it was set at a high volume to some of the latest music from some of the most popular bands. He saw my reaction and immediately turned the music off. I was in shock. Having for almost two years listened almost solely to the gentle sounds of nature, I was totally unprepared for this introduction to what lay ahead of me. Steve did not turn the radio on for the duration of our journey to his home in Richmond. However, on the way, he stopped at a very large hall to introduce me to some of his acquaintances. At one end of the hall, a band was preparing to rehearse, while Steve and I stood at the other end. The music began, and I had to put my hands over my ears for fear of damaging my eardrums. The wooden floor beneath my feet was vibrating. I quickly made an exit. I don't recall for certain the name of the hall, but Fillmore is a possibility.

The plan was for Steve to take me the following day to a section of San Francisco known as Haight-Ashbury, introduce me to some acquaintances of his, and leave me to fend for myself over the next four days, after which he would pick me up at a designated place. His expectation was simple: I was to meet people, explore the situation, and determine if Haight-Ashbury and the surrounding environs would become my first congregation. He said that for the next few days, I would have to look after my night lodgings and my meals in any manner I saw fit, which could mean "begging, borrowing, or stealing," since the amount of money I had in my pocket would not take me very far, and his budget was limited.

Early the next morning, after a hearty breakfast provided by his wife, Robin, I embarked on my voyage of discovery. The sequence of the next four days is a blur, but the events are clear. Steve introduced me to a few friends he felt would be good contacts for me to have, people who could be counted on to help if I ran into trouble. Then he went back home.

Steve's friends were pleasant, sensitive, intelligent, and willing to do what they could to acquaint me with the landscape and its offerings. A peculiar odour was immediately apparent to me; when I asked about it, they informed me it was "pot," or marijuana, and asked if I would like some. The offer was spontaneous and casual, like asking a guest if he would like a cup of tea. I declined for a few reasons: first, I didn't smoke; second, they told me inhaling was essential to get the full effect, and as a teenager I had once experimented with a cigarette and found that I couldn't inhale; and third, I was a purist and had been through two years of natural highs. They told me to let them know if I changed my mind.

In our discussions, Steve's friends helped satisfy my curiosity about many things: the drug culture (the use of mind-altering substances of all kinds was readily apparent), the hippies (who were they?), the flower children (where were they, and what did they do?), why all this was happening, what the hippies and flower children wanted to achieve, how they were all being treated by regular society and by the police, and who their leaders were. I'm sure there were many other topics I squeezed in as we talked. In a nutshell, this is what I heard:

Taking mind-altering drugs releases a person from normal perceptions of reality, a reality that is all too often stunting and crippling. Drugs take one to a place of peace, sometimes enlightenment, to a place of greater awareness where an appreciation for oneself, others, and all of creation is enhanced. Cares of the day retreat, and troubles either diminish or evaporate. In essence, drugs make one feel good. Some people suggested that the more powerful drugs, like LSD, give one an experience of what real religion is all about (a position taken by Timothy Leary and Aldous Huxley). In the coming days, this comment on religion was to take on greater significance.

(My only previous experience with a mind-altering substance took place in Cincinnati. One day a classmate asked me to serve as his "ground" while he ingested morning-glory seeds. At the time, this was in vogue and had not yet been banned by the government. He downed twenty-three triple-sized gelatin capsules filled with powdered morning-glory seeds Shula and I had ground up in our pepper grinder. The next several hours found him sprawled on our couch, going through a series of mind-altering experiences. At one point he thought he was going to die, which prompted us to want to take him to the hospital, but he refused to go. He recovered but was out of commission for the next twenty-four hours.)

As for hippies and flower children, these were the very people I was talking to. Perhaps they were too close to themselves and the situation to clearly define the terms; it seemed to me that there was some overlap between the two groups. My experience on the streets and in dialogue with an assortment of individuals indicated that hippies were carefree persons who rejected the norms of society and were prepared to test the boundaries of conventional mores, laws, and interpersonal relations. Experimentation with living arrangements and sexuality was a hallmark of the hippie culture, giving birth to communes and free love. (I sometimes think that the O'Neils' book *Open Marriage* had its roots in the hippie culture.) The flower children, who may or may not have been hippies, seemed to be more single-minded. I observed young women walking down the streets of Haight-Ashbury with bouquets of fresh spring flowers in their hands, handing them out to passers-by. I was among the recipients. Their message was to spread love, and the flowers were the symbols of their message. Every flower child I encountered had a big smile on his or her face.

As to why all this ferment was occurring, the macroscopic view of the people I talked to was that the world was in trouble, something had to be done, and someone had to do it — why not them? They were part of a revolution to change society one step at a time, and as they saw it, theirs was the first step. I have since come to see their statement as a protest against rationalism, empiricism, and the Industrial Revolution and its failed promise of a better and more humane life for all people.

Their thinking about their treatment by the so-called "establishment" was mixed. Some felt people rejected them and saw them as a nuisance, perhaps a threat, while others felt many saw them as a breath of fresh air, perhaps even as modern-day prophets. Whatever the case, they did not engender indifference. The police tolerated the hippies as long as they obeyed the law and didn't stir up trouble. In the context of the bubbling cauldron that was Haight-Ashbury, this seemed to me an oxymoron. Some hippies felt the police were threatened by the societal disturbance, in particular the message of softness and love — "flower power" — that challenged the policeman's image of himself. The police, they argued, had to feel they were "real men" in the Western mode, and to prove it, as one young woman remarked, "they wear their cocks on their hips." I don't recall seeing a single policeman taking a flower that was offered to him, or wearing one. No doubt, even if one of them had wanted to, it would have gone against regulations.

No one had a clear answer on the question of leadership, although people could point to some individuals who were more vocal than others. Poets like Allen Ginsberg were admired, as were Tim Leary and Aldous Huxley. (Other names were mentioned, but they escape me at the moment.) In the following days, however, I did encounter three people who, in my opinion, were leaders of this counterculture.

Steve's friends directed me to the first such person. His name was Allen Cohen, and he was editor of *The Oracle*, the main voice at that time for the hippies, the flower children, and others who bought into their zeitgeist. I went to Allen's office, introduced myself, and asked him if we could talk. He said he would be happy to talk with me, but at the moment he was busy. He invited me to come to his "pad" at 7:30 that evening and gave me directions. At 7:30 I showed up and knocked at the door a few times, until finally a young woman came and invited me in. I found myself in a large room with several people, all of whom, it seemed, lived together in this one space. The walls were covered with posters and other hangings. Loud but somewhat familiar music was playing from floor speakers, and again there was that peculiar odour — only this time there was also visible smoke and cigarettes in plain view. I told my hosts that Allen had asked me to meet him here at this time. They informed me that Allen had gone to a certain theatre to meditate. I asked the location of the theatre and went to it, hoping to track down my elusive editor. The place was packed, and finding Allen would have been like finding the proverbial needle in a haystack. On the stage sat a man in saffron robes giving a discourse on meditation. Spotting an empty seat, I sat down. A few minutes later everyone was meditating, and I joined in, remaining there about an hour, during which there was chanting and more discourse from the man on the stage. I don't recall who he was, but he had the attention of those present.

I left the theatre and walked the streets, deep in thought. I had failed to find Allen Cohen, but I did discover that some kind of shift was in process. At first it didn't come to me, but then I began to see that the man in saffron robes was filling a need with no odour, no smoke, and no ingestion of chemicals — he provided simply deep breathing, chanting, and speaking. It was a reflection of my life for the past two years at the ashram.

In the late '60s, yoga and meditation were in their infancy in North America. What was happing in San Francisco was to presage the coming decades, where figures like Maharishi Mahesh Yogi (transcendental meditation), Yogi Bajan (Kundalini Yoga), and my own teachers, Swami Vishnudevananda and Swami Radha, would bring ancient practices to maturity in our land. Yes, pot is still around, and there are still those seeking chemical highs, but drugs are no longer in the foreground the way they were in those days. Both yoga and meditation are commonplace, found in churches, synagogues, community centres, recreational buildings, children's camps, spas, and locations dedicated solely to their practice, including many ashrams across our vast continent. The same can be said of other countries around the globe.

The next day found me in a Zen temple. It was located on Bush Street, and the roshi (head person) was very gracious, allowing me to sit in and meditate with his students. He gave me a round, black, firm pillow, which I placed under me, and then instructed me on how to sit and what to do. The main difference I perceived between Zen meditation and the practice I was taught at the ashram is that in the former, one meditates with the eyelids slightly open, so students stay awake. The roshi informed me that from time to time he would swat me with a stick, to make sure I hadn't drifted off and to keep my mind alert. The stick was a bit like a straw whisk, and when he hit me it didn't hurt, but I was certainly startled. I was also startled every time I heard the stick come down on another meditator. Later in the day, the roshi kindly gave me the pillow to keep, and it remains in my possession.

On my last evening in Haight-Ashbury, I was again walking the streets. I had no particular destination in mind; I was just looking, and thinking about what my decision would be when Steve came to pick me up the next morning. Then I heard, in the far distance, some familiar music. I walked in the direction it was coming from, and soon I was at the entrance of the I-Thou Coffee Shop. With a smile on my face, I entered. There, at the far end of the narrow shop, was my old friend Shlomo Carlebach, strumming his guitar and leading a packed house in songs he had written. (Zalman first introduced me to Shlomo in the sixties and we remained casual friends from that point on. Both he and Zalman had studied at the Lubovitch Yeshivah in New York where they received their ordination as rabbis.) He waved at me as if no time at all had passed since we last saw each other and said, "Hi, Jerry!" Immediately I was drawn in and began singing along with everyone else. After about a half hour, Shlomo, with all of us following, danced his way out into the street, and we all formed a circle around him while he continued leading us in song. As we whirled around this gifted rabbi, singing our hearts out, I said to myself, "Haight-Ashbury has its hippie rabbi. They don't need me!"

Between Shlomo Carlebach, Allen Cohen, and the man in saffron robes, I felt that both Jews and non-Jews in Haight-Ashbury were in good hands. The next day Steve picked me up, and the day after, I returned to the ashram.

As a footnote to the last story, Rabbi Carlebach went on to become well known in Jewish and even some non-Jewish circles around the world. He established Houses of Love and Prayer in San Francisco, with branches in New York and Jerusalem. His songs continue to be sung in synagogues, camps, and many other venues, and his recordings are numerous. Several years ago he passed away.

Looking back, I can see that the young people of Haight-Ashbury made a difference in our world. They helped start something positive that flowered and grew, affecting millions of people. They had a vision that helped all of us see more clearly, but that still has miles to go before it is fulfilled.

SWAMI RADHA ALSO had a vision, which was realized in the establishment of Yasodhara Ashram, and within the ashram she had another vision: that one day the ashram would build a temple, and it would be dedicated to honouring the religions of the world. However, she was hampered in this vision by a lack of funds and by the more immediate needs of the ashram. Yet, in spite of constraints, somehow she was able to put a small amount of money aside to at least make a beginning. So, in the second year of our residence, under Prem's supervision, construction began. That initial effort resulted in a large round platform that was to serve as the floor of the temple. The platform overlooked the lake and was positioned for a breathtaking view. One day during its construction we had a consecration ceremony. A small round piece of wet cement was laid at the base of the platform, and we all gathered around it. Like a pie, the cement was divided into eight sections, and the symbols of eight religions were engraved into it. I had the pleasure of imprinting a seven-branched candelabra, the ancient symbol of Judaism and one associated with the first and second temples. It was a wonderful day, full of promise, and we all looked forward to a time when the Temple of All Religions would be completed.

Top: Temple of Divine Light, outside view (circa 1992)

Bottom: Temple of Divine Light, inside view (circa 1992)

Alas, the structure stood unfinished for close to twenty years and eventually was taken down so a new temple could be built from the ground up in the same location. I don't know what happened to the centre stone with the religious symbols, but I do know that in 1992 I was invited to the dedication of the new temple building, named the Temple of Divine Light. It is a magnificent structure, with every detail, inside and out, carefully designed according to Swami Radha's wishes. The chandeliers that adorn the main sanctuary, for example, she saw clearly in her mind before they were produced. Like the entire ashram, the temple is a tribute to the vision of a great lady and the commitment of those who walked with her. Over the years, several other structures were built on the grounds, and the ashram continues to thrive as I write.

We left the ashram toward the end of the summer of 1967. We stayed on into August to conduct workshops for visitors, something we continued to do each summer thereafter for several years. During these summers, I had three experiences that significantly affected my life, although the significance of one of them I was not aware of at the time.

The first experience relates to my keen interest in dreams. I learned from Swami Radha a technique for working with dreams that I applied whenever I was assigned to help a visitor with dream work. One day a student of mine from the University of North Dakota, where I taught for five years, came to the ash-ram and asked that I help him interpret one of his dreams. I applied Swami Radha's technique diligently for about an hour, but we couldn't seem to get to the crux of the matter. I was about to give up when I felt a strong intuition to do something I had never done before. I asked my former student to lie down and close his eyes. Then I asked him to repeat the dream in the first person, present tense, as if he was dreaming it over again. Nothing happened. I asked him to repeat it. Still nothing happened. I decided to give it one more try. As he was repeating it for the third time, I noticed a change in his breathing and a subtle shift in his demeanour. He appeared to be having the dream again, only this time there was someone there to guide him. Within a short period of time he was experiencing deep emotions, and within about a half hour he had, with only a little prodding from me, resolved the dream with a great sense of relief.

This was the beginning of my development of the dream interpretation technique I have named "re-dreaming and figure identification." It's a power-ful tool and, in the hands of a skilled therapist, can bring extraordinary results to clients or patients. I have completed a manuscript describing the technique and how to use it, and hope in the near future to have it published.

My second experience had to do with mountain climbing. Across from the ashram and a short distance up the road toward Nelson is a mountain, the top quarter of which is covered by ice. It's known as Kokanee Glacier and used to be where the Canadian National Ski Team did its training. One summer when Shula and I were at the ashram, Krishna's brother was visiting with some of his friends, and they decided they wanted to climb the mountain, beginning below the edge of the glacier. I was invited to come along, as was Joe Reuter. We drove up the mountain as far as we could, parked the car, and began our trek.

Along the way we came across a glacial lake. This is a lake whose water is a degree or so above freezing. By the time we reached the lake, we had done a fair bit of climbing and were perspiring. Joe decided that he needed to take a dip, so he removed all his clothes, ran into the water, and submerged himself. Then I heard a yell, and Joe came galloping out of the lake. He was in shock. I don't remember how he dried himself, but as soon as he had his clothes on, he sat and shivered while his lips, and probably some other parts of his body, turned blue. When Joe caught his breath we continued our climb, with him shivering for most of the next hour.

Once we reached the glacier, the climb became much more difficult. We were walking on crushed ice, and with each step my foot sunk in several inches. This made climbing exceedingly difficult. As we got higher and the oxygen thinned, I also found myself quickly running out of breath. The others were in better shape than I was and, except for Joe, much younger. So I told them I would meet them at the top, and they went on ahead of me. As much as I tried, I was not able to take more than seven or eight steps without

Rabbi on the rocks circa 1970

having to stop and catch my breath. Finally, I saw the top of the mountain and made my way to it. However, as I reached its summit, I realized this was only a peak on the way to the top. The real top, which I couldn't see before, loomed before me not too far in the distance. How I ever made it to the next peak I'll never know, but when I got there I realized I was still not at the summit, only at another peak on the way. As I plodded up the glacier to my destination, I could feel my heart doing double-time and thought it would burst the boundaries of my chest.

I stopped to take stock. I had only a short way to go, but I felt that my physical safety might be in peril and that a fatal heart attack was imminent. The question was whether to go on. It was time for some serious talking to myself. The prudent thing to do, I reasoned, was to turn back before it was too late. On the other hand, if I turned back when I was so close, I might never forgive myself for not trying. The thought then occurred to me that if I gave up now, I would have to live with this defeat, and someday, perhaps, I would want to return to prove to myself I could do it. The thought of going through all of this again when I was older and not in such good shape was the deciding point. I would go on, even if it killed me. And I did. It took about twenty more minutes, but I arrived at the peak where the others were waiting. And I was still kicking.

The view from the top was exquisite. (I was about to say "breathtaking" but changed my mind. My breath had already been taken.) We sat there for perhaps an hour, ate a late lunch, and then started back, which was also an experience. We all decided to ski down on the heels of our climbing boots. I angled my toes upward and began a very quick descent, taking care to avoid crevices, which could have swallowed up any one of us.

The lessons of that day have stood me in good stead ever since. First, don't give up when you're so close to completing a task. Second, reaching one peak serves to bring other peaks into view that previously could not be seen. Many times since, I have committed to a task trusting that I would be shown the way, even though my vision was limited.

I often think of that mountain.

The third experience occurred in the summer of 1972 while Shula and I were teaching at the ashram. I had a disturbing dream about Shula:

You stood
     with your back to the balcony
          on the second floor
   suddenly
       you were sucked away from me
          back
           back
        through the door
          over the railing
           to the cement below
  I ran
     ice gripping my heart
     and saw you lying there
         still
     and I shouted
        screamed
    I've lost her
    I've lost her
and awoke
     trembling
        sweating
   awakening you
    telling you my nightmare
and somewhere inside
      you shuddered
    because you knew it was true
  while I calmed down
      whispering
    thank God
     it's only a dream

It took several months before I began to realize that our marriage was in danger.

My stay at the ashram, and the visit to Haight-Ashbury, laid the foundation for two future jobs, one with the University of North Dakota and the

other with the federal government of Canada. But first and foremost, it gave me a deeper spiritual awareness that I could bring with me as I made my way in the world.

I remained in touch with Swami Radha and others at the ashram for many years and still hear from them on occasion, although Swami Radha has now passed on. I have also, over the years, suggested to many that they visit the ashram and take advantage of the many gifts it has to offer. Some have done so.

Eventually, after many years and at different times, all four swamis left the ashram and married.

Swami Radha and me (circa 1992) the last time we were together. Swami Radha passed on in 1995.

LEAVING THE PULPIT

Winnipeg 1967–1972

Ultimately
        there is a very deep aloneness
                        that sets in
                where neither God
                                nor the angels
                        dare intrude
                here is determined
                        the quality of life
                                to yet be lived
                        and the quality of death
                                to yet be known

While visiting my parents in Winnipeg early in 1966, I was put in touch with some members of a fledgling Reform congregation. Our discussions led to an invitation for me to come to Winnipeg once a month to serve as their rabbi for one year, beginning in the fall. (At the time, I was serving the Reform congregation in Vancouver on a similar basis.) Winnipeg was the place I wanted to be in the long term, and I felt that taking this congregation for 1966–1967 might lead to a lengthier and full-time contract. Indeed, toward the end of the year, the congregation asked me to stay on as their rabbi for five years. So, near the end of the summer of 1967, Shula and I left the ashram and came to Winnipeg.

Temple Shalom was a small group, numbering at that time around thirty or forty families, so they couldn't pay me very much, certainly not enough to live on. I asked my friend Zalman, at that time a professor at the University of Manitoba, if he knew of any jobs I might do to supplement my income. He told me that he thought the University of North Dakota, a two and a half hour drive south of Winnipeg, was looking for someone to teach a course on Judaism in its religion department. He arranged for me to go down and have an interview that led to an appointment on their faculty. At the same time, the Canadian Jewish Congress was looking for a prison chaplain for Jewish prisoners in the federal penitentiary and in the provincial and municipal jails, a job I gladly accepted. Two years later, in 1969, Zalman, who had become chairman of the Department of Near Eastern and Judaic Studies at the University of Manitoba, hired me to teach courses in Jewish history and Jewish literature. So, after two years in Winnipeg, I was making $12,000 in total. Granted, this was not much money, even for that time, but it sustained us. Having my parents there also helped, as they were very generous when we needed major items, like a car and a house.

Shula and I stayed with my parents for a few weeks until we found a place to live, in the upper level of a home at 722 Weatherdon Avenue. We stayed there for about a year and a half and then, when Shula became pregnant, we moved to a newly built home at 18 Purdue Bay in Fort Richmond, near the University of Manitoba. It was an attractive three-bedroom bunga-low in a very friendly neighbourhood and would provide a lovely setting for us and our soon-to-be-born child. Not long after, Zalman and his new wife, Mary Lynn, moved into a similar house just a few blocks from us.

Then came one of the greatest joys in my life, the birth of our son, Meher, on February 12, 1969, to be equalled only four years later by the birth of our daughter, Dahlia. I drove Shula to the Women's Pavilion at the Winnipeg General Hospital early that morning, looking forward very much to being present at my child's birth. The doctor told us that it would be many hours before the birth would take place, so Shula suggested I go home and look after some things that still needed doing. I left the hospital and drove home, which took me about twenty-five minutes. As I was putting the key in the door, I heard the phone ring and rushed to answer it. A nurse at the hospital said that Shula wanted me to come back right away, as she was about to give birth. I rushed back, cautiously running a few red lights, and ran into the pavilion, only to be told that my son had arrived. I waited impatiently outside the deliv-ery room until finally a nurse brought him out. I was overwhelmed and could only whisper, "Welcome, son," at which point he opened his eyes, as if to say, "Thanks, Pop. Good to be here!"

By the time Meher was able to roll over onto his knees, we began to real-ize that he harboured some kind of talent. We had attended a production of the operetta *Carmen* while Shula was in her eighth month, and we had noticed that the child in her womb started moving vigorously when the toreador song came on. One night, an hour or so after we put Meher to bed, we checked on him and discovered the crib had moved to the other end of the room. He had rocked himself from one wall to the other. When he was a little older and we were able to put him in a car seat, he would rock the whole time, so much that we could feel the movement sitting in the front of the car. With Meher, there was always a beat in whatever he did. Today, he is a professional musician, delighting audiences at home and abroad.

We thought it would be a good idea for Meher to have a dog. I loved Dalmatians (possibly under the influence of *101 Dalmatians*), and after care-fully researching the breed, had a male pup flown in to us from Vancouver. He was beautiful, and we named him Tevya, after the main character in *Fiddler on the Roof*. Meher was delighted with Tevya and they quickly became friends. We took Tevya to training classes when he was a little older but found him to be a slow learner. I learned later that Dalmatians and Irish setters have a reputation for having minds of their own and look upon their owners as objects to toy with. Tevya was certainly in that category.

I decided, shortly after his arrival, that Tevya should have only the best food for his growth and health. Again, some research informed me that fresh meat was the best, and in a class far superior to anything one could buy in a store or pet shop. So I found an outlet on the outskirts of Winnipeg where they shot retired horses and ground up the meat for dogs and other carnivorous animals, probably beasts in the Winnipeg Zoo. Tevya took to ground horse meat like a newborn calf to its mother's milk. And he grew — and grew — and grew. Before long he was the biggest Dalmatian I had ever seen, and as strong as a horse, if the reader will pardon this expression, given the situation. He would bowl Meher over whenever he went to greet him, such that my son began to fear our friendly, well-meaning dog. When I had him on a leash, it was all I could do to hold him back; he seemed to enjoy taking Meher and me for walks. But he did learn some manners, and on occasion we actually had a pleasant, non-eventful stroll. When we left Winnipeg in 1972, we found him a good home, as circumstances in Ottawa would not permit us to have a pet.

TO COMPENSATE FOR the small salary, my contract with Temple Shalom specified that I was only to work for them part-time — more precisely, half-time — so that I could seek other employment to make ends meet. Initially it all sounded fine to me, but as I got into my work with the temple, I began to realize there was no such thing as part-time for a rabbi, especially when the congregation was young, desirous of growth, and trying to make a name for itself in a very traditional community that was not particularly open to the concepts of Reform Judaism.

The magnitude of what I was trying to do became evident to me as I tried to juggle my four jobs. As the five-year period progressed, I found that I had little or no time for my family, and no time for myself outside of work. Fortunately I enjoyed my work, for the most part, and this helped to compensate for a gruelling schedule. However, toward the end of five years, I was worn down and, unbeknownst to me, my relationship with Shula was hanging by a thread.

The fact that my congregation and I were bucking the tide in a community not receptive to us as Reform Jews was another challenge I had to deal with. This became apparent quickly in my first year, when I submitted an article to the local Jewish newspaper, and it was rejected on the grounds that it would be too controversial. I countered with a letter to the editor stating that everything I was saying could be backed up by references to Jewish sources. Eventually, after back-and-forth letters and phone conversations, the article was published and the community didn't fall apart. In essence, the article was about intermarriage in the bible, showing that there was a case to be made both pro and con, depending on where one looked. On the pro side, I mentioned Moses and Joseph, among other great Jewish leaders, who married non-Jewish women. On the con side, again using Jewish sources, I pointed to the teachings of Ezra and Nehemia, who not only condemned intermarriage, but also said that Jewish men who were intermarried had to divorce their wives. I suppose, if I had only talked about the con aspect, there would not have been any hurdles to overcome, except for protests from Jews already married to non-Jewish women. As time went by, other articles I wrote for the paper were printed without protest.

Ever since becoming a rabbi, I have had frequent requests to perform intermarriages. This is defined as marriage between a Jew and a non-Jew. I have always declined, on the grounds that as a rabbi, my duty and obligation is to marry only Jews when called upon. Neither from the tradition nor from my own feelings of what is right am I inclined to deviate from this position. My view on this is shared by my colleagues in the Greater Toronto area and, for the most part, across the country. However, in the early years of my rabbinate I decided that while I would not marry a couple unless both parties were Jewish, I would make myself available to be present at the intermarriage ceremony and give the bride and groom a blessing, along with a few words grounded in the Jewish tradition, as long as someone else officiated and did all the required signings. I held this position as I felt it would make things easier for the couple and, in particular, would help the Jewish family present feel more at ease about the ceremony. Also, it was my hope that, by being accepting in this manner, perhaps I could help the non-Jewish partner become receptive to the idea of converting to Judaism. (Many of my colleagues south of the border hold to this view and, for this and other reasons, do perform intermarriages.) Some of the weddings I participated in went smoothly, but others did not, and as the "did nots" increased, I eventually decided it was simply too much trouble and aggravation.

Let me give two examples of the "did nots." In one case, the wedding was being performed by a Christian minister who was sensitive to the situation and asked to sit down with me and go over the service. Unwittingly he had included references to Christ without using that name per se, which would have made the Jewish family present very uncomfortable. When I pointed this out to him, he apologized and removed the references from the service, but situations of this kind were common, and I grew tired of always feeling I had to be extra vigilant to make sure all went well. The second oft-repeated scenario was that the Jewish partner or his/her family would insist that there be Jewish wedding symbols and rituals in the ceremony, such as a *chupah* (canopy) and a breaking of the glass. My response was always that this was not a Jewish wedding and nothing in the ceremony should indicate that it was. This usually led to disagreement and argument, until finally the family either agreed to my terms or decided not to have me present — usually the latter. In one instance, I lost an acquaintance with whom I had a warm relationship. Finally, I threw in the towel and said, "no more."

A colleague in Toronto has recently informed me that in the United States, the pressure on Reform rabbis to do intermarriages has become so strong that many congregations will not hire a rabbi unless he or she agrees to do them. I find this situation most unfortunate and believe that no rabbi should have to even think about compromising his or her integrity to please a congregation, especially when difficult economic times are a factor in the rabbi's decision and jobs are scarce. On the other hand, I also understand the congregation's position: they want a rabbi who will meet their needs, and if those needs include intermarriage, so be it. However, as a rabbi, one needs not only to serve, but to lead. If the rabbi has an important conviction with which the congregation is not in accord, then the rabbi must decide whether to compromise his/her position or move on. To the best of my knowledge, in most instances, when a rabbi already has a congregation, the rabbi stands by his or her convictions and tries to persuade the members to agree. Failure to do so, when the matter is significant enough, usually leads to the rabbi's departure. If a rabbi interviewing for a new position has principles at odds with those of the congregation, he or she is not likely to get the job.

My five years with Temple Shalom were certainly a voyage of self-discovery. Perhaps the most important trait I uncovered in myself was that I was a lousy politician, lacking the understanding and finesse to manoeuvre through the minefields of congregational politics and personality conflicts among members and between members and myself. This is not to say that I didn't have friends in the congregation. One of them is among my closest friends to this day, and others I kept in touch with long after leaving Winnipeg. I believe I can also say that while I did some good work during my tenure in Winnipeg, I was certainly not without fault. A few examples of the conflicts I encountered, the good seeds I sowed, and mistakes made follow:

It was my belief that if Reform Judaism was to take hold in Winnipeg, Temple Shalom would have to be creative, innovative, and resolute in its understanding of Judaism, especially in the realm of social action, and so I endeavoured to show vision and leadership in this domain.

An example of this is a program I initiated at Stoney Mountain Federal Penitentiary, on the outskirts of Winnipeg. The penitentiary was for inmates whose sentences went beyond two years. There were several Jewish prisoners at Stoney Mountain, and all except one were serving time for white-collar crimes. The one exception was a man who had committed murder; though I attempted several times to see him, he never agreed to a visit. Besides visiting and talking with the prisoners, I brought them books to read and, just before Passover, would have a small *Seder* with them in a room provided. The prison personnel were very co-operative, realizing that warm and caring input from the outside was beneficial to their inmates. I made visits to the penitentiary at least once a month, more often if needed. I also saw Jewish prisoners at the other penal institutions serving the city and province. Then I had an idea.

I made an appointment one day with the warden of Stoney Mountain and proposed to him that I take prisoners out for Shabbat, provided I could find homes in my congregation to receive and welcome them. The warden liked my idea and was willing to go along with it, so long as the prisoners were picked up around 4:00 p.m. on Friday and returned by their hosts to the penitentiary before midnight. I asked two or three selected members of my congregation if they would be willing to take part in this experiment. The response was positive, and the prisoners were picked up, brought into members' homes for a Shabbat meal, and then taken to services. After services they interacted with the congregation over coffee and pastries; we introduced them as visitors and left it up to them whether they wanted to disclose the circumstances of their presence. As it turned out, there were no complications. The families enjoyed the prisoners, and the prisoners enjoyed the families. And they were always returned on time.

After this had gone on for several Shabbats, and word about the program had spread throughout the congregation, I came to a board meeting and suggested that the board make this initiative an official project of the congregation. The discussion that followed was, to say the least, divisive. The greatest fear was that the prisoners might harm the families. A lesser concern, but nevertheless important for certain board members, was how to explain the prisoners' presence to their children. I assured them that the members who had already taken part in this experiment had had no problems on either account and found the experience gratifying. They felt they were making a difference in the prisoners' lives by showing them warmth, kindness, and hospitality, not to mention offering them a positive exposure to Judaism. Two of the members on the board had hosted prisoners, and they backed up my words. I emphasized that the prisoner program was in the finest tradition of Reform Judaism's emphasis on social action and gave some supporting quotes from scripture. Not to mention, I said, that it would also put us on the map in Winnipeg, since nothing like it had ever been done there before. Finally a vote was taken on a motion to adopt the prisoner program as an official activity of Temple Shalom. It was defeated.

I was stunned. I couldn't believe what had happened. "Of course," one member of the board, who had voted against the motion, quipped, "anyone in the congregation who wishes to have a prisoner in their home and bring him to services has the right to do so." One or two others expressed concerns about even bringing the prisoners to services, but since this had already been done without incident, the objection was not taken to a vote. Several members of the congregation, to their credit, were also very upset and disappointed by the board's decision.

A week or so later, I received a phone call from a reporter representing one of the two major newspapers in Winnipeg, who wanted to interview me and do a feature article on the temple and the prisoner program. I told him that there was no temple prisoner program, but only individual families who were members of the temple and were hosting prisoners. So, no interview was given. In retrospect, had I been politically astute, I would have given the interview anyway and let the chips fall where they may. My guess is it would have created a stir in the congregation and perhaps forced the board to reconsider its position. Alas, hindsight always comes too late, and often at a price.

The effect the prisoner program had on some of the inmates may be seen in a letter from one of them:

> April 28, 1970
> P.O. Box 101,
> Stoney Mountain,
> Manitoba

Dear Jerry, Shula & Meher,

I am not now nor have I ever been much of a correspondent until prompted. I am prompted by the until-now unbelievable fact that someone is really trying to help us. In my particular case, as I am coming in and out of myself, I am finding many things hitherto impossible, possible, with some genuine no nonsense on my part. Had I but known this feeling many years ago, it is quite possible that I would not even be here.

What I am going through now is beautiful, fascinating and frightening.

But what kind of a person am I that writes once in a "blue moon" and when he has to burden those to whom he writes?

What I really wanted to say so many lines ago but is hard for me to express because to me it still sounds a little odd though it is not, is — Thanks Jerry. Thank you and your wife and your son and your congregation for all that is building and releasing within me now. Also, thanks to all concerned in sending us special foods in the penitentiary and Farm Annex. But most of all to those who thought of five lonely boys in this prison.

Where before there was nothing ahead, there is now hope of becoming a respected and accepted member of not only the Jewish community, but of all peoples as well.

I really did not expect to write this long of a "note," but as I said, many impossible things before are possible now.

Say "hi" to Shula and Meher for me.

Be in good health,
(name withheld)

The reader may have noticed that the letter was addressed to Meher as well as to Shula and myself, with comments about my family. Almost all the letters I received from the prisoners included our son, even though he was only about two years old at the time. Most letters that I received from other people (non-prisoners) did not include him. For some reason, the prisoners took to our little guy, and he to them, as the following incident further illustrates:

One Friday evening we had a prisoner to our Shabbat dinner. As I had picked him up early, we had some time at our home before the meal. Shula asked me to go to the nearby grocery store to pick something up. I was about to leave when the prisoner said he would be happy to run the errand for us. Since Meher had become friendly with the man, he wanted to go with him. I hesitated for a moment (shades of the board meeting) and then said, "Sure." The image remains very clear in my mind: the prisoner, who had a black belt in karate and would have been a formidable foe for anyone, walking away with his enormous hand holding Meher's hand, which totally disappeared in his gentle grip. It was a scene of great tenderness and trust. Many years later, when Meher was grown up, I told him the story. He looked at me, and with a grin on his face, chided, "Dad, what were you thinking?" Recently I showed Meher portions of some of the letters where he was mentioned, and he was touched by the prisoners' interest in him. I can only guess that for the prisoners, the tenderness that Meher brought out in them had a positive impact on their lives.

About two years after our arrival in Winnipeg, Shula and I invited three prisoners to an early Yom Kippur dinner at our home on Purdue Bay. After dinner, the three men, all big and husky, squeezed into the back seat of my small Rover 2000 sedan, and along with Shula and me (Meher was with a babysitter), headed across town to Council House, which at the time was where our congregation held services. Upon arriving at Council House, I couldn't find the key to my trunk, where I had all the prayer books for the service. I voiced my dismay, whereupon I heard a voice from the back seat casually say, "Not to worry, rabbi." A minute later I found the key, but I have no doubt that had I not found it, the prayer books for the service would have nonetheless quickly become available.

THERE'S A CERTAIN charm in a small congregation. For one thing, it's easy for the rabbi to get to know all the members by name, including their children (and sometimes even their relatives). And when the congregation is new and meeting in the warmth and intimacy of members' homes, as was the case with Temple Shalom for the first two years, the members are more open to experimentation. An example of this was the congregation's receptivity to my suggestion that one Shabbat service each month be a creative service, developed and organized by a different member each time and reflecting what that member felt would be meaningful to the member and the congregation as a whole. The congregant could call upon others — including myself — for help, or could put the entire service together independently. These services were delightful and sometimes very moving. Some congregants closely followed the traditional liturgy, with readings from different sources interspersed among the prayers; others featured original prayers written by the congregant. Some services were mostly musical; others were poetic or philosophical. Every month they were eagerly awaited by the congregation, and attendance was most often exceptional. Once we moved to Council House (also known as the Jewish Golden Age Club), the creative services ceased, partly because the ambiance was not as warm and inviting to creativity, but also, I believe, because the creative wells were drying up.

In Winnipeg, I had difficulties with many of the other rabbis in the community, most of whom were orthodox, and with the Rabbinical Council, the *Vaad Ha-iyr*, which refused to accept me as a member unless I agreed to their orthodox terms. These terms were simple but profound. The council said I could join if I agreed to observe an orthodox lifestyle, which meant keeping kosher and observing Shabbat according to their very strict rules. This was not my idea of pluralism. I was a rabbi, ordained by the oldest yeshiva in the United States, and a member in good standing of the largest rabbinical organization in the world, so I felt entitled to belong to any local rabbinical council that represented the city in which I lived. They didn't see it that way and viewed me as a threat to the way they believed Judaism should be presented to the public. I told them that I did observe a kosher lifestyle and did observe Shabbat, but not as they felt I should. In fact, we kept a very kosher home, buying only kosher meat and having two sets of dishes, one for milk and one for meat. But I ate in restaurants; I avoided pork products and shellfish when eating out, but otherwise, I ordered what was on the menu. I also drove on the Shabbat; I did so as little as possible, but I had to get to services on the other side of town, and besides, I did not consider driving a car a desecration of the biblical injunction against lighting a fire on the Sabbath. My interpretation of the biblical prohibitions was not what my Winnipeg colleagues (and the orthodox in general) considered acceptable. Winnipeg was in those times the bastion of orthodoxy in western Canada, and the encroachment of Reform Judaism was anathema to the orthodox. Having once been orthodox myself, I could understand where they were coming from, and I had no desire to try to convince them to change their ways. My point was simply that Judaism, throughout its history, has always incorporated and included divergent views, the Talmud being the prime example of this principle, as exemplified by the schools of Hillel and Shammai, which were often in disagreement. I put my arguments to them, but to no avail. I was never allowed to attend their meetings.

On occasion I debated in public with one or two of Winnipeg's orthodox rabbis. My main opponent at these debates was Rabbi Yitzchak Witty who later became director of the Jewish Bureau of Education in Toronto. In spite of our differences, Rabbi Witty and I got along; years later, in Toronto, whenever we saw each other it was always a warm experience. One time he told me he was not well, and I could see that he wasn't in the best of shape. I suggested that he might want to begin exercising, and he replied that this wasn't for him. So I said to him, in a good-humoured way, "Yitz, don't you realize that it's a *mitzvah* [good deed] to keep oneself healthy, and exercise promotes life, and the Torah teaches us that we should always choose life? In fact," I went on, "the Talmud says that every Jew should learn to swim." He looked at me, paused for a moment to think, and replied, "I don't know how to swim, and I have some fear of water." I responded that I would be happy to teach him and would do so in a large public facility — Garnet Williams Community Centre in Thornhill — that had a lap pool, which is a pool where one swims lengths for exercise and where the water is never more than about four and a half to five feet deep. This meant, I explained to Yitz, that at any time, he could stand up and his head would be above water. He thanked me for the offer and said that if he decided to learn to swim, he would call me. I never heard from him, and a few years later he passed away.

IN THE FALL of 1971, the prime minister of what was then the Soviet Union, Alexei Kosygin, made a state visit to Ottawa. His visit prompted a reaction from the Canadian Jewish Community, because of the USSR's treatment of Jews, who were not permitted to leave that country. A call came out for a protest demonstration to be held in front of the Parliament Buildings, consisting of a twenty-four-hour vigil and led by rabbis from all denominations of Jewry across Canada. Approximately seven thousand people showed up and marched in the streets. As I recall, the demonstration's lead rabbi was Gunther Plaut of Holy Blossom Temple in Toronto. Rabbi Plaut was one of the foremost Reform rabbis in the Reform Movement, a man of impeccable reputation, and his congregation was a leader in social action.

There was no doubt in my mind about going to the protest rally. My only problem, given my financial situation, was how to pay for the trip. As it was a common practice in such situations for a congregation to foot the bill, I called my president and asked him if the congregation would support me and pay my plane fare, about two hundred dollars. I would look after the lodging on my own. He said he would have to call some members of the board and see what the consensus was. He called me back an hour or so later and said that the members wished me well on my journey, but would not agree to pay or contribute toward my fare. I told him that somehow I would find the funds and that when I returned, I would submit the bill to the congregation, and asked him if he would personally support me in this action. He said he would not.

The demonstration in Ottawa was very moving and very meaningful. We did a round-the-clock vigil, taking shifts and standing near the eternal flame that burns in front of the Parliament Buildings. When Premier Kosygin arrived, we rushed to his car holding high placards and chanting, "Let my people go!"

Upon returning to Winnipeg, I submitted my bill to the president. He called a board meeting on the same night that a local radio station interviewed me for over an hour about my experience in Ottawa. The congregation received considerable exposure that evening, but no one on the board heard the interview because of the meeting. A few days later I received a letter, signed by the president on behalf of the board, censuring me for my actions and upholding their earlier decision to not pay for my fare. To say I was incensed would be an understatement. I told the president that I was going to send a letter to every member of the congregation explaining what had transpired, and that I would include in my letter the letter from the board.

The next day, a former president of the congregation, Gabe Broder, a true gentleman and a great supporter of Israel and the Jewish people, called me and asked if we could meet the next day for breakfast. We met at the Pancake House on Pembina highway and, over pancakes and coffee (the best in the West), I outlined for him, step by step, all the events of the past few days. Gabe completely supported my position and asked me if, before I sent off the letter to the congregation, I would be willing to come to a board meeting and present my case. I was reluctant to do this — pride got in the way — but nevertheless agreed to his request. The meeting was contentious and seemed to solve nothing, even though Gabe supported me as strongly as he could. I did not leave in a good mood.

A few days later I received another letter from the board, apologizing for their previous letter and commending me on my actions on behalf of Soviet Jewry. It was accompanied by a cheque to cover my expenses. Apparently, after I left, Gabe convinced them that what I had done was no less than what any self-respecting rabbi would have done in my situation, and that they should be proud that someone represented the congregation for such a worthy cause.

Following is the motion passed by the executive and sent to me:

Nov. 14/71

Whereas:
Temple Shalom joins with the rest of World Jewry in urging the Government of the Soviet Union to allow the Jews of the Soviet Socialist Republic to live as Jews and to emigrate,

And Whereas:
Temple Shalom congratulates Canadian Jewry on its peaceful and organized demonstration on behalf of Soviet Jewry during the visit of Premier Kosygin to Canada,

Therefore,

In accordance with the social action program of Temple Shalom, Temple Shalom commends its Rabbi and spiritual leader for his initiative and leadership in travelling to Ottawa and lending the support of Temple Shalom along with other Canadian Jews, in voicing our concern for our Jewish brethren in the Soviet Union,

Therefore,

The executive of Temple Shalom reaffirms its decision to reimburse the rabbi for his expenses incurred during his trip to Ottawa,

And Furthermore,

The executive urges all the members of Temple Shalom to support the actions of its Rabbi and executive by making a financial contribution to help cover said expenses.

Within a few months of our Ottawa demonstration, the Soviet Union began to slowly open its doors to Jewish emigration. Some of my colleagues and I like to think that our demonstration had something to do with this, but of course we realize that our action was only one small part of the worldwide pressure being put on the Soviet Union to change its policy.

ANOTHER AREA OF contention between the congregation and myself had to do with my position regarding gala evening events for *bar* and *bat mitzvahs*. I felt that evening celebrations should be modest, to avoid competition among families, which might adversely affect those of modest means. When I was *bar mitzvah*, my family and friends cooked and baked and provided a large number of guests with a delicious meal in the modest venue of our Talmud Torah, the building that belonged to the community and housed almost all of the religious and social events of the congregation. When my son, Meher, was *bar mitzvah* in Toronto, once again family and friends prepared the food, and the venue was a relative's home. This kind of experience had been common among my friends in Regina, and this shaped my philosophy on *bar/bat mitzvahs* and brought me into conflict with Temple Shalom. Members with means wanted an evening celebration with a dance and orchestra, to be held in a hotel ballroom or other venue of their choice. I explained my position to the board and encouraged them to adopt the policy I was recommending. They said they could not, as it was an infringement on the rights of members to celebrate in whatever manner was pleasing to them, and even if they did adopt this policy, it would have no teeth. I understood, and realizing it would be a losing battle I simply said that while I would do everything in my power to assure that each *bar/bat mitzvah* service was beautiful and meaningful, I could not, in good conscience, attend evening functions. I stuck to this policy for the five years that I served the congregation in Winnipeg, much to the chagrin of some members.

In later years, and after much reflection, I altered my position. I was influenced by a conversation with a friend, who suggested that life was so full of difficulties and sadness that once in a while, when the opportunity to rejoice presents itself, why not go for it, even if it does cost a substantial amount? I thought a lot about this, and concluded that he was right and people should celebrate in whatever manner pleased them. Life is short, and happy moments are to be cherished and proclaimed. Why didn't I see this sooner? In looking back, I can only think that early on in my rabbinate I did not have the maturity to fully appreciate what life is about. But I still balk when, on a rare occasion, I attend an evening *bar* or *bat mitzvah* celebration and find it over-done and ostentatious.

Another mistake I made while in Winnipeg was to join a "T Group" that comprised only members of my congregation. The "T" stands for "Therapy," and the groups are sometimes also referred to as "Sensitivity Groups." Such groups were in vogue in those days, and I led many myself, but in this case the leader was from outside the congregation and not Jewish. The group had initially formed without me, and had already been active for a few months when I asked to join, not in any leadership capacity, but simply as a member. In this way, the other members and I would be on an equal footing, and I thought we could get to know each other on deeper and more intimate levels. The group voted on this, and by consensus, I was admitted. Almost immediately, the group wanted me to open up and reveal my personal life. I tried to do this, and they tried to open up about their own lives. But somehow my presence was unhealthy for them and for me, and before long the group began to stall. I suppose that as I was their rabbi, they were not able to separate me from the title and were hesitant to reveal some of the nuts and bolts of their lives. And probably I, too, held back on my personal life. Since the purpose of the group was to be entirely open and, as the expression goes, "let it all hang out," my presence impeded its function. Before too long, I left, realizing that what Rabbi Davis had said many years before was true: "A rabbi is not a rabbi only when he is with other rabbis." My apologies to the members of that group for being a disrupting influence.

Members of Temple Shalom who were critical of me had one major complaint, which I heard again and again: "Rabbi, you don't listen!" Most of the time, the complaint came from women, for some reason I didn't quite understand. At first, in my naiveté, I would ask them to tell me again what they were saying; perhaps the second time I would hear it better. This didn't seem to help. Then I tried repeating back to them, often word for word, what they were saying. As I had a pretty good memory, they would agree that these were indeed their words. But this didn't help either. The same criticism kept coming at me. Finally it dawned on me that I was hearing them very clearly but that I disagreed with what they were saying. For example, regarding *bar mitzvah* celebrations: "Rabbi, you should attend all *bar mitzvah* celebrations in the evening and not be critical of how they are done." Since I was in fact critical of this, I did not hold back on informing my congregation of my position. And when this was brought up to me, I acknowledged what was being said and then went on to defend my position, whereupon they would continue to say I wasn't listening. I would then reply, "Yes, I am listening, I do hear what you are saying, and I disagree." This pattern repeated itself on different issues when individuals or groups didn't like what I was doing or not doing, or saying or not saying. Finally, I gave up trying to defend my position and simply retorted, "I hear you. I disagree. Let's agree to disagree." When they saw that they weren't going to convince me, as a final jab they would say, "Rabbi, you're stubborn!" To which I would reply, "No, I'm not stubborn. I'm persistent." (Actually, sometimes I am stubborn.)

ONE DAY, AS I sat in my office at the University of Manitoba, there was a knock on my door. I said, "Come in," and two young men entered, dressed in saffron robes. They introduced themselves by Hindu names and asked me if I had heard of Hari Krishna. I told them that I had some familiarity with the organization, and this seemed to please them. They said that they and a few others of their group would like to come to my home that evening and cook dinner for my family and five of them. Our only obligation would be to provide the food; we could sit back and relax while they did the rest. I was a bit leery but also wondered whether they would eat at all if I refused. So I called Shula and we decided to accept their offer, after which I went out and bought food according to their specifications.

The group showed up at our home around 7:00 p.m. (it was a Friday evening, so we were going to share our Shabbat with them) and began preparing and cooking. They completely took over the kitchen. On two or three occasions, they took meditation breaks while food cooked on the stove. They sat on the carpet in our living room, chanting and talking, while Meher, who was then two years old, wandered among them, curious about what he was seeing and trying to be friendly. Not once did any of the group acknowledge his presence. No one smiled at him or said hello or reached out a hand. They were totally preoccupied with themselves and with the grand repast soon to be delivered.

By nine o'clock, they still hadn't finished cooking, the kitchen was a mess, and Shula, Meher, and I were starving. (It being Shabbat, we let Meher stay up late.) We were concerned about the condition of our kitchen, but they reassured us that everything was going to be fine, and in just a little while we would eat. At one point Shula and I retreated to the bedroom, sat down, and discussed throwing the whole bunch out. We were angry at the way they were treating Meher and at the damage taking place on one of our counters.

Finally, at about 10:00 p.m., dinner was ready. They ate voraciously, as it appeared this was their only meal of the day. The meal, entirely vegetarian, was decent but certainly not gourmet. By 11:00 p.m., it was all over. The kitchen was in a shambles, a pot was burned, and the counter was in need of repair. They had cooked more than what was needed and, with our consent, took the leftovers with them, possibly part of their strategy so that they would have something to eat for breakfast. Shula and I never begrudged them the food. It was, after all, a *mitzvah* to feed the hungry. But we vowed, given the disrespect with which we and our home were treated, to never again allow the Hari Krishna to visit us.

While on the subject of food: Shula and I had decided to keep a strictly kosher home so that any Jew would feel comfortable dining at our table. Toward the end of our sojourn in Winnipeg, we invited a visiting friend who was an orthodox rabbi to dinner. While I assured him everything was kosher, he said he would appreciate if he could have a vegetarian meal. In effect, he was saying that he didn't trust that our kosher home was as kosher as he needed it to be. This incident made it clear to us that no matter how kosher we kept our home, no orthodox Jew was going to eat in it without imposing additional conditions. So Shula and I decided that we would eat in our home the same as we were eating outside of our home: no biblically forbidden foods (red meat only if it is from an animal that both chews its cud and has a cloven hoof, and seafood only if it has both fins and scales), but nothing more strict than that. This is still my practice today.

GIVEN THE FINANCIAL state of Temple Shalom, we did not initially have our own Torah. When we needed a Torah for Shabbat morning services, the High

Holidays, and at other times, we borrowed one, though I no longer recall from where; perhaps it was the YMHA (Young Men's Hebrew Association). Then I learned that a considerable number of Torahs had been rescued from the Nazis in Czechoslovakia and were being housed at the Westminster Synagogue in London, England. They were available for the small fee of $300 to any congregation that would give them a good home. The board of Temple Shalom approved the purchase and was later informed that a Torah had been selected for them and would be shipped to Toronto at some point in the near future.

I sent a letter to Rabbi Davis, my contact person in New York who would facilitate our procurement of the Torah.

> Rabbi Jerry Steinberg,
> 18 Purdue Bay,
> Winnipeg, Manitoba,
> Canada
> July 20/69

Dear Rabbi Davis, Shalom,

I am most pleased to enclose a Money Order in the amount of $300.00 (U.S. Currency) for the acquisition of a Sefer Torah from the Westminster Synagogue in London, England. My congregation will of course also assume responsibility for the shipping expenses which may be sent C.O.D. or in any other manner suitable to the sender. I would like to request that the Torah parchment be between 18 & 22 inches as per your recommendation that this be stated clearly in this letter. If possible we would like to receive as much information as is possible on the background of this Torah. By this I mean not only the name of the city from which it comes, but if such information is available, the name of the synagogue with some it its history. The presentation of this Torah will be a major event in our Temple & we hope also in the general Jewish community. So whatever information you can supply us with will be greatly appreciated.

The Torah may be sent to the following address:

> Temple Shalom,
> Mr. Hy Cohen,
> 957 Beaverbrook Street,
> Winnipeg 9, Manitoba,
> Canada.

I wish to thank you on behalf of my congregation for the help and direction which you have given us in this holy matter. It was a great pleasure meeting you & I shall look forward to seeing you again on my next visit to New York.

Warmest wishes and blessings,
Rabbi Jerry Steinberg

P.S. I thought you might like to know that the money was collected from the members of my congregation rather than from just one person. The congregation felt that obtaining such a Torah was a great honour & they wanted to participate in the *mitzvah*. It was a very dramatic response.

The news quickly spread through the congregation, and we were all excited to know we would soon have our very own Torah. In Jewish circles, the advent of receiving a Torah is a case for considerable rejoicing. Usually a Torah, which is written over a period of about nine months, is donated by a wealthy individual, often to honour someone of his or her choosing. I say "by a wealthy individual" because a new Torah can cost, depending on its size, anywhere from about $20,000 to $50,000. Producing such a Torah is highly labour intensive, and the scribe must be very skilled, not only in the writing itself, but even in the preparation of the ink. And he must be very careful as he writes, for a single mistake means rewriting the entire section that he is working on.

On the eve of Yom Kippur in 1969, the president of the congregation received a message that our Torah would arrive the next morning. "Of all times," I thought. "On Yom Kippur, the holiest day in the Jewish calendar. How appropriate!" The next day, the president and one or two members of the congregation went to the airport to pick up the Torah. Meanwhile, I was conducting Yom Kippur services at Council House, hoping that the Torah would arrive in time for that part of the morning service where it is read. Everyone knew what was happening, and there was a buzz throughout the congregation. God must surely have been smiling upon us that morning. About twenty minutes before the Torah service, the president walked in carrying the Torah. I could hardly contain myself. It was placed in the *Aron Kodesh* (ark), and later in the afternoon brought out to be read. (The Torah we had on loan had already been prepared for the morning service.) The Torah was very large, and the script clear and easy to read. After the afternoon reading, instead of the usual ritual of someone carrying the Torah among the worshippers to be kissed, I brought the Torah to the closest person sitting in the assembly, and it was passed throughout the entire congregation, some hundred or more persons, so that everyone could hold and kiss it. We had adopted an orphan, a survivor of the Holocaust, and it was safe in our arms.

Each year at the congregation's annual general meeting, I gave an overview of my thoughts on our activities of the past year. In my May 1970 report, my comments included this reference:

> Torah Dedication:
> Few events since the beginning of our congregation have been met with such response as the receiving of our own Torah, rescued from the Nazis in Czechoslovakia, and preserved by the Westminster Synagogue in London, England. I believe that more than any other single event, it was the highlight of the year. The congregation's provision of the necessary funds to obtain the Torah was prompt and generous. The dedication itself was beautiful and moving and I felt a wonderful spirit in our congregation that enhanced the event immeasurably. I shall not say more on this, for I believe that the feelings in our hearts, from the executive meeting last spring to the Torah's arrival on Yom Kippur morning and our reading from it Yom Kippur afternoon, to its Dedication at Chanukah, are still in large measure with us. May we always be moved when we see this Torah taken from the ark.

At this same general meeting I tried to make clear to the congregation my ideas on the role of the rabbi:

> Each congregation has its own particular ideas of what a rabbi is supposed to do, and each rabbi has his own particular ideas of what a rabbi is supposed to do, both of these ideas often changing as rabbi and congregation grow together. Due to its very young age, our Temple has never had another rabbi by which there could be a basis for comparison. Likewise, I have never had another congregation, other than part-time pulpits. So in a sense we're both in the same boat.
>
> Now I would like to express to you very briefly a few of the ideas that I consider to be important in the role of rabbi.
>
> Let me say, as a general statement, that I believe one of my purposes is to make the congregation as independent of me as possible. By this I mean that the congregation should become so knowledgeable and dedicated to Judaism that each member will be deserving of the title "rabbi,"

and that we may indeed be a congregation of rabbis and not laymen. I, of course, realize that for a long time this will be the dream and not the reality. Nevertheless, it is towards this goal that I strive, and I would hope that the congregation would join me in this pursuit. Until this goal is achieved I am willing to serve as a conveyor of life's ceremonies — birth, marriage and so on — and also to be available as a source person in various areas. I am willing to serve as teacher, preacher, confidante and friend, to represent you in the community, to rejoice in your joys and to weep in your sorrows. I will take pride in your achievements and I'll sting you when I see the mark of apathy and nearsightedness. I'll also do those things that I consider necessary for my growth. I will take time to study, to write and to become involved in projects that I deem worthwhile, whether they are in the congregation or in the community at large. I will take time to pray and to meditate and to be with my family. One thing more — I will be your rabbi but I will not be your father. Some of you have suggested that I wait until you have learned to crawl before I expect you to walk or run. Some of you have suggested that I present potentially controversial things to you with a sugar coating, slowly and gently. All these suggestions I reject. I will not condescend to you; I will give you things straight, without the polish of a politician. Only in this manner can we relate as equals.

All these things then constitute my role as your rabbi, as I presently see it. I now await your ideas on the role of this congregation.

I then went on to talk about the relationship between a rabbi and his congregation:

The relationship between the rabbi and his congregation is always in a state of flux. This point is a very basic one and must be understood and appreciated by both rabbi and congregation if the relationship is going to exist and continue to develop. This state of flux not only exists between the rabbi and the group as a whole, but also between the rabbi and individual congregants.

During the past year, the flux has been more vigorous than in the previous two years. While I have enjoyed deepening my relationship with you as a group, and in several cases individually, this deepening has not been without its strains and tensions. At times you have elevated me and given me reason to sing, and at other times you have depressed me and made me very angry. No doubt there are those among you who have been angry with me. Some of the matters leading to this have not yet been resolved. Hopefully soon they will be. We can expect, though, that other issues will arise, bringing with them conflict, cooperation, disappointment, harmony and a whole host of feelings, attitudes and moods. Such is the nature of this relationship between rabbi and congregation. I'm sure it is our mutual desire that the conflicts and disappointments will diminish, and harmony and cooperation will increase. This, however, can only come about through a deeper understanding of each other, through a deeper appreciation of each other, and through a deeper love of each other.

As I look back upon my statement to the congregation on the role of the rabbi, I smile. Perhaps I was over-optimistic about the proximity of the Messianic age. Also, I wish I had a statement reflecting my congregation's view on the role of the rabbi, and I wish I'd had it at the beginning of my tenure with them. No doubt it would have been sobering and given me pause for reflection. More important, it would have helped me modify my views and be more effective in my role, assuming of course that I would have listened. However, as I noted in my address, both the congregation and I were young and inexperienced. True, I took the required course in practical rabbinics at my yeshiva, but it hardly touched upon the myriad situations a rabbi in the pulpit has to deal with. I would have been better prepared had I spent a few years under the wing of a senior rabbi in an established congregation.

One challenge that I don't think any amount of preparation would have helped me with was how to explain to the members of a congregation that their rabbi is not an employee, at least not in the usual sense. Yes, they pay the rabbi's salary and expect him or her to fulfill certain functions according to a job description, but the demands they can make of their rabbi are limited. For example, no congregation has the right to preview a rabbi's sermon for approval. The role of a rabbi, and indeed any clergyperson, is unique. The rabbi is comforter, source of inspiration, critic, counsellor, spokesperson to the Jewish and non-Jewish community, pastor, overseer of adult's and children's Jewish education, interfaith representative, and much more. In all that he or she does, the rabbi is expected to show leadership. For the congregation, this may create a conundrum: If you pay someone, should you not have the right to tell that person what to do? Why should that individual be given any more or less consideration than an employee in any other job? Some may argue that for the rabbi, work is a *calling* and not just a job. Others reply that this may well be the case with other professions as well, such as medicine. And so, I still feel I have never found a satisfactory way to explain why a rabbi is not an "employee" as customarily understood. When I talk to my colleagues about this, they suggest that you have to be a rabbi to really understand. Perhaps so. However, I like to think that maybe somewhere there is a very sensitive congregational president with extraordinary communication skills who can succeed where I, and all those I know of in my profession, have failed.

AROUND 1970, SWAMI Radha was passing through Winnipeg, and I invited her to address the congregation at a Shabbat service. She did so and was well received. Not long afterwards, building on her address, I announced from the pulpit that Shula and I would open our home every other Tuesday evening for meditation and that everyone in the congregation was invited. The evenings would consist of my teaching meditation techniques, followed by discussion and refreshments. For the next two years, until we left Winnipeg, many people, Jewish and non-Jewish, came to our home for these gatherings—but not one person from the congregation ever showed up, not even my closest friends and allies. To this day I have not been able to figure that one out. Not one! It seemed to defy the laws of chance.

My friendship with Swami Radha remained strong, and every summer when we were living in Winnipeg, Shula and I returned to the ashram to give classes. The summers were glorious. What could be better than living in paradise and teaching what we loved? When Meher came into this world, he of course accompanied us on our summer excursions, receiving abundant affection from everyone around. Earlier, we had asked Swami Radha if she would be Meher's godmother, to which she happily consented.

Although Shula was the one giving the courses on dreams, following along on Swami Radha's dream methodology, the subject was also of considerable interest to me. As a young boy, I was always an avid dreamer. I recalled dreams with ease, but never gave much thought to interpreting them until my sojourn at the ashram, where Swami Radha introduced us to her technique of interpretation, which relied heavily on free association. She would ask the dreamer what he or she associated with the symbols appearing in the dream and, through discussion, help the dreamer arrive at an interpretation, with her input. The technique was often quite effective and helped people obtain insight into their lives. This is the method by which Shula and I worked on our dreams every day during our two-year residence at the ashram.

Beginning at about the age of nine or ten, I found that I often had what decades later came to be called "lucid dreams." A lucid dream is a dream in which the dreamer is aware he or she is dreaming. In my case, I would say to myself while in the dream state, "Hey, this is a dream. I can do anything I want and get away with it." At that time in my life there were mainly three things I desired: to drive a car, to fly, and to have sexual relations with women. When I became aware that I was dreaming, I would direct myself to a car, which somehow was always around; the keys would be in the ignition and off I would go — no worries about accidents or cops or anything else. Or I would find myself on the roof of a high building and, knowing it was a dream, jump off, spread my arms and, like an eagle, soar into the wild blue yonder (for some reason I was never able to get above the clouds). As puberty arrived, I could find in my dreams all the women I desired and never had to worry about my sexual advances being rejected — they were always willing, able, and beautiful.

I was a prolific lucid dreamer until my early twenties, when I slowly began to lose this ability. I'm not certain why; perhaps, since I had many times over-satisfied my fantasies, sometimes even in reality, I didn't find the skill useful any longer. It wasn't until the incident with Shula and her headaches that I started to realize that dreams could be directed for specific purposes, such as healing, and that one could program dreams before going to sleep. This awareness came to me after my *boba* dream, which indicated that questions could be answered and issues resolved while a person was asleep, such answers coming from realms of reality beyond normal cognitive processes. At this point I regretted having let my lucid dream skills recede, since I saw uses for lucid dreaming at age thirty-one that were not in my consciousness at age twenty-two. This became increasingly evident to me as I delved further into this unusual aspect of dreaming. I tried in various ways to recapture my ability, but with only occasional success, as for example for the very ill young friend of the ashram for whom I was able to recommend wheat grass. What became, and remains, clear to me is that dreams are a key to resolving issues in all areas of life, including medicine, science, religion, and social intercourse. I am confident that as research into this subject progresses, the efficacy of the dream state will rise above anything conceived of by Freud or Jung, and that mankind's well-being will be enhanced in proportion to such research efforts.

> I must sleep now
>   in a different way
>   sleep
>   to know
>   to understand

> sleep
>> to pull the pearl
>>> from its bed
>> and set it
>>> in a necklace of stars

One other experience I have had in dreams many times over the years is hearing music. Most of the time the music is classical, and sometimes I awaken and remember a few bars of what seems to me music I've never heard before, although I can't be certain of this. While hearing such music is always an exciting and uplifting experience, it is also frustrating, in that I am not able to write down what I remember because I have no training in any aspect of music, let alone composition. I sometimes feel that had I been afforded such training, I would have become a musician and devoted my life to composing. I do, however, take considerable satisfaction in my son becoming a professional musician with a flair for writing songs, some of which I believe are excellent. Also, my father in his early years played the saxophone.

There is another facet of my dream experiences, one that has occurred on and off throughout my life and for which I still don't have an adequate explanation. This is where I have a dream within a dream within a dream. In other words, I am dreaming, then I awaken—only I awaken into a lighter level of dreaming. Then I awaken again, into a still lighter level of dreaming. Then finally I wake up completely. I can only conclude that there seem to be different levels of dreaming, the significance of which eludes me. Perhaps there are many levels of consciousness, beginning with the awake state, that also apply to the dream state. To explain this, I imagine a straight horizontal line that I call *consciousness*. There are many levels above this line, each with its own reality. There are also many levels below this line, also each with its own reality. The levels below are an expansion of the sleep state, while the levels above are an expansion of the awake state. At present, more seems to be known about awake states of expanded consciousness (creative states, "in the zone" states, psychic states, and so on) than about the asleep states of expanded consciousness, although there are some Jewish mystics who speak of sleep as a state in which a curtain is drawn back to reveal other realms of reality. Are these realms spoken of by the mystics the same as what I'm calling dreams within dreams? I don't know.

My childhood dream experiences, in combination with my work on dreams at the ashram, brought me one day to a fresh insight about Judaism. It is because of dreams that the Jewish people were spared going out of existence.

If we are to take the Joseph story in the bible seriously, then Joseph, as a result of his dreams, was taken captive into Egypt and later saved the Jewish people from starvation by bringing them to Egypt, where there was food and shelter. All this because he was able to interpret Pharaoh's dreams. Then, four hundred years later, having greatly multiplied, the Jewish people made their exodus from Egypt, and so began a new and highly significant phase in Jewish history, in which the commandments, including our major holidays and festivals, were given to and initiated by Moses. All because of a dream.

IN 1971, DURING one of our summer stays at the ashram, my parents came to visit us. It was their first time in the interior of British Columbia, and they loved the scenery. After a week, Shula, Meher, and I, along with my mom and dad, packed into my car, and off we went on a tour of the province, or at least a small part of it. Our first stop was in Trail, where there lived someone my dad had met years before while being treated for arthritis and polio at the Banff Hot Springs. The gentleman's name was Bruno, and it was a warm reunion. From there we headed for the Okanagan Valley, an area famous for its fruit. It was the peak of peach season, and for a small fee we went into an orchard, where we plucked ripe peaches from the branches. We took a large bag filled to the brim with us to the car, and had eaten them all by the time we arrived in Calgary several hours later. I have not been able to fully enjoy a peach since that day, because nothing I come across in supermarkets or even fruit specialty stores comes close to what we tasted on that occasion. If there ever was such a thing as a Platonic ideal for a peach, it would have to be a product of the Okanagan Valley.

In Calgary we stayed with Shula's relatives, Ben and Sima Herman, survivors of the Holocaust and the nicest people one could hope to meet. On our second evening with them, the discussion got around to how we came to name Meher. Shula and I told our hosts that shortly after our son was conceived, Shula had a dream in which an old man came to her and told her to give him the name of Meher (giver of light). He further informed her that when Meher grew up, he would be a builder. Ben and Sima listened very carefully to the story. Then they asked Shula if she could describe the man in the dream. She described him as best she could, and I saw Ben and Sima blanch. She was describing a deceased relative of the family, someone whom Ben and Sima had known but who had died before Shula was born. And no photos of him survived the Second World War. We are still unclear about the "builder" part, but Meher is young, and this may yet unfold.

> Fingers reach
>> from distant years
>> to impart wisdom
>> fingers
>>> needing to inscribe
>>>> once more
>>> upon a new heart
>>>> the destiny of an old soul

When I first came to live in Winnipeg, my parents introduced me to one of their customers, Clayton Purcell, who was studying for the priesthood. Clayton and I took an immediate liking to each other and became friends. Some years later, shortly after I became a rabbi, I received an invitation to attend Clayton's ordination at one of the large Catholic churches in the city. I was honoured to be there, and Clayton acknowledged my presence in his ordination speech. After that, we lost touch for a while and then regained contact when I came to Winnipeg as rabbi of Temple Shalom. We would meet every once in a while and engage in theological discussions as well as just ordinary chitchat about our lives. Then I lost touch with him again, this time for many years, as he was posted in some remote part of the province. Finally, several years ago, I looked him up when I was visiting Winnipeg and found him in a Catholic retirement residence on River Avenue. I walked in one day while he was organizing a choir for Christmas carols. We embraced, talked briefly, and promised to stay in touch. Not long after, I visited him again, and this time found him in a wheelchair. He had undergone open-heart surgery and had to be very careful about his activities. We had lunch together in a nearby restaurant and updated each other on our lives. I remember him saying to me that somebody should be doing a story on the rabbi and the priest being buddies and having a meal together. After that, I saw him only one more time, when I returned from a trip to Israel in 2005 and brought him a rosary and cross from a monastery on Lake Kinneret (Sea of Galilee). I have since spoken to him a few times on the phone and hope, all being well, I'll see him again the next time I'm in Winnipeg.

WINTERS IN WINNIPEG can be brutal. This creates challenges when a rabbi has to do a funeral and the temperature is thirty degrees or more below zero Fahrenheit, much worse if the wind is howling. First, it takes special machinery to open the ground for a grave, as the earth is frozen solid like stone. Then, when the mourners take shovels to cover the coffin, the thud of the frozen earth on the wood sends additional shivers through their bodies. On some days, it was so cold that to take the time to fully cover the coffin (a practice in many Jewish communities) would have endangered those present, especially older folk, so the covering was left to the gravediggers and their front-end loaders. My experience growing up in Regina taught me how to dress for such occasions. Admittedly, my outfit wasn't much of a fashion statement, consisting of a parka with a hood, a toque, thick gloves, wool trousers, galoshes, and a scarf, but I was warm.

Speaking of the weather, on January 17, 1972, my parents celebrated their fortieth wedding anniversary with a party at our home in Fort Richmond. At about 2:00 p.m. on that day, a storm began to make its way into Winnipeg, and by 6:30, when dinner was to begin, there was a full-scale blizzard in progress, with very limited visibility. Yet, in spite of this, almost thirty guests arrived, braving the elements to honour my parents, who were dearly loved by one and all. Only two couples didn't show up, and one of those came close but made a wrong turn and got lost. Shula and I couldn't get over the fact that so many came, given the conditions, and we felt it was an extraordinary tribute to my mother and father.

One small and humourous incident occurred later on that evening as the celebration began to wind down and people prepared to leave. Among the guests was my uncle Jack, who was married to my father's sister, Jean; the couple ran a ladies' ready-to-wear store in St. Boniface, just around the corner from my parents' menswear store. Jack, a Holocaust survivor who was at that time in his sixties, was rather stern and pulled no punches when he expressed himself. But behind his gruff exterior was a man of compassion and humour. On this particular evening, when Jack went out to start the car and warm it up for Jean, the engine wouldn't turn over, not unusual in such freezing conditions. He came back into the house and announced that the car wouldn't start. So my dad and I went out with Jack to see if we could help. Indeed, it wouldn't start, no matter what we did — at which point Jack opened the hood and began looking around. My father said to him, "Jack, what are you doing?"

My uncle replied, "I'm looking under the hood."

"Do you know what you're looking for under the hood?" asked my father.

To which Jack retorted, "No, but isn't this what you're supposed to do when you can't start the engine?"

My father and I started laughing, Jack closed the hood, and we all came back inside. Then one of our guests said he had booster cables and went out to give Jack a boost.

Our favourite eating place in Winnipeg was Simon's Deli on North Main Street. When my parents took us out to dine, it was most often at Simon's. The ambiance was about as simple and Spartan as one could imagine, but the food was exceptional. Although the restaurant was called Simon's, the owner was Mr. Solomon, and his wife and daughter-in-law were the cooks. It was one of the few restaurants I've been to where the term "home cooking" genuinely applied. Mr. Solomon can best be described in appearance as a smaller version of the actor Charles Lawton, jowls and all. The family's origins were in Romania, as are my family's, so the cooking reminded me of what my *boba* used to serve back in Regina. When we sat down at a table, Mr. Solomon would bring us the menu and five minutes later come to take our order. The dialogue would go something like this:

Mr. Solomon (with a Yiddish accent): So, you know vat you vant to order?

One of us (usually my dad or me): What do you recommend today, Mr. Solomon?

Mr. Solomon: You vant ze brisket or ze chicken (no question mark).

One of us (after consultation): We'll take the brisket.

Mr. Solomon: Ze chicken iss better.

One of us (after consultation): Okay, we'll take the chicken.

Mr. Solomon: Kasha or potatoes?

One of us (after consultation): Potatoes.

Mr. Solomon: Ze kasha iss better.

One of us (after consultation): Okay, we'll take the kasha.

Ten minutes later our meals arrived on large plates, so full that the food was almost falling off. Unless one was a lumberjack, it was not possible to finish everything, so when Mr. Solomon came by to pick up our dishes, he would often see that there was still food on them.

Mr. Solomon: Vat's ze matter? You don't like mine food?

One of us: The food was wonderful, Mr. Solomon. But so much!

He would take away the plates, not looking terribly pleased, and return a few minutes later.

Mr. Solomon: Vat you vant for dessert?

One of us: What do you have, Mr. Solomon?

Mr. Solomon: Today ve haff prunes or *flomen* [Yiddish for prunes].

One of us (after consultation): Four prunes and one *flomen*.

There was never a time when we didn't repeat the routine—same main dish, same side dish, same dessert. We loved it.

Note: Occasionally, he recommended the brisket.

IN WINNIPEG, I was called upon one day to perform an unusual wedding. Most Jewish weddings take place in the late afternoon or early evening and occasionally around noon. This couple wanted to get married at the turning of the summer solstice — which, that year, took place at 1:13 a.m. The wedding party gathered late in the evening for a pre-celebration dinner at an upscale restaurant, then met at the bride's parents' home around midnight for cocktails and other refreshments. At 1:00 a.m. we assembled under the *chupah,* and I began the service, adjusting my pace so that the vows would be exchanged as the solstice was changing. After the ceremony, dessert was served, and guests mingled until about 3:00 a.m. It was my one and only solstice wedding.

IN ADDITION TO providing me with a source of income, my work at the University of North Dakota in Grand Forks became a significant part of my sojourn in Winnipeg, both spiritually and intellectually. At my first interview, I met with the dean of Arts and Science, Bernard O'Kelly, and the chairman of the Department of Religion, Gerry Potter. O'Kelly was a former minister, possibly Episcopalian, and, if I remember correctly, married to a Jewish woman; Potter was a Catholic priest. From the first moment, there was a chemistry between O'Kelly and me, an ease and mutual respect that remained throughout my five years at the university. O'Kelly was of medium build with reddish hair, a man of considerable energy who had no problem speaking his mind. Potter was tall and slim. I often stayed overnight at his home when bad weather made driving dangerous, and I noticed a formidable rifle on one of his walls. He told me he hunted deer.

The Department of Religion consisted of three full-time professors: Gerry Potter, Al Mattson, and Ben Ring, who was chairman of the Department of Philosophy with, I believe, a cross-appointment in the Department of Religion. My job would be to teach a course in basic Judaism; after some discussion with O'Kelly and Potter, I was given the title "Assistant Visiting Professor of Religion."

Grand Forks had a very small Jewish population; only three of my students over a five-year period were Jewish. The others were primarily, if not entirely, from Christian backgrounds, and most had never had any exposure to Judaism. I enjoyed my students, and besides teaching basic Jewish concepts, I was able to dispel myths and stereotypes about the Jewish people, such as all Jews being wealthy (I was an example to the contrary) and Jews being of dark complexion with pronounced noses (I'm fair-skinned with a normal nose).

The university required that all students take exams at exam time. This may at first glance seem obvious, but I objected to having to give exams on the grounds that they only show a part of what a student knows, and also because some good students get very nervous at exam time and don't perform well even though they know their stuff. Potter understood my position but said this was how the university functioned, and there were no exceptions. I got around this one by having the students write essays and weighting the essays equally with the exams, that is, fifty per cent essay and fifty per cent exam. This seemed acceptable to the university.

In 1968 a problem arose about a month before the beginning of the second semester, which started towards the end of January. O'Kelly and Potter asked me to come to a meeting in O'Kelly's office. The three of us sat around a small table with coffee and tea on it, and O'Kelly launched into what he wanted to discuss.

O'Kelly: Steinberg, what are you going to teach for the second semester?
Steinberg: I have no idea. I haven't thought about it.
O'Kelly: Neither have we.
(Pause. Silence. We look at each other. Finally O'Kelly breaks the silence.)
O'Kelly: What would you like to teach?
Steinberg: I don't know.
O'Kelly: We need to know today, because the second semester starts in a few weeks, and we have to let students know well in advance what you're doing, so they can register for your class. Any thoughts?
Steinberg (swallowing hard): Well, I don't know if you would be open to this, but how about a course in comparative mysticism and meditation?
O'Kelly: Steinberg, that's the biggest bunch of nonsense, rot, quackery, and a few more words that I won't say in polite company that I've ever heard of, but I think the students would love it.
Steinberg: You sure?
O'Kelly: Let's do it!
(Potter nods in assent.)

With those words, O'Kelly endeared himself to me ever after. In my opinion, he was a great man, and before leaving the university five years later, I reminded him of that meeting and told him of my warm and respectful thoughts.

On the first day of the second semester, at about 1:45 p.m., I went to the Department of Religion's office on the second floor of the Arts and Science building to find out in which room my class was being held. The secretary told me the room number and gave me a class list, which I put into my briefcase without bothering to look at it. I walked down the long hall, scanning the room numbers for 212, which was to be my room for the two-hour lecture beginning at 2:00 p.m. I passed room 210 and saw, outside the doorway of the next room, a long line of students. Thinking this couldn't possibly be my room, even though the number sequence suggested that it was, I didn't bother to look at the number and continued on down the hall to the next room, which was clearly marked 214. I turned back and looked at the number on the previous room. Sure enough, it was 212. I tried to enter the room, but was told by a student standing near the front of the line that I should go to the back of the line and wait my turn. I said I was the prof, and the students made way for me to enter. Entering the room was difficult, as not only were all of the thirty or forty seats taken, but every bit of floor space was also occupied by students sitting and waiting for the class to begin. I carefully stepped over several of them to reach my desk, only to find that someone had taken my chair. The only place left for me to sit was on top of the desk. And this is from where I conducted my classes for the next five years.

Let me note that the only public announcement of this class had been a notice on a bulletin board somewhere in the building. O'Kelly had said it couldn't be included in the annual calendar that contained all the classes for the year, since that was printed well before the first semester. Also, the overwhelming response had nothing to do with me since, as a visiting professor, I was virtually unknown on campus. Although it is true I had taught a class in Judaism in the first semester, and although I believe I did a decent job of teaching that class, it was not the kind of stellar performance that would have made me a household word at the university. There had to be, I concluded after some thought, another reason.

In a nutshell, I believe there was a spiritual hunger on the campus. It was disguised in the rather uninhibited use of LSD, pot, and whatever other psychotropic substances the students could get their hands on. They were influenced by what was happening in San Francisco (the "spring of the flower children" had happened several months earlier), and the shift from drugs to meditation that was spreading across the country. Drugs gave them an experience of altered consciousness, and when it was a positive experience, they felt they were touching a realm of reality not accessible to them in normal states. The message coming through from various quarters, like Transcendental Meditation (TM) and Hari Krishna, was that these other realms of consciousness that gave spiritual satisfaction could be accessed by natural means. However, Grand Forks, North Dakota, was far from the cutting edge of the innovative spiritual experimentation that was happening among young people on the west coast. My students had heard about the movement, but at that time, contact with it had not yet filtered down to the University of North Dakota campus, or for that matter, to most American campuses. I therefore believe that the stage was set for a course that included in its title the words *mysticism* and *meditation*. Bernard O'Kelly must have known this, and he was able to transcend his intellectual objections and allow me to teach a subject that he believed would be meaningful for the young men and women whose academic prowess he oversaw.

So I sat, semi-cross-legged, on top of the desk, and began my lecture. In the following years, the course was always oversubscribed. Only seniors and juniors were permitted to register, on a first-come basis, while sophomores and freshman had to wait their turn. To the best of my knowledge, "Comparative Mysticism and Meditation" was the first credit course of its kind at any university in the United States.

Each class was divided into two sections. For the first hour and a half, I lectured on trans-cultural and trans-denominational mysticism and mystical practices. For the last half hour I taught the class a meditation exercise — a new one each week. The students practised the exercise in class for ten to twenty minutes, after which I asked anyone who so wished to describe his or her experience. I then took questions. My homework assignment, in addition to readings like *The Varieties of Religious Experience* by William James, *Siddhartha* by Herman Hesse, and *Childhood's End* by Arthur C. Clarke, was for each student to practise the meditation technique at least once a day for ten to fifteen minutes until next week's class. At the next class, the students were asked to hand in reaction reports on what, if anything, they had experienced while meditating. I specifically requested that they not put their names on these reports, as I didn't want a desire for marks to colour their accounts. They complied on all accounts. Over the duration of my teaching at the university, I collected these reports, and they have had a profound influence on my thinking about meditation.

From my first contacts with Swami Vishnudevananda and Swami Radha, I had the impression that meditation was difficult to master. Through my own attempts at meditation, especially at the ashram, this impression deepened. Even though I practised mediation almost every day for two years, and even though at times I broke through and had deep and profound experiences, I rarely found it easy. My most consistent benefit was a feeling of peace and contact with something at a metaphysical level that was beyond my normal consciousness. I realized that even if this was all that I, or anyone else, could receive from the meditative state, it was a lot. I was also intrigued by the possibility of *peak experiences*, a phrase used by psychologist Abraham Maslow to describe unusual and extraordinary states of awareness that, once achieved, were often transformative to the individual but were usually difficult to come by. These were the states I was exposing my class to in the trans-cultural literature I was giving them to read. And these were the states talked about, and sometimes experienced, by myself and others who lived at the ashram. At times in the readings these states were equated with enlightenment, although some in the field of mysticism believe that enlightenment goes beyond this. My view is that enlightenment has many dimensions and no one, including Moses, Jesus, Mohammad, and the saints of the east, has tapped into all of them. Experiences of enlightenment are not easy to come by, and no one, in my opinion, has the last word on what these states are all about.

What I learned from my students — few, if any, of whom had ever practised meditation before — was that if a person wasn't ripe, that person was unlikely to have a profound meditative experience, no matter how hard he or she tried. I learned this from the reaction reports, some of which touched on experiences I had read about in the great mystical literature of the ages and sometimes encountered in my own meditative adventures. What *ripeness* means is a readiness to have a significant mystical experience — which could also mean an experience of enlightenment — as a result of mainly unconscious forces at play in the psyche or soul. To a person with this readiness, such an experience will occur with very little prompting, which is why some of my students had powerful experiences while others didn't. Rarely does one know at the conscious level that one is ready for such an experience, and in most instances it comes as a surprise.

It must also be said that meditative techniques are not the only modality for inducing mystical experiences. Among others are music, art, dreams, strong emotions, and even deep depression. In the nineteenth century, Rabbi Nachman of Bratslav once said that some individuals only reach transformative experiences when they are at the lowest ebb of their lives; that they have to reach bottom before they can rise anew. Or, in my terms, depression can be the modality and catalyst for ripeness, though certainly not the desired route.

I meditate
into realities unknown
that beckon
and draw my soul
to touch God

I cannot claim that the extraordinary experiences described by some of my students were indeed transformative: without names on the reaction reports, there was no way for me to follow up on the experiences. I can say that, if nothing else, the students were introduced to possibilities of expanded consciousness, and some of them benefited from their experiences. I think they came to realize that there are natural, drug-free means of achieving spiritual highs.

Below are a few examples of reaction reports from my students:

> It is the first time I reacted to a lab period. In past labs I had not been able to feel anything. However, this time I actually felt the light pouring through me.

> Your chant sent vibrations up and down my body and it felt very good. When I opened my eyes I felt spaced out, as though I had been smoking dope. It lasted for a couple of hours and I meditated during the week alone with even more lasting results.

> I had a feeling of complete relaxation when I allowed the light to invade my cranial cavity... My whole body just sparkled inside and it felt so good.

> As the light coursed through my body, I could feel my body glow. I felt very alive. It seemed I had an excess of energy—I could do anything. As the lab continued I began to tremble with excitement.

> I felt and still feel very refreshed and revitalized; my physical discomfort is still suspended. I am on surgical recuperation. I wonder how long this painlessness will last.

When I first arrived at the university, the third full-time member of the Department of Religion was Al Matson, a gentle and lovely man. He too had been a minister, but I don't recall from which Christian denomination. Al was the faculty member with whom I had the most in common, as he had a keen interest in mysticism. Also, like Gerry Potter, he would house me from time to time when the weather was bad. In our many after-class discussions, Al and I would wander far afield into the esoteric realms of religion. Like myself, he believed that the soul was separate from the body and that at death it entered a different domain of reality. Al's interest led him to the world of mediumship, and he attended seances from time to time. Unfortunately, about halfway through my appointment at the university, Al suddenly and unexpectedly passed away, and I was one of those asked to speak at his funeral. At one point in my eulogy, the lights in the church began to flicker. I had heard of some studies where it was claimed that the dead sometimes contact the living by means of electricity, so, looking up, I smiled and said, "Hi, Al!" There was a chuckle among many in attendance, some of whom I'm sure joined me in the greeting.

ONE DAY AN Arts and Science faculty meeting was held over lunch. I was invited to attend because, shortly after lunch, I was to deliver an annual lecture to the Arts and Science students. As we chatted over the meal, somehow the topic came around to the importance of silence, and I stated that I had found that most people had considerable difficulty staying quiet for even five minutes unless they were doing something. One or two of those present challenged me on this and thought I was overstating the case, so I suggested an experiment. Since my lecture was going to be on Siddhartha, and silence was a pillar of his life, I would begin with five minutes of silence. But, I said, if I was going to do this, I needed the co-operation of all the faculty present at the lunch. In other words, they too would have to remain silent and help restore order if things started to get out of hand. They agreed.

There were anywhere between six hundred and a thousand students in the large lecture hall; all I remember with certainty is that it was full. I sat near the podium, and after the introduction I walked up to the microphone, looked at the audience, checked my watch, and closed my eyes. Everything was still for about a minute, the students wondering what was going on. Then a soft murmur issued from the crowd, followed by a "shush," which led to another forty-five seconds or so of silence. Then a louder murmur, talking, and rustling. By the three-and-a-half-minute mark (I kept checking my watch), my fellow faculty members were busy trying to control the students, who were laughing and whispering as they fidgeted in their seats.

Finally, at exactly five minutes, I looked up, cleared my throat, and said, "Ladies and gentlemen, the past five minutes was the essence of my lecture." (The thought passed through my mind that I might sit down at this point, but I resisted the temptation.) "For Siddhartha, the subject of today's presentation, nothing was of greater importance than silence, not just five minutes like today, but five hours, five days, five months, and even five years." I talked for about forty-five minutes about various aspects of silence and other facets of Siddhartha's life. The audience was very silent and contained for the entire lecture.

After the lecture, the professors I had challenged at lunch acknowledged, all credit to them, that sitting in silence for five minutes was harder than they had ever imagined, for themselves as well as the students.

THERE ARE ALWAYS special relationships that develop between a teacher and his or her students. Each year at the University of North Dakota (and also at the University of Manitoba), certain students, for different reasons, stood out in my eyes, and bonds were formed. Once, I received a phone call at my home in Winnipeg from one of my North Dakota students, who told me that his sister, who was visiting him in Grand Forks, was having a problem and asked if they could drive up to Winnipeg for a consultation.

The next day, he brought his sister, and Shula and I sat down with them in our living room. Normally for a counselling session there would be no one present but the principals; however, the house was small, and Shula had nowhere to go except to lock herself in a bedroom or leave, which I didn't feel was fair. I had informed the sister and brother of this before they came up, and said that Meher would probably be taking his afternoon nap. They said they were fine with this arrangement.

The woman began to relate her story. Her opening statement set the tone for the next hour or more. "I'm pregnant by the Devil," she said casually. She went on, redundantly, to say that she was carrying the Devil's child. (I don't believe in the Devil, but this was her story.) How she had gotten pregnant by the Devil was somewhat unclear; she was nevertheless convinced that this was the case. I had her close her eyes, do some deep breathing, and then talk to the fetus she believed was growing in her womb. As she spoke to the fetus, four different personalities inside of her competed for turns to speak. I began to suspect that I might be dealing with a multiple personality disorder, although this particular term had not yet entered my vocabulary. I had witnessed individuals who practised channelling, so I was not deterred by unusual voices and personalities emerging from someone's mouth. I was also aware that when there was more than one voice, usually some voices were malevolent and some (perhaps only one) benevolent. In this instance, that was exactly the case: three voices expressed negativity and one tried to be a positive influence. As I worked with her, the three negative voices became one, and a competition developed between the negative voice and the positive voice. It was like a classic case of the war between good and evil as found in literature, religion, and the movies. I was aware that such voices, usually the negative ones, sometimes possessed psychic abilities, in particular telepathy and clairvoyance. I decided to take a chance and see if I could confuse and confound the negative voice; success would be a step toward defeating it.

I began by telling the negative voice that voices like itself often had psychic powers and asked whether this was so in its case. It replied that this was indeed so. Then, laying my trap carefully, I gave the woman a pad and pen and asked the voice to spell my Hebrew name for the woman, so she could write it down on the pad. (No one in the room, with the exception of Shula, knew my Hebrew name.) The woman's hand began to move on the pad, and she slowly wrote down Y, o, n, a. My Hebrew name is Yona, from the book of Jonah in the bible.

I realized that my scheme had temporarily backfired. I also knew, from my training at the ashram and other sources, that the display of psychic ability by a malevolent discarnate voice was a ploy to convince us of its superior status and thus gain control over its host (the woman) and its audience (the student, Shula, and me). So I confronted the voice more directly. I told it to leave the woman alone and return to wherever it came from, and that I was going to teach the woman the Divine Light Invocation as an antidote to its influence. At this point, the positive voice began to assert itself, assuring the woman that she was going to be fine. After the session ended, I did teach the woman the Divine Light Invocation and asked her to practise it each day for the next year.

About eight months later I received a call from my student, who told me that his sister was really pregnant and that she and her husband were looking forward with excitement to the birth of their first child. And I was informed, when the birth occurred, that mother and child were doing well.

I have kept the sheet of paper with my Hebrew name on it in my files.

Strange things happen in this business.

TOWARD THE END of my tenure at the University of North Dakota, I decided to hold a weekend workshop on inner growth, open to any students who might be interested. I had a brochure printed up and distributed to my class and to the rest of the Department of Religion. I used the Hebrew word *Kol* (meaning *voice* or *all*, depending on the Hebrew spelling); the cover page of the brochure read: *Kol — A New Experience in Inner Growth*. This was to be the first of many forays of mine into running a group for personal growth, later workshops included dreams and psychotherapy. The *Kol* brochure described the workshop as follows:

KOL is an all-encompassing approach to the process of inner growth. No dimension of human experience is foreign to *Kol* or outside its range of concern.

Man functions on many levels — social, psychological, spiritual and physical. All of these levels must work together harmoniously for man to realize his highest potential.

It is the goal of *Kol* to integrate these levels, to relate them one to the other, and to bring to the fore aspects of our nature that are essential to our growth.

To achieve its goal, participants in KOL will be involved in the following areas:

Sensitivity-Encounter experiences

Yoga

Meditation

Dreams

Sound

Dance and Creative Movement

Practice details and a short bio of myself followed, and the back page read, "It is the Inner Life which permeates our being."

The workshop was well attended, with about eighteen participants. In every workshop I have conducted over the years, I have always learned at least one new thing and often several. In the *kol* workshop, I learned something from a young woman that has served me well. We were discussing the topic of love, and I asked each participant to tell us his or her thoughts. What each had to say was different, with some overlap. When it was this young woman's turn, she told us that she loved everyone and then went on to say that she loved the whole world. When I probed and she talked more about love, she began to cry. She confessed that she was lonely and did not have any love in her life, and expressed an almost desperate desire to be loved. The people in the group gave her as much support as they could over the two-day workshop, and when it ended she was in better shape than when we began, although certainly this improvement was only temporary; her loneliness would remain until she found someone. What I learned is that when someone talks extensively about love in general, it's usually because they do not have love in particular in their lives. It is a sign that a deep personal need is going unfulfilled. I have encountered this dynamic over the years more times than I care to remember.

LATE ONE SUMMER, on our way back to Winnipeg from the ashram, we passed through Regina and stayed with my aunt Goldie, my cousin Sorrel's mother. I learned that Maharishi Mahesh Yogi was giving a lecture while we were there, so we attended. The auditorium was packed as we awaited the arrival of the maharishi. He eventually came on stage and sat down, surrounded by many bouquets of flowers. His talk lasted about an hour, during which he picked up one flower after another and plucked off the petals. By the end of the lecture he was surrounded by strewn petals covering the floor; I don't recall what he said, but I retain this clear image in my mind. I must have been distracted. After the talk, I was introduced to one of his followers who, upon learning I was a rabbi, asked me if I would like to meet the maharishi the following day at a venue in Lumsden.

Shula and I arrived at the venue and were greeted by the person who had invited us. In the foyer of the venue, a display of works written by the maharishi was set up, including translations of Hindu holy books like the *Bhagavad Gita*. A few minutes later, we were ushered into a room and introduced to the maharishi. He received us warmly and told me that I was the first rabbi he had ever met. He asked me some questions about Judaism, then I asked him some questions about meditation. Our dialogue went something like this:

> Jerry: What is the goal of meditation?
> Maharishi: The goal of meditation is God consciousness.
> Jerry: Is there anything higher than God consciousness?
> Maharishi: Yes. Cosmic consciousness is higher.
> Jerry: Is there anything higher than cosmic consciousness?
> Maharishi: Universal consciousness is higher than Cosmic consciousness.
> Jerry: Is there anything higher than universal consciousness?
> Maharishi: No. Universal consciousness is the highest.

I felt that the most important thing I learned from our meeting was that the goal of Transcendental Meditation (TM) was a spiritual connection and that all the other benefits of TM research — relaxation, reduced stress, better work performance, etc. — were spinoffs. It seemed to me that the spinoffs were inducements, emphasized because they spoke to the Western mind in a language it could relate to, whereas "spirituality" would only have attracted a very small audience. In other words, it was clever marketing. Some years later, Dr. Herbert Benson, a Harvard-trained cardiologist and one of TM's big guns, showed that by meditating and chanting the word "One" as a mantra instead of the mantras given by TM, one could achieve comparable results.

Today, when I give lectures or workshops on meditation, I stress that the goal is a connection with God, what in Hebrew is known as *d'veykut*. I say that the word "yoga" means "connection," and that all the exercises people do (known as *asanas*) are to give the practitioner a healthy body and particularly a healthy spinal cord and nervous system, so the practitioner is a more fit receptacle for spiritual awareness, knowledge, and power. In Judaism we call this the *Shefa* (divine influx).

Before I left the company of the maharishi, he told me that he would like to invite me to India to learn TM but could not do so because I was a rabbi. I asked him what this had to do with my learning TM. He replied that the TM tradition had to be transmitted in a pure form and that since I was committed to a tradition other than his, he was afraid that this would not happen. However, within a few years he did bring one or more rabbis to India for training, and I don't think TM was compromised by my colleagues.

THERE'S NOT A lot to say about my appointment at the University of Manitoba to teach Jewish history and Jewish literature. I enjoyed my classes and the company of Zalman, Neal Rose, and Moshe Stern, who were the other faculty members. I even had my own office for one year while Neal was away. I enjoyed just being in a university environment. Shula was also on campus, taking courses in the School of Art, where her major influences were George Swinton and Ivan Eyre. The latter told her that she was probably wasting her time in art school, since she was already an artist and had to learn just a little technique. Her unique talent blossomed, and today she has pieces in homes around the globe. In later years, she also earned an honours degree in art history from Carleton University in Ottawa, with a special interest in Eskimo art.

One of the exciting aspects of living in Winnipeg at that time was witnessing the birth of the Jewish Renewal Movement, with Zalman as its founder. Jewish Renewal is today a branch of Judaism that emphasizes the Hassidic attributes of joy and mystical experience while encouraging artistic expression and living in harmony with the environment. Back in those days, it was but a glimmer in Zalman's eyes, initially to be loosely patterned on the early Essene communities. Its first name was *B'nai Or* (Sons of Light), which, for egalitarian reasons, was later changed to *P'nai Or* (Faces of Light) and much later to *Aleph* (the first letter of the Hebrew alphabet). Today it is referred to by two names, *Aleph* and Jewish Renewal. While its roots are in Winnipeg, the dynamic phase of its development occurred when Zalman moved to Philadelphia to teach at Temple University. He now lives in Boulder, Colorado, and Jewish Renewal exists in many communities across the United States, Canada, and abroad. It has a retreat centre in New York State called *Eylat Chayyim* and gives rabbinic and cantorial ordination in an at-large program (there is no central teaching school). It also sponsors a one-week conference on various university campuses across the country every two

Zalman in later years

years (where I have had the privilege of teaching on several occasions), attended by six hundred to eight hundred Jewish supporters. Every January, graduates of its various programs meet for a few days in Boulder.

My relationship with Zalman in Winnipeg was very close. We were friends, colleagues, and he was my boss at the university. At one point during his tenure at the University of Manitoba, Shula and I had the pleasure of having Zalman stay with us for a period of time. The circumstance that prompted this

was a breakup with his wife, leaving him temporarily without a place to live. Around the same time, the Jewish community in Winnipeg assailed him for speaking openly about the religious highs one could derive from psychotropic substances. It was no secret that Zalman had become friends with Timothy Leary. Between the breakup of his marriage and his outspokenness, Zalman became persona non grata among the Jews of the city, and at one point they tried to have him ousted from his position at the university because of his influence on the students. To their credit, the overseers at the university stood behind Zalman and his right to academic freedom. All of this was unfortunate, for Zalman had made a major contribution not only to the Jewish community of Winnipeg, but to the city as a whole and to the University of Manitoba. It reminded me of Socrates, who was accused of corrupting the youth of his day and ended up taking hemlock. Fortunately, Zalman's fate was otherwise, and he has gone on to make a significant contribution to the entire Jewish world and beyond, not only through Jewish Renewal, but as well through lectures, interfaith dialogues, and numerous publications. I feel fortunate to have had him in my life as a guide, teacher, and cherished friend.

In the early spring of 1972, I could see the writing on the wall regarding my future in Winnipeg. The congregation was split, some wanting me to leave and others wanting me to stay. At a general meeting on April 23, 1972, I delivered my last report to the congregation. I reviewed my five years with them, dwelling especially on missed opportunities to make a mark in the community through high-profile social action programs. It was my contention that little was done while much was asked for by various groups and organizations in the city. The congregation's failure to respond to such requests, to creatively initiate their own programs or to endorse those started by one or two members or their rabbi, reflected a lack of will and a lack of vision. And, as I did not see any indications that the situation was going to change, I made this final suggestion to them:

> If however, this kind of commitment to the future cannot be made tonight, then I do not believe it will be made at another time. This is the governing body of the Temple and what happens here within the next hour or so can, with little doubt, be taken as an indication of what is going to happen during the coming year. If nothing happens, that is to say, if no inner and outer-oriented programs are adopted, then this Temple clearly has no future. In such case I would recommend that a motion be brought forth to abandon the elections and dissolve the congregation. There is certainly no shame in admitting defeat when such admission is warranted. There is shame, however, in perpetuating a body that has lost its soul.

Two votes were taken at this meeting. I survived the first vote on a motion to keep me on as their rabbi, two-thirds for and one-third against. The second vote had to do with increasing my salary so I could live, since my jobs at both universities were coming to an end, and all I had left was the job of prison chaplain, which provided only a quarter of my wages. The funds were not available, and the motion was defeated. The conclusion was simple: I had to leave.

I knew that, for many reasons, leaving Winnipeg was going to be difficult. I had made close friends, I liked the community, I liked the congregation in spite of the difficulties, and saying goodbye to my parents would be painful, especially as they were getting on in years.

My first thought was to look for another congregation. Fortunately, the rabbinic organization to which I belonged (and still do) had a placement director and an excellent system in place that enabled rabbis to find employment. My first offer came from a congregation in Colorado Springs, but this did not interest me. The next offer I was very interested in. This was a congregation in Highland Park, Illinois, a suburb of Chicago, whose rabbi, Arnold Wolf, was moving on. Arnold was a well-known and highly respected rabbi, and his congregation, Solel, had a reputation for being perhaps the most avant-garde temple in the Reform Movement at that time. This appealed to me, since it seemed to be in tune with my own thinking. I was invited to come for an interview.

Between twenty-five and thirty members of Solel showed up; I presumed they were mostly, if not all, members of the board or a very large search committee. The interview lasted over two hours, and I was queried on my views on just about every aspect of Judaism. I did not hold back from expressing my thoughts about mysticism or anything else they asked me to talk about. They seemed to be in accord with most of what I was saying, except for my perspective on the Chosen People concept, which was different from what they were used to hearing from their rabbi and what they had come to accept. I sensed their uneasiness when I told them that I did not believe in the conventional ideas about chosenness but did believe that, as Jews, we are a unique people with a special destiny. A few weeks later, I received a letter from them in which they expressed their appreciation for my visit and for my candour, but said they didn't think we would be a match. I was certainly disappointed.

My choice was to continue searching for another congregation or to do something else. If a congregation like Solel was not open to my ideas, I thought, then who would be? I kept my hat in the placement ring just in case something came along, but, Solel aside, I was beginning to realize that perhaps I was not cut out for the pulpit. I was smarting from my congregational experience at Temple Shalom, which in its last two years was anything but pleasant. But I had a family to support, and what else could I do? My other options were a Jewish organizational position or a post at Hillel, and such jobs were not readily available.

DURING THAT SPRING, I was invited to give a major paper and I was invited to two conferences. All three of these events were significant in determining my future.

My friend Steve Forstein, who had asked me to come to San Francisco and be the hippie rabbi, was with a congregation in Topeka, Kansas. A member of the congregation had recently given an endowment for an annual presentation, the Pusitz Library Memorial Lecture, and Steve invited me to come down and deliver the second such lecture. I had little time to prepare for this talk, so Zalman managed to get me a small research grant from the university. I used it to pay one of my students, Hart Mallin, an excellent research assistant without whom I would never have been able to prepare the paper. I went to Topeka and gave my talk, titled, "Light and Sound in the Jewish Experience." The subject matter was revelation in the bible and post-biblical literature and its relation to some current scientific findings. In their congregation flyer, I described my talk:

> I hope to show how light and sound have played a dominant role in the Jewish religious experience from biblical times to the present, particularly in the mystical expression of these phenomena. I would also like to touch on the universal experience of light and sound as well as bringing in some of my own experiments in this area.

Unfortunately, I had prepared too much material and after two hours, Steve and, I'm sure, others were getting antsy. However, no one left before I finished, so I suppose the subject kept them interested.

After the talk a woman and her daughter approached me. The woman thanked me for my presentation and suggested that I might want to come to her husband's lecture the following evening at the Menninger Foundation. I had never heard of her husband, Dr. Elmer Green, but she said that he was doing research into altered states of consciousness and biofeedback. I told her I would try to attend, but I had a dinner engagement with a family in Steve's congregation, and I didn't know when it would end. As it turns out, in Topeka, dinner engagements during the week are exactly that—you eat, chat while you eat, and then leave. Everyone I met in Topeka was involved in some kind of research, and time was precious. So, by 7:45 dinner was over, and I was delivered to Dr. Green's lecture. After the lecture, he and his wife, Alyce, mentioned that the Menninger Foundation and the Institute for Transpersonal Psychology (bringing together science, psychology, and spirituality) were having a conference in June at a camp facility about two hours west of Topeka. Elmer told me that attendance at this conference was limited to ninety people and the roster was full, but he would try to get me in if I was interested. I was.

A few weeks later I was on a plane to St. Louis where a shuttle bus delivered me and other attendees to the White Memorial Camp. The conference lasted five days and had a profound impact on me. In attendance were about thirty-five psychiatrists, many from the Menninger Foundation (one of the foremost neuropsychiatric institutions in the world), plus physicians, psychologists, spiritual healers, and other researchers in the area of human development and potential. I learned that the conference was secret and no press were allowed because the subject matter was on the fringe of science and some people were concerned that their reputations, and even jobs, might be on the line if their attendance was discovered. Many others did not feel this way and had no hesitation in talking about the conference after they left. It was at this conference that I had the pleasure of meeting and talking with Elizabeth Kubler-Ross, author of *Death and Dying*.

The early seventies were a time when some of the first inroads into the interface between science and spirituality were being made, and the Council Grove Conference (the conference I had just attended) was an annual meeting of pioneers in the field. Many who attended these conferences went on to become household names in the Human Potential Movement (which promoted the development of the potential in every human being), like Charles Tart, Robert Monroe, Daniel Goleman, Walter Houston Clark, Norman Shealy, Jack Kornfield, Stanley Krippner, and of course Elizabeth Kubler-Ross, to mention but a few. I felt honoured and privileged to be in the company of these men and women and found that no matter whom I spoke with, I always came away feeling I had learned something. In a sense, I had come home, and for the second time in my life (the first time having been at the ashram), I could speak freely and know I was being heard by all present.

Excerpts from the agendas for 1972 and 1973 may give the reader a better sense of what the Council Grove Conference was about:

Values and Consciousness: Some Key Issues. Keynote address, Willis W. Harmon, Director for the Center for the Study of Social Policy, Stanford Research Institute.

Address by Elmer Green, Director of the Voluntary Controls Program, Menninger Foundation. Title of his address: Physiological Correlates of Values.

Mad Bear: Iroquois spiritual leader. Assisted by Doug Boyd, author of "Rolling Thunder" and "Swami," cross-cultural investigator.

Domo Geshe Rinpoche, Njigme, spiritual successor of the former Domo Geshe Rinpoche, Ngawang Kylsang. Assisted by Gayle Williamson, Cultural Anthropologist.

Chairman of the Day: Irving Zaretsky, Cultural Anthropologist and student of law at the University of Chicago Law School and Divinity School. He is concerned with the social, political and legal regulations of altered states of consciousness and the adaptation of findings in this field to the utilization of the scientific method and problems associated with the development of transpersonal and consciousness values in different members of families at different rates. The issue of how one integrates these values into everyday work, especially when one may be working with people who do not share the values, will be addressed. Small group leaders for the day will be: John Heider, Director of the Human Potential School of Mendocino; Elizabeth Kubler-Ross, author, teacher, and psychiatrist working in the area of death and dying; Robert Monroe, author of "Journeys Out Of The Body"; Daniel P. Brown, Experimental and Clinical Psychologist & Historian of Religion.

> The Mystical Aspects of Consciousness by Rabbi Herbert Weiner
> The Impact of Science on the Study of Consciousness, by Stanley Krippner

Interspersed among the various topics were sessions in meditation, body movement, music, and special movies on topics of healing and creativity.

At the two annual conferences I attended, one individual in particular stood out for me. Jack Schwartz, originally from Holland, I believe, was a chiropractor by training, but this appeared to be the least of his abilities and talents. Jack was a healer of extraordinary measure, not only of others but of his own body. One of the movies I attended showed Tony Agpao, a psychic surgeon from the Philippines, giving a mind-altering display of surgery without medical instruments. When it ended, one woman in the audience was so disturbed by what she had seen that she went into a state of shock and cried out for help. Although there were many medical doctors, psychiatrists, and psychologists present, all eyes turned to Jack. He immediately responded; within minutes, the woman was calm, and by the end of a half hour she was restored to her normal self.

For a better understanding of Jack Schwartz, here is a brief and unusual description of the man from a statement in the 1973 conference program:

> Jack is willing to do a demonstration for medical groups or others along the following lines: 1) Put a needle through his arm without any flow of blood. 2) Change his heart rate at will and keep his heart rate constant while the needle passes through his arm. 3) Temperature control experiments: he will raise his temperature as much as 16 to 17 degrees within a few minutes. 4) Blood flow control changes. 5) Have somebody extinguish a cigarette on his arm without any burn.

Before I left for one of the Council Grove conferences, Zalman told me about a friend of his somewhere in the eastern United States who had a very serious medical condition relating to his heart, a condition that had not yet been fully diagnosed. The doctors were trying to treat it based on the knowledge they had at that point from various tests, but it wasn't going well. I mentioned all of this to Jack one evening and asked him if there was anything he could do. Almost instantly, he gave a diagnosis of the condition and how it might be treated. I immediately phoned Zalman and gave him the information, which he then relayed to his friend. A short while later the concluding diagnosis was made, and it was exactly what Jack had told me. Zalman's friend, to the best of my knowledge, did not follow Jack's treatment regime. A few months later his heart gave away and he passed on.

Attending the conferences and following developments in the field of the Voluntary Control of Internal States and related healing modalities, I felt a growing frustration. It seemed to me that what this field was offering was a view of healing outside the normal parameters of classical medical practice, a view that promoted non-invasive and drug-free procedures. (Unfortunately, I have seen little of the benefits from the research done in this area appearing in the more standard medical journals and in doctors' offices. It's not that relevant articles have not been published in abundance — to find them, one need but consult the *Aldine Annual on the Regulation of Bodily Processes and Consciousness*, published by Aldine-Atherton of Chicago and New York, whose editors, Johann Stoyva, Theodore Barber, Leo DiCara, Joe Kamiya, Neal Miller, and David Shapiro, were well-known figures in the field of medical research. It's that the research seems to have remained isolated in a small corner of the medical profession and is largely unknown to the general practitioner, much less the general public. Even biofeedback, the best known of all the more esoteric modalities, has receded into the shadows, despite its considerable promise of effective treatment for a variety of medical conditions. Granted, there have been exciting advances in medical research in recent years, such as gene and stem-cell treatments, but very little that I am aware of in the area of voluntary control over one's bodily processes, an area where the mind augments or even replaces the scalpel and the pill.)

I returned from the 1972 Council Grove Conference on a high note, excited by what I had learned and by the people I had met. Of course, when I landed back in Winnipeg, I was still faced with the reality of not having a job and not knowing where to look. Then a series of events led me to being hired for a position that was unique in the history of Canada.

Around 1970, the Government of Canada, through its Department of Health and Welfare, set up a unit known as the Non-Medical Use of Drugs Directorate. Its mandate was to try to find ways to counter the growing "drug problem" in the country, since there was an outcry from the public for the government to do something about it. The directorate created five regions in Canada, of which Manitoba and Saskatchewan were one, and appointed a director for each region. The Manitoba–Saskatchewan director was Ron Wally. Ron and I had become friends, so one day, as I was looking for a job, I approached him and asked if he thought the government might be interested in having me do some kind of pilot project in Manitoba on drugs and altered states of consciousness. My thinking was that if young people were looking for highs, perhaps I would have something to offer through meditation and the like. He suggested I put together a proposal, which he would send to the head office in Ottawa. I did so, and waited, hoping that the proposal would be accepted and funded, thereby allowing me to remain in Winnipeg.

One day, while sitting in my office at the University of Manitoba, I received a phone call from Ottawa. The gentleman at the other end introduced himself as Jack Nightscales and told me that he and others had read my proposal and wanted to invite me to a clergy conference on drug abuse that was taking place in Toronto in a couple of weeks. He assured me that all expenses would be covered. I accepted.

I arrived in Toronto and checked into the Hyatt Regency on Avenue Road. It was the hotel's opening day, and I was customer number nine. I jokingly suggested to the clerk at the desk, who was processing my registration, that the first ten customers should get a free room (though, of course, I wasn't paying for my room anyway). He chuckled and said he would like to oblige, but it wasn't his decision.

The conference lasted four days and was attended by about a hundred clergymen from across the country. I was the only rabbi. About midway through the third day, it occurred to me that, given the amount of material presented each day in talks and literature, perhaps some of the clergy would enjoy a little relief in the evening through a session on meditation. I presented my idea to the conference director, Tom Foran, and he concurred, telling me he would arrange for a room. As our final meeting of the day was concluding, I raised my hand and announced that at 8:00 p.m., I was going to conduct a meditation session for anyone interested. At 7:45 I found the appointed room, only to discover that it was a ballroom, not the cozy space I was hoping for. So I arranged about ten chairs in a circle and placed a candle on a plate in the centre. By 8:00 o'clock, thirty-five people had arrived, and the circle had to be widened. Tom came by to see if I needed anything, and I asked him if he could figure out how to turn the lights out in the room, since I had tried and failed. After some searching he found the switch, and suddenly the room was in darkness except for the glow of the candle. Tom looked at everyone sitting around the candle, commented that this looked interesting, and said he was going to skip the meeting he was supposed to attend and sit in.

I conducted a forty-five-minute meditation, guiding the group through various techniques. This was a long period for people not accustomed to meditation, which was the case for probably everyone there. As no one left and no one seemed fidgety, I concluded that things probably went well. And according to the feedback Tom received from the group that evening and the following day, that did indeed appear to be the case. Later that day, Tom took me aside and asked me if we could forget about my project proposal. Instead, he said, he wanted me to come to work for the government in Ottawa, although he would have to get approval from the assistant deputy minister of Health and Welfare. Shortly after the conference the government flew me to Ottawa to meet with the minister, and that summer at the ashram, I received a letter confirming my new job, with the title of Consultant to the Federal Government of Canada in Yoga, Meditation and Altered States of Consciousness as an Alternative to Problems of Drug Abuse.

THE GOVERNMENT'S YOGI

Ottawa 1972–1977

Winds blow in strange ways
caressing my heart
entering my soul
always with purpose
that eludes me
until I open my eyes
and see what was always there

M y job title was not assigned to me until I arrived in Ottawa because they didn't know what to call me. So, a week or more after I took up my yet-to-be clarified duties, a man came to see me with the purpose of writing a job description, giving me a title, and assigning me a rank. The rank was the easy part. I was to be at a level called PM 6, which meant Project Manager, Level 6. The job description and title were another matter. My working title when I first came aboard was Project Manager — Meditation, as my acceptance letter attests:

Place Vanier, Tower "A,"
333 River Road,
Ottawa, Ontario, K1A 1B6
October 5, 1972

Miss M.K. Smith,
Staffing Officer,
Staffing Unit "A,"
Administrative Staffing Program,
Public Service Commission of Canada,
Place de Ville, Tower "A,"
Ottawa, Ontario, K1A 0M7

Dear Miss Smith,
    I thank you for your letter of September 25, 1972, offering me a position at the Program Administrative level 6 with the Department of National Health and Welfare as Project Manager — Meditation. I am most pleased to accept this offer and appreciate your good wishes for the future.
                            Sincerely,
                            (Signature)
                            Rabbi G. Steinberg,
                            National Program,
                            Non-Medical Use of Drugs Directorate

Before this title designation was broadened, my job description was oriented primarily toward meditation, as may be seen in excerpts from the job description memorandum. I present this material for the reader's interest as, to the best of my knowledge, from the standpoint of a national government, I believe it is unique and precedent-setting:

Non-Medical Use of Drugs
National Program Division
Project Officer — Meditation

Basic Functions
The Project Officer — Meditation will be responsible for:
  - developing and conducting programs in meditation
  - conducting research programs to determine effectiveness of meditation as an alternative to drug dependency
  - developing training programs to train professionals and community workers in the techniques of meditation

Duties
  1. Develop and conduct educational programs in meditation by:
  - presenting courses in meditation as an alternative to drug dependency to persons associated with the drug problem, e.g., doctors, social workers, nurses, etc....
  - presenting courses or briefings to various institutions of learning (e.g., public and high schools, universities) on the meaning of meditation to the Western mind.
  - preparing written and other literature on yoga for the public.
  - preparing audio-visual material on yoga as a medium for information and/or training.

  2. Conduct research programs to:
  - determine scientifically the effectiveness and value of meditation as a viable alternative for drug users.
  - determine the physiological and psychological effects of sound on persons.
  - examine and evaluate the existing programs on yoga in terms of their suitability for drug users, and consider what they may contribute by way of ideas, procedures, etc....

3. Develop training programs to:
   - train a core of persons in the art of meditation and send these people out to work with the drug culture in hospitals, outreach houses, community centres, schools, therapeutic communities, street clinics, etc.
   - prepare a feasibility study on establishing a centre concentrating on yoga and related disciplines to work with drug users.
   - prepare a feasibility study on contracting teachers of yoga already trained and orientating them towards a program directed specifically towards drug users.

4. Develop other programs such as:
   - working with parents via an information program in meditation to familiarize them and give them a deeper understanding of certain segments of our youth, thereby hopefully influencing in a positive manner the home environment in which our young people grow up.

That first week, after lengthy discussion and probing, the man and I revised this description to include lecturing to select groups across the country, attracting appropriate individuals and groups to apply for funding from the government for relevant projects, reviewing project applications when they came in and making recommendations, and doing some in-house teaching on meditation. Then we worked together on a title to reflect all of this, and came up with the aforementioned designation: Consultant to the Federal Government of Canada in Yoga, Meditation and Altered States of Consciousness as an Alternative to Problems of Drug Abuse. It was a mouthful, but we didn't know how to shorten it and still cover everything. So it remained. However, those who couldn't remember the full title or just found it awkward called me the "alternatives consultant," and the government also provided a more concise job description:

1. To develop a conceptual and operational model of alternatives to drug abuse problems.
2. To consult with and/or advise colleagues and clients in the area of drug abuse as this relates to alternatives.
3. To identify persons capable of doing research in the area of alternatives.
4. To stimulate interest among research scientists in the area of alternatives.

5. To evaluate research proposals related to the area of alternatives.

6. To give lectures to professionals in the area of drug abuse on the alternatives approach, particularly in the field of self-regulation of physical and mental processes.

7. To conduct workshops for professionals in the field of drug abuse.

8. To keep up to date on research and programs in the area of alternatives to drug abuse.

As the reader may discern from this job description, the Canadian government wasn't quite sure what to do with me. I combined the two job descriptions and went to work.

During my first few weeks in Ottawa, I lived in a hotel, and Shula and Meher remained in Winnipeg while I looked for housing. My most exciting memory of those initial days is of the first Canada–Russia hockey series. I was glued to my TV every evening when there was a game. During the day, I acclimatized myself to my office and to my job. I use the term *acclimatize* because I didn't like what I was given. Open-office space was in vogue in the 1970s, and that's exactly what I had — a wide-open cubbyhole off in a corner. There were portable buffers, like padded screens, to give me and others some modicum of privacy. These kept us from seeing each other, but conversations, either on the phone or face-to-face, were easily overheard by whoever was on the other side of the screen. I felt that I had to constantly monitor what I was saying and suggest the same to those coming to see me.

My first office was in the Ottawa suburb of Vanier, but after about a year we moved to Kent Street, closer to the centre of the city. Here, those at my level and above were given private offices with closing doors. "Halleluyah," I said to myself. "My own space." My only problem was the fluorescent lights, which I didn't like for two reasons: they were bright and harsh, and they emitted a hum. I ordered a small desk lamp, unscrewed the fluorescent bulbs, and was a happy man. I liked to meditate for a short time each day, and I could close the door and not worry about being disturbed: a closed office door at that time (and probably still today) meant "do not knock unless urgent."

My first day on the job was very enjoyable. Tom, my new boss, took me around and introduced me to the twenty or so other employees, always with the title "Rabbi," immediately after which I said "Jerry." I could see no reason for formalities in this setting, but I think Tom got a kick out of introducing me in this manner and watching the surprised looks on the faces of my co-workers, who didn't quite know what to make of having a rabbi in their midst. For a while afterwards, when one of them approached me, they began with

"Rabbi," until eventually I weaned them away from the title. I jokingly warned those with Ph.D.s that if they insisted on calling me "Rabbi," I would call them "Doctor." After that, everyone in the office was pretty much on a first-name basis, except for a few who felt that persons with titles should be addressed accordingly. It sounded stuffy to me.

About a week after my arrival in Ottawa, I found my family a home at 23E Deerfield Drive in Nepean, a suburb of Ottawa. It was a brand-new three-level townhouse, with an exit off the main floor leading out onto a large field. We had three bedrooms on the upper floor: one for Shula and me, one for Meher, and the third I made into a kind of chapel or meditation room, as I had done at our home in Winnipeg. I used it often, and frequently brought Meher in with me to meditate. As in Winnipeg, he would sit on my knee, and as his reward for remaining still and quiet, he could blow out the candle that I always lit to begin the meditation. It was a special time for my son and me to be together; he remembers it clearly to this day.

A few weeks after I began my new job, word somehow got out that a rabbi was working for the federal government. Just why this was news remains a puzzle to me, but a reporter for the *Globe and Mail*, Canada's national newspaper, called me and asked to come and interview me. I cleared it with Tom, and the reporter arrived a day or so later, for lunch and an interview that took almost three hours. I liked the reporter, a young man who struck me as pleasant and with a sense of integrity. Having not had a lot of experience at being interviewed, I readily answered all of his questions, including the amount of my salary. When he asked me what I was going to be doing in my job, I outlined my job description and added that it still wasn't all that clear and I didn't know everything that I would be doing. The reporter told me that his write-up of our interview would be edited by someone higher than him, but that he would do everything he could to be sure it accurately reflected what I told him.

Later that evening I had an appointment with Dieter Schneider, a gifted massage therapist. About midway through the massage, his phone began to ring. He at first ignored it, but it kept on ringing until finally, thinking it might be urgent, he picked up the receiver. He said it was for me, and that the person at the other end said it was indeed urgent. I got up off the massage table and took the phone. The caller was from another newspaper based elsewhere in Canada, and he said that he had gotten wind of an article about me that was to appear in the *Globe and Mail* the following morning. He wanted to interview me on the phone right then and there. I told him that I hadn't yet read the article and didn't want to respond to something I hadn't read. He said he would read to me what he had on hand. I rejected this offer and told him that I was in the middle of a massage and not interested in being interviewed at that moment. This ended our conversation. I went back to the massage table, and the phone again rang. It was another newspaper wanting to interview me. I refused this one as well, and asked my masseur to either disconnect the phone or not pick it up. He completed my massage, but all through it I kept wondering what was going on. I found out the next morning.

When I got to the office, there was a hubbub in the air. "Did you see the *Globe and Mail*?" one of my co-workers asked me. "No, not yet," I replied. He handed me the paper and, upon glancing at the front page, I sat down. The bottom third of the page was devoted to the interview, and the headline read, "$18,600 a Year Rabbi Says He Doesn't Know What He's Doing."

After reading the article, I didn't know what to do with myself. To say I was in shock would be an understatement. I told my boss that I had trusted the reporter to be discreet, and he had assured me that he would be. Then I remembered that he also told me that his writing would be edited by someone above him. Whoever that someone was, he obviously saw an opportunity for a catchy headline and did not hesitate to pursue it.

All that day, the Non-Medical Use of Drugs Directorate (NMUDD), the branch of the government's Department of Health and Welfare for which I worked, was inundated with phone calls from newspapers across the country. The callers all wanted to interview me, but only one or two were given the opportunity, since it quickly became apparent that if a curb wasn't placed on interviews, this whole matter would deteriorate into a circus. However, with the permission of the assistant deputy minister of health, who had interviewed me for the job, a few papers sent reporters to my office to talk to me. I believe the ministry hoped that in these additional interviews, I might partially rectify the damage that had been done to the government's reputation: I would have the chance to correct, if not refute, what the *Globe and Mail* said. One of the reporters, remembering that I was also a yoga teacher, asked me if I would stand on my head in my office so he could take a picture. Being now a little sensitized to this reporting business, I politely declined.

The damage, however, had already been done, and the topic was picked up the following morning in the daily editorial cartoon of the *Globe and Mail*. It depicted Prime Minister Pierre Elliott Trudeau talking to his cabinet, all sitting cross-legged, yoga style, on the floor, with the caption, "Rabbi Steinberg said nobody knows what he's doing, either." Alex Morrison, the assistant deputy minister, got such a kick out of this one that he had the cartoon enlarged, framed, and placed on the wall of his office. At my request, he had a copy of the enlargement made and sent to me; I still have it.

In retrospect, this was one of the funniest moments of my life. I never tire of telling the story, and I'm always rewarded with peals of laughter. However, it was not so funny at the time, and I was asked to lie low and not attract any further attention. I was only too happy to comply.

'Rabbi Steinberg said nobody knows what he's doing, either.'

(© *Ed Franklin/The Globe and Mail*)

I WAS CHARMED by Ottawa. Like many capital cities, it was a showpiece, and I enjoyed it to the full. For example, there is nowhere else in Canada, and probably very few places in the world, with such an extensive system of bicycle paths. Upon becoming aware of the paths, I bought a ten-speed bike that became my main mode of transportation to and from work during clement weather. I would wind my way to the Experimental Farm (a government facility), pass by its barns, pastures, and other structures, and then pedal along the Rideau Canal to within a few blocks of my office building — all in all, a distance of about ten miles. After securing my bike, I would go down to the cafeteria and have breakfast. In the evening I would return home by the same route, always with a good appetite for dinner. In the winter, I shared a car pool with others in my office; my preference would have been to skate to work on the five-mile-long canal, but this only made sense if you lived within walking distance of the canal, which I did not. Many who did skated to work with small backpacks, changing into their shoes in one of the warm-up huts placed strategically along the way. Occasionally, on the weekend, just for the sheer pleasure of it, I drove to one end of the canal, put on my skates, and took off to the other end, where a friend would pick me up and return me to my car. I was spoiled, and after I left Ottawa I found I could no longer take pleasure in an ordinary skating rink, where you have to go in circles.

In general, the city had a lot to offer, and my family and I partook of museums and art galleries, as well as the lakes and hills that surrounded us. Also, we bordered the province of Quebec, which is just across the Ottawa River, and within two hours we could be in beautiful Montreal or the Laurentian Mountains.

AS AN EMPLOYEE of the federal government, I travelled back and forth across the country giving lectures and workshops on meditation and altered states of consciousness to a wide assortment of audiences, from alcohol- and drug-related institutional staff to police and military personnel. The reader might be bemused by an excerpt from the schedule of the Canadian Armed Forces' drug conference, titled "Command Drug Education Co-ordinators' Conference," in March of 1974, where I gave a talk titled "Altered States of Consciousness." It was possibly the only time anyone has ever been invited to speak on a topic so far removed from the military to a military audience. No doubt there were substance abuse issues in the Armed Forces, but the title of my talk did not address this, although the content of my presentation did link to it:

Wednesday, 6 March, 1974
0900–1000 Agenda Items
1000–1015 Coffee Break
1030–1230 Rabbi Jerry Steinberg H&W [Health and Welfare] Canada
   "Altered States of Consciousness"
1230–1400 Lunch
1400–1515 Agenda Items
1515–1530 Coffee Break
1530 Closing Remarks—Major J. Harder

The main thrust of my talk was that being a soldier involved a lot of stress and that modalities such as meditation and biofeedback, as well as other forms of altered states of consciousness, could reduce negative stress, the result being a better military man. Over the course of two hours, I presented a considerable amount of material to back this up. While altered states of consciousness can be linked to spirituality in the non-denominational sense, I did not expand on this association, since I felt that with a military audience my responsibility was to present material that was more objectively credible and supported by scientific studies.

I had many opportunities to address audiences across the country, and I found that most of the events I was invited to were pretty straightforward and uneventful; I would give a lecture and lead some meditation exercises. At other times, however, there were interesting incidents.

On one occasion, I was invited as a guest lecturer to a drug and alcohol rehabilitation conference sponsored by the province of Saskatchewan. It took place at Fort San, which many years earlier had been a sanatorium for sufferers of tuberculosis. There were two to three hundred attendees, representing many different branches of the field, such as social workers and addiction counsellors. At one of my evening presentations, I conducted a meditation session, and nearly everyone at the conference attended. It took place in a large, rather plain room, with everyone seated. I tried to adjust the lighting, but it wasn't set up for this kind of event, so I had the lights turned off and lit some candles. The mood created by this subdued lighting was something I sensed most of those present were not used to. Before we began, I mentioned that the session would include a lengthy period of silence. At first there seemed to be tension in the room, but as the meditation progressed, people relaxed, the shuffling of bodies and chairs ended, and only my voice could be heard. It was a lengthy meditation, as I guided them through different aspects of breathing, visualization, and chanting. When the active part of the meditation was over, the silence began. After about ten minutes, someone began to laugh. Like wildfire, it quickly caught on and in about thirty seconds, the entire group of men and women present were laughing. I joined in. The laughter continued for about five minutes and then gradually subsided. When everyone, including myself, had caught our breath, I commented, "Ladies and gentlemen, laughter is a part of meditation. It doesn't always happen, but when it does it's quite wonderful. So thank you all for making this happen and helping me to laugh along with you." My words seemed to have some impact, as everyone left the gathering in a good mood and spoke well of the meeting next day.

Fortunately, this was not the first time I had encountered laughter in the midst of meditation, although it was certainly the first time this had occurred with such a large group. If I were to retroactively make an observation on this phenomenon, I would say that sometimes meditation brings a huge release of tension and, with it, a sudden feeling of well-being and joy, which is expressed through laughter, although on occasion it has other results, such as weeping.

Another time, I was a weekend guest with a group of high-school students who were participating in a program on drugs and alcohol. This event took place in one of the large hotels on the Canadian side of Niagara Falls. I conducted a session in meditation with a group as large as that at Fort San, only this time we met in a very nice ballroom, which gave the session a more comfortable ambience.

The meditation went well, lasting about a half hour. Upon concluding, to make certain that everyone was okay, I asked each student to say hello to the person on his or her left and then the person on the right. If, I told them, some did not get a response to their hello, they should immediately tell me. I waited. Then one of the students said she wasn't getting a response from the girl sitting next to her. I went over and asked the girl who was not responding what her name was. She didn't answer. Someone spontaneously offered me her name (to protect her privacy, I will call her Mary), and I said, "Mary, can you hear me?" I had to ask this question several times before she said yes. The ensuing conversation went something like this:

Jerry: Mary, tell me what's happening.
Mary: Nothing.
Jerry: Nothing?
Mary: Nothing.
Jerry: Do you know where you are, Mary?
Mary: Yes.
Jerry: Tell me where you are.
Mary: I'm on the ceiling.
Jerry: On the ceiling?
Mary: Yes.
Jerry: What are you doing on the ceiling?
Mary: Resting.
Jerry: Resting?
Mary: Yes.
Jerry: How long would you like to rest there, Mary?
Mary: For a while.
Jerry: Okay, Mary. You rest there for a while and I'll get back to you.

I turned to the students and said, "Everything is going to be fine. Mary just needs to rest for a little while, so we'll all sit quietly for a few minutes and then I'll talk to her again." I could see that my words brought relief to some worried students and teachers, but there was still concern on their faces. I waited for five minutes and then began to talk to Mary again.

Jerry: Mary.

Mary: Uh-huh!

Jerry: Where are you now?

Mary: I'm still on the ceiling.

Jerry: Mary, everyone here would really like it if you would come down from the ceiling and join them. Do you think you could do that?

Mary: I'll try.

Jerry: Good, Mary. We're all waiting for you.

(Pause.)

Jerry: Mary, what's happening?

Mary: Nothing.

Jerry: Where are you, Mary?

Mary: I'm still on the ceiling.

Jerry: Okay, Mary. I'm going to help you come down from the ceiling. I'm going to count to ten, and with each succeeding number you will find yourself moving further and further away from the ceiling, and at ten you will be back with us on the floor. One, two, three, moving away from the ceiling, four, five, further and further away from the ceiling, six, seven, eight, almost down now, nine, ten. Where are you, Mary?

Mary: I'm down.

Jerry: We're all very happy that you're down now, Mary. How are you feeling?

Mary: Fine.

Jerry: Good! Now, Mary, in a moment I'd like you to open your eyes. But first I want you to put your hands over your eyes with your fingers together. Now, I'm going to count to three, and at three, I want you to open your eyes, but keep your hands over them so you can't see anything. Okay, one, two, three. Are your eyes open?

Mary: Yes.

Jerry: Now I'd like you to part your fingers just a very little bit so you can see through the openings. That's it. Now a little bit more. Good. Now take your hands completely away from your eyes. (Mary is now looking around at everybody.) Welcome back, Mary. How are you feeling?

Mary: Good. (She commented later that she felt "well rested.")

I addressed the group again and told them that on rare occasions, these things happen, and that even if someone meditated alone and experienced what Mary had experienced, after a little while they would come back to normal on their own, or perhaps just fall asleep. However, as a caution, I asked one of the teachers present to keep an eye on Mary and let me know if anything further occurred. It didn't, and Mary was fine the next day.

The third event took place in Manitoba. Ron Wally, who had been instrumental in getting me the job in Ottawa and was the director of the Manitoba–Saskatchewan region of NMUDD, asked that I be sent to work with staff at an Indian reservation a few hours north of Winnipeg. The reservation had a hospital, with accompanying medical and other support staff, as well as facilities for handling those in trouble with substance abuse, especially alcohol. I was to be with them for a week, conducting sessions in meditation and yoga with two goals in mind: to give the staff some tools with which to handle the stress they were under in their work, and to train them to pass on these skills to those who came under their care. Again, the overall objective was to present alternatives to substance abuse.

I should say a few words about the philosophy with which I approached my job, and which allowed me to obtain my position at NMUDD in the first place. This might also help the reader understand more clearly why I was asked to work on an Indian reservation, and with alcohol- and drug-related agencies in general.

It was my belief that at the root of substance abuse was the desire to escape from reality and the pressures of daily life. Alcohol and drugs provided the escape, but they did so in a manner that was often detrimental to the individual and society. This was the secular reason for substance abuse. I also believed that there was a spiritual component, namely that every human being had a soul, and every soul longed for connection with a being greater than itself — a being, entity, or power we call God. This longing manifests itself in various ways, and for a certain segment of the population, religious institutions and philosophies provide a means of achieving this connection. But not for everyone. Some felt that drugs designed to alter one's consciousness (LSD, marijuana, peyote, etc.) were a better and quicker way to satisfy this longing. In other words, besides providing an escape, drugs were a vehicle for attaining altered states of consciousness. The expression used in those days was to "get high." I proposed that the same motivation applied to alcohol and that a spiritual need was at the basis of drinking to excess. It was as if an elixir was needed to attain a taste of Eden, only the elixirs in vogue had dangerous side effects. I advocated for a natural process to attain Eden — a process that discouraged external substances, that rarely had negative side effects, and that reduced stress.

In my years with the government, I wrote an in-house paper explaining my position. It was titled "A Little Philosophy on Substance Abuse." Following are some brief excerpts from that paper, written in 1974. (The addressee, "Ed," is fictional and was used to give the paper a conversational tone.)

Dear Ed,

From time to time you have asked me to explain my philosophy of drug dependency. Up to the present I have hesitated to do so, due to the fact that certain points needed to be worked out more clearly and fully in my own mind before committing them to writing. I think I've now reached the point where I can give you some kind of a cogent, though by no means definitive, philosophical position.

As I have mentioned to you in previous discussions, every philosophical position must begin with some kind of a presupposition. That is to say, I have to start somewhere, so I begin with a statement that to me is self-evident. If this statement is also self-evident to you, then we can proceed in our discussion. If not, we can exchange views but not very likely reach a mutually acceptable understanding of the major issue.

Let me begin with my self-evident statement which is: *man is innately endowed with the potential to achieve any psychological or spiritual state without recourse to ingesting external substances other than those necessary for his biological survival...*

There is a corollary to my statement which says that *any psychological or spiritual state achieved with the assistance of external substances can be surpassed without the use of such substances...*

While my paper went on at length, the above is the essence of what I had to say.

So here I was at an Indian reservation in the middle of Manitoba, teaching meditation techniques so that staff and patients might have the opportunity of incorporating natural processes into their search for peace and joyous mental states. It was my hope that the techniques would mitigate, if not eliminate, the need for ingesting harmful materials foreign to the body, particularly, in this case, alcohol.

Most of my sessions on the reservation took place in the evening after dinner, because everyone worked during the day. However, I did see staff privately during the day, if they had time, or were on their day off, or if it was urgent and they were able to get away. I taught them a number of meditative techniques and also some of the techniques that I had developed for interpreting dreams. The dream part was intended to help the staff understand better what was happening in their inner lives, but it was also for the Native people they were looking after. I felt that since aboriginal history had a high regard for dreams, some knowledge in this area would help facilitate communication and help their efforts to leave alcohol behind and live rich and fulfilling lives.

On the fifth day of my sojourn at the reservation, I received a long-distance call from a newspaper reporter in Winnipeg. He told me that a complaint had been lodged against the federal government for advocating practices of witchcraft on an Indian reservation. Since I was the specific person being fingered, he wanted to know what I had to say about it. Fortunately, the reporter was Manfred Yaeger, whom I knew personally; there being a mutual liking, we were able to have a warm and friendly conversation. I asked him what this was all about. He said that two women who worked on the reservation, and who were fundamentalist Christians, had passed by the house during my evening sessions and had seen candles burning. I told Manfred that I had indeed lit candles, for purposes of meditation, as there were some meditative techniques that focused on the candle flame. I also explained the broad purpose for which I was at the reservation, namely, to give staff and patients tools to cope with stress and substance abuse. Manfred had no trouble understanding and believing what I told him and said he would quash the story, which he did. And no more was heard about it. I breathed a sigh of relief. I didn't need another story on the front page of a major Canadian newspaper, especially one associating me with witchcraft.

I left the reservation with fond memories and a prayer that my work there would bear fruit.

BESIDES THE *Globe and Mail* interview, another humourous incident in my time with NMUDD had to do with meeting one of the medical icons of the last half of the twentieth century, Hans Selye. At the time, Dr. Selye was the foremost authority in the world on stress, and I hoped to convince him to submit a proposal to get funding for research relating stress to drug abuse. I called his office at the University of Montreal, and his secretary, after consulting with him, said he would be happy to meet with me. An appointment was made, and two weeks later I came to Montreal.

I arrived at the University of Montreal and, after some searching, found the building that housed Dr. Selye's office. I introduced myself to his secretary, and she alerted the good doctor to my presence via intercom. A few minutes later a tall, slim man, possibly in his sixties, came out of a side door and greeted me warmly. I must confess I was honoured to be in the presence of this great man and humbled that he was willing to see me on such short notice. At this point, the usual protocol would have been for Dr. Selye to point me in the direction of his office and follow me in. Instead, he asked me to follow him, turned his back on me, and led the way. His office was large, with a high ceiling and wall-to-wall bookcases, all totally filled. We sat down facing each other, without a desk separating us. After exchanging a few pleasantries, he asked me if I noticed anything when I followed him into his office. I thought for a moment and replied that I hadn't seen anything unusual. "That's good," he responded. "You weren't supposed to! You see, I've had two hip replacements, and the fact that you didn't see me walking any differently from anyone else attests to the excellent job that the surgeons did. In fact, I bicycle on a regular basis and am not restricted in any of my activities." I commented that I was very pleased to hear this, and added something about the wonders of modern medicine. Then he asked me another question: "Rabbi Steinberg, would you like to see my hip?"

I looked at him, not knowing what kind of facial expression I was supposed to convey at this very delicate moment, or, for that matter, what to say. Very quickly, what went through my mind was something like, "Well, if such a great man as Dr. Hans Selye wants to show me his hip, who am I to refuse such an invitation?" "Yes," I replied, "that would be interesting."

He got up from his chair, took me over to one of the bookcases on the far wall, and pointed to a container filled with liquid. He informed me that the object immersed in this liquid, which turned out to be formaldehyde, was his hip. I don't recall him showing me both of his hips. Perhaps he only decided to have one pickled. After that, we got down to business about what kind of project he might submit to me for funding. I never did receive a proposal from him, but to this day I recall our encounter very clearly.

IN THE LATE sixties and early seventies, a Bulgarian physician by the name of Georgi Lozanov developed a system for learning languages known as Suggestology. His thesis was that given the proper environment, almost anyone could learn a foreign language quickly and easily. The proper environment consisted of music in the background, subtle suggestion, and specially trained teachers. His work was initially written up in a book by two Canadian women, Sheila Ostrander and Lynn Schroeder, titled *Psychic Discoveries Behind the Iron Curtain*.

Since Dr. Lozanov's approach seemed to involve some kind of altered state of mind, it was within my professional area of interest, and it occurred to me that if his method was credible, it could be very useful to the Canadian government, which required many of its civil servants to be bilingual in English and French. I therefore approached my bosses and suggested that I go to Bulgaria to check all this out. They agreed, and things were set in motion. About halfway through the process, I was required to have a preparatory session with the RCMP (Royal Canadian Mounted Police), who would brief me for my journey to a Soviet country. In a clandestine room, I met with officers of the force, who, among other things, cautioned me about how I should act in public. When I conversed with someone, for example, I should make sure it was out in the open — say, near a fountain in the middle of the city. Then they presented me with a paper to read, but wouldn't give it to me. The officer held it up in front of my eyes and told me to read it quickly. Being a slow reader, I managed to get halfway through before he snatched it away and wouldn't bring it back for me to complete. I asked him why not, and he spoke some words that made no sense to me. What I did manage to read had something to do with my restrictions in a foreign country, none of which I can recall, since by trying to read so quickly I missed out on most of the comprehension. After that, I was dismissed, and I left with the feeling that either I had done something wrong, or it was expected that I might do something wrong. (My other encounter with the RCMP was when I was invited to give a lecture to some members of the force, as I had to the Canadian military, but that was quite a pleasant experience.)

In the end, my journey to Bulgaria did not materialize, again for reasons not given. Perhaps the force felt I was some kind of risk. I doubt that I'll ever know.

This, however, is not the end of the Lozanov story. Another civil servant in another department, Gerry Duclois, also knew about Suggestology, and he wanted to bring it to the civil service in Ottawa. He organized a conference on the subject, with Dr. Lozanov as the principal speaker. I was invited, along with about a hundred other government personnel. Dr. Lozanov gave an eloquent speech in which he presented evidence for the efficacy of his method. It was all very convincing, so much so that the conference spawned an experimental project, to take place in Ottawa.

The project consisted of Lozanov-trained instructors (Canadians, I believe) teaching classes to civil servants, some learning French and some learning English. About halfway through the program, myself and a few others were invited to sit in on the classes and note our impressions. Yes, there was music playing, and the teachers seemed competent, while the students appeared to be learning their new languages quite well. All this was designed and evaluated by trained research workers with skills in experimental design and statistics. The Lozanov groups were matched against non-Lozanov groups, and the conclusion at the end of the experiment was that the Lozanov groups did better than their counterparts, but not a lot better—the gap was not statistically significant. In discussing the results with others interested in the program, I suggested that perhaps the better result for the Lozanov group had to do with a Hawthorne effect. This is the phenomenon whereby groups selected for experimental purposes often do better than regular groups because, for the short duration of the experiment, they are highly motivated to produce good results, since they feel special to have been selected. The problem here is two-fold: first, the Hawthorne effect wears off before long, and second, often the effect does not carry over to other groups that have not been given any special status. My comments were noted. The Lozanov methodology, to the best of my knowledge, was never adopted by the Canadian government. Perhaps the factors Lozanov used in Bulgaria were not all being employed properly in Canada, although I'm not sure why this might be the case. Another possibility is that the reports from Bulgaria were not properly evaluated, and therefore the method's effectiveness was overestimated. I rarely heard of Lozanov again.

ON TWO OCCASIONS I had the pleasure of addressing staff at the Addiction Research Foundation (ARF) in Toronto. I spoke about my philosophy of addiction and substance abuse and conducted exercises in meditation. The feedback from those who participated in meditation was similar to what I heard after most of my presentations across the country: people felt relaxed, peaceful, and elevated. The consensus at ARF and elsewhere was that meditation was a useful tool in the war against drug abuse. However, no one seemed to be quite sure how to implement a program using this tool within the context of a federal or provincial institution. To me it seemed quite simple. Do something along the lines of what I had done on the reservation: send staff for training in meditation, then let them teach residential patients and outpatients. To my knowledge, for reasons that were never clear to me, no one acted on my recommendations, even though they acknowledged the benefits of meditation. I began to feel that my efforts were a cry in the wilderness.

While I was working for NMUDD, the government funded a commission, headed by Gerald LeDain, to gather information and present a report on substance abuse in Canada. The report came out in the middle of my tenure with the government, and was made available to senior staff at NMUDD before it went out to the public. I recall many of us poring over the commission's findings into the wee hours of the morning. In the end, the commission minimized the effects of heroin, marijuana, and LSD and its derivatives on the population of Canada, and stated that the real problems were alcohol, tobacco, and prescription drugs like Diazepam (the base ingredient of tranquilizers). So, despite the public perception of the so-called drug problem as something that came from outside the home, the real culprits were in the nation's medicine cabinets, liquor cabinets, and cigarette packs. In other words, the pharmaceutical, tobacco, and alcohol industries—the Big Three—were mainly responsible for the country's descent into substance addiction and abuse. I don't recall the LeDain Commission putting it quite this way, but I could see no other conclusion.

I saw an illustration of this when NMUDD sent me to attend a conference of the Canadian Psychiatric Association. The pharmaceutical companies had booths set up all over the venue, encouraging psychiatrists to pick up samples and prescribe their particular tranquilizer or antidepressant pill. One booth was handing out "worry stones," small, one- to two-inch smooth stones you were meant to rub to relieve stress. On each stone was an inscription that read, "For your stress, rub the stone, but for your patients, prescribe [name of medication]." To me, this said it all. Big money was at play, and it was highly unlikely that the federal government would take the LeDain Report seriously, for to do so would have meant a massive reduction in the national treasury (and no consideration was given to how much money would be saved by the reduction of health problems related to products from the Big Three). And indeed, the report was dismissed and pretty much never heard of again. Of course, before long, the same fate would befall NMUDD, which from beginning to end was a political ploy to quiet the perceived anger of the public. After all, they even hired a rabbi to deal with the "drug problem."

My cynicism grew whenever NMUDD held a conference for all of its senior staff. The meetings usually took place at some comfortable venue within a two-hour drive of Ottawa. I recall a moment on the first day of my first such gathering, while everyone was still arriving. One of the regional directors opened the trunk of his car and, with some help from others, hauled out case after case of beer. There may also have been some hard liquor, but I don't recall this. At mealtime, wine flowed. I don't wish to give the impression that I'm against alcohol. I'm aware today of studies that tout its health benefits, and in moderation, I see its value as a social lubricant, not to mention its place in religious ceremonies and events. However, the next morning, part of the staff was hungover and trying desperately to cover it up. I realized that a government agency formed to solve a problem was perpetuating this same problem in its midst, and nobody seemed to mind or care.

Maybe I'm a bit stodgy or naive, but there seemed to be a disconnect here.

As a project manager, one of my main tasks at NMUDD was to develop a project to mitigate the "drug problem" in Canada. After pondering my task for some time, I began to realize that however one defined the nature of the problem, it was endemic to our society, and nothing short of a change in attitude toward drugs, tobacco, and alcohol would have a positive impact. This, of course, would be a paradigm shift for a culture that advocated, both subtly and not so subtly, the use of agents outside of ourselves, such as drugs and alcohol, to fix whatever was wrong. I felt that to begin to correct this unhealthy perception, we needed to tackle things at the grassroots level. My target population was high school students. I told my main boss, the director general (in government there are levels upon levels of bureaucracy), that if we could begin to engage our young people in healthy activities, and teach them life skills and how to derive pleasure from accomplishments in the arts, sports, and related endeavours, then we would create a generation of individuals who would leave an enviable legacy to their children. The literature identifying lifestyle as a factor in overcoming substance abuse was overwhelming. I wanted to try this idea by introducing many diverse lifestyle opportunities for students at one high school as a pilot project, and follow up on the results over a number of years. I had already spoken to the principal of an Ontario high school, and he was excited by the concept and ready to come on board. My boss and others at NMUDD bought into the idea and were prepared to lend their expertise. In fact, my boss told me that the integrity of NMUDD was at stake with my idea, and he fully endorsed it. Yes, it would take money, but it was well worth the risk, and if it didn't work out, then it was likely that no other approach would either. I was ready to commit the next several years of my life to seeing this project through, and was pursuing it diligently, when all of a sudden I was called into my boss's office and, after working for the government almost three and a half years, was notified that my position was being terminated.

No reason was given, other than words to the effect that my services were no longer required. And no amount of probing on my part uncovered what was really going on. I can only guess that politics, and my not seeing eye-to-eye with one or two colleagues, fed into the mix. So "Project Put-Put," as I whimsically called it, never got off the ground, and my chance to contribute something meaningful to my country on a national scale evaporated. My contract, being loosely worded, afforded me little protection and my small amount of severance pay, which included unused sick days, was quickly used up.

During my relatively short time with the government, I did have some opportunities to help obtain government funding for groups that were oriented toward helping young people who had lost their way, such as the 3HO (Happy, Healthy, Holy) Yoga Organization. Unfortunately, as a condition for funding approval, I required these groups to include in their proposal a rigorous evaluation component. My own Project Put-Put, on a larger scale, would have had this component as part of its design. But the evaluation component proved much too stringent a requirement. Most organizations, including the ashram, simply did not understand what it meant, and so I felt I could not recommend them. In hindsight, this was a mistake, and I regret it. A lot of good could have been done with a little leniency on my part.

I had the pleasure during my stay with the government to be asked by the Canadian Medical Association to review a book that had just come onto the market by a then-little-known physician by the name of Andrew Weil. The title of the book was *The Natural Mind*. I enjoyed it, and found that Dr. Weil's thinking and mine were pretty much on the same page, both of us believing in the efficacy of altered states of consciousness and natural approaches to mind expansion. A few statements from Dr. Weil's book:

> . . . altered states of consciousness have great potential for strongly positive psychic development. They appear to be the ways to more effective and fuller use of the nervous system, to development of creative and intellectual faculties, and to attainment of certain kinds of thought that have been deemed exalted by all who have experienced them. . . . People who begin to move in a spiritual direction in connection with drug experimentation sooner or later look for other methods of maintaining their experiences. . . . The real risk of using drugs as the primary method of altering consciousness is in their tendency to reinforce an illusory view of cause and effect that makes it ultimately harder to learn how to maintain highs without dependence on the material world.

Since 1972, when this book was first published, the name Andrew Weil has become almost a household word, certainly for anyone interested in approaches to health both conventional and beyond.

IN EARLY JANUARY of 1973, Shula became pregnant with our second child, Dahlia. Her pregnancy came at a difficult time, as we were struggling in our relationship. In the beginning the pregnancy was touch and go, and, for medical reasons, we weren't sure if she would be able to hold onto the child. Fortunately, our daughter was determined to be born and made her entrance on September 28, the second day

294 · ROGUE RABBI

of Rosh Hashanah, the Jewish New Year. I told Shula that day that no matter what happened, I wasn't going to leave the hospital and risk not being present in the delivery room when our child was born, as had been the case with Meher. I remained by Shula's side until mid-afternoon, when she went into labour. The nurses tried to locate her doctor, but it seemed he had left the hospital and could not be reached. They waited as long as they could, and finally took her to the case room, where the nurses would perform the delivery. I stayed close and went into the room with them, but one of the nurses turned to me and said I would have to leave. I told her that the doctor had said I could be there for the delivery. She replied that in their hospital, that was only allowed if the doctor was present. So, much to my chagrin, I waited in the hallway until I heard a very loud cry when Dahlia made her entrance.

When I went in to see her and Shula, I was beside myself with excitement and joy, but I couldn't believe that this was my daughter. She was plump, with jet-black hair, and didn't remind me of anyone in my family or Shula's. However, as she got older she began to resemble Shula's mother, who had passed away eleven years earlier. In fact, many years later, Dahlia felt a special kinship with her grandmother, whom she had never known and whom she was named after. Even her grandmother's name, Bronia (*Brachah*, "Blessing" in Hebrew), had special meaning for her. Meher was somewhat bewildered by his sister's arrival but quickly adjusted, and except for one outburst of jealous anger several months later, became her much-loved brother, a love that was reciprocated in kind.

During my stay in Ottawa, I took up playing the piano. Well, not exactly. Because of what Shula and I perceived to be Meher's innate musical talent, we enrolled him in the Suzuki method of learning piano, which meant that the parent who drove him to lessons had to sit at a piano next to him and play along with him and the rest of the class. We also bought for him a very inexpensive portable piano so he could practise at home, with my help, which he quickly outgrew.

A very frightening incident with Meher occurred one day at the beach in Ottawa. We were together in the water just a few feet from shore when something distracted me, and I looked up for about five seconds. When I looked down to continue keeping my eye on my son, he had disappeared below the water. I very quickly reached down and pulled him up. He was fine, but I wasn't. In later years, when I mentioned this incident to him, he told me that he remembered being below the water and just looking around, not feeling in any kind of distress. This experience obviously did not have any negative effect on him, as years later, in Toronto, he took swimming lessons and was at the top of his class. By age fourteen, he had completed all the swimming courses available to him, with the next step being the level of bronze medallion. However, the rules at that time, and perhaps still today, were that one had to be at least sixteen to take the test for the bronze medallion. Unfortunately, by the time Meher was sixteen, he was no longer interested in swimming. To this day I ponder whether, due to the rules, Canada might have lost an Olympic contender.

By 1974, before I received notice that my job was ending, things for me at NMUDD had slipped into a routine, with occasional breaks that took me out to meet interesting people, deliver lectures, and conduct workshops. I have never been very good with routine, always feeling that to be happy and feel alive I had to be on the cutting edge of things. I was also encountering frustration around my ideas, particularly with Project Put-Put. Meanwhile, at 23E Deerfield, the home fires were barely burning. Back in Winnipeg, I had worked four jobs to make a meagre living, but in Ottawa almost all of my evenings and weekends were free. I had hoped that the extra time spent with my wife would begin to heal our differences and bring back the spark that keeps spouses happy and able to deal with the downs that inevitably occur in all marriages. Unfortunately, this did not turn out to be the case and, by 1976, Shula and I made the decision to part. Meher took this very hard, crying and fiercely stating, "We're not going to be a family anymore." His words to this day echo in my ears and in my heart. Dahlia, being but two and a half, did not have any overt reaction, but I know she sensed that things were not well and that all of this had a strong impact on her as well.

The decision to end our marriage came closely upon the termination of my job with NMUDD. I was reeling. For the first time in my life I went into a deep depression. I was not suicidal, but for a period of many months, death would have been a friend. I felt I was a failure as a husband, as a breadwinner, and as a man.

As the days and months passed and Shula and I drifted further apart, we agreed that while we lived under the same roof, we would occupy separate bedrooms. It was also by mutual agreement that each of us would be free to see and be with other partners. A few months later, while visiting my parents in Winnipeg, I met a woman who began the process of restoring my feelings of self-worth. Our relationship was brief, but I will always be grateful for what she did for me.

You looked at me
        and said simply

                    you have beautiful eyes

    no woman

            had ever said that to me

before

I stared at you

in disbelief

surely you must be joking

but you weren't

I was almost dead

when you said those words

parched and dried up

not touched

or loved

for years

you let me drink from your well

enough

for new stirrings

in my loins

in my heart

in my soul

enough

to bring blossoms

into my desert

In addition to losing the woman I had deemed my life partner, the most painful and disturbing aspect of our parting was that I felt I was losing my children. I knew I would have rights, but I was aware that this was not going to be the same as seeing them grow up on a day-to-day basis. Fortunately, my will to live, my love of my children, and the support of my parents and dear and treasured friends brought me out of my depression. Then, in Ottawa in the fall of 1976, I met a beautiful woman who enjoyed everything I had to offer and showered me with love.

Gabriele was a gentle and sensitive soul. We met at a dance, and shortly afterwards she came to a dream workshop that I was conducting near Ottawa. I was taken by her beauty, both inwardly and outwardly. Over the next four years our relationship blossomed, and she came to be very close and loved by both Meher and Dahlia. Shula, too, at a later point, came to like Gabriele and on one occasion appreciated her hospitality when she stayed overnight at Gabriele's home.

I remember the holy moments

when I took sanctuary

in your arms
you cradled my soul
in your wings
and breathed new life
into my heart
even as I remember
a stillness enters my being
your presence
fills my spaces
and your voice speaks softly
I love you

With the end of my job, I had to make a decision about what to do with my life. My first concern was how to support my family. Shula was working, and her income, though not sufficient, was all we had, except for my three months of severance pay from NMUDD. I was put on a so-called preference list by the government, which meant that if a job came up for which I qualified, I would be given consideration, along with whoever else was on the preference list. The only call I got was from a government alcohol agency, but when I went for my interview, I was told that I was overqualified for the job. I asked the interviewer what exactly this meant, being "overqualified." He hemmed and hawed for a few minutes and finally came out with it: "It means that before long you will probably get bored with the job and quit." I tried to argue with him to hire me, especially since I was desperate to find work. But he held his ground. Later, when I thought about it, I realized that the man saw me well, much better than I saw myself at the time.

The decision on my future could not wait any longer. I toyed with the idea of going back into the rabbinate and taking a pulpit. But this would, in all likelihood, have meant moving to the United States or elsewhere. Given my family situation, this was not something I could do, as it would have meant separating myself from my children. Also, given the last two years of my experience as a pulpit rabbi in Winnipeg, I had little stomach for another congregation.

As I mulled over my situation, I asked myself a simple question: "What is it I would really like to do?" The answer came quickly. I always had a strong interest in dreams, and the ashram experience consolidated this. I wanted to be a dream therapist. This would bring together my experience as a counsellor, my training in psychology, and my development, under Swami Radha, as someone who could help others interpret their dreams. The thought excited me and grew with a force that took me by surprise. But, I countered to myself, "How can I make a living doing this? Where do I start? Who do I talk to? Is there a need for my services? And where do I find clients?" With all of this in the mix, I hesitated. Finally, it came to me that sometimes in life one has to leap before looking. And there was no time like the present. So I jumped.

THE PLACE WHERE I held my first dream workshop was called Strathmere, in North Gower, on the outskirts of Ottawa. It was run by a kind and irascible Scotsman by the name of Alex Sims. (This continued my romance with Scotspeople, which was also buttressed by my colleague at NMUDD, Ian Henderson, a fine physician and gentleman who was very supportive of my ideas.) Strathmere was an old large farmhouse on many acres of land and was also a working farm. Alex had turned his home into a venue where people offering courses or lectures on human potential and growth could come and make presentations. He was a man without pretense and honest as a plumb line. I liked Alex, and I believe the feeling was mutual, so I worked out with him an arrangement for me to conduct a dream workshop on his farm. Then I had posters and brochures made at the lowest cost possible, and had them distributed. Applications came in from about fourteen people, enough for me to go ahead with my plans.

The workshop began on a Friday evening with a light dinner served by Alex. Upon entering the dining hall, I noticed that Gabriele, whom I had recently met, was there. She quickly avoided my glance, which I took to be a good sign. After dinner, I met with the group in the large living room, which had a wonderful fireplace. On the hearth of that fireplace, I sat and conducted that workshop and many to follow.

The program for the weekend began with the participants introducing themselves and saying a few words about why they wanted to come to a workshop on dreams. I explained to the group that I would teach them some tools to help them understand their dreams and that we would work on their individual dreams, either in pairs or together as a group. In the course of this and many workshops that followed, I presented a number of dream interpretation techniques that I had been developing over the years. These are all compiled in a manuscript titled *DreamTime — A Manual for the Interpretation of Dreams*.

The first workshop at Strathmere, like many others there and elsewhere, was in-residence, meaning that participants stayed together for the whole weekend, from Friday evening until Sunday after lunch. Strathmere had enough bedrooms to accommodate everyone, and Alex, along with some help, prepared and presented tasty and wholesome food. His specialty was a porridge that must have taxed his imagination, it had in it so many ingredients.

On the second night of the workshop, I explained to everyone what REM was. For those unfamiliar with the term, it means "rapid eye movement," movements visible on the eyelids of a sleeping person; sleep researchers discovered that the movements indicate the sleeping person is dreaming. To demonstrate this, I asked the group to pair up, and one person in each pair to close his or her eyes. The people whose eyes were open were to watch their partners' eyelids at very close range while I gave those with closed eyes this instruction: "Imagine that you are watching a tennis match." The observers saw their partners' eyeballs slowly and steadily moving from side to side. "This," I said to them, "is not rapid eye movement." I continued: "Now, imagine that you are sitting in a movie theatre and watching a movie that is full of action happening all over the screen." The eyeballs moved quickly and erratically, not slowly and steadily. "This," I emphasized, "is REM."

After this explanation, each participant selected a partner for REM watching. I gave instructions that each person should leave a light on next to their bed. At about 11:00 p.m., everyone except me went to bed. At 1:00 a.m. I awakened one of each pair (they had decided who would go first), and that individual went and sat next to the bed of his or her partner. Their task was to watch for REM for the next two hours. When they saw REM, they were to let it go on for about a minute and then quietly but firmly say to their sleeping partner, "Tell me your dream!" At this point what usually happened was that the dreaming partners would awaken very slightly, enough to speak or mumble some words about what they were dreaming. When finished, the watching partners were to encourage them to continue talking by saying, "Tell me more!" Everything related by the dreaming partners was written down verbatim by the watching partners.

After two hours, the dreaming partners were woken up completely and came to the kitchen for some coffee or tea, while the watching partners went to sleep. An hour later, the roles reversed, the process would be repeated for another two hours.

Extracting dreams in this manner was often successful, but not always, and various obstacles had to be overcome. Sometimes it was not possible to extract any dreams at all; on other occasions, the observer never stopped writing for the better part of the two hours and later complained of writer's cramp.

Even when the exercise did not work, all participants learned a valuable tool for culling dreams from a partner, sometimes the technique of last resort when people have difficulty remembering dreams on their own.

After breakfast the last morning, participants, both dreamers and watchers, described their experiences during the night. Then, as a group, we worked on one or two of the dreams that had been written down and presented by the watchers.

One of the most important observations I made over the years of doing dream workshops was how quickly the people in a group bonded with each other. I have done other workshops, not on dreams, and have found that while bonding does take place, it usually takes longer and is not as deep. There is something about presenting another person with one's dream that facilitates the bonding experience. Perhaps it's because the dream is a part of one's soul, and by presenting it to others, you are trusting that if there is something there that is painful or embarrassing, they will treat it gently and with understanding, as you will with theirs. I have often suggested to parents that by sharing dreams with their children at breakfast each morning, or perhaps just on weekends, even without attempting any interpretation, they will find that over time, the dream brings about a dimension of closeness surpassing most other family experiences.

IN MY MANY years of working in the field of dreams, I have frequently been asked by concerned parents how to help children who are having recurring nightmares, usually involving a monster of some kind. What I present to these parents is a technique that I discovered in working with Dahlia. She began having frightening dreams at the age of three years and three months. She would wake up crying during the night or, upon awakening in the morning, would be disturbed by what she had experienced. Over the next five months, I conducted an experiment to try to influence her dreams so as to mitigate her upsetting experiences. The technique is called "Taming the Monsters." The basic premise is to suggest, in dialogue with the child, that he or she has the ability to affect his or her dreams and tame the threatening monster. The taming procedure involves asking the child to make friends with the monster. This can be done in a variety of ways, as I will show with examples from my daughter's experience. The child may first need to do battle with the monster before coming to peaceful terms with it.

Here are the instructions I give to parents:

Step One: When your child awakens in the morning, ask her what she has dreamed. (In this section, I will use the female pronoun, for simplicity's sake.) This is to be done immediately upon waking so that the child, if very young, learns by proximity what is meant by the term "dream." However, if she asks what a dream is, you might answer that it is pictures that are seen, or sounds that are heard, while sleeping. You should ask questions about dreams, every morning, until she is able to identify pictures or sounds during sleep as dreams. If she wakes up frightened during the night, you may say, "Did you have a bad dream?" This question, following upon a dream, helps the child associate the word "dream" with visual and auditory experiences occurring while asleep. It would be wise to emphasize that there are also good dreams, so that she doesn't interpret the word "dream" in only a negative sense. Once the child understands what a dream is, you may proceed to the next step.

Step Two: Ask your child to tell you the dream, and record it using a tape recorder or digital recording device. When she stops talking, prompt her with, "What else did you dream?" in case there is more. When you feel that she has no more to say, ask her whether she would like to hear her voice played back. My daughter always wanted me to play back her telling of her dream, so she could hear her voice. This, as time went on, became an incentive for her to relate her dreams first thing in the morning.

Step Three: Upon putting your child to bed, ask what she thinks she could do so the monster won't scare her anymore. If she suggests something, encourage her to try it; emphasize that in a dream, she can do whatever she wants. If your child does not come up with anything, you might suggest that she try to make friends with the monster. Another suggestion would be to beat up the monster, if that is more to her liking. Some parents might be hesitant to suggest that their child do something violent, even in a dream. My experience, however, has been that if a child is harbouring feelings of anger or resentment toward someone, and this person is represented in a dream by a monster, it is better to give the child a safe and harmless outlet through which she can express her feelings than to let the feelings linger in the unconscious and potentially come out in the awake state. Usually, once a child has tamed her monster, either peacefully or aggressively, in a dream, I have observed that she tends to be more at peace and less inclined toward hostility in the awake state.

Step Four: When your child indicates which approach she wants to take — making friends or battling with the monster — ask her how she would like to go about accomplishing her goal. If she doesn't know, you can make a suggestion. Here are some possibilities:

For making friends:
- Give the monster something to eat that she thinks it might like.
- Play with the monster.
- Take the monster to Disneyland.

For battling the monster:
- Hit the monster with a bat. (Place a very light plastic baseball bat, or one made of soft material, next to the child's bed, and tell her that she can use this in her dream.)
- Put glue in the monster's mouth.
- Squirt water in the monster's face.

This four-step process can take several weeks or even months. Continue to record your child's descriptions of her dreams to monitor her progress. The process can be discontinued when some kind of resolution is reached and the monster is no longer frightening your child. From time to time, however, you may wish to ask your child about her dreams, in case the monster returns or something else indicates that your child is struggling with an issue. Dreams are often an excellent barometer of your child's emotional well-being.

Following are excerpts from my experiment with my daughter, Dahlia, showing how the process of "Taming the Monster" can evolve. These excerpts have been culled from recordings made over a period of five months. I have not edited her language so that the personality and charm of a three-year-old might come through.

December 14/76

Dahlia: I dreamed about an animal—a horsy—it was hurting me. It was eating my hair. My hair was bleeding. I had to ask mommy for a bandage. [pause] I smell flowers—red flowers and pink flowers and black flowers. And I was dreaming about a monster. The monster scared me.

Daddy: What was the monster like?

Dahlia: Ugly! A scary, scary, biggest monster—on top of my head. The monster hurt my fingers—'cause it bleed myself with a knife. That's all!

December 19/76

Dahlia: I dreamed about a horsy. I killed hiself. He died into the fishes water and the fish bites the horsy.

December 26/76

Dahlia: Daddy, the giant hurt me. I saw Bigfoot. I smell flowers. I dream the big fish hurt me. The fish was dead—I hit it. It was biting my finger. It died. [pause] I dreamed a scary monster. It get bleeding. I put some glue in his mouth and he got dead.

January 12/77

Dahlia: I dreamed about scary monster. Flowers. The monster was eating all our food. He took away my food. He did something to me. He killed me!

Daddy: Why would he do that?

Dahlia: Because I would take your gun and kill him.

Daddy: Why don't you do that? Take my gun and kill him next time. [In reality, I have never possessed a gun.]

Dahlia: But he's not dead.

Daddy: If he comes back you can maybe give him something to eat and then you can become friends with the monster.

Dahlia: And then he would take all our food.

Daddy: Well, maybe he's just hungry and if you give him something to eat he'll be friends with you.

January 18/77

Dahlia: The monsters did something to me — they tickled me. They didn't take all my food. I dreamed about a bug. Then it got in my throat and then the monster came and bites the bug and then the monster bites me too and then I killed it.

March 8/77

Dahlia: Uh oh! I dreamed about a monster. It gave back our food.

Daddy: And then what happened to the monster?

Dahlia: I didn't kill it. It was nice to me. It kissed me.

April 15/77

Dahlia: A big monster camed — a snake. It killed me behind my lip.

Daddy: What will you do to the snake next time?

Dahlia: I will kill it and hit it.

May 7/77

Dahlia: I dreamed about a monster but it didn't goed away. Then I was thirsty and hungry. Then I gave cookies to the monsters and milk to the monsters so they won't be thirsty.

Daddy: What happened then to the monster?

Dahlia: I hit it!

Daddy: You know, sweetheart, sometimes if you just feed the monster then you don't even need to hit it because if you feed it, it gets very nice and is very happy that you fed it — and it will be friends with you.

May 10/77

Dahlia: Yesterday I dreamed about a nice monster and then he eat all the food up. He got the food from this fridge and then I had lots more 'cause he didn't eat too much.

Daddy: Who gave him the food?

Dahlia: I did.

Daddy: Then what happened to the monster?

Dahlia: I kissed it.

Daddy: What did the monster do when you kissed it?

Dahlia: He kissed me back.

Daddy: Beautiful, sweetheart! That's just lovely!

Dahlia: Then you know what? He was laughing.

Daddy: So what did you do?

Dahlia: I got a secret for him and I told him to have a birthday. He can have a birthday with me to be friends.

Daddy: That's a beautiful idea.

May 12/77

Dahlia: The monster let me go to his party.

Daddy: What did you do at his party?

Dahlia: I gave him some chips and some ketchup and some bread and some relish on some bread for me. And then the monster let me come to his home.

Daddy: What did you do in his home?

Dahlia: I played with him and he had cars — red and green and orange and blue.

Daddy: What kind of home does the monster have?

Dahlia: A red home.

Daddy: Is it a nice home?

Dahlia: Ya! A bootiful home.

Daddy: And what does the monster look like?

Dahlia: The monster looks like my friend.

Daddy: What does your friend look like?

Dahlia: Big Bird!

After this, I never again heard Dahlia mention nightmares.

WHENEVER I CONDUCTED "Taming the Monsters" workshops, I always played portions of Dahlia's tapes and discussed various approaches. Many participating parents tried these methods. Some called or met with me later to tell me about the results they had with their children. The following is one such report:

First of all, I'd like to relate what happened before the last dream workshop, with regards to my youngest daughter. She's three years old and she was having monster nightmares that she would recall to me sometimes in the middle of the night and sometimes the next morning. Before the dream workshop, I dealt with it by having her "program" her dreams by thinking of something pleasant before she went to sleep. Then she would say, "Okay, I'm going to dream about Easter or Christmas or my birthday," or something that was pleasant to her.

What would happen sometimes is that she would wake up in the night and start crying, and I'd go in to see what had happened, and she would say, "Mommy, I can't find my dream!" And she would be all upset because she had decided that she was only going to dream about that one thing. So then I tried to solve that problem by mentioning four or five different nice things for her to dream about. So she tried that, but she was still having monster nightmares occasionally.

Then, at the dream workshop, Jerry related what he had done with his daughter about feeding the monsters. So, when my daughter had her next nightmare, I asked her if there was something she thought she could do with this monster in order to solve the problem. Well, a three-year-old doesn't know how to communicate very well, so she said she didn't know. She couldn't think of anything, and I said, "Well, do you want to be friends?" She thought that was a good idea. But how? So she thought—well maybe some candy because she liked candy, well, maybe the monster would like candy too. I said, "Yes, you could feed the monster something." And she said, "Well, what about water? If I want to give him a drink of water, does that mean I have to get up in the middle of the night and go to the bathroom and get some water from the sink?" And I said, "No!" And I explained to her that her dreams were her own and she could do whatever she wanted. She could have what she wanted and produce what she wanted.

So that night she went to sleep and she dreamed about the monster and in the morning she woke up happy and she ran into the room saying, "Mommy, guess what? I gave him a carrot and a dish of water and he was fine. Nothing happened!" And she was all excited about it. So, there hasn't been any recurrence of any problems with her monsters. She's handled them quite well.

One last and memorable encounter on the topic of dreams. I had the plea-sure one day of meeting with Charlie Roberts, an Ottawa psychiatrist who trained other psychiatrists to be analysts. Over lunch, we talked mainly about dreams, as his interests and mine coincided in this regard. Dr. Roberts had an open mind and knew that there was far more to dreams than what was discussed in psychoanalytic theory. When I told him about my experiences with healing dreams, he was eager to tell me of an observation that he had made repeatedly with some of his patients over the years. These patients had come to him with dreams of illness, usually relating to some organ in the body, such as the liver or kidneys. With his respect for dreams, Dr. Roberts did not want to take any chances, so, in case the dream was actually indicat-ing a health problem, he would send the patient for tests to determine the health of the organ in question. He told me that inevitably the tests did not show any evidence of a problem. Following the tests, however, within two to three months the patient would become ill, and further tests would deter-mine that it was indeed the organ the patient had dreamed about that was affected. Our discussion on this phenomenon developed into a theory that, at a subconscious level, the psyche picks up signals from an organ that is in the beginning stages of illness, too early to be diagnosed through medical tech-nology. The dream therefore becomes the vehicle through which the body transmits information about the organ to the brain.

We were both amazed at how sensitive the psyche must be to pick up the subtlest of cues and translate them into dream forms. We realized the impli-cations of this, namely that each person has within him or her the ability to know well in advance when something is wrong in the body — indeed, far enough in advance that remedial action can be taken to prevent the problem from escalating and becoming a serious health threat. Of course, one has to be open to the concept that dreams are far more than an expression of psy-chological issues, a concept that has not made a lot of progress in Western philosophy and science to date.

AS THE READER has probably gathered by this point, the concept of spiritual heal-ing has also failed to make significant inroads in the scientific community and in the public mind, except as presented in religious texts and in publications of an anecdotal nature. So I will close out this chapter with the story of a healing experience of the kind I have encountered many times in the literature and in the testimony of others. Only this time, it happened to me.

Sometime in 1974, I received a phone call from friends in Montreal,

Marilyn Zweig and John Rossner, informing me that they had as a houseguest a very unusual and powerful healer visiting from Sri Lanka. They wanted Shula and me to come and meet the man. I discussed it with Shula, and after making arrangements for the children, we got in the car and drove the two hours from Ottawa to Montreal. Marilyn is a gifted psychic and John an Anglican priest. Both have been instrumental in educating people about the hidden potential that all human beings possess. They have also sponsored many conferences, bringing unusual individuals to Montreal to share their ideas and perspectives on the world of psychic phenomena and spiritual development.

We arrived at John and Marilyn's home in the early evening and were greeted warmly by them. They said we would have to wait a while to see the healer, since there were a number of people ahead of us. They also told us that the man didn't speak a word of English, so either Marilyn or John would accompany us to a session and translate as best they could. Neither of them knew his language, but they had somehow learned to communicate with him, perhaps with some initial help from a translator. At the very least, they were familiar with his methods and could figure out most of his sign language and expressions.

Marilyn suggested we bring to the man some medical problem for him to treat. Being aware that some healers are good at helping medical problems that are responsive to suggestion or psychosomatic processes, I felt that if I was going to find the man credible, I had to present him with something of substance, whose healing could not be attributed to suggestion — or, at least, not to any kind of suggestion that I was familiar with. The problem was that I was very healthy and could think of nothing that was wrong with me. If Shula and I had made the effort to come this far in such a hurry, I wanted at least to have something healed that would be empirically convincing. Then I remembered that I had a cyst on my back, about the size of a dime, that had been with me for many years. It had been checked by a dermatologist, who felt it was nothing serious and that I shouldn't worry about it. This I knew was beyond suggestion and psychosomatic influences.

Finally my turn came. Marilyn took me upstairs into one of the rooms and introduced me to the healer, a tall, slim man in his late seventies or early eighties with a soft face and warm smile. He motioned for me to sit down on a chair in the centre of the room. Marilyn explained to him what I wanted healed; she pointed to my back, and I lifted my shirt so he could see the cyst. I was told to close my eyes and not open them until told to do so. Since my eyes were closed for the whole session, which took about a half hour, I can't relate to the reader much of what he was doing. I do recall that at one point he blew on my head and that toward the end of the session, he sprinkled some water on me. Then I was told to open my eyes, go out of the room, and walk the full length of the hallway, back and forth, a few times. I did as asked. Finally, through Marilyn, I was instructed not to touch the cyst for twenty-four hours. However, I was only able to contain myself for about two hours; then, slowly, my fingers wandered over to the cyst. It was half its original size. I couldn't believe it, and checked a second time. It was so. Over the next several days it got smaller until it was about a quarter of its original size. I have no explanation for what the healer did, or the nature of his method. I only know what I felt on my back and later saw in the mirror. The cyst remained at quarter size for many years and then grew a bit before settling in to where it is today. I keep wondering what would have happened if I had listened to the healer and waited the full twenty-four hours.

A NEW BEGINNING
Toronto 1977–1986

She stepped into his heart
treading softly
not disturbing his pride
whispering melodies
          that brushed his soul

I n the early spring of 1977, Shula was offered a job in Toronto with the Ontario Arts Council. She asked me if I would be willing to move to Toronto so that Meher, Dahlia, and I would not be cut off from each other. I could have refused her request and entered into a legal battle to keep the kids in Ottawa, but I decided against this, because I was tired of fighting and also because I had no resources to support a sustained legal battle. Also, if Shula had a solid job, the kids could be properly looked after while I struggled to get back on my feet. In addition, I had a feeling that Toronto would turn out to be good for me. Eventually this hunch was realized well beyond my hopes and expectations.

Gabriele (circa 1980)

It was, however, one thing to move with my family to another city and something quite different to make such a move knowing that the family was no longer intact. I couldn't stop thinking that I was no longer going to be there each night when my kids went to bed, or be around all the time to help them with school and share in their daily joys and tribulations. I somehow couldn't get my head around this. All I knew was that it hurt, and there was nothing I could do to soften the pain.

To add to this, I had to leave Gabriele at a time when our relationship was just beginning to blossom. She was as upset as I was. We worked out a system whereby I would come to Ottawa for a week or so each month, and occasionally she would come to Toronto for a weekend. My trips to Ottawa frequently combined business and romance, as I had a few private clients there who wanted to continue seeing me, and I would do workshops from time to time at Strathmere. When school schedules permitted, I would take the kids with me to Ottawa, as Meher and Dahlia got along well with Gabriele, who showed both children a lot of care and loving. They would also often be with us when she came to Toronto. So there was a considerable amount of commuting for me as I made the five-hour trip between us at regular intervals. For the most part, the travel was enjoyable, with interesting discoveries along the way.

Another difficulty I had to face was living in a big city. Since I was a small-town boy, Toronto was never my idea of a home base. A visit now and then I could deal with, but to live there was, for me, a daunting prospect. Fortunately, as the years went by, the city grew on me. (Thirty-five years later, I boast about Toronto whenever I have the chance, especially to American visitors, who always make positive comments to me about the "Little Apple.")

Arriving in Toronto in the late summer of 1977, I had two immediate issues to deal with — where to live and how to make a living. With barely two nickels to rub together and no shelter, I spent the first few months sleeping on friends' couches, including Shula's. In January 1978, I found a small apartment with low rent, where I lived until 1986. The apartment was above a beauty salon, so my unit was usually well perfumed from the hairsprays that wafted up through the vents. The building was two storeys high, with a music store on the ground floor in the corner section. There, I bought a new harmonica, which I had learned to play on my first visit to Israel in 1954. Why the harmonica? It seemed to be a popular instrument in Israel in those days, and I took to it. Not that I was ever an accomplished musician, but I did learn how to play a single reed at a time, one of the first obstacles an aspiring harmonica player needs to master. I could usually get people's attention with my version of "Michael Row the Boat Ashore" and "Shenandoah." It gave me many hours of pleasure.

As for making a living, I began by having business cards printed, advertising that I did general psychotherapy with a specialty in dreams, past-life regression, and psychogenic illness (illness not responding to conventional medical treatment). My first client came to me quite by accident. I needed to have a dream workshop brochure photocopied, and a kind librarian offered to do several copies for me without charge while I was in the library. When, after a few minutes, she brought the copies back to me, she said she couldn't help but notice the subject matter, and told me that she had some dreams that puzzled her. Although she didn't come to the workshop, she did become my first private client in Toronto and remained with me, on and off, for many years.

To do psychotherapy, I needed some kind of venue where the rent was cheap and the location appropriate. At this point I met Dr. Sheila Pennington, a psychotherapist, who had a large room above a convenience store on Yonge Street, just north of Eglinton, which she was willing to rent to me on an as-needed basis. Sheila and I did a lot of anger work with clients, and part of the therapy involved clients pounding with a plastic bat on a padded leather block and screaming to their hearts' content. The room had to be somewhat soundproofed, so the floor had a thick foam covering overlaid by a heavy canvas. However, the sound could still to some extent be heard in the store below us, and when a client really got into the swing of things, the light fixtures hanging from the ceiling of the store would shake. Sheila told me that one time, before I came onto the scene, a client's screams were so loud that they carried out onto the street, and the convenience-store owner called the police because he thought someone was being murdered above him. Sheila had to do a lot of explaining to the policemen, who were not reassured until the client himself appeared and vouched for what she was saying. After a search, they left. However, the writing was on the wall, and eventually we moved to a basement unit under a bank on Eglinton Avenue West. It was perfect, as there were no windows and the bank's ceiling was many feet thick as a security measure. For us, this meant excellent sound insulation, and in our many years there, we never received a complaint.

Our mutual interest in Meher and Dahlia kept Shula and me in constant contact, which, in retrospect, helped us work through difficult personal and legal issues. However, even with regular contact it took about five years for us to develop a sustainable friendship, which has since grown considerably. Twice a year we enjoy our children's birthday parties together, and we are also together on certain Jewish holidays. As well, my many cousins here in Toronto always include her in family gatherings. My parents, even during the most difficult periods of the divorce, kept an open heart for Shula and always treated her like a daughter.

While I struggled to make a living, Shula was doing well in her new job. Having an honours degree in art history from Carleton University, she was a natural for her position at the Ontario Arts Council. With her income, she was able to make a down payment on a new condo in Thornhill, a suburb north of Toronto. Eventually, this building also became my home.

Building my practice to the point where I had a good income took all of five years. Slowly, word got out about my specialties, and interest grew. I had numerous radio and television interviews about either dreams or past-life regression, and this brought in clients, at times so many that I had up to a six-month waiting list. It was not unusual for my day to begin at seven in the morning and end twelve to thirteen hours later. I never worked a fifty-minute hour, as was common with many psychotherapists, and my time with a client could last from an hour to two or three hours. I believed then, and still do, that some clients need a lot of sustained time to get to the point where they can make a minor or major breakthrough, and one hour often isn't sufficient. Granted, there is always the next appointment, but it could take the entire hour or more to get back to the point where we had left off, only to have a repeat of the previous situation. I felt that sometimes a client purposely, though without conscious awareness, engineered our session so it wouldn't be too long, in order to avoid having to deal with difficult and painful material. However, arranging my appointments without a specific time limit could be tricky, as I had to guess how much time I might need with a client and schedule other clients around this. At our first meetings, I would always tell new clients that they might have to wait a considerable length of time in the waiting room before I could see them, but by the same token, if they needed more time, someone else would wait for them. Once I got to know a client, I was often able to determine quite accurately how much time to allow for the next session. It was rare that I received a complaint from anyone about waiting too long.

My general philosophy toward psychotherapy was that if the therapist could get something to move in the client's psyche, then good things would follow. I jokingly referred to my approach as "gum ball therapy," as I explained it to my clients using the analogy of a gum ball dispenser. When you put a coin into the machine and remove a gum ball, or two or three, the remaining gum balls rearrange themselves into an altered configuration. In a similar manner, change could occur in the client. Most of the time I found that when something was stuck in my client's psychological makeup, shaking it up would produce healthy progress. Usually the shaking up needed to be at the emotional level, and for this reason I tried to work primarily with feelings. However, from time to time I met a client for whom this approach did not produce change, but for whom things began to happen when we switched to the intellectual level — talking and analyzing. For these individuals, gaining insight with the mind rather than through feelings often resulted in profound changes. Generally, however, the intellectual route was slower and not as effective.

Occasionally I would attend workshops to learn new theories and techniques that I might integrate into my practice. As an example, I learned about Gestalt therapy from two individuals who visited the ashram when I was living there, and a few years later, I attended a workshop in Toronto where I witnessed it in practice. On occasion, I use some elements from Gestalt therapy in my work, and find it works well. I also looked into bioenergetics, Hakomi, and forgiveness therapy. Whatever I felt might contribute to my knowledge and my clients' well-being was grist for the mill. I also did not hesitate to draw from my rabbinical training when I felt this was appropriate. One of my favourite stories to tell clients who persisted in intellectualizing every-thing and not doing anything comes from the Book of Exodus, chapter 24, verse 7. "Then [Moses] took the record of the covenant and read it aloud to the people. And they responded, 'Everything that the Lord has said we will do and we will hear.'" I would explain to my client that sometimes one has to act ("do") before thinking too much about a situation, and that only through action will one come to understand ("hear") the value of the action. In other words, if the reader will forgive the juxtaposition, as the Nike ad suggests, "Just do it!"

I discovered another technique as a result of a relationship I had in 1984 with Dona, a gifted astrologer. I used to attend her workshops to learn more about this field, but I never quite caught on to it. However, one aspect of Dona's work intrigued me. She said she was often able to determine, from a client's astrological chart, talents that lay hidden in the person's subconscious. It occurred to me that if, with Dona's help, I could help a psychotherapy client develop one or more hidden talents, this might be highly beneficial to the client's well-being. I suggested to selected clients that they might want to have Dona give them an astrological reading, which we could then use in therapy. A few clients were willing to do this, and after their sessions with Dona they brought the readings (usually eight to ten pages) to me.

My approach was to read to the client very slowly what Dona had writ-ten. As I read, I frequently looked at the client to see if there was any emotional reaction, such as a change in breathing, tears, hesitation, or flushing. When something along these lines manifested, I asked the client to talk more about this. Sometimes this lasted for the rest of the session, in which case we picked up again at the next session, when I continued reading aloud.

I found this to be a very effective way of drawing forth from my client emotions that he or she might not have been able to access otherwise. Also, when I came to those items in the reading that touched upon hidden talents, the mention of these usually evoked strong responses. Later, in discussing this with my clients, most acknowledged that they had always had a yearning to express themselves through these talents. Dona's readings encouraged them to consider exploring their hidden possibilities.

Unfortunately, my relationship with Dona was brief, and I was not able to continue referring clients to her.

DURING MY EARLY years in Toronto, I would often return to Ottawa where I had a small following. I did most of my work at Strathmere and occasionally at Gabriele's place.

On one visit to Ottawa, I received an unusual request from a client. From time to time it was my practise, when I felt it would be appropriate and to the client's advantage, to suggest that she or he visit a loved one's grave alone and talk to the deceased out loud. This was a way of trying to find closure on some issue that lingered between the client and the deceased, and I found it often brought clients relief. In this particular case, the departed loved one was the client's mother, and I agreed to accompany the client, a middle-aged woman, to the cemetery. This was something I had not done before, but she said she didn't feel she could go unless I was with her. We agreed that she would pick me up at 10:00 a.m. in front of Gabriele's apartment building. That morning, as I awaited her arrival, I heard a motor revving in the distance. A moment later she pulled up on her motorcycle—leathers, helmet, and all. "Hop on," she said, handing me the spare helmet. We drove through the city and into the country, eventually arriving at the Jewish cemetery. We walked awhile and, coming upon her mother's grave, she said, "Hi ma! I've brought the rabbi!" With little encouragement from me, she began to talk to her mother, and soon was deep into her monologue. When I realized she didn't need me any more, I excused myself, telling her to take as much time as she liked and that I would wait for her near the entrance. About a half hour later she joined me and took me to a nearby pub, where she bought us both a drink and wished me a *L'chayim* (to life), as she felt unburdened and was looking forward to a new chapter in her journey. Then she took me safely back to where I was staying. And to think I got paid for all of this.

In London, Ontario, which is about a two-hour drive west of Toronto, I trained a group of five people to do dream therapy using the re-dreaming and figure-identification technique mentioned earlier. I also had two students in Toronto, one a physician and the other a tai chi teacher, whom I trained in this technique.

One individual I had the pleasure of befriending when visiting London to work with the group was Macleary Drope, a gifted artist whose work has been on display at the National Gallery in Ottawa. "Mac," as we in the group called him, once took me on a walk through some woods in Ontario, which is an experience I'll always remember. He had a very keen eye and kept pointing out to me things in the landscape, such as shapes and forms in the earth and foliage, that I would never have noticed on my own. I drew from this an important lesson—there is so much all around us we never see or hear unless we have cultivated a special sensitivity. I extrapolate from this to the spiritual realm, where I believe that while some individuals are gifted spiritually, most of us can be trained to expand our awareness to dimensions of reality that are beyond conventional apprehension.

As networking was an important part of developing a client base, I would attend relevant conferences and social gatherings where I thought participants might be interested in my work, either as clients or as professional contacts; my hope was that the physicians, psychiatrists, and other appropriate health professionals I met might refer patients to me. Such referrals came to me regularly until I began retiring from my practice, around 2004.

I was always very careful not to take on clients I felt were borderline psychotic or in other ways highly unstable. I made exceptions when such clients were referred to me by a psychiatrist or medical doctor practising psychotherapy. As long as the referring doctor and I could work together, I would accept the client knowing that if I needed backup, in the form of access to medication or hospitalization for the client, it was available. Usually when a medical professional referred someone to me, it was because the professional had exhausted his or her expertise and the patient was floundering. In other words, I became, for many patients, "a court of last resort." I would like to be able to say that I always came through for them; however, such was not the case. While often I was able to help, there were certainly situations where my best efforts were for naught. In such cases I always felt bad that I couldn't help the individual, but eventually I learned to be at peace with such failures, realizing that I, like everyone else, had limitations. And, when my best efforts were unproductive, I would refer a client to someone I thought might be able to help.

In addition to individual therapy, I worked occasionally with couples and with groups. Doing group therapy was always satisfying and exciting. I found that when one member of a group was courageous and opened up about his or her life, it gave other members permission to do the same. In addition, issues presented by one person frequently reflected issues in other group members' lives. One of the great advantages of group therapy is that people realize they are not alone in their troubles, and this gives comfort. It also gives participants tools: they see how someone works through a particular problem, thereby seeing often what can be done with their own similar situation.

I always found couples therapy challenging and difficult. Often, by the time a couple got to me, their relationship was in such disarray, and so much damage had been done, that there was little I could do but help them separate with some degree of amicability. Sometimes, not even this was possible. When I did help a couple find each other again and bring their relationship to a healthier level, I rejoiced with them and always felt good about the work we had done together. As part of the therapy I had a simple recipe for those couples who were struggling but whose relationship was still intact. I suggested that they take one weekend a month and go away, without kids, to a hotel or cottage or whatever was available and affordable, and just be together, without external interruptions. I learned this recipe from a psychiatrist friend who told me this story: "After twenty years of marriage and three kids, my wife and I finally got away for a weekend alone together. It was an odd and unfamiliar experience, but at the end of two days, we rediscovered one another and were reminded why we got married in the first place."

I originally held to the position that a good couples therapist should be able to work with both partners. This meant that I would see each partner alone and would also meet with them both together at specified intervals or when needed. I found this worked for me, although as time went on and I became more experienced, I came to appreciate the perspective of those who advocated seeing only one partner of a couple and leaving the other partner to work with another therapist. It's certainly easier to be supportive of one individual than two when those two are in conflict, and if the therapist is in denial about his personal bias, it makes matters even more difficult.

I'm not one to become easily depressed. In my psychotherapy practice I would hear horrific stories, to which I always tried to respond with compassion and empathy. But, unless it was an extraordinary situation, such as a client with suicidal leanings, I could close my office door at the end of the day and leave everything behind. There was, however, another exception, and this was when I was dealing with a parent who had lost a child. In the spring of 1989, as fate would have it, I had a series of parents whose children had died for one reason or another, from illness to accident to fetal abnormalities. (With one Jewish client, I conducted the burial service for the infant.) I wasn't aware of the toll this was taking on me until one day I recognized that I was in a state of depression. Eventually I figured out the reason for this and then had to decide what to do about it. My solution was radical, given that while my income had improved considerably, I still had to watch my expenses carefully. I decided to buy a new car. So, building on my romance with the automobile, I began to work on finding the right vehicle and arranging financing. The whole process lasted about two months and engaged me so totally that, as my excitement grew and the day to pick up the vehicle came near, I realized that my depression had lifted. By the time I drove away in my new Pontiac Bonneville sse, I felt normal again. The car lasted until 2001 and gave me twelve years of pleasure.

IN ADDITION TO my practise as a psychotherapist, I continued some activity as a rabbi, responding to requests for weddings, funerals, and other life-cycle events. Also, in my early years in Toronto I was very active in the Jewish Information

Class (JIC), a class for individuals wishing to convert to Judaism. Rabbi Gunther Plaut, at that time the senior rabbi at Holy Blossom Temple and a fine Judaic scholar, arranged for me to oversee the candidates and give rabbinic direction. Besides giving me much-needed income, this job was to my liking, as I have always enjoyed working with individuals wishing to embrace the Jewish faith. My function was to meet with students in the class on a regular basis, keeping my eye out for actual or potential problems and being supportive when support was needed. I believe I was up to the task, and on only one occasion that I know of did I let an inappropriate candidate slip between my fingers.

A young woman in the class whom I'll call Joan (not her real name) was an excellent student, very bright, sensitive, and committed to becoming Jewish. Her teachers had high praise for her, and the required essay she wrote was well researched and impressive. She easily passed the *Bet Din* (tribunal of three rabbis who examined her at the completion of the program); after that she went to *mikveh* (ritual immersion), the final step in becoming Jewish. A few weeks later, in a ceremony at one of the Reform congregations in Toronto, she and several of her classmates received their Hebrew names. During the reception she introduced me to her father, who was very proud of his daughter, and we chatted awhile.

Ordinarily the story would happily end here. However, there is a postscript: A few years later, when I was visiting with some friends on a late Friday afternoon before Shabbat, someone asked if any of us had ever been to a Jewish-Christian service. Puzzled by the term, I asked for clarification. I was told that there was a congregation where Jews practised Judaism and believed in Jesus. For me this was a contradiction in terms, but I also found it somewhat intriguing and wondered what this was all about. So I went along with the group to the service, held in the rented space of a hotel. Lo and behold, who should appear to conduct the service but Joan's father, wearing a *kippah* and *tallit* (prayer shawl). Close behind was Joan, who seated herself at the piano and led the musical part of the service, while her father conducted the liturgical aspects. To say I was flabbergasted would be an understatement. I was tempted to get up and leave but, upon reconsidering, decided to stay and view it as an educational experience. (Perhaps I was rationalizing a little.) I squirmed every time Jesus' name was mentioned, not because I have anything against Jesus, but rather because his name did not belong in what was supposed to be a Jewish service. When the service ended about an hour later, Joan and her father came over and wished me a *Shabbat Shalom* (Sabbath Peace) before I could make my exit. I was polite, given the setting, but I felt duped. Had I or anyone else known that Joan intended to be a "Jew for Jesus," she would never have been allowed into the JIC course, let alone become a Jew. She and her father undoubtedly realized this, and so I did not feel very kindly toward either of them.

MY RELATIONSHIP WITH Gabriele, and my monthly trips to Ottawa to spend time with her, continued until 1981. It was a good four years, and we did many interesting things together, including peeing on the Chicago freeway. This happened one day when we had been visiting friends of mine in Highland Park, a northern suburb of the Windy City. We left their place to begin the journey back to Toronto, but decided to first stop for a cup of tea at a lovely tea room restaurant that our hosts had recommended. I don't recall the name of the tea we tried, but it had something in it that so stimulated our bladders, we couldn't drive for more than twenty minutes without having to find a place to relieve ourselves. As we got onto the freeway (having made sure to take care of business first), we looked at each other, crossed our legs (at least she did—I was driving), and hoped for the best, which would be, at the very least, a convenient exit. Sure enough, fifteen minutes on the freeway and the urge began to mount. We kept looking for someplace to get off, but finally, realizing that we only had minutes before the unthinkable would occur, I pulled over near a guardrail and opened both doors on the passenger side. The space between the doors became our bathroom and, as cars whizzed by, each of us in turn paid tribute to that old Coca-Cola ad, "The Pause that Refreshes." We made it to the outskirts of the city and into the countryside, where ample opportunities for pausing presented themselves.

My dear friend Harry Prosen, former chairman of the Department of Psychiatry at the University of Manitoba, was in Toronto one day when Gabriele was visiting me and we were fighting over some issue without resolution. I suggested to her that I give Harry a call at his hotel and see if he could help us resolve the conflict. Harry invited us up and, after a while, realizing that the conflict was not going to be resolved, gave us a piece of general advice I have never forgotten. He said, "When you and your partner have exhausted all avenues of discussion and find yourselves at an impasse, stop trying to fix the situation, and simply be physical with each other—cuddle, make love, and then at a later point, perhaps a few days later, if things still haven't been resolved, go back and try to talk about it again." Later that evening, Gabrielle and I were smiling. His advice has stood me in good stead on numerous occasions ever since.

IN THE EARLY eighties I learned to downhill ski. Having grown up on the Prairies, where one had to search to find a hill, I didn't know one end of a ski from another. A week at Grey Rocks, an excellent ski school in the Laurentian Mountains about two hours north of Montreal, turned me into a decent intermediate skier. Later, when Meher was ten years old, I introduced him to skiing at Grey Rocks, and some years later Meher and I gave Dahlia her first lesson at Upland's ski hill in Thornhill, just north of Toronto.

During one ski vacation with Meher at Grey Rocks, I waited in the dining room at lunchtime for my son to join me, as we had separate classes that were determined according to one's level. As time passed and I didn't see him, I began to worry. Finally, someone came to my table and told me to go to the front desk. I was told that Meher had had a ski accident and was at a clinic in St. Jovite, a twenty-minute ride from the resort. When I got there, the doctor told me he suspected a fracture in Meher's leg, gave me the X-rays, and suggested I return immediately to Toronto or take him to an orthopaedic surgeon in St. Jerome, about an hour away. I returned to Grey Rocks, packed our things, checked out, and went back to St. Jovite to pick up my son — literally. I carried him on my back. (The manager at Grey Rocks was terrific. He sympathized with my situation and only charged me for the portion of the week that we had used, even though we had committed to a weekly plan.)

In St. Jerome, the orthopaedic surgeon looked at the X-rays and said that there was a fracture and that he could operate on Meher, or I could take him back to Toronto for surgery. I opted for Toronto. To keep Meher comfortable and his leg stable for the journey, one of the residents put a cast on his leg. On the way back, we stayed overnight at Gabriele's place in Ottawa and in the morning continued our journey. Upon arriving in Toronto, I took Meher immediately to his pediatrician, Dr. Sydney Rosen. He examined Meher and told us he was going to call a friend of his, Dr. Bobechko, at the Hospital for Sick Children and arrange immediately for a consultation. He called the hospital and was informed that Dr. Bobechko was in surgery. He told the receptionist to patch him through to the surgical ward, then asked the nurse there to put the doctor on the phone. I'll always remember the conversation Dr. Rosen had with his friend: "Hello, Walter. It's Sydney. So how are things? What are you up to? Listen, I have a kid here who had a ski accident. Can I send him down now for you to have a look at the X-rays? Great! Thanks, Walter. Talk to you soon." I imagined Dr. Bobechko standing there in the operating room with scalpel in one hand and phone in the other. I guess it was all in a day's work.

At the hospital, an orthopaedic resident was sent ahead by Dr. Bobechko to have a look at the X-rays and give an opinion. He concurred with the orthopaedist in St. Jerome: Meher would need surgery. Finally, Dr. Bobechko appeared, looked at the X-rays for about twenty seconds, and concluded that with a little physiotherapy, Meher would be fine. And he was. No surgery — just the eye of an experienced and excellent physician.

I tell this story because from it I learned a valuable lesson. I discovered later that Dr. Bobechko had an international reputation in pediatric orthopaedics. He was, in other words, a surgeon's surgeon. His discriminating eye, with years of experience, saw what lesser surgeons failed to see. After that incident, whenever one of my children had a medical problem, I sought out the best I could find in the field and would rarely trust a first opinion, or, as in the case of Meher's leg, even a second. This stood me in good stead when Dahlia had recurring sore throats year after year. A specialist examined her, drew me some sketches of pus pockets in the throat, and said she would have to have her tonsils out and then everything would be fine. I took her back to Sick Kids to get a second opinion, which was that she would probably outgrow the problem in a few years. Within two years she was fine, and today, about thirty years later, she still has her tonsils.

My visits to the Laurentians were not only for skiing. One summer I spent several days at Vishnudevananda's yoga camp near Val-Morin. After much hard work, Vishnu had purchased a piece of property and made it into a retreat where his followers and others could come and spend a week or longer doing yoga, meditating, and participating in various kinds of spiritual encounters. The week I was there about a hundred people showed up, with some sleeping in cabins and others in tents. On Friday evening, Vishnu invited an Israeli woman and myself to conduct a creative Shabbat service for all present. The service went well and involved the usual Shabbat rituals, with the woman lighting the candles and me making the blessing over the wine. Normally, wine is not permitted in a yoga setting (like the ashram in British Columbia), but because it was for religious purposes, Vishnu didn't mind. During the service I gave explanations about the Shabbat and Judaism, since most of those present were not Jewish. After he established his retreat in Val-Morin, Vishnu founded other yoga retreats in different parts of the world, including the Bahamas. It was in Val-Morin, however, that I saw Vishnu for the last time. Several years later he passed on.

DURING MY JOURNEYS between Toronto and Ottawa to see Gabriele, I always drove through a small town called Tweed, which was at exactly the halfway point. As I exited Tweed on my way to Highway 7, a distance of about ten miles, I passed a sign on my left that advertised some kind of an artist's camp or colony. I made a note of this and told myself that on one of my excursions, I would drive in and explore exactly what was there. Finally, after driving by umpteen times over the four years I was with Gabriele, the day came that I turned off the road and into the establishment.

First I noticed a house at the top of a small elevation and knocked on the door. I explained to the woman who answered that I had seen their sign and was curious about what was being offered. She told me it was a school for artists and that, if I wished, I could go down to the studio and visit freely.

The studio turned out to be a large room, like a social hall. About a dozen adults were busy, each on his or her own, painting in acrylics, oils, or watercolours. No one approached me to ask what I was doing there, so I simply walked from station to station and looked at the work being produced. For the most part, I was not very impressed. It all looked pretty amateurish until I came upon a man in his forties, intensely focused on what he was doing. I watched him, not wanting to disturb his concentration, for perhaps ten or fifteen minutes, until he looked up and saw me. I said hello and told him I was visiting and that I liked his work very much. He thanked me, and we began to talk. As it turned out, he was the teacher. Our conversation deepened until he felt comfortable enough to tell me about a major concern in his life.

The man had recently been diagnosed with a serious heart condition. His doctor told him that he had to remain calm and relaxed and not get too excited or his life might be endangered; if he followed these orders, he could have a normal lifespan. His problem was that, as an artist, he had to be passionate about his work or what he produced would be only mediocre. He felt that, since his diagnosis, he was painting far below his standards, and he was feeling very frustrated and unfulfilled. Passion and a weak heart were not good companions. He asked me if I had any thoughts about what he should do. I wasn't sure what to tell him, although I knew what I wanted to say. Finally, after some hemming and hawing, and with encouragement from him to speak my mind, I told him that I didn't feel one's life should be measured in terms of quantity but rather in terms of quality. A shorter life lived fully and

with passion was, in my view, a better choice than a long life without fulfillment. And, I added, a life with meaning can contribute to one's health and
possibly prolong a person's life. The artist looked at me and for a few minutes
was silent. Then he took my hand and thanked me, upon which I wished him
well and took my leave. I don't remember his name and I'm not even sure he
gave it to me, nor do I remember giving mine to him. I trust and hope that he
went on and lived a good life in the manner that most pleased him and that
his work graces the walls of homes across this country and beyond.

> We are all angels
> delivering messages
> one to another
> We are all angels
> revealing secrets within
> beyond understanding
> We are all angels
> drawing from beyond
> sustaining our souls

Upon our arrival in Toronto in 1977, one of my first concerns was my
son's Jewish education. (Dahlia was still a bit too young, and later she followed Meher to attend the school at Temple Har Zion). Toronto offered a
number of options, but the one I most preferred was to enroll Meher in a
Jewish day school, where I felt his needs would be best served. However, we
arrived late in the summer, so I did not have the opportunity to set all this up,
and instead we registered him at the local elementary school, E.J. Sands,
where he went for that first year. E.J. Sands is nestled among the woods in
Thornhill, an idyllic setting for children. On weekends, I would sometimes
go with Meher to the school playground and push him on the swings, or take
advantage of some of the other facilities available. Whenever we did this,
before leaving the playground, Meher would always want to spend some time
in his favourite tree, a big old oak.

One day, toward the spring of 1978, I told Meher I wanted him to spend
half a day visiting a classroom in the Leo Baeck Day School, which at that
time was housed in Temple Emanu-El, also located in a beautiful park setting. I explained to him my reason for taking him there, and he was at first
resistant, until I assured him that the final decision would be his. I know
that where a child receives his or her education is usually a parental decision,

but in this case, because of all the disruption created by the breakup of the marriage and leaving his Ottawa school and friends, I didn't want to cause Meher any more distress. He enjoyed the class at Leo Baeck, but when I asked him if he would like to go there from now on, he said no. I asked him why and he replied, "I don't want to leave my tree!" I thought about his reply, and something deep in me resonated as I remembered the tree I sadly left in Regina when we moved. And that was the end of the story. Meher went on at E.J. Sands (Dahlia joining him after two years) and graduated there some years later.

A VERY CLOSE and cherished friend came into my life while I was living in Ottawa. Yvonne McKinley was a yoga instructor in Toronto, and on one of my visits on NMUDD business, she invited me to a gathering of yoga students who were the followers of the teacher Amrit Desai. His organization was called Kripalu, and he was meeting with his disciples at one of the hotels in the city. Yvonne and I arrived at the venue, a very large hall in which about two hundred people were standing and talking, and situated ourselves at one end of the room. Suddenly, a voice cried out something, and a tall, handsome man in robes entered the room at the other end. The next thing I knew, everyone prostrated themselves on the floor, which left only two people standing—Amrit and me. I looked at him and he looked at me. Anyone entering the hall at that moment could not have been sure whom everyone was bowing down to, Amrit or myself. I felt embarrassed and wanted to disappear, but there was nowhere to go. Someone on the floor nearby motioned for me to bow down, but I refused. A little later, Yvonne took me over and introduced me to Amrit, being certain to use my title of "rabbi" (she always got a kick out of having a rabbi as one of her best friends). We chatted a short while and toward the end of our conversation I asked him, "So, Amrit [everyone else called him *Gurudev*—beloved guru], what's this business about all these people bowing down to you?" He replied, "They feel they need to do it!" I said nothing, but thought, "Well, I think you need it more than they do, or you would tell them not to do it." I held my peace until a few years later.

That day came about five years after the meeting, when Yvonne was director of Yoga Centre Toronto, at that time perhaps the largest yoga centre in the country. She asked me if I would help her drive several yoga students in a van to Amrit's ashram in Pennsylvania for a four-day retreat. She added that my room and board would be taken care of at the ashram, in exchange for my giving a talk on dreams. I accepted the invitation, and we headed down to the States. The drive was not without incident, as the van broke down about fifty miles outside of Toronto, and we had to spend the night in a motel. We arrived at the ashram the next day, about a half-day later than originally expected.

The ashram was very lovely, except that there was nowhere I could find privacy. Even out of doors, it seemed that the hedges had been cut and almost all the trees had been removed, so that, no matter in what direction one looked, everything was open. Even if you sat behind a tree, you were exposed. This was certainly not conducive to clandestine meetings between men and women. In fact, like the ashram where I had lived, anything sexual was discouraged. There weren't any signs or posters conveying this message, but it was nevertheless loud and clear. I was bunked with several other men and the women with other women. I asked one of the residents what people did with their sexual inclinations, and he answered that they subdued them and channelled them into spiritual directions. "Hmm!" I thought. "I wonder how successful they are." However, upon further reflection and remembering my own ashram experience, I concluded that the sexual suppression here was so strong and privacy so absent that the subduing of sexual desires was facilitated by the atmosphere. Nowhere and at no time did I witness any physical affection between the sexes, even among those few who were married. I don't know what they did in their habitats, but it wouldn't surprise me if abstinence was the order of the day unless procreation was desired.

On the second day of our visit, we were summoned to an audience with Amrit, who welcomed us as he sat cross-legged with a disciple on either side. Our Toronto group asked him a number of questions, while I remained in the background; Amrit did not seem to recognize me. Toward the end of our audience, which lasted about two hours, one of the group asked Amrit what the secret was whereby so many people from India reached such high spiritual peaks. He waxed eloquent on this topic and concluded that vegetarianism and sexual abstinence were key ingredients for producing the greatest spiritual masters the world has ever known. With this statement, I could no longer contain myself. I raised my hand and said, "Amrit, I come from the tradition of Judaism. My faith has produced individuals like Moses, Isaiah, Jeremiah, Amos, and Elijah, all prophets of great spiritual stature and recognized all over the Western world as such. My scriptures abound with such individuals, yet none of them, to the best of anyone's knowledge, were vegetarians or abstained from sex. In fact, the first commandment in our Holy Scriptures tells us to be fruitful and multiply. How do you account for this?"

He looked at me and said, "What do you do?"

I replied, "I'm a rabbi!"

"Oh," he responded, "Jewish people like to debate!" End of conversation.

Word got out that I had challenged the guru, and I was soon notified that my dream lecture scheduled for the following day was cancelled. I couldn't wait to leave but had to bide my time for the sake of the group.

Yvonne, who remained an admirer of Amrit, wasn't in the least fazed or upset by my interaction with him; in fact, shortly afterwards she asked me if I would serve on the board of directors at Yoga Centre Toronto, which I did for a few years. I also became involved in the centre's yoga teacher-training program, teaching the trainees communication skills so they could have a better rapport with their future students.

Yvonne and me dancing to "Never On Sunday" at her 65th birthday (2000)

My relationship with Yvonne continued to grow over the years, and every now and then we would go ballroom dancing. I mention this because, to this day, Yvonne and I laugh and brag about a dancing contest we won in Toronto. A few years later, I was the MC at her sixty-fifth birthday party, a gathering of about sixty family and friends. At one point, I took the microphone and said, "Good friends and family, rumour has it that over these many years, Yvonne and I have been having an affair. I wish to clarify. I love Yvonne dearly, but we have never been sexually involved and in this regard our feelings are mutual. It's been strictly platonic." To which everyone, as if on cue, responded, "Aww!" Our friendship continues as I write, although she is currently quite ill, and I worry about her.

While on the topic of yoga: As I've mentioned, while working for NMUDD I had become acquainted with the 3HO Yoga Ashram on Palmerston Boulevard in Toronto. When I lived in Toronto, I was invited to teach Israeli folk dancing there one evening. I arrived with a cache of Jewish records (vinyl) and set things up in their largest room. About thirty members showed up, most with white turbans wound around their heads. I began with a *hora* but didn't have to teach any steps for this dance, as many of the participants, turbans and all, were Jews. It was a great evening.

They hadn't forgotten that in addition to being yogis, they were also Jewish.

Later that year, I was asked by one of the Jewish organizations in Toronto to give a lecture on the similarities between Judaism and Buddhism, as a way to help give those Jews who had gone over to Buddhism a bridge by which to come home. The organization felt that with my background in meditation and Eastern religions, I might have something meaningful to say to the group. At this well-attended lecture, the question most often asked, albeit in many different forms, had to do with the inner life. Many of those who had turned to Buddhism (and Hinduism) felt that Judaism had a strong external form but little to say about what one does on the inside. They had been attracted to meditation and soul growth, not realizing that Judaism had a great deal to offer in both of these areas. My response to their questions was an affirmation, backed up by examples, of the importance of the inner life and meditation in Judaism, from biblical times onward. I could see by their faces and body language that what I was offering was new to them and that the parameters along which I spoke had never been presented to them. I don't know whether my words had any lasting results, but I hope I at least gave those present some food for thought. Perhaps, too, I was able to reach them because while I understand what it is to be Jewish, in some inexplicable way, I also understand what it is to not be Jewish.

This jewish world
        flows past me
I am of it
        and out of it
weaving in and out
                        of david's star
                not knowing my place
                        then landing
                            briefly
                            re-rooted
        but always now
                            briefly
                before moving on
                                into galaxies
        where jew is not
        returning to solar dust
                            our common mother

ON ONE OF my trips to Ottawa, a psychotherapy client told me she needed to dance naked in front of Jesus. I asked her to explain. She said it was always a vision of hers that if she could do this, it would feel like a complete spiritual giving of herself, and that this would make a major difference in her life. I suggested that there were other ways of doing this, and she agreed, but remained convinced that this particular act would advance her psychologically and spiritually more than any amount of therapy or religious ritual. She convinced me that this was important to her, so I set about to try to arrange it. I approached a friend of mine, a Christian minister at one of the Ottawa churches, and explained the situation to him. He was sympathetic and said he would see what he could do. A few days later, he called me and said he had a plan. We got together and he told me that the church was very quiet between 12:00 and 1:00 p.m., as most of the staff went out for lunch. The plan was to have my client alone in the sanctuary, with all doors locked and the door windows covered with a sheet. He and I would stand guard outside the doors while my client went through her ritual. She was overjoyed to hear the news, and she came at the established time, did her naked dance, then dressed and came out to thank the minister. I then went with her to a room and helped her process her experience. She was radiant and had what some might describe as a "born-again" appearance. This concluded our relationship.

Over the years, I have from time to time thought about my client's wish to dance naked before Jesus. I have tried to imagine the nature of the primitive forces that compelled her in this direction. As I pondered, the image of Adam and Eve in the Garden of Eden appeared in my vision. There was, it seemed to me, a naturalness in their nudity, a purity of spirit and a sense of wholeness that transcends morality, culture, and convention. For them, clothing was still a foreign concept.

On this topic, one day during my early years in Toronto, a lady friend invited me to visit a nudist colony located about an hour's drive from Toronto. I accepted her invitation and, on a beautiful summer's day, we entered the colony. It was a lovely setting, with an artificial pond for swimming and areas for sunning or sitting in the shade, according to preference. It might have been any resort, except that everyone was nude, including us. For a few minutes, the scene felt unnatural to me, and then that feeling dissipated as my friend and I lay on the grass, along with everyone else, and sunned ourselves. Later, we swam in the pond and strolled the grounds, in a manner no different than if we were wearing clothes. For the first time, I had a glimmer of what my client was desiring: freedom, simplicity, naturalness, and rejoicing before

God in a dance of gratitude for life and the magnificence of the human body. When we left the colony later that day, I had a feeling of liberation, and I was just a bit awkward in the clothing that again covered my body.

AS IT HAS always been my practice to have a yearly medical checkup, shortly after coming to Toronto I searched out a doctor to look after my health needs. Before long, someone was recommended to me, and I went to see him for a first appointment. The man seemed competent and thorough, though somewhat distant and not very talkative. In my third year with this doctor, he noticed a lesion on my chest. It had been there for many years, since long before I ever met this doctor, so I was a bit puzzled as to why he was just noticing it now. I wasn't too worried, as I had had it looked at some years before by a dermatologist, who said it was a little suspicious and to keep my eye on it. I guess I had assumed my current GP had seen it when he first examined it, but said nothing because he wasn't concerned. Now, however, he seemed very concerned, and, after putting a magnifying glass to my chest, said to me in a rather nonchalant manner, "It's cancer!"

I almost fell off the examining table. "Cancer?" I gasped.

"Yes," he replied. "But just to make sure, I want you to meet me tomorrow morning at 9:00 a.m. in the emergency room at Branson Hospital. I'm going to cut it out and send it to the lab for analysis. Hopefully it's just on the surface and hasn't penetrated further into your chest." I left his office in shock.

My dilemma was whether to go ahead with the surgery or wait while I tried to heal it myself or find someone else with healing abilities, like the man in Montreal, who unfortunately was no longer around. I wrestled with this predicament and talked to some friends, one a nurse, and all suggested I go ahead with the surgery.

The next morning I was on the table in the emergency room. The doctor gave me a local anesthetic and cut out the lesion, which I saw pass before my eyes as he placed it in some kind of vial. Then he stitched up the incision and told me to go home. He said it would take a few days to get the results, and he would call when they came in.

Over the next few days, I was in turmoil. If it was cancer and had penetrated deeply into my chest, then I might soon die. All kinds of thoughts went through my mind, like how was I going to tell my kids, was my will up to date, how would I spend my last days on earth, and so on. I waited anxiously each day for the phone to ring and the verdict to be proclaimed. Was I to live or die, and if the latter, how soon?

After four days the doctor called. I picked up the phone and he said, "Mr. Steinberg, I was right! It is cancer." There was a note of glee in his voice, based, I presume, on the fact he had made an accurate diagnosis. He went on to tell me that he had cut enough beyond the lesion to allow the lab to determine if healthy flesh existed close to it. He said everything was fine and the lesion was shallow. I asked him if he would send me a copy of the diagnosis. He did, and I learned that the term used for the lesion was "basal cell carcinoma." Having never heard this term before, I did some research and spoke to a physician friend in another city, who informed me that basal cell carcinomas were very common and rarely dangerous. In fact, he said, a fair percentage of the population have them and die *with* them, but not *because* of them. I was angry. I felt that my doctor could have told me all of this at the time of the examination and saved me a lot of anguish. Also, it bothered me that he seemed more interested in making a correct diagnosis than he did in the mental and emotional condition of his patient. I decided to look for another physician.

Good fortune smiled upon me a few months later when I met Mel Borins, a Toronto physician, at a holistic health conference. We took to each other right away, and at the end of the day, he offered to give me a ride home. On the way, he told me about a holistic heath group that met once a month, each time at a different member's home. He invited me to their next meeting, the following week. It was a great group, consisting of people from all streams of the health profession: physicians, chiropractors, dentists, psychologists, psychotherapists, and many others from allied disciplines. I immediately fit in and felt I was with my own kind, as I'd been at Council Grove. Before long, I was invited to give a presentation on dreams. We all learned from each other, and I always looked forward to the meetings and the presentations by members, each of whom had a creative outlook on health. A few of them became my friends, but, as I write today, only Mel has remained close to me, with one or two others on the periphery.

After a while, I asked Mel if he would be my physician, and he agreed. One might think that this would create a conflict of interest, but it hasn't to this day, some twenty years later. I consider Mel one of my closest friends and am close to his family — in a sense, an extended family member. Mel, in addition to being an excellent doctor of physical medicine, also practises psychotherapy and over the years has referred several of his patients to me. We have worked well together, consulting whenever needed on relevant patient issues. I will mention Mel again, as he played a crucial role in another medical dilemma that I faced.

IN THE EARLY eighties, myself, along with some like-minded acquaintances in the field of psychotherapy, started a group in Toronto for the study and expression of past-life experiences. We called our group A.P.L.E, which stands for Association for Past-Life Experiences. The study component of our group consisted of meetings, held a few times a year, while the expression aspect played out in lectures and workshops for the public. Our study meetings, held usually in a restaurant over a meal, were always stimulating, and I looked forward to them. This camaraderie eventually developed into a larger project when two of the group invited me to join them and some others in the formation of a training institution for psychotherapists. This got off the ground around 1985, and we named it the Centre for Training in Psychotherapy (CTP). Most of the founders were ex-priests and nuns, many of whom had come through a unique and creative organization called Therafields. It was the philosophy of those running Therafields that persons needing psychotherapy would improve more quickly if they lived together in houses designated expressly for that purpose. The organization acquired large houses, each with an in-resident therapist, and put the philosophy into practise. People I spoke to who had been involved in this told me that it was an exciting and productive experiment that went on for many years, each house offering individual and group therapy. I'm not aware of a similar model for psychotherapy existing elsewhere. Eventually Therafields came to an end, and the houses were sold.

CTP put out a brochure to attract students. The brochure began with a mission statement:

> The Centre has developed a programme unique in its comprehensiveness. Its competence to offer broad-ranging theoretical courses, highly developed physical approaches to psychotherapy, learning through personal participation, and case supervision makes this Centre one of a kind.
> The Centre holds that psychotherapists are developed through
> - their own inner struggle for maturity
> - their experience of the struggle of others
> - their careful study of significant literature.

I drafted my own mission statement for the program, which included the text in the brochure as well as some different views. This eventually brought me into conflict with many of the other faculty. Here is my text, with the controversial material in italics:

Psychotherapy is an art which, at its best, takes into account all aspects of the human experience. These aspects include the emotional, intellectual, physical *and spiritual*. While it may not be necessary to address all of these aspects in working with a particular client, it is an asset for a psychotherapist to have a working familiarity with each, or at least be able to recognize problems whose etiology may be in one or more of these areas and know where to refer when it is out of the realm of personal experience.

I believe it is important for each student taking the training program to have exposure to all of the above areas, with learning and experience through personal therapy, clinical supervision and didactic material. Such learning *does not require that a student personally subscribe to any particular therapeutic philosophy or approach*, but rather that he/she be familiar with as many as possible and *know at least one in an erudite manner.*

Ultimately, the goal of psychotherapy, from my perspective, is to help the client achieve a satisfying integration of all the above-mentioned aspects. Just when such a level of integration is achieved is a *matter of intuitive perception on the part of the client* and may be further enhanced through discussion with his/her teacher. There are, however, degrees of integration en route to a full integrative experience and one degree or another is what most clients and therapists achieve. The fully integrated therapist is more an ideal than an actuality. Perhaps such persons exist. I have yet to meet one.

By the time the third year of the program came around, I was finding increasing divisions between my colleagues and myself. For example, I noticed that I was being excluded from parts of the training—in particular, so-called "body-work," a technique of working with the body in order to release emotional blocks. Whenever I brought this up, I was told that they had forgotten to put me in as one of the therapists in the groups where "body-work" was being done. I bought this the first time, but not the second or third. I also felt that things were going on that I was not aware of and that I should know about. At first I attributed this to a mild paranoia on my part, but I discovered my suspicions were valid when two of the more friendly members of the faculty told me I was being undermined by some of my colleagues and that they (the friendly members) regretted not doing more about this.

Finally, my instincts told me that I had to confront my colleagues about my discontent, even though I didn't know the extent to which my position on the faculty had been eroded. At the next faculty meeting, I gave a letter to each faculty member:

March 2, 1988
To my colleagues at CTP:

The events of our last meeting, spurred by [name withheld]'s attack on me, have left me with a lot to think and feel about. Though I would prefer the gentlemanly art of dueling at 30 paces, nevertheless I feel some appreciation to [name withheld] for forcing me to wrestle with some issues which have been rumbling around inside of me, though not too clearly. I still can't pretend to clarity, but things are a little more focused and I want to share with you some of my thoughts and feelings.

First, at the feeling level: I'm sensing a heaviness in our institute, both among students and faculty. As we move deeper into our program, there seems to be a growing rigidity and tightening of requirements. I get the feeling sometimes that we're almost afraid to graduate any students, out of fear for how they will reflect upon us as a faculty. It's as if we're trying to be super-credible as a means of self-protection. The image comes to me of our institute as a mediaeval castle, symbolic of the entrenchment of arcane values and stodgy theories, struggling for some breath of fresh air and occasionally glimpsing enough sunlight to continue the struggle. I think we're becoming stuffy, somewhat pompous, and about to take our place as another conservative institution in an overly conservative society. The freshness and excitement of the dream with which we first began is beginning to fade, yielding to some kind of obtuse reality which dims our sense of vision and blunts our creativity.

At the practical level: The following are some ideas which I like to think will put us more on track as a dynamic, creative and innovative centre for training in psychotherapy.

1) That we implement, along the lines already suggested by the clinical committee, but augmented, a comprehensive screening program aimed towards selecting candidates who can begin to practice psychotherapy under supervision during their first year at CTP.

2) Following on the above, that candidates entering our program be given clients whom they will do psychotherapy with over the duration of a one-year period, on a once-a-week basis, under supervision.

3) That in the second year of training, the candidate be given two clients, each on a once-per-week basis, under supervision by a different faculty member for each client. This would mean three different faculty advisors for the candidate during this two-year period.

4)   That case study seminars be the main emphasis for students over a two-year period, there being seminars held one evening per week, in small seminar groups of four students, led by faculty members.

5)   That lectures on theory be given one evening per month for nine months over a two year period, with two one-day intensives each year.

6)   That psychotherapy groups be reduced to a maximum of eight persons per group to facilitate a shorter and more intensive experience, and that

   a -   during the first year, students participate in their group along regular lines.

   b -   during the second year, students take turns as group leaders, a faculty member being present for all sessions, and that as part of each session, an analysis and feedback of the student's work be presented to him/her by fellow students and faculty members.

7)   That individual therapy hours as a precondition of entering our program be dropped, such hours being available to the student while participating in our course.

8)   That there be no set number of hours for individual therapy, neither minimum nor maximum, the student's progress and development over a two year period determining how many hours are needed, this being monitored and assessed by the faculty in conjunction with the student on a regular basis.

9)   That there be leeway for exceptional students, rich in life experience and rich in introspective and extrospective skills, to be given the option of having individual therapy or not.

10)   That we graduate students at the end of two years, except for extenuating circumstances, e.g. — having, for financial or work load reasons, to spread the program over a longer period.

11)   That a third, so to speak, honour year, be available to those students desiring advanced training. For example, a student may wish to have more intensive group or family training and could be a co-therapist in one or more groups or family situations.

12)   That there be a concerted effort to facilitate more social interaction between students and faculty. Some suggestions along these lines would be

   a -   more parties

b - faculty-student weekends in the country (at a retreat house or
some other suitable place)

c - faculty open houses once a month

I look forward to hearing your thoughts about my thoughts.

Jerry

My letter did not receive a warm welcome, and thereafter things deteriorated rapidly. Finally, at a meeting of the faculty, it was suggested that my
resignation would be welcomed. They could not pin down a solid reason for
asking me to resign, though one member accused me of not believing in the
unconscious, as if to say that such a non-belief was tantamount to heresy. In
actuality, I have a strong belief in the unconscious, so where he got this idea
from, I'll never know. Technically, I was one of the founders of CTP and there
was no legal mechanism whereby I or anyone else could be dismissed.
However, realizing that to continue on would be masochistic on my part, I
submitted my resignation. The unkindest cut of all was when the two people
who had originally asked me to help found the institute did not support my
staying on, and in fact turned against me. I felt I was betrayed, and I do not
react well to betrayal. Many years later, at a meeting of a different group, one
of these two men approached me, hand outstretched, wanting to engage me in
conversation. I was polite, said a few words, and walked away. If there was a
lesson for me in all of this, it was to trust my instincts more and act upon them
early, rather than waiting until matters progressed beyond repair. This lesson
has proved invaluable in subsequent years.

Love me until it hurts
Praise me until I blush
Criticize me until I repent
Yell at me until I cry
but
Don't betray me

In the basement of 2043C Avenue Road, below the music store, was a
Christian book outlet called the Reformation Book Store. It was run by a
lovely gentleman by the name of Bob Schraeger. Over the years I lived on
Avenue Road, Bob and I became friends, and on many occasions I would visit
with him and look over his extensive inventory. One year, as Passover

approached, I asked Bob if he had ever been to a *Seder*, which is the Jewish celebration of Passover, commemorating the exodus of the Jews from Egypt about three thousand years ago (the exact, or near exact date is still debated among scholars). He said he hadn't, and since it was common knowledge (now disputed) that the Last Supper was a *Seder*, he would be very interested.

At the *Seder*, attended by my children, Shula, and some friends, Bob was all ears. Besides partaking of some good Jewish cooking, some of which was provided by my guests, he took away with him a sense of what he thought it might have been like to be present with Jesus when he ate his last meal with his disciples. He was grateful for the invitation, and our friendship continued for many more years.

THE JEWISH RENEWAL Movement had a branch in Toronto that was organized and spearheaded by Shelley Duke, an energetic and well-organized woman with a strong commitment to Judaism who, unfortunately, has since passed on. Shelley would often ask me to help out with a lecture or a service. The most memorable of these events arose out of our mutual interest to have a second-day Rosh Hashanah healing service. Rosh Hashanah can be one or two days, depending upon custom. The healing element of our second-day service was at that time seldom, if ever, found in second-day services. It consisted of spiritual readings about healing from Jewish sources, in addition to the regular liturgy. As well, after the service, for those who wished to have direct hands-on healing, we placed three chairs at the front of the room. I and two other persons stood behind the chairs and laid our hands on the heads of those who came forward and sat down. It was a deep and profound experience for all of us, both the healers and those who received the healing. Hands-on healing, especially at a Rosh Hashanah service, is virtually unheard of in Jewish practice.

A word about hands-on healing. Its premise is that ultimately all healing comes from a spiritual source, be this God, an angel, some other kind of spiritual intelligence, or even an individual's own inner soul. By laying on hands, the healer becomes a conduit through which healing energy from a higher source flows into the one wishing to be healed, or catalyzes the recipient's own inner healing resources. At the very least, the recipient leaves feeling better, even if for a short time; at most, a physical, emotional, or spiritual healing is brought about that lasts a long time. Spiritual healing of this nature has its roots in both Jewish and Christian scriptures.

My interest in unusual and non-orthodox avenues of healing led me, in 1983, to the idea of using dreams and other non-conventional modalities to treat sick children. This idea had been incubating for a long time, beginning with my own lucid and controlled dreams as a child, then being augmented by my dream-healing experiences at the ashram. It occurred to me that if dreams could diagnose, prescribe, and heal — this being my own experience, supported by reports from the healing temples of Aesclepius in ancient Greece — then surely something could be done to bring this modality into play in modern times. I selected children as the group to begin with, as I felt they would be most open to non-conventional approaches and were, by and large, devoid of the resistance and skepticism that in this area unfortunately plagues most adults. If, I reasoned further, a hospital could be built that focused entirely on very sick children who were not responding to the usual medical procedures and who would continue to suffer and probably die from their illnesses, then there would be nothing to lose by introducing unusual methods of healing. As a spinoff from this, I believed that much could be learned that might later be applied to an adult population. Further fuelling my idea was my awareness of the scientific research that was being done on the effects of the mind on the healing process. In other words, mind control, through such discoveries as biofeedback, was already being tested with encouraging results. For example, B.V. Basmajian of Queen's University in Kingston, Ontario, presented a paper describing his research. For the reader's interest, I present the abstract from his paper, titled "Control and Training of Individual Motor Units," as an example of the healing potential of the mind:

> Experiments clearly demonstrate that with the help of auditory and visual cues, many can single out motor units and control their isolated contractions. Experiments on the training of this control, interpreted as the training of descending pathways to single anterior horn cells, provide a new glimpse of the fineness of conscious motor controls. After training, subjects can recall into activity different single motor units by an effort of will while inhibiting the activity of neighbours. Some learn such exquisite control that they soon can produce rhythms of contraction in one unit, imitating drum rolls, etc. The quality of control over individual anterior horn cells may determine rates of learning.

This is one small but significant example of the plethora of scientific research done in the field of mind over matter. I could also mention the collection of studies done by Larry Dossey in his book *Healing Words*, which presents research into the effects of prayer upon those who are ill. Readers may be aware of Christian Science, that branch of Christianity that believes implicitly in the power of prayer to heal all things, based on the stories of Jesus' healings of the sick. In my own tradition, Moses, Elijah, and Elisha give us powerful renderings of their abilities to heal through word and touch.

I put together a proposal to present to anyone who would listen:

CHILDREN'S HOSPITAL FOR HEALING RESEARCH

The purpose of the Children's Hospital for Healing Research is to explore, from a scientific and intuitive perspective, alternative modalities in the healing of chronic and/or life-threatening illnesses. Research will be encouraged in such areas as healing dreams, active visualization, hypnosis, therapeutic touch, prayer, music, colour and sleep suggestion. Other approaches of merit which are encountered will also be considered.

The hospital facility will initially consist of 18 patient rooms, specially designed and equipped to foster the research mentioned above. Laboratories and other needed facilities will be provided. Consideration will also be given to further expansion of the hospital when such need arises.

A carefully selected staff of core researchers and treatment personnel will fill faculty positions in the areas of physiology, psychotherapy, religion, medicine, nursing, cell biology, bio-medical engineering and research methodology. Visiting faculty will include persons with demonstrated abilities in the art of healing.

Illnesses such as asthma, leukemia, rheumatoid arthritis, sickle-cell anemia and neurodermatitis will be researched. Other illnesses as well will be considered.

The hospital will publish its findings as meaningful healing evidence is accumulated. The findings will also be looked at in the light of their possible application to the adult population.

An initial capital expenditure of $20 million is required for the purchase of land and for building and equipping the hospital. An additional $20 million is required to provide interest for upkeep and payment of staff. The hospital will operate as a non-profit charitable institution.

The hospital is to be situated within a 50-mile radius of the city of Toronto, and in a rural setting where full advantage can be taken of the healing benefits of nature.

Children will be admitted in accordance with the highest ethical standards. Selection will be based on need and propensity for research.

Parents will be invited and encouraged to participate in the healing process of their children and will be asked, where appropriate, to take an active role in administering treatment.

The enclosed paper, "An Investigation into the Healing Properties of Dreams," explains more fully the concept of alternative approaches to healing, using dreams in this instance as the specific modality.

Rabbi Jerry Steinberg
Toronto, Canada
February, 1983

As an act of confidence in seeing this proposal to fruition, I registered the name "Children's Hospital for Healing Research" with the province of Ontario.

I made an appointment with Quentin Ray-Jones, who was then the head of pediatrics at the Hospital for Sick Children in Toronto. I had met Quentin some time before, while working at NMUDD, and tried to interest him in submitting a proposal to the government for funding. That didn't happen, but Quentin and I liked one another, so I received a warm welcome from him when I came to see him at his office. I brought with me the paper "An Investigation into the Healing Properties of Dreams," which he quickly looked over after I explained to him my overall purpose for coming. He gave me a sympathetic hearing and told me that if it was his decision alone, he would make the project happen at the hospital. However, he explained, any proposal to the hospital would have to go through a series of committees, including ethics and finance. He said that in all honesty, he didn't think my proposal would have a chance. So ended my attempt to introduce an exciting research proposal to a hospital with an international reputation.

Some years later, a pediatrician at the children's hospital in Buffalo, New York, who was in charge of training pediatric residents, invited me to give a talk to his residents on my thinking. The talk was well received but didn't lead to anything, possibly because the pediatrician moved shortly afterwards to Chicago.

Having exhausted my opportunities to work in a hospital, I turned to announcing, whenever I had the opportunity, that I was available to work with sick children on a one-on-one basis, without charge. My announcement caught the attention of someone who told me of a family just north of Toronto who might be interested. I spoke with the family and learned that their nine-year-old son had leukemia, with a poor prognosis. They gave me permission to visit him at the general hospital in Newmarket, a half hour's drive from Toronto. I went to the hospital, and the boy's parents took me to his room and introduced us. My plan was to get to know the boy simply by talking to him and then, on subsequent visits, begin to work with him on his dreams. However, I encountered an obstacle on my first visit—his parents wouldn't let me be alone with their son. This meant that the boy could not talk freely, and both he and I would be under constant and intense scrutiny. I could understand the parents' concern, seeing that I was a complete stranger, but it didn't bode well for my being able to work with the boy without restraint, which I felt was necessary if I was to have any chance of success. In fact, even after a rather benign conversation with the boy, in which I was careful not to say anything off the beaten track, I was not encouraged to come back and work with him. This was most unfortunate, as he passed away not long afterwards. I'm not suggesting that I could have saved him, but perhaps I could at least have helped prolong his life and give it quality. And then again, who knows, perhaps he might have encountered that most elusive experience of "spontaneous remission of symptoms."

My efforts to build a hospital did not end here. At a party in 1984, for no apparent reason, I suddenly got the idea to create a board game. The concept came to me clearly, but the details had to be worked out. What evolved was a game of extrasensory perception; the game board had a drawing on it that was a disguised model of the basic architecture for the hospital I wanted to build. My hope was that if the game was successful, it would provide the funds I needed to at least get started. I spent many months and considerable money creating the game, which I called simply ESP. The initials were stylized and all joined together. I even had the game copyrighted and the logo registered. The cover of the instruction booklet read:

> A game of extra-sensory perception
> For the whole family
> ESP
> Four to any age.
> For one-to six-players.
> ESP is a game of Fun, Competition and
> Cooperation. It is designed to challenge and
> develop Extra-Sensory-Perception abilities.

Some excerpts from an introduction to the game:

> ESP is a board game that is fun to play, while at the same time stimulating the development of telepathy and clairvoyance. The game may be played alone, with a partner, or in teams of two (up to six players). There are also versions of the game for very young children. In addition, the game presents various levels of ease or difficulty, depending upon the inclination of the players.

ESP is intended for general family use and capitalizes on the current media emphasis on the power of the mind. Interest in the game has been keen, as evidenced by the testing, to date, of over 200 persons, spanning a wide and highly diverse population, with an age range of from five to eighty-three.

A 1982 Gallup poll gives some indication of how much the belief in ESP is part of the fabric of American society:

"Slightly more than half of those polled in the general American population believe in ESP, but the figure rises to nearly two-thirds for those people with a college background." (George Gallup Jr., *Adventures in Immortality*, McGraw Hill, 1982, pp. 136–137)

The feedback I received from the many who tested the game for me, in particular those in their mid-teens, was very gratifying. I was sure I had a winner, and I even found a game company near Toronto that was keenly interested. Unfortunately they went out of business before they had a chance to seriously pursue production. Not long after, I found a man who was interested in partnering with me, but he was unable to raise the necessary funds to have the game produced. Recognizing that my strength was in the creative aspect of the game and not in funding and marketing, and also feeling that the wind had been taken out of my sails, I packed up the game and put it away. I still believe that it has great potential and could be adapted to the electronic age. Perhaps it will yet be resurrected.

IN THE SPRING of 1983, I was invited to attend a workshop given by Nell Thomson, a gifted psychic. The title of the workshop was "Nonlinear Thinking (Intuition) in Therapy, Research and Personal Growth." Attendees at the workshop included physicians, naturopaths, nurses, social workers, Ph.D.s from various disciplines, and others, mostly in professional and academic fields. The workshop was held at Innisfree Farm, a venue associated with the University of Toronto. The main purpose of the workshop was to introduce individuals with a scientific leaning to experiences and phenomena that do not fit into the scientific mould; in other words, to expose them to different and unusual material that did not follow, or that defied, the laws of nature as commonly understood.

The conference was organized by Dr. Paul Grof, a faculty member of the Department of Psychiatry at McMaster University in Hamilton, Ontario. The following are excerpts from a letter by Dr. Grof introducing the concept of the workshop to potential participants:

New insights in therapy and personal growth, as well as scientific discoveries, usually seem to take place through a mixture of rational and intuitive, linear and nonlinear thinking. In research, intuition has frequently been considered a dirty word, yet it has played a major role in new discoveries.

The history of science shows that many breakthroughs have taken place at the intuitive level first; real validation came much later. To wit, the heliocentric system was postulated intuitively in Alexandria during the 2nd century, B.C. and rationally fought out in the 16th and 17th centuries. Gauss, a famous German mathematician, described a similar sequence when he wrote in 1810, "I have had my solutions for a long time but I do not yet know how to arrive at them."

Similarly, when you look at many important problems, there is frequently a phenomenal amount of facts already available, yet some meaningful integration might take place through the intuitive process. Intuition, well balanced by experimental and rational assets, seems important for new understandings.

Nell Thomson is a very accomplished teacher of intuitive skills. She has been spreading her message during her travels across Canada. She is very willing to teach her skills and, indeed, very motivated to do so. I have found her very helpful in dealing with some difficult, treatment-resistant patients, as she can integrate complex material in new, meaningful, and unorthodox ways.

I no longer have a copy of the weekend program, but would like to share with the reader the one exercise Nell taught us that I believe had the greatest impact on most of the participants, and certainly on myself.

On the second evening of the conference, Nell brought in a box and emptied its contents, a large assortment of spoons, onto a table. She then told us that she was going to teach us to bend the cutlery with our minds. We each selected a spoon and held it in our hands. Then, under her tutelage, we practised certain meditation techniques specific to the task at hand, such as visualizing the spoon bending, using our hands only to guide the direction of the bend, applying little, if any, pressure. We were also told that we could gently rub the neck of the spoon as we continued our meditation. I must admit that while we were all eager and excited to try this exercise, I could also feel the skepticism in the room, including my own. Nevertheless, with honest intention, I and the others proceeded under Nell's instructions.

To my utter amazement, I found that not only was I able to bend my spoon with a light touch, one that certainly could not under ordinary circumstances have had any effect whatsoever, but that I was able to tie my second spoon into a knot. Two or three members of the group were able to hold the spoon by the tip of the handle with one hand and then watch it bend all the way over, as if it was made of heated wax. The buzz in the room was palpable.

Following this exercise, I conversed with several of the attendees about the implications of what we had experienced and witnessed. The overall conclusion was along these lines: If, with our minds, we can have such an influence upon an external object, then there was an enormous potential for us to so influence our own bodies for the better and to have some say in healing our own ailments. Also, we could perhaps have an impact on our patients and clients by visualizing them in a positive manner.

All of this was not new to me. At the ashram, through the Light Invocation, we had tried to influence unwell people whose names had been submitted to us. Research by Dr. Basmajian and Dr. Elmer Green and others in the field of biofeedback gave a clear scientific basis for the effect our minds can have on our well-being. More recently, the work of Dr. Larry Dossey, as presented in his book *Healing Words* makes a case for prayer as a healing modality. But bending spoons was one of the most impressive methods to show just how powerful our minds are. The reader may remember that Uri Geller, who did spoon bending regularly in public, was accused by some of trickery; but it wasn't trickery, as attested to by my own experience and those of my friends and colleagues. In fact, almost anyone can do it. I still have in my possession various pieces of cutlery, including forks, that in the months following the workshop, I bent and knotted.

BETWEEN MY WORK in healing dreams, the ESP game, and bending spoons, the reader may have a good sense of my interest in psychic phenomena and the spirit world. When I speak to Jewish audiences, it is not unusual for someone to question me about the Jewish view on such phenomena, and in particular to mention that the bible prohibits getting involved in anything psychic: "Let no one be found among you...who is an augur, a soothsayer, a diviner, a sorcerer, one who casts spells, or one who consults ghosts or familiar spirits, or one who inquires of the dead" (Deuteronomy 18:10–11). This admonition is repeated in different ways and places in the bible. My response is that the bible was written over a period of many centuries, and different schools of thought had divergent views on this topic including positive views on psychic phenomena. For example, precognition (seeing the future) is clearly evident in Joseph's dreams (Joseph himself practised divination—Genesis 44:5), and later Jacob, on his death bed, tells each of his sons what will become of them: "Gather about and I will tell you what is going to happen to [each of] you in the future" (Genesis 49:1). Examples could also be given of clairvoyance (seeing with the inner eye that which is out of sight), telekinesis (moving objects with the mind), telepathy (communicating from one mind to another mind without benefit of the normal senses), and clairaudience (hearing voices), which pervades the Hebrew scriptures. We even have an example in the First Book of Samuel where a woman conducts a seance and conjures up Samuel's ghost: "And the woman said to Saul, 'I see a godlike being coming up out of the earth'. And he said to her: 'What does he look like?' And she said, 'An old man comes up and he is covered with a robe.' And Saul perceived that it was Samuel, and he bowed with his face to the ground and prostrated himself" (1 Samuel 28:13–14). Jewish literature in the post-biblical period up to the present day is also replete with examples of psychic occurrences.

In my lectures and sermons, I strongly advocate that people develop their psychic abilities because I believe that such development is a step in expanding one's consciousness into other domains of reality — in other words, a step toward deepening one's sense of the spiritual. Whether through dreams, bending spoons, visions, or voices, the many avenues of psychic growth are given to us as precious gifts in the pursuit of spiritual authenticity.

From the strictly Jewish perspective, dreams have played a major role as a link between man and God, or in my preferred terminology, other dimensions of reality. The dreams of Jacob, Joseph, and Daniel are all clear statements that we can connect with God in our dreams. In the eleventh century, Maimonides, the great rabbi, physician, and theologian, wrote that there are twelve levels of prophecy, and dreams occupy six of those levels. A study of other religions will reveal to the reader the importance of dreams for revelation, inspiration, and healing.

While I have a good rapport with my rabbinical colleagues in Toronto, most, to the best of my knowledge, do not share my interest or belief in other dimensions of reality and the spiritual derivatives of such a belief, which include the psychic world and the power of the mind. We do, nevertheless, have many other interests in common.

When I arrived in Toronto in 1977, I automatically became a member of the Toronto Board of Reform Rabbis. Toronto has the largest number of Reform congregations in Canada, and consequently the most Reform rabbis — at times there have been as many as twenty-six, if we include the entire Greater Toronto Area. Excluding the months of July and August, we meet monthly to discuss issues relevant to our profession, such as conversion, intermarriage, Israel, our congregations, and social action. By far the issue most frequently talked about at our meetings is conversion. We have large classes, and our prospective converts go through a nine-month program, after which each must individually appear before a group of three rabbis, who ask questions and determine if the candidate can proceed to the final steps of the process. For a woman this means going to *mikveh* (ritual immersion), and for a man it means first circumcision (unless he is already circumcised) and then *mikveh*. I have spoken about my early involvement with the JIC class and the case of Joan — not a pleasant memory, but an interesting one.

As part of our monthly meetings, we take turns leading study sessions on the Jewish scriptures, including post-biblical literature, with the material presented at the leader's discretion. The teachings are usually discussed, often with considerable vigour, and I always look forward to our meetings, which are also a time of fellowship and sharing of our concerns and joys. Issues sometime arise, which spur heated debate, and certainly we don't always agree on everything, but at the end of the day, there is for me always a sense of time well spent and friendships deepened. I have heard other Reform rabbis living outside of Toronto, especially in the States, say that our rabbis' group is quite special.

The other organization I belong to is the Toronto Board of Rabbis (TBR). This group is for rabbis from all streams of Judaism — Orthodox, Conservative, and Reform — although we have only a few Orthodox rabbis, as most of the Orthodox in Toronto have formed their own group and generally don't associate with us except in events that concern all Jews, such as a Holocaust memorial or a rally in support of Israel. I also enjoy the TBR's monthly gatherings, where we address issues that are more broadly communal than the ones discussed in the Reform group, such as the status of *kashrut* (keeping kosher) in the community. Once a year, the rabbis of the TBR and the cantors of the synagogues represented by the TBR get together to celebrate Chanukah. Most often this means meeting for a lunch of latkes (potato pancakes) and other delicacies, followed by a singsong led by the cantors. This camaraderie across religious lines is something I would like to see more often, particularly in Israel.

In September 2009, I spoke with a Conservative rabbi and his wife who were visiting Toronto from Israel. Both had extensive experience in Jewish education. Both commented to me, after a brief tour of the Jewish education system in Toronto, that to the best of their knowledge, the system in this city has no equal anywhere in North America. I was surprised to hear this, thinking that cities such as New York, Chicago, and Los Angeles would surpass anything we had here. They assured me this was not so. As is the case all too often, one doesn't fully appreciate what one has until it is validated by a credible outside source.

ABOUT FIVE YEARS after arriving in Toronto, I was walking one day on Davenport Avenue near Avenue Road and passed by a karate studio. Since, as a young man, I took up boxing and wrestling, martial arts were somehow in my blood, probably because I so often had to defend myself while growing up in Regina. Karate at that time was unknown in Canada except perhaps among those of Japanese descent. It wasn't until much later, in the 1980s, that it became a household word, and Toronto was replete with karate dojos (schools). My interest was therefore piqued when I saw the sign on Davenport Avenue indicating a dojo on the premises. I went in to check it out.

The studio was located on the second floor of an old building, and one accessed it by climbing a long set of stairs. The room was large, with a bare, light-coloured hardwood floor covering ninety per cent of the space. Only a small office and a change room, at the far end of the studio, interrupted the floor's continuity. A class was in session, consisting of about twenty students wearing white *gis* (karate outfits) with belts of varied colours. A diminutive man with a black belt came over to greet me. His last name was Tsuroka and he told me he was the *Sensei* (master) of the dojo. I said I had some interest in finding out more about karate and asked if he would mind if I watched the class for a while. He said that was fine, and if I had any questions, I shouldn't hesitate to ask him. By the end of the class I was hooked, and a week later I became a student of *Sensei* Tsuroka.

The karate workouts were grueling. After a few minutes of meditation, followed by bowing to the black-belt conducting that particular class and then bowing to the *Sensei*, we went at it. For me, the most difficult part was stretching, as I found that I was pretty stiff compared to the others, in spite of my yoga background. I became keenly aware by the second or third class that stretching was extremely important; one had to be flexible and loose in order to perform all of the karate moves. Equally important were focus and power, the two being closely connected. To enhance focus and power, we were taught to scream "*kiyii*" when delivering a punch or a kick. Once I learned to co-ordinate the scream with the punch or kick, the power of my delivery greatly improved.

Classes were divided into four parts. Meditation was part one. Part two consisted of practising *katas,* which are stylized, dance-like movements. There are many different *katas,* each one designed to teach a series of offensive or defensive moves, which are important to know if one is in combat. Part three had to do with no-contact sparring. Usually the lower belts (white being the lowest and black the highest) sparred with higher belts, because the higher belts supposedly had more control over their punches and kicks, and therefore there was less risk of the lower belt being injured. However, it didn't always work out this way, and on more than one occasion I was hurt by a higher belt who didn't know his own strength. I remember one black-belt hitting me in the chest, thinking it was a light blow, but I had trouble breathing properly for days afterwards. Fortunately, nothing was broken. Part four, which consisted of watching demonstrations by the higher belts, occurred periodically but was not presented at each class.

The dojo had no air conditioning, so on very warm days the sweat on the floor had to be mopped up several times in the course of a two-hour workout. It was the task of the white belts to do the mopping, although from time to time, to emphasize humility, higher belts were called upon.

For me, the most fascinating part of karate were the *katas*, and I never tired of watching the black-belts go through their movements. *Sensei* Tsuroka's son, David, came third in the world one year at a tournament in Japan. On rare occasions, he performed *katas* for us, and I marvelled at how he combined power and grace in every movement. To this day, in my mind, I can see him in motion, hear the snap of his kicks and punches, and watch the poetry of his moves.

I took karate for two years and then left after one too many injuries. None of them were serious, but I got tired of the pain. Nevertheless, I remain grateful to *Sensei* Tsuroka and always remember what he told us one day: "The highest level of karate is when, just from looking at you, no one wants to bother you, and you never have to fight." I saw this as a very wise spiritual statement.

As I learned to use my hands as weapons, I couldn't help comparing them to fire, in the sense that just as fire can burn or warm, forge or destroy, hands can harm or create, inflict pain or heal. In fact, it occurred to me that many things in life have multiple purposes, all depending on the intention of the user. As I look back upon my life, it seems that there has always been a need for me to express myself with my hands in a variety of ways. In Cincinnati I took up baking; at the ashram in British Columbia I built a clothes rack; back in Winnipeg I was introduced to sandal-making by an American fleeing from the Vietnam conscription; in Ottawa I took a course in fabric making and dyeing; and weaving its way through all of this was my writing, which began with a pen, graduating to a typewriter, and then a computer. And for two years at the dojo, I studied how to use my hands as weapons. Although I never advanced beyond a yellow belt, I felt able to defend myself better than at any time previously in my life. It was a good feeling, the residue of which remains with me many years later. And it will come as no surprise to the reader that upon leaving karate, I unconsciously sought out another way to employ my hands.

Having practised hands-on healing over the years, I was excited one day to receive an invitation to take a course in reiki, a Japanese form of working with one's hands for the purpose of healing others emotionally and physically. I had been doing this already, but I welcomed the opportunity to learn more about a practice I felt was important and whose healing qualities I believed everyone had the innate ability to express.

I was told at my first class that the essence of reiki was to have a positive intention to heal when laying one's hands on someone. After that, the process was to cover the person's body over the course of an hour or so by moving one's hands over different sections, beginning with the head, and every five minutes moving the hands to a different spot. When addressing the chest area of a woman, the instruction was to have her lie on her stomach and place the hands on her back opposite the breasts. The theory of reiki is that the healing energy penetrates through the whole body, so one can work from either side and even through a cast. Also, in cases where the patient can't be touched, such as where there are severe burns, the hands can be held an inch or so above the burn areas, and the healing will still take place. In my practice as a psychotherapist, I used my reiki training from time to time on my clients when it was warranted and always received positive feedback from them. So the course provided me with a name for what I had been doing all along and added to my knowledge and understanding of the healing process. I still do reiki occasionally when called upon, but I also digress from the formal practise when my intuition so guides me.

MY MAIN TECHNIQUE in working with dreams is Re-Dreaming and Figure Identification. The essence of the technique is to guide the clients to a state where they are re-experiencing the dream with vivid recall and emotional impact. Once they are in this state, without suggesting any kind of interpretation or content, I guide them to explore the dream and its meaning. I use open-ended questions such as "What do you see?" and "What happens next?" I help them identify figures that appear in the dream. Often such identification uncovers the meaning of the dream and brings both insight and relief to the client. Sometimes the figure is an animal or a monster or a shadow, which, upon probing, usually turns out to be someone the dreamer knows. I have found that Re-Dreaming and Figure Identification is a powerful tool for any therapist wishing to help a client or patient at a deep psychotherapeutic level.

In the '80s, my friend Harry Prosen was chairman of the Department of Psychiatry at the Universtiy of Manitoba and asked me to give a seminar on

Re-Dreaming and Figure Identification to several of his psychiatric residents. One of them, Brian Plowman, now a professor at the University of Calgary, tried using the technique and sent me a letter after the first time he tried it on one of his patients:

When I first learned about Re-Dreaming, I could not wait to try this exciting new method. Having developed a theory of the process, I decided to give it a try on my own. I had a young lady in therapy and her complaint was that she did not feel very enthused in her marriage or life in general. She felt depressed and did exhibit a slight vegetative shift. There was no history in her family of psychiatric difficulty. Therapy had been under way for a short while and little had changed. She presented a dream and it seemed very interesting. It was very short. She was on the edge of a small town and she noticed a baby carriage. That was the dream.

I instructed her to lie down on the couch and repeat the dream in the first person singular over and over, until she was in a trance. I then instructed her to describe any and all of the scenery as she walked to the edge of town. She described buildings and in particular one of them which was a school. I instructed her to go over to the school. She did and she climbed a number of stairs to the front door. She entered the door. There was one room with a few rows of desks. There was no one else in the room. She sat in one of the desks and a teacher came by and looked at her. The teacher smiled approvingly and left. She described children's drawings on the walls and writing on the black boards. She then left the school. She continued to walk and came across the baby carriage again. It was black and just sat there alone. There was no one around. I instructed her to go over to the carriage. She did and looked inside. There was something black there. It looked like a book at first but was a binder. She took it out of the carriage and began to read it.

At this moment, the door to the therapy room burst open and there stood a huge man pointing a handgun directly at my head. I nearly died on the spot. It turned out that he was a policeman and he was looking for a criminal who had just robbed the business next door. My young patient was essentially not fazed by this and finished reading the binder. To this day I cannot recall one word of what she read. She wrapped up the dream. How, I cannot remember. She then left and returned once after this episode to tell me that her symptoms had completely disappeared and to thank me. She was now quite happy in her marriage and in her life and did not require any further therapy.

I felt very gratified when I received Dr. Plowman's letter.

I was given the opportunity to present Re-Dreaming and Figure Identification to a Toronto audience of about sixty physicians who, as part of their practice, did psychotherapy. After describing the theory to them, with some case examples, I offered to do a live demonstration if there was a doctor present who would volunteer a personal dream. A young physician, Adrian Sohn, offered to share a dream and work on it with me using the Re-Dreaming technique while his colleagues watched and listened. The session went well, and later Dr. Sohn called and asked if he could meet with me to discuss something he had in mind. We met for dinner a few weeks later and he wanted to know if I would be willing to take him on and train him in the use of the technique and, in general, my manner of doing psychotherapy. I was happy to, and this marked the beginning of a very rich and deep friendship, which has lasted and continues to grow. Dr. Sohn, an excellent and much-loved physician, practises in Guelph, Ontario.

My first nine years in Toronto were a time of settling in and accepting that this was to be my new home, possibly for the rest of my life. Not being generally a fan of large cities, I had to go through a period of adjustment, but by 1986 I realized that not only was Toronto a great city, I actually enjoyed living here. There were more opportunities to develop a practice, and the Jewish community was rich and vibrant. I looked forward to the years ahead.

THE JOURNEY CONTINUES
Toronto 1986–2011

We bind our souls
                in jungle vine
        whispers of eagle wings
                        and jaguar feet
        souls
                        echoing the night cry
                                of solitary birds
                                        in night plume
            whispers of dying leaves
                        and magic potions
        souls
                        taking in the breath of God
                                the moist flesh
                                of animal spirit
                        seeking to entwine
                                with eternal embrace
    We bind our souls
                in jungle vine

etween 1981 and 1986, the ending of two relationships had a powerful emotional impact on my life. To keep myself from bottling up all my feelings about the relationships, I returned once again to the writing of poetry, which I had been doing throughout my life, off and on, and which always helped me work things through. The difference was that the words were pouring out of me in such a torrent of feeling that at times I couldn't stop writing. It seemed, furthermore, that once the floodgates were opened, many thoughts and feelings about things other than the relationships presented themselves for expression. The result was a large volume of poems, a selection of which was published by ECW Press in Toronto under the title *Melting: Poems of a Frozen Man* (1992). The book launch took place at the University of Toronto, and I must admit I very much enjoyed autographing the copies that were sold that evening. About two years later, I was invited to do a poetry reading at the Harbourfront Reading Series, an experience I will always remember, including the signings after the reading. Over the years I have received mixed reactions from readers of *Melting*. Some readers have been very moved by the poems, and some, both men and women, have even thanked me, while others have been less impressed. I admit that some of my poetry is quite raw, but I believe it's honest and expresses the thoughts and feelings of many men, who would write in a similar manner if they had the desire to put on paper their innermost thoughts and feelings. A few of the poems included in this work are from *Melting*; others are more recent.

With the breakup of two relationships, there was another, even more powerful undercurrent of emotion festering in my unconscious that I had been in denial about for nine years. One day in 1986, I was sitting with my treasured friend Sharon Letovsky and told her that I felt there was a hole in my heart. Being a very good listener, she slowly and patiently drew me out, until finally I was able to identify what this hole was all about. I missed my kids. Yes, I was seeing them on a regular basis and going on trips and holidays with them, but somehow this wasn't enough. When Sharon asked me what I wanted to do about this, I replied that the best solution I could think of would be to move into the condo building where they lived. Once I understood clearly what my empty feeling was all about, I was able to act. I met with Shula and told her what I wanted to do. She thought it was a great idea. Then I met with Meher and Dahlia, and they, too, thought it was a good idea. On Shula's suggestion, I went to talk to the superintendent to find out if there were any units for rent in the building, though, since it was a condo, the chances of this were slim. Fortunately, the superintendent told me that a family had just moved out of one of the units, and its owner wanted to rent it. I immediately pursued this, and within six weeks I was a new resident in the building.

I quickly realized that I had made the right decision. Both Meher and Dahlia had keys to my new home and could come and go as they pleased. It was particularly handy for them when the selection in Shula's fridge was not to their liking, as they would come to explore what I had. The contents of my fridge were also not always to their liking, but still, two fridges are better than one. Or, if one kid wanted to watch a particular program on television and the other wanted to watch something else, one of them could just come down from the fourth floor to the second. At times, for one reason or another, either kid would sleep over. Dahlia even lived with me for a short time. To put it mildly, I was ecstatic to be near my kids again and have them in my life on a daily basis. The hole in my heart began to heal, and within a few months the emptiness was filled.

Meher and Dahlia were always very close to my parents so, in the early eighties, when Meher was about fourteen and Dahlia around ten, together with Shula, we planned a special surprise for their grandparents' anniversary. The surprise was to secretly fly both kids to Winnipeg and present them to my parents. I flew in alone a few days early, and then, on the evening of their anniversary, I told my parents that I had to visit somebody for a little while, but that I would be back in an hour or so. I drove to the airport, picked up Meher and Dahlia (all of this with Shula's co-operation back in Toronto), and brought them in through the back door of my parents' home. The children waited very quietly in the hallway, out of sight. I went into the living room, where my parents were sitting, and told them to close their eyes and keep them closed until I said to open them. I motioned to the kids to tiptoe into the living room and had Meher stand in front of his grandmother and Dahlia in front of her grandfather. Then I told my parents to open their eyes. The surprise and look of sheer delight on their faces was nothing short of wonderful. It was for them and us one of the best anniversaries ever.

As Meher and Dahlia moved into their early teens, both became interested in cars, not unusual for young men and women approaching driver's licence day. Being a "car guy," I wanted to make sure that both had proper driver training, so they took classes at a good school when they came of age. Initially they learned to drive a car with an automatic transmission, but once they became comfortable and reasonably skillful on the automatic, I taught them both how to drive a stick shift, which was what my car was at the time. My reasoning was that if they could drive stick, they would be able to drive any car. This paid off for both kids: as the years passed, they found themselves in situations where a manual gearshift driver was needed and no one else around qualified. Later on, when Dahlia needed a car to get to and from school, I bought her an old BMW 5 series stick shift with 190,000 miles on it. It was still in good shape, as the owner ran a BMW shop and had given the car to his daughter until Dahlia came along. She loved the car and learned, among other things, to appreciate the sound of a good engine and the joy of revving it when changing gears. A few years later she was T-boned by a large taxi cab with such force that it bent the frame of her car, making it a write-off. Fortunately, because the car was so well built, she walked away from the accident. This is a plug for good-sized heavy cars for teenagers learning to drive. Actually, even for experienced drivers.

MY GOOD FRIEND and colleague Danny Gottlieb was for many years the director of the Canadian Council for Reform Judaism. In that capacity he oversaw all the Reform congregations in the country and occasionally was called upon to send a rabbi from Toronto to serve a congregation elsewhere. One day he called and asked me if I would like to go to Regina to conduct services for the High Holidays. I gladly accepted. Not only was I always happy to return to my birthplace, but, as a Reform rabbi, it would give me particular satisfaction. The reason for this is that when I lived in Regina, it was a bastion of orthodoxy — there was no one espousing Reform Jewish views, and anyone who did would have quickly been ostracized. And, until recent years, all the rabbis there were Orthodox (indeed the Orthodox community is still intact and today is led by Rabbi Jeremy Parness, recently ordained under the auspices of Jewish Renewal). So, coming from Regina, I found a certain sweetness in being invited to conduct High Holiday service for a nascent Reform congregation. It was a small group, and they met in rented quarters for Rosh Hashanah and Yom Kippur and gathered in members' homes during the rest of the year.

My visit there, and my childhood memories of the season, are fresh in my mind as I write, since I am taking a week off for R & R and to do some writing, having just finished conducting services for the High Holidays with my congregation near Toronto. What stands out among my memories from many years ago as a child in Regina at this time of year is observing the act of blowing *shofar*. The *shofar* is a ram's horn that is hollowed out and made into a semi-musical instrument. In biblical times it was used, among other things, for sounding battle; according to scripture it was used by Joshua to destroy the walls of Jericho. I remember that on Rosh Hashanah, when the time came to blow the *shofar*, everyone held their breath because blowing seemed so difficult, and we all wondered whether the blower would get any sound at all out of the horn. The blower would place the narrow opening to his lips and usually, after several tries, sound would emerge. Many different forms of sound had to be made, so it usually took a while to get through the ritual. After the service the *shofar* blower was usually commended on his effort, even if the efforts had not been entirely successful.

As it turned out, the moment I put the *shofar* to my lips for the first time, I was able to blow it quite well, and I improved with practice over the years. So, on my trip to Regina as a rabbi, I was eager for the opportunity to blow *shofar* for the Reform congregation. However, I was told that there was a member of the congregation designated to blow *shofar*, so my services in this regard were not needed. I was a little disappointed, as I wanted to show off my horn prowess to the congregation. When the time came in the service for the blowing, a man in his forties came forward and with each of the many successive prompts sounded the appropriate notes. Never in my life have I heard the *shofar* blown with such skill and beauty. I sat there in complete awe of what I heard coming out of the wide end of his ram's horn. Not a note was missed and each emerged with a purity I can still hear ringing in my ears. After the service I met this man, who was very humble and accepted my compliments almost with apology. I asked him what he did for a living, and he told me he was the head of the music department at the University of Regina, and his principal instrument was the trumpet.

Today, in my own congregation, just before the time of blowing the *shofar*, I call all the children up to the *bimah* (the area, usually elevated, at the front of a synagogue where the service is conducted) and tell them a story I've made up about a man who tries to blow the *shofar* and can't. In the story, a number of people in his congregation try to blow it and they can't either. Finally, a little boy (or girl) offers to try, and everybody laughs. After all, if the husky butcher and the powerful blacksmith and the robust farmer can't do it, why does this little kid think he or she is going to be successful? However, little Joseph comes up, and lo and behold, he puts the *shofar* to his mouth and out comes a clear and uplifting sound (at which point I blow the *shofar*). Then, with two additional *shofars* present, I invite those who have come forward to try to blow. Before each attempt, the cantor calls out the note to be blown — in this case, *Tekiah*, a note of moderate length — and after each child's turn, I swab the mouth of the *shofar* with isopropyl alcohol, to disinfect it. Sometimes, a child does get a sound out of the horn, at which point everyone in the congregation spontaneously applauds. Then, at the end of the service, I invite anyone with a *shofar* to come up and join us in the final blowing. Several members of my congregation have gone out and purchased *shofars* for their children and themselves.

While in Regina for the High Holidays, I of course paid a short visit to the Army and Navy Store, wandering up to the second-floor coat department. Early on in this work, I described my love of fur coats and how I used to visit my mother when she worked here, losing myself between the mouton and the mink. There was something special about the smell and softness of the fur, and the thought that it was the hide of an animal gave the fur a life of its own. In later years in Winnipeg, and then in Toronto, I developed a liking for working with leather. This initially came about through contact with an American Vietnam protester (spoken of earlier) who was a skillful leather worker. He taught me some of the fundamentals, after which I went to a leather foundry and bought a processed hide and some tools. Upon entering the foundry I immediately felt at home: I found the smell intoxicating, in the best sense of that word. For years afterwards I was engaged in making sandals, belts, and purses. I can't claim to have ever mastered the process of leather craft, but it was a lot of fun and I presented many people with gifts. The most challenging project was making a pair of sandals for my father, whose one foot was badly deformed as a result of his childhood polio. It was the only pair of sandals he was ever able to wear in his life, and it gave both him and me immense pleasure. The only vestige today of my love for leather and fur is my sheepskin winter coat — made and purchased in Winnipeg, where they know how to make winter coats.

IN THE FIRST chapter of this book, I spoke about a mysterious room in the basement of our synagogue in Regina. Although I never did solve the mystery, it had occurred to me that perhaps the room had something to do with the ritual washing of the bodies of the deceased, a holy task in Judaism. Later I became convinced this theory was wrong, especially when I realized that our congregation had a small funeral home, on the nineteenth block of Toronto Street, which was probably where the washing took place. I can only guess that my childhood fascination with death (no doubt related to my equal fascination with guns) led me to the earlier hypothesis. It will come as no surprise, then, that while attending a Jewish Renewal conference in Philadelphia in 1995, I selected a workshop dealing with *tahara*, which is the Hebrew word for the care of the body after death. I had known for a long time that in Judaism the body is treated with great respect, but I had never witnessed the procedure.

At the conference, Anne Brenner, who has since become a rabbi, shared with our group of about fifteen, her expertise in the area of Jewish death and mourning. She wanted to demonstrate the procedure, so we gathered, on a bright and sunny day, in a grassy area at Bryn Mawr College, where the conference was being held, and she led us through the process. Of course, we were missing a body, so one of the group volunteered and pretended to be dead, which meant keeping his eyes closed and being as limp as possible. He made a fine corpse, except for the bathing suit. Step by step, we washed his body and purified it, reciting the appropriate prayers and pouring the required number of buckets of water over him. It was all done with great reverence, although at times it seemed a bit strange. After all, how often do people practise washing the body of someone pretending to be dead in the middle of an Ivy League college campus?

That was the closest I have ever come to the actual experience, although some years later a cousin of mine passed away, and his brothers asked me to conduct the funeral. It took place in North Dakota, and there wasn't a Jewish funeral home anywhere nearby. The day before the service, I went with the brothers to the non-Jewish funeral home, and the funeral director told us he had a Jewish *tahara* manual, giving step-by-step instructions and with sketches, for the washing and preparing of the dead. He had acquired it years before from an Orthodox rabbi in New York, and he said he would be happy to let us use it if the brothers and I wanted to do the honours. I was willing, but they demurred. And frankly I was relieved, although I am sure it would have been an experience I would not soon forget. At my request, the funeral director made a copy of the manual and gave it to me. (The *tahara* is not easily available, and I wanted a copy for reference.)

While on the topic of death in the family, in 1986, while I was visiting Winnipeg, my mother died. I was at a friend's son's *bar mitzvah* at the moment of her passing; when informed, I immediately left, picked up my dad, and we went together to the nursing home. We entered her room, sat down beside her, and wept. The nurse's assistant, who was with her at the moment of death, told us that she asked for a glass of water, put her head back on the pillow, and passed on. She died as she had lived, simply and with dignity. Meher and Dahlia flew in right away and were pallbearers at her funeral, which I conducted at the Hesed Shel Emet funeral home on North Main Street.

Then, six years later, in December 1992, at age eighty-eight, my father joined her. I had brought him to Toronto in 1991 to live out his days in the presence of his family, who adored him and visited often. Leaving Winnipeg was very difficult for my dad, not because he was hesitant to leave the city itself but because it meant he had to leave behind his treasured sister, Jean. I will always remember the day we finished packing the car and drove over to say goodbye to Jean. Because he had difficulty walking, my father remained in the car, and Jean came out to see him. Paula, Jean's daughter, was visiting from Calgary at the time, and we stood a short distance away, watching Jean talking to my dad through the passenger-side window. We commented to each other, with lumps in our throats, that this would most likely be the last time they saw each other. We agreed that we would stay out of their sight so that they could have as much time together as they wanted. We knew that they were as aware as we were of the significance of this moment. Finally the time came and they said goodbye. As we drove away, beginning the three-day journey to Toronto, my dad was silent. I knew what he was feeling, and because I too loved Jean, I felt a small measure of what he was going through. It was indeed their last time together, and a few months later Meher, Dahlia, and I had to break the news to my father that Jean had passed on.

My father was a very strong and stoic man with a tender heart. He was not afraid of death, but neither was he eager to embrace it. However, he was a widower, and with Jean and, soon, his brother Jay gone, he was also the last of seven siblings. All these losses took their toll, and I could see on his face that he was beginning to retreat into his soul. To add to this, he developed a gangrenous foot, and because nothing could be done to heal it, he was facing an imminent amputation, something he dreaded. I knew his time could be measured in days; and then it was hours.

Meher and I were at his bedside throughout his final night. At about 6:00 a.m. his breathing became laboured, and the nurse told us that he was in the final stage of dying. My dad had instructed us that he didn't want any heroics to keep him alive, and at a family meeting, Shula, the kids, and I had agreed unanimously to honour his wishes. Meher and I did our best to talk him through the process, assuring him that everything was going to be okay and that he would soon be with my mother, his beloved Betty. We assured him that we, his son and grandchildren, were going to be okay, and we told him that he was going to blend into the light, and all would be well. At about

6:30 a.m. on December 9, 1992, he took his last breath. I immediately informed Shula and Dahlia, who had been standing by at home throughout the night, and also Stacey, my girlfriend, who was sleeping at my place. They came to the hospital to spend some time with my dad's body and to say good-bye, each in her own way. Then, as we were about to leave York Central Hospital, Dahlia, bless her heart, suggested that we go to the maternity ward and see a newborn baby. We all thought this was an excellent suggestion. The nurse in the maternity ward was very accommodating after we explained the circumstances. She found a mother willing to part briefly with her infant, and brought the child to us. We found this very comforting and asked the nurse to please thank the gracious mother.

Then, amidst a very bad snowstorm, we saw to it that my father's body was returned to Winnipeg according to his wishes, to be buried next to his wife. Again, Meher and Dahlia were pallbearers.

I try to get back to Winnipeg every three or so years so that I can visit my parents' graves and update them on the latest happenings in my life. I always find this monologue comforting and very moving; I feel that somehow they hear me — wherever they are. And sometimes I even tell them about humourous incidents in my life, so we can have a laugh together.

EVERY RABBI HAS stories to tell, some funny, some unusual, and some sad. When I was a student at the Hebrew Union College in Cincinnati, one of the best stories I heard had to do with the blowing of the *shofar*. It goes like this: In a small town somewhere in the midwestern United States, one of our rabbinic students had a High Holiday pulpit and observed a strange act. When it came time to blow the *shofar*, the gentleman who had this privilege walked up to the open ark where the Torahs are, turned his back to the congregation, stuck his head into the ark, and blew the horn. After the service, as the story goes, the student rabbi asked the gentleman why he turned his back to the congregation as he had never heard of this practice. The *shofar* blower replied that he believed this was the way it was supposed to be done, as he had always seen his predecessors perform it in this manner, ever since he was a small child. Not being satisfied with this answer, the student approached one of the most senior members of the congregation, a gentleman in his nineties, and asked him the same question, figuring that at such a venerable age, the man might know a little more about the history of this custom. The elderly member took the student rabbi aside and, in a subdued voice, told him that when the congregation was formed, the first man given the honour of blowing *shofar* was elderly and had false teeth, which interfered with his performance. To prevent embarrassment, he placed a small glass of water in the ark, and when he opened the ark with his back to the congregation, he removed his teeth and placed them in the glass in such a way that nobody saw what he was doing. Then he blew the *shofar* as required, and at the end replaced his teeth. Since no one in the congregation knew any different, this became the custom. Later, the student rabbi discovered that the man who told him the story was the congregation's original *shofar* blower, by then very aged but not without a twinkle in his eye.

Now, some humourous stories of my own:

Throughout the years, the weddings I have conducted have been pretty straightforward — until recently. In 2007, I had two weddings on the same day, not unusual for a rabbi. The first wedding was at noon and took place outdoors on a beautiful sunny day. As most readers probably know, especially if they have attended a Jewish wedding, at the end of the ceremony a glass is broken. The glass is usually wrapped well, so that fragments won't scatter and become a hazard. It is the groom's pleasant task, and only the groom's, to bring his foot down on the glass, at which point everyone shouts, *"Mazel tov!"* At this particular wedding, the groom wanted his elderly grandfather to come up just before the glass was broken and say a few words to him and his bride. The grandfather, a distinguished-looking gentleman with a white beard, sat in the front row, elegantly dressed, and awaited his call. When the time came, I motioned for him to come over. He got up, walked right up to his grandson, stomped on the glass, and said, *"Mazel tov!"* Instead of the usual joyous response from the guests, a hush came over the gathering. No one, including myself, had ever seen or heard of anything like this before. I had to think quickly, and, with a smile on my face (not sure how I managed that), I announced, "Today we have a double *Mazel Tov*, and now, it's the groom's turn to break the remaining glass more completely!" — which he did, followed by a chorus of *Mazel Tovs* from the guests and music from the band.

That day I also had an evening wedding. In recent years, Jewish gift stores have been selling specially designed pouches for the glass to be broken in. The pouch consists of an attractive cloth bag with a drawstring at one end, which is tied after the glass is inserted. Some couples are given this special pouch as a pre-wedding gift, and it's my job, as with all glasses at my weddings, to give it to the groom's father to perform the honour of placing it at his son's foot. However, since I didn't know, or had forgotten, that a cloth pouch had been given to this couple, I brought along the kind of well-wrapped drinking glass I use at all my weddings, leaving it in my briefcase when I saw the pouch. When the moment came to break the glass in the pouch, the groom brought down his foot with perfect aim, and the glass, fully intact and without breaking, shot through the drawstrings, shot out of the sack, and raced across the floor. Somebody had not tied the drawstring tight enough. Rather than go chasing after the erratic glass, replacing it in the pouch, and then tying it properly, which would have taken too long, I reached into my satchel, pulled out my own glass, and the groom did his duty, this time without incident. The family thanked me later for having a backup glass ready. Who would have thunk?

My most unusual wedding story, however, came from a couple who had three children, the youngest still an infant. It was a small, intimate house wedding, and while I was conducting the ceremony, the bride held the infant in her arms. At about the midway point of the service, the baby began to cry. The mother tried rocking the baby, but to no avail. So, without missing a beat, she sat down on the floor under the *chupah* and began breastfeeding the child while I went on with the prayers, and the cantor sang his liturgical pieces. And this is how the ceremony ended. She was still on the floor as the groom broke the glass. No one batted an eye.

The thought has occurred to me to collect such stories from my colleagues and present them in a book of their own. Perhaps at a later point in my career, I'll pursue this.

MY RELATIONSHIP WITH Stacey, who accompanied me to my father's funeral in Winnipeg, began in 1991. This beautiful woman came into my life and led me on adventures I would not otherwise have experienced. Although there were many exciting and dramatic events in our four years together, two in particular stand out.

Stacey had relatives in Phoenix, Arizona, whom she wanted to visit. Since I had never been to Phoenix, and Arizona had for some time attracted me, I was happy to accompany her. We visited many sites and went briefly across the border into Mexico (my first time). But the crowning event of our two-week stay, and a spiritual experience in its own right, was the Grand Canyon. I know this has been written about and shown on the screen for decades; however, no amount of words or pictures can possibly do justice to this wonder of nature. And my writing about it doesn't add much, except to express my reaction and tell the tale.

We began our downward trek in the morning so as to reach the ranch below in time for dinner. It took us seven hours on the trail, carrying our own water, since there were no watering holes on the way down. We had been told to make sure we drank water, even if only a little, at least every fifteen to twenty minutes, thirsty or not. Apparently the nature of dehydration in this sort of clime is such that your body can be dangerously water deprived without your even knowing it. We heard stories of people who had died from dehydration with full canteens because they became delirious and couldn't think straight. We made sure to drink, one of us always reminding the other if necessary.

There are two ways one can explore the Grand Canyon: by foot or by mule. We chose to do it by foot because we wanted to have the experience of doing it under our own steam, and also because we wanted to explore at our pace and not be subject to the mule train's schedule. And there was another reason. Someone had mentioned to us that occasionally a mule went over the edge. I figured if I was going to die in the Grand Canyon, I would prefer to do it under my own aegis rather than that of a tired or careless donkey.

One might think that going down would be easy. It wasn't! Yes, we had gravity on our side, but we had to watch every step, and we were constantly fighting gravity so we wouldn't go too fast and endanger ourselves. I had purchased a new pair of running shoes for the occasion and was confident they would make a positive difference on the hike.

Stacey (circa 1992)

Each time we went around a turn, a new and always spectacular sight awaited us. I couldn't get over how varied the scenes were, some of which took my breath away. As it was early October, the trail was dry and dusty, and the air, while still hot, was also very dry. I've always enjoyed dry heat, perhaps a vestige of my prairie upbringing. After about five hours of walking, we could see the bottom of the canyon, highlighted by the rich blue strip of the Colorado River. I commented to Stacey that I couldn't wait to get to the bottom and take a dip. She felt the same.

We reached the river at about 4:30 in the afternoon. After a quick change into our bathing suits behind some bushes, we joined a number of other hikers who had the same idea for cooling off. And it was indeed a cooling off, as the water was frigid. I lasted all of five minutes before I had to get out. But it was certainly invigorating and gave us the strength for the forty-five-minute trek to the ranch.

The ranch was like an oasis, with ample vegetation and places to just sit and relax. The dining room was large, and nearby were several cabins for sleeping. The meals, delicious and copious, told us that the owners were well aware that after a day's hike, a hearty meal was needed and appreciated. Our arrangements to stay at the ranch had been made months in advance, as occupancy was in high demand. Sleeping quarters were camp style, with bunk beds, and the sexes slept separately in different cabins. By 9:00 p.m., most everyone was in bed, getting a good night's sleep for the upward climb early the following morning.

We were awakened at 5:00 a.m., ate a hearty breakfast of steak, eggs, pancakes, and all the trimmings, and by 6:30 began the upward journey. We were told it would take eleven to twelve hours to reach the top, which was one of the reasons for such an early start. "You don't want to get stuck on the trail after dark," one of the trail rangers had told us. (Incidentally, we found out that if someone had to be rescued from the canyon, there was always a helicopter standing by, ready to take your credit card before you board.)

The upward journey took us until about 5:30 in the afternoon. It wasn't as arduous as I had expected, partly because there were several watering stations along the way, which meant we could drink to our hearts' content without worrying about rationing our water supply. Along the trails, both going down and coming up, the canyon rangers patrolled to help anyone in trouble. These men (I didn't see any women rangers) had to be in superb shape, as they spent each day patrolling the full range of the canyon's trails.

When we reached the top, each of us felt exhilarated and quite proud that we had accomplished the hike both ways. A shower later that evening capped off the day in grand style.

The next morning, feeling something strange about my feet, I took a closer look and found that both of the toenails on my big toes were coming off. Shortly afterwards, I was nailless in Arizona. Apparently I should have worn hiking boots to keep my feet properly secured, as each time I took a step on the downward journey in my running shoes, my big toes rubbed against the shoes' front. After seven hours of grinding and bumping, my toenails gave up. It took about six months for them to fully grow back.

We climbed the canyon
     dust in our eyes
each step grueling
     stones on the path
silence our companion
     lips crying for water
pain in the air

blisters gnawing
seeking a ridge
our breath heavy
standing at last
together

In the spring of 1993, Stacey came to me with a proposal. She would pay part of my expenses if I accompanied her on a trip to the rainforests of Peru. She explained that a friend had told her of a wonderful shaman who lived there, and that two or three times a year junkets were arranged for groups to go down and spend two weeks with the shaman at his compound. She said that, for her, part of the purpose of the trip would be to take a psychotropic mixture called *ayawaska*. She had some issues that she wanted to clear up, she explained, and she felt that this experience might just do the trick, and that my companionship in Peru would give her extra security in case things got rough. I resisted at first, since I had no interest in travelling to Peru or ingesting psychotropic substances, but I finally gave in when she assured me that whether I took the substance was entirely up to me, and she would not exert any pressure in that direction. Done deal!

Augustine, 1993

After getting the necessary shots and stocking up on water purifiers, we flew to Miami, met the rest of the junket group, and got onto Elmer Fawcett Airlines bound for Iqhitos, Peru. The plane was one of my favourites, a Lockheed L1011, though it had seen better days. Still, I had confidence in the craft, as I knew a little about its excellent safety record.

At the airport in Iqhitos, we were greeted by a Peruvian wearing a baseball cap. He looked no different from anyone else in the vicinity. He introduced himself as Augustine, and, upon further inquiry from one of the group, told us he was the shaman, and if we would be a little patient, he would soon have us through customs and on our way. He spoke briefly with one of the customs officials, and very quickly we got through and onto a bus. We were taken to our lodging for the night in preparation for our journey to his home in the rainforest early the next morning.

Augustine Rivera was a diminutive man and very unassuming. He emitted a confidence, gentleness, and strength that won all of us over. There were no airs about him, and he went about his business easily and clearly. At our overnight lodging, he made sure that everyone was comfortable and that we were properly fed before retiring. In a sense, he was to be our father for the next two weeks, and that sense took on many aspects over the following days and nights.

The room in Iqhitos where Stacey and I stayed was somewhat primitive by North American standards, especially the bathroom, in which there was no partition on the floor to separate the toilet and shower. Consequently, when one of us took a shower, the water flowed partly down the drain and partly into the toilet area. Eventually, after some hours, it evaporated. This was interesting but not pleasant if one of us had to use the facility during the night. Rubber boots were not provided.

Our boat on the Amazon

In the morning, after a simple breakfast, our group of twenty boarded a two-level motorized boat, with the baggage underneath and all of us on the top deck. We began a five-hour trip down the Amazon River, and Augustine warned us not to try to dangle our feet overboard or touch the water, as the river was polluted and there was a risk of disease. This was not a pleasant way to begin the day. However, before long I began to enjoy the journey and the company of my fellow adventurers, among them a newly married couple who were making these two weeks their honeymoon. Along the way, the motor broke down but was quickly fixed by the captain. I can't say that the boat ride was interesting, since the scenery on the banks was pretty much the same: trees and more trees, with an occasional break for a small village whose inhabitants waved to us as we passed. Yet it was enjoyable enough, every passing mile augmented by the excitement of coming closer to an adventure we were all looking forward to, even though none of us knew exactly what to expect. I told Stacey that I was reconsidering my position on not taking *ayawaska*. I figured if I was coming all this way, I may as well join the party.

When we finally came ashore, a contingent of women met us, unloaded our suitcases and duffle bags, and placed them on the ground. Once the boat had been emptied, each woman took a piece of baggage and, regardless of its size or weight, placed it upon her head. Then they quickly disappeared into the forest. There was a kiosk at the place where we landed, and among other things it sold cold Coca-Cola. Stacey and I bought a large bottle, downed it, and followed Augustine into the trees.

Top: Coke never tasted so good
Above: Our sleeping quarters. Protruding at the back on the left is the kitchen

Our trek took about an hour and a half, with Augustine stopping every now and then to be sure everyone was present. About halfway we passed a cemetery, and I noticed that the graves had crosses on them. Christianity seemed to be the dominant religion in Peru, with local customs and beliefs blending into it, especially in the area of the occult. In due course we came into a clearing, and there was the compound.

Augustine's compound (we learned later that he had a more opulent home elsewhere in Peru) consisted of several structures. There was an open kitchen and dining room, housed under a thatched roof, that was home to a cook with a warm smile. Next to the kitchen and a few steps away were our sleeping quarters. These were in a two-level structure, mounted on stilts about ten feet above the ground so the local wildlife could not visit us at night, and well covered by a fine netting to keep the insects out. The first level was a very large floor where most of us slept. There were no partitions of any kind, and since there was no lighting, undressing at night was not a problem. The second level was an open space where there hung several one-person hammocks. A few of the group preferred the hammocks; the rest of us made our beds on the floor, with thin mats for cushioning. The married couple had their own small but private hut, compliments of Augustine, to honour their marriage. Augustine also had private quarters where he lived with his partner, a charming and lovely Peruvian woman. There were several other men at the compound, all hired by Augustine for different purposes. At night they would sit on the porch outside our sleeping quarters and talk into the wee hours. I found their speech very soothing: to my ears the language they spoke sounded musical and soft. It lulled me to sleep. About fifty yards from the compound was a double-seated outhouse, with a thin wall of bamboo separating the two stalls. This served for both men and woman on a first-come, first-serve basis. You never knew who your neighbour was, unless a conversation ensued and there was voice recognition. This, too, became a non-issue after a few days. The walkway to the outhouse was an elevated narrow plank with a railing, whose height kept us from being attacked by ants and other crawling creatures. We were advised to avoid using the facilities at night unless absolutely necessary, and if we did, to be very careful not to fall from the plank, because one never knew what one would find on the ground. Besides, once on the ground, unless there was a full moon, finding one's way to either the outhouse or the compound could be a problem. We made sure to do what we had to do before retiring for the night, but in case of emergencies, taking along a flashlight and, if possible, a friend was always a good idea.

Top: The original co-ed outhouse
Above: Kitchen and dining room

The meals were always very plain but tasty and wholesome. The chicken that wandered around during the day became part of our meal in the evening. A kind of bread was plentiful, and the pineapple, freshly harvested, was the best I've ever tasted. There was always plenty of coffee, and we were told that drinking the water was not a problem. I had doubts about this, so every time I wanted a drink, I first put in a few drops of the purifier I had brought from Toronto. It tasted awful. A couple of days of purified water was all I could take before I succumbed to the regular drinking water. Neither I nor anyone else had any ill effects — at least, not from the water.

Running through the compound was a stream of very pure and clear water. Stretched across the stream, which was perhaps twenty feet wide and shoulder deep, was a low wooden sitting area where we could perch when washing clothes or just chatting. Everyone wore bathing suits the first day or two. After that, slowly, one man or woman, then another, bathed or sat in the nude. Before long, no one brought anything to the stream, not even a towel, as the weather was warm and we dried off in the breeze. Even walking from the compound to the stream, a distance of about eighty yards, we rarely wore anything, unless it was for protection from the sun or it was late in the day and a bit chilly. At all other times we wore clothing.

Our bathing stream

Adding to all this natural beauty were exquisitely coloured birds, some in the air and some perched where we could approach them and enjoy their company.

In some ways, the compound and the surrounding area reminded me of what I had at times imagined the Garden of Eden to be like before Adam and Eve went on a clothes-shopping spree. Everything came from nature; for the most part, nothing unnatural had a place here. Before long, I began to feel that even organized religion would be a stranger in the rainforest.

On the second day at the compound, Augustine gathered us together to prepare us for that evening's *ayawaska* ceremony. He told us that as protection from any unwanted animals, an armed guard would accompany us on our walk to the temple, which was a half hour away. We were to wear all-white clothing so that we could be easily seen in the dark in case we got lost, and he suggested that we take along insect repellent in case the mosquitoes were bad, although, he added, "sometimes the mosquitoes respect the *ayawaska* and stay away." Augustine took questions from the group about the ceremony, and only one posed a problem for him. The honeymooning couple wanted to come to the ceremony along with everyone else, but they did not want to take the *ayawaska*. Augustine said that everyone who came to the ceremony had to participate fully. The discussion went back and forth, until finally Augustine told the couple that they could come and observe without taking the *ayawaska* under the condition that they remained for the entire ceremony, no matter how long it took, and that they did not speak the whole time. The couple agreed.

Just before nightfall, led by Augustine and one guard with a rifle, we walked to the temple along a narrow and winding path. The temple was not like anything I had imagined. The elaborate and very large structure I had envisioned yielded to a relatively small and humble assemblage of tree railings surrounding an area of about fifty by twenty-five feet. A slight elevation of compacted earth bordered the inside of the area right next to the railings. This was where everyone sat in horseshoe formation, with a table at the open end that accommodated various unfamiliar ritual objects and also a goblet and a flask. We made ourselves as comfortable as we could, most of us leaning back against the railings. Augustine then gave us our final pre-*ayawaska* instructions. Each of us would come up to the table, one at a time, and drink the brew that had been prepared by one of Augustine's fellow shamans, who was also there. We were to drink the entire contents of the goblet, which he would then refill from the flask for the next person. He told us that each person's reactions to the *ayawaska* would be different and highly individual and that the amount of time needed for the mix-

Temple

ture to take effect would differ from person to person. We were also told, and this point he emphasized very strongly, that no one was to leave the temple for any reason except to go to the outhouse, which was a short walk away and visible from the temple during daylight.

Augustine assured us that everyone would come through this fine, and that he and the other shaman would be there constantly to attend to our needs. Some questions were asked by the group, after which Augustine poured *ayawaska* from the flask into the goblet. To my surprise, before calling up the first person, Augustine himself drank the contents of the goblet. He completed his drink with the comment, *"Bueno!"*, Spanish for "Good!" The way he said it gave me some cause for concern. As we later found out, the brew, prepared by the other shaman, was stronger than usual, which was what prompted Augustine's rather pointed remark.

One by one, each of us took the potion, some bravely and some with trembling fingers. It took about twenty minutes to go around, by which time one or two of the group were already beginning to feel the effects, as evidenced by soft sounds of sighing and other subdued vocal expressions. By the forty-five-minute mark, most of the group were feeling the effects, and the sounds emanating from their throats were no longer subdued. At about the hour-and-a-quarter point, the pretty and innocuous *ayawaska* leaf had unleashed its magic. The place felt and sounded like bedlam.

I sat on the earth mound listening to the groans, shrieks, and undistin-

Augustine holding Ayawaska leaves

guishable utterances of my fellow travellers, wondering when my turn would come. It was almost an hour and a half since I had ingested the brew and, like the honeymoon couple, I was feeling like an observer rather than a participant. Then a very subtle feeling began to develop in my chest, like a soft fluttering, which over the next several minutes grew in intensity until I felt my heart pounding so hard I thought it would break through my chest cavity. My whole body was in a state of trauma, and I thought, contrary to Augustine's earlier assurances, that I was going to die. To his credit, Augustine picked up that I was in distress and came over, stood in front of me, played his harmonica with great intensity, danced and moved his arms and hands as if warding off spirits, and stayed with me for a period of time. His presence was comforting, and only when he saw that I was

doing better did he move on to help someone else. The other shaman, the one who mixed the brew, was performing the same function as Augustine, moving back and forth among the group, assuaging wounded souls and comforting ravaged hearts. He did not play the harmonica.

Many of us needed to vomit. Augustine had earlier prepared us for this possibility and said that when the urge came, we should turn around, lean over the railing, and expel the contents of our stomachs onto the ground just outside the temple area. I did so on several occasions over the next few hours. Also, on two occasions I had to relieve myself in the outhouse. The first time I found my way there, but coming back I got lost and the flashlight was of little help. Fortunately, even with the *ayawaska* in my system, I had the presence of mind to remain standing in one spot and wait until someone else came along who needed to use the facility. I didn't have to wait long, and that person pointed me in the right direction, which was sufficient to bring me back to the temple.

At one point during the evening, about midway through the *ayawaska* process, Augustine suddenly doubled up and pressed his fists into his stomach. A split second later we heard the distant roar of a jaguar (usually referred to in Peru as a tiger). In discussing this among ourselves the next day, some of the group concluded that Augustine was so in touch with nature that he picked up on the presence of the jaguar even before it made any sound. I was inclined to concur with their speculation, and later that evening Augustine confirmed our assessment.

At about five in the morning, the last effects of the *ayawaska* departed from the group. Augustine was clearly aware that it was time to return to the compound and equally aware that some of the group were in no shape to make the journey. He informed us that since it was daylight, those who wanted to could remain behind and sleep on one of the cots that stood a short distance from the temple, each cot surrounded on the top and sides by a gauze-like netting. I don't recall if anyone took up his invitation, or whether we all preferred to make the trip back, no matter how difficult. Those of us who were more able helped those less so. Everyone got back safely and spent the rest of the day sleeping and resting, since physically and emotionally we were drained and exhausted.

That evening, Augustine assembled the group in our large sleeping area and asked each of us to recount to him all the details we could remember about our experiences. He allowed us as much time as we needed, and no one was rushed. To the contrary, he made an effort to draw from us more than we initially remembered or were at first able to share. The stories varied considerably, each being a snapshot of some part of the individual's life, such as a buried memory, a sad or tragic event, an unresolved conflict and, in a few instances, perceived memories of lifetimes lived before the current one. In almost all cases, the experience had to do with unfinished business, either emotional or spiritual. Issues of abuse, belittlement, abandonment, early death of a loved one, sickness, disappointment, and unrequited love were among those presented. It was as if the *ayawaska* was a therapist in disguise, opening up areas of the heart and soul, draining the psychological pus that had accumulated over a lifetime (or lifetimes) and bringing to each a cleansing, in part or in full. Many tears were shed as people told their stories, and each ended by stating what, if anything, the *ayawaska* had done for them.

Augustine listened carefully to each story. When the person was finished speaking, he would give him or her feedback, often bringing insight into their experience or comforting them in a way that was compassionate and at times profound. He advised those who felt their issues were still not fully resolved and needed more work to remain patient; he said in the next two *ayawaska* sessions they might find the resolution they were looking for.

When my turn came to speak, the only thing I could think of to say was that during the times I was vomiting, I felt like an eagle with its neck stretched way out in flight. Other than that and the fact that I felt like I was dying, with my heart pounding like a jackhammer in my chest, nothing much had occurred. Augustine thought about this but had little to offer by way of comment. I felt a little shortchanged, but on the other hand I wasn't giving him the kind of dramatic material that was being provided by others.

It took about seven hours to process everybody. Three days later we went back to the temple for our second *ayawaska* journey.

This time around, I needed to do some unusual and dangerous preparation. Stacey had an issue from back in her childhood that she felt I didn't really understand. No matter how many times she referred to it, I didn't give her the response she needed because, she said, I was afraid to deal with a similar issue in my own childhood. She asked me to go into the second *ayawaska* experience with the clear and determined intention of trying to understand her issue without fear. It occurred to me that if I came out of the second experience without any further understanding of her issue, she would still claim that it was because I hadn't overcome my fear. At first, this appeared to be a no-win situation. Then I thought that if I could find some way to show her I wasn't afraid and that I could face whatever *ayawaska* brought me, she would believe that my effort was sincere. I loved Stacey and wanted to do whatever I could to improve our relationship. Finally, it came to me.

The second *ayawaska* ceremony was to take place on a Sunday evening, so at eleven o'clock Saturday night, I quietly got up, dressed, and went to the kitchen, where I performed the Jewish ceremony of *Havdalah*, which marks the closing of the Sabbath. Then, with flashlight in hand and a flask of water, I started out for the temple. It was totally forbidden for any of us to wander away from the compound for two reasons: we could get lost, and there were tigers in the area. But I believed that if I could find my way to the temple and sleep there for the night on one of the cots, this would prove to Stacey that I wasn't afraid of anything: I was risking my life to make good my intention.

With grim determination, at about midnight, I took off into the Peruvian jungle. I felt a slight bit of security from having the flashlight. I had learned in my youth that if a dog tried to attack you at night and you had a flashlight, you could keep him at bay by shining the light in his eyes. However, I wasn't sure this would work on a tiger.

I had not walked for more than a few minutes when I realized I was not in familiar territory. Something didn't seem right. I recalled that near the beginning and end of our first journey to the temple, we had passed over a small bridge. I had walked far enough to have encountered the bridge, and it wasn't there. So I backtracked to where I had started out and noticed that there was another path. Apparently I had taken the wrong fork in the road. I came upon the bridge and continued from there to the temple area without incident. I found the cots near the temple, chose one, and laid down with the mosquito netting surrounding me and giving me a false sense of protection. I could hear the wind blowing through the trees and quickly was lulled to sleep.

At about 2:00 a.m. I suddenly awoke, feeling the hairs on my body bristling. The sound of feet running toward me made me realize that I was about to be attacked by a tiger, and the gauze-like netting would mean nothing to the animal. I was its next meal. I found myself out of my body, as if my soul had departed ahead of time to protect me from the beast and from having to endure any suffering. I looked down on my body and waited. I don't remember how long I remained in this state. All I know is that eventually I found myself back in my body, unharmed, but I was frozen to the cot, and the only movement I could manage was to open my eyes and stare straight in front of me into the darkness for what seemed an eternity. Finally I began to slowly move my head so I could look around. This, of course, didn't do me much good,

Sitting on the cot where I spent the night and encountered the tiger in the wind

since the night was black and the slim moon didn't help. After what I would estimate was a half hour, I concluded that I must be fully back in my body because I had the strong urge to urinate. This naturally meant getting up, parting the netting, and walking into the night. I wasn't ready to do this, and fought the biological pressure until I couldn't take it any more. Even the thought of the tiger being there was overcome by the urgency. Finally, trusty flashlight in hand, I emerged from the enclosure and relieved myself. Then, figuring that the tiger must no longer be around, since I had survived this far, I laid down on the cot and slept till daylight.

When I awoke, Stacey was standing beside me. She said that she had seen me leave the night before and had started to come after me, but then said to herself that she shouldn't interfere and that I must have a good reason for what I was doing. So, out of respect for what she thought were my wishes, she held back but worried about me throughout the night. It was good to see her, and I quickly explained why I did what I did. She was very touched by what I told her and replied that she had full confidence that I wouldn't be afraid to face the next *ayawaska* experience, given the ordeal I had just been through. We returned to the compound hand in hand.

That night saw us at the temple again, going through the preparatory *ayawaska* ritual and ingesting the substance. The response of the group was similar to the first time, if somewhat more subdued. Perhaps because it was our second time and we knew what to expect, it wasn't as powerful, or if it was, it wasn't perceived as such. My experience was mild, and I only threw up once.

As we returned to the compound the next morning while it was still dark, our guard with the rifle stumbled and fell off the path. Fortunately the rifle did not discharge. Later in the day, I told Stacey that nothing had come up for me that related to her issue. After that, she did not bring the subject up again. At a later time, I told Augustine about my tiger incident, wondering if all I'd really heard was the wind. He responded that it very likely was a tiger, and that he intuitively felt this to be the case. He said nothing about the fact that I had broken the rules.

The next evening we again went through the process of relating to Augustine the events of the previous night. This session was shorter. Some of the group found it meaningful, bringing to a closure unfinished business from the earlier *ayawaska*, while for others nothing was added. The honeymoon couple took the *ayawaska* on our second venture and, it being their first time, had more to recount than the rest of us. I again had little to say, but in response to my account, Augustine asked me if I would like to spend two years with him as his apprentice. He said he would help me build a tree house and would teach me the ways of the shaman. I thought about his offer, but before leaving I told him that although I was honoured by his gesture, I needed to return to my home and my family. He understood and wished me well.

There was to be a third *ayawaska* ceremony, which Stacey and I decided not to attend. As it turned out, the mosquitoes were so bad that everyone returned before taking the potion.

On one of the days between *ayawaskas*, Augustine asked us all to come to an old tree that had large above-ground roots running in all directions. He told us to form a circle around several sacks on the ground that were filled with fresh cow dung. Next, he instructed us to take off all our clothes, and with the help of two of the group, he emptied the sacks onto the ground. He described this as a purifying ritual and told us that each of us in turn would come and lie in the dung. I believe that more than one of us thought this was a crazy idea, but here we were in the middle of the Peruvian jungle, being guided by one of its native sons. I figured he knew what he was doing, since he was a very religious man, not to mention a shaman, which I believe means more or less the same thing. So I went for it, along with everyone else.

I laid in the dung, which was so fresh it was still slightly warm, with several members of the group kneeling around me. I noticed, to my surprise, that I couldn't detect any odour. At Augustine's signal, the others covered me completely with the dung while he knelt at my head and, a few moments later, told me to open my mouth. I did so, and he put a handful of dung into it, adding emphatically that I mustn't swallow. (Thank God for small mercies.) It all happened so quickly I didn't have time to even think of protesting. Expecting the worst, I was quite taken aback to find that the taste wasn't in the least offensive. After two or three minutes, he told me to spit it out. This was the ritual that everyone went through, and not one person objected. When we were all done, Augustine suggested we go bathe in the stream, and make sure we were downstream from where we normally bathed and swam. We gladly obeyed. Some of the group said that their skin felt unusually soft and clean, and there were jokes about marketing a new cosmetic product.

I related this story fifteen years later to my naturopath, who also had spent time with Augustine, and he thought that the shaman was playing a joke on us. Maybe, but at the time it didn't seem to be the case, although I must admit, in retrospect, some humour does come to mind.

Top: Preparation for the dung dip
Above: Assisted dung bath

Later it occurred to me that perhaps the dung didn't smell or taste bad, because the cows from which it came did not receive injections of any kind, nor did they have chemical supplements added to their food. They simply grazed the available grass and drank the available water. What went in was pure, and what came out was pure.

On another morning, Augustine assembled the group and told us we were to drink something he referred to as *ohey*. He said it was a very strong laxative, and its purpose was to cleanse us inside. He suggested that we have lots of toilet paper handy and that if we couldn't make the outhouse in time, we should just squat wherever we were and let go. He also said that after downing the solution, we would need to continually drink water for the next hour, to dilute the *ohey* so it wouldn't burn our insides. So, there we were, with large jugs of water in our hands and rolls of toilet paper strung around our necks. And he wasn't kidding.

Stacey and me in our spiritual-marriage tuxedos

For the next two hours we ran around in fierce competition for the outhouse, but for the most part ended up fertilizing the fields. Modesty had gone out the window on the second day of our visit.

All in all, by the end of our two-week stay, most of us felt very clean, physically, psychologically, and spiritually.

One more thing to mention. Stacey and I got married in the rainforest — well, sort of. Three couples, us included, had a spiritual marriage ceremony, conducted by Augustine and the woman who led the group. It was a lovely and touching ceremony, and Stacey looked very beautiful, dressed all in white with flowers in her hair. However, the tension and stresses between us that had plagued our relationship on and off almost from the beginning surfaced with force once we returned to Toronto. In some ways, subtle and otherwise, perhaps the *ayawaska* played a part. Unfortunately, after a few months we went our separate ways, although over the years we have continued to have occasional contact. I believe there will always be a spiritual bond.

During my time with Stacey, she and Dahlia formed a strong relationship. Stacey attended Dahlia's dance performances with me, and the occasional musical events by Meher. Even after we stopped seeing each other, she followed Dahlia's career and attended events without me.

SPEAKING OF MY kids' talents, two of the proudest moments in my life were when they graduated from their respective colleges, Meher from the Humber College School of Music and Dahlia from the School of the Toronto Dance Theatre (TDT). Meher excelled in jazz piano and Dahlia in modern dance.

As part of Meher's graduation, he was required to present a recital of approximately forty-five minutes. Being the quiet rebel he has always been, he extended this to an hour and a quarter, much to the smiling chagrin of his main teacher, who later gently chastised him. He got a slightly lower grade for this extension, but it was well worth it as everyone present, family, friends, classmates, and teachers, were treated to a wonderful recital.

I had a small part in Meher's performance. About six weeks before the recital, a friend gave me a clarinet that had belonged to one of her children who didn't want it anymore. I immediately took a few lessons, in the hope that I would be able to make a cameo appearance at Meher's recital. I practised "When the Saints Come Marching In" until I was blue in the face. With Meher's permission, I was introduced midway through his recital and began to play, with his buddies backing me up and Meher on the piano. Well, talk about a hoot! I started out fine but quickly ran into trouble, squeaking and squawking between notes, until finally the place was in stitches, and I, too, couldn't stop laughing. I finished the song and everyone applauded loudly. Somewhere in my files I have a copy of the recording of Meher's recital, including my virtuoso rendition of "When the Saints."

I attended many of Dahlia's dance performances throughout her studies at TDT. She, too, was required to give a recital, for which she had to choreograph a dance and present it to an audience. With a flair for choreography, she presented a well-received performance and also participated in her classmates' performances. At her graduation, she and a fellow student were honoured with an award for leadership over the four years of their studies. Shula, Meher, and I beamed as she went up to accept her award.

In the summer of 2002, Pope John Paul II visited Toronto on World Youth Day. In honour of his visit, the band that Meher played with, White Cowbell Oklahoma, put together a skit for a performance at Lee's Palace, a popular Toronto club. The skit, with musical accompaniment by Meher and the band, had the Pope and Stephen Hawking arguing about some conflicts between science and religion; I recall it being mainly about evolution versus creationism. As the debate heated up, Hawking and the Pope got into a fight, and as they began to tussle, I, in the role of rabbi, entered the stage, broke up the fight, and told them that there was a solution to their problem — namely, that both positions are valid. I then added that the best solution of all was for both men, as the Torah prescribes, to love one another as cherished friends: "You shall love your neighbour as yourself." With these words, the standing-room-only audience broke into cheers and applause while the Pope and Hawking joined arms and danced in a circle. For some reason I still can't fully understand.Meher and some members of the band remind me from time to time of this event and how much it meant to them and everyone there. They think my words were "brilliant." I have difficulty with this, as I'm sure any rabbi, or for that matter many lay people, could have said the same thing. Still, I feel honoured to have made what seems to have been an impression on so many young minds.

Top: My dad — Brighton Beach, New York (circa 1992)
Above: And his 88th birthday cake

Shula's and my pride in our children has continued over the years, as they continue to create in their respective fields, much to the delight of those they entertain and serve. Meher has expanded into writing and recording. Dahlia has also performed professionally, her most memorable performance being the lead role in a choreographed version of *The Little Prince*. Both kids have done considerable touring, giving much pleasure to audiences at home and abroad. Dahlia has moved on to teaching yoga and Pilates, with a special sensitivity to dancers who can benefit from her expertise, and in 2010 she started a two-year course to become a massage therapist.

Both children have always had a soft spot for their grandparents, so on September 8, 1992, when we had a surprise party for my dad's eighty-eighth (and last) birthday, Meher and Dahlia brought a photograph of my father to a cake artist. In the photo, which I had taken earlier in the year at Brighton Beach in New York, my dad is on the sidewalk of a busy street, sitting in a chair that just happened to be there, smoking a cigar. It's a classic picture of my father, who loved his cigars. The cake artist and master baker used cake icing to make an excellent replica of my dad, based on the photo. We had this done because the kids and I had decided to make his eighty-eighth birthday a cigar birthday party; we asked the many who attended to bring cigars as the only present. Everyone complied. The collection of cigars my dad accumulated that day was profound. After the party, he spent several weeks sitting outside of his assisted-living quarters in the country, smoking them one by one and enjoying every puff. As for the cake, it was a hit, and my dad's very surprised reaction to it will be remembered for a long time by all who were there. He stared at the cake for several minutes, hesitating to cut into it, until finally he took a full, strong breath and blew out the candles.

My poetry book, *Melting: Poems of a Frozen Man,* was dedicated to my father, who unfortunately passed away just three months before its publication. The inscription reads:

> To my father
> who sings and hums
> in death's shadow

IN 1994 I completed a collection of stories (unpublished), *The Magic Touch — True and Unusual Stories of Healing and Hope*. The stories were gleaned from my practice as a psychotherapist. These are stories I recorded on tape as they unfolded before me with my clients in a state of regression, brought about either by the Re-Dreaming technique or through intensive breathing. These stories are among the most exciting moments I have experienced in working with clients over a period of thirty years. I present here, for the reader's interest, three of these stories in abbreviated form. Names and other identifying material have been changed to protect confidentiality. In the first two stories, where perceived past lives are involved, I cannot testify to the factuality of these accounts. Also, as a therapist, I believe factuality in cases like these is of secondary concern, since it is my view that even if the entire story is fabricated, it's the result that's most important. Sometimes, as with psychodrama, the subject needs free rein to construct the narrative that will best facilitate the healing process, whether this is based in fact or not. Also, in my many years of doing past-life therapy, not one of my clients, to my knowledge, has ever tried to ascertain the facts of his or her story by delving into history, even when such tracing was within the realm of possibility. It seems that once they have finished with the session, clients do not feel any need to pursue the matter further.

Since some of these stories take place in the perceived past-life state, let me mention briefly the incident that began my work with past-life therapy.

In 1976 I was asked by the owner of a restaurant to work with one of her employees, who was giving her considerable difficulty but whom she couldn't bring herself to fire. I began our work with the re-dreaming technique, using one of two recurring dreams. As the man did not believe in anything metaphysical, it came as a surprise when suddenly, while in a regressed state, he began to recount an event he described as happening during the period of the French Revolution. From this point on, the session lasted about two hours, during which he went through an intense emotional catharsis, which is described in detail in *Magic Touch*. Suffice to say that in the end, one of his problems, acrophobia (fear of heights), was completely eliminated, as was demonstrated in subsequent situations where, for example, he was required to climb ladders. My time at the ashram, where I was exposed to the concept of past lives, had prepared me for this moment, and while I was surprised when he began describing another lifetime, I was nevertheless able to work with him and bring the session to a positive conclusion. From this point onward, I began doing past-life work on a regular basis, partly because I started looking for clues in people's dreams that might indicate the recall of other lifetimes, and partly, I believe, because at an intuitive level, people consciously or subconsciously sensed that I was open to hearing this kind of material.

THE WOUNDS OF WAR
CHRONIC STOMACH AILMENT

GREG, IN HIS mid-forties, had suffered with stomach problems all of his life. Diarrhea, cramps, and discomfort or pain were frequent symptoms. A round of medical specialists and various medications over many years were unable to bring him relief. He was told he had a nervous stomach, something akin to colitis.

Greg related all this information to me on the telephone when he first called. He had seen me interviewed on television and was willing to try anything, even past-life regression therapy, if it might help. I told him I would be willing to give it a try, but cautioned, as I do in all cases, that regression therapy doesn't always work, and even when it does, there was seldom a way of telling if the lifetime experienced was real or a fabrication of the mind. He replied that he would take his chances.

A week later, Greg walked into my office. There was a look about him that I have come to recognize after doing regression therapy for many years. Something in his eyes told me that he was already well on his way into the regression state before he even sat down. There was little for me to do except ask him to close his eyes, take a few deep breaths, and tell me what he saw.

I see a green hill. There are men in uniform. They have their bayonets fixed. They're not moving.

I see a white stone cliff and an ocean. The waves are coming in.

The men are wearing khaki uniforms. They're First World War British soldiers. They have puttees around their legs up to the knees. They're not wearing helmets. It's Macedonia, 1915.

I asked Greg to continue looking at the soldiers and to tell me whatever he saw.

One face is very clear. It's a round face with a very large, black moustache. He's bent over, with a rifle and bayonet in one hand. He's been wounded and is in pain. He's been wounded in the stomach.

No one is moving. They're all still like statues.

Who is it you're looking at?

I don't know!

Ask him who he is?

John Soames.

How old is he and where is he from?

Twenty-eight years old, born in London, February 10, 1877.

What is the connection, if any, between you and John Soames?

It's me! I have stomach pains. I have suffered all my life. That's the connection.

Why is no one moving?

They're all dead!

How were you wounded?

With a bayonet.

By whom?

The Turks.

Describe the scene of the wounding.

We're advancing over a hill, and we're attacked by the Turkish infantry. There's a lot of shooting and hand-to-hand fighting.

Can you describe the person who wounded you?

He's a corporal. He's wearing a long overcoat, and he's lost his hat. He has black hair, and he's young. He has a stubble beard, not shaved, and a small black moustache. A dark complexion. I shot him in the chest as I fell. He's dead.

What happened after you were wounded?

I died three hours later from loss of blood.

Where were you buried?

In a graveyard in a valley. I see mountains in the background and a small village, like a Greek village.

Go to the grave and describe to me what you see.

I see a white cross. It's like a Greek cross. There's a circle on top of the cross, and the top of the circle meets at the top of the cross.

Is there any inscription?

Yes!

What does it say?

John Soames

The Warwickshires Regiment

Died of Wounds

May 1915

Can you describe to me the grave that is next to yours?

Sgt. William Penn

Killed in Action

May 1915

What is the main lesson of that lifetime?

I shouldn't have killed him. He was very young. I should have known better, even though he was the enemy. I've been paying for that with my stomach problems.

Can you ask him for forgiveness?

I do. I understand now.

At the conclusion of the session, Greg told me that his stomach felt fine.

Four months later, he called again to tell me that since our session together, he had been pain free until a few nights ago. Now he was again suffering. I asked him if there was anything that he was doing that might account for the return of his condition. He said that he couldn't think of anything, unless maybe it had something to do with his starting to read a war novel a week or so earlier. I suggested that he not read war novels or watch war movies or in any way be involved with anything military for the rest of his life. He said he wouldn't.

Six months later, I called Greg to see how he was doing. He told me he was feeling well. The stomach pains and diarrhea had not returned, and he had not gone near anything having to do with war.

Note: When clients have come to me with physical complaints, it is not unusual for them to feel relief from the symptoms after only one session. While I am pleased that there is relief, I am not convinced that it is more than temporary. It is only with time and the persistent absence of symptoms that I feel the therapy has produced a more substantial healing. This seems to have been the case with Greg.

REACHING FOR THE SKY

A BLENDING OF ACROPHOBIA AND CLAUSTROPHOBIA

DONNA WAS SUFFERING from a case of severe acrophobia. It was a condition that had haunted her all of her life, although she could not think of any incident to account for it. Her work required that she use the elevator every day, and she often had to go to the upper levels of high buildings, which terrified her.

A recurring dream, beginning at age seven, found Donna lying face down on the floor of an elevator:

My hands and legs are stretched out, spread-eagle. I can't get out of the elevator. I'm completely out of control.

This dream occurred once a month until she was thirteen, then once about every six months thereafter for many years. Presently it was occurring once or twice a year. When I asked Donna to close her eyes and start the re-dreaming process, she began recounting an entirely different dream, in which she was going, all alone, deeper into a black, empty hole. At the end of this tunnel was a figure, a man, who wouldn't let her out. She identified this figure as the devil and called out for help. Slowly she came to the awareness that she had done harm to someone, and asked for forgiveness. The dream then continued on in a circuitous manner.

What I found curious about this dream was that it seemed to have little to do with her acrophobia, at least not directly. Yet three weeks later, when Donna came in again to see me, she reported that her fear of heights had considerably diminished and that she could go to the thirty-fifth floor of any building with ease. Somewhere in her deep unconscious, a partial healing had taken place.

At this session, Donna again regressed to the tunnel experience of the previous session and this time found herself in a past life as a Jewish girl running from religious bigotry.

I see a little girl, chubby, with big brown eyes and long hair. She's playing. We're watching each other. Her mother just came and took her away. Her mother doesn't like me being there. She doesn't like me talking to her little girl. I'm different. She doesn't want my kind there, my race. I'm not Christian. I'm Jewish! She thinks I'm disgusting. [Donna, in this lifetime, is Christian.] *My father is very orthodox and has curls on the side of his head. My home is very small and my bedroom is part of my parents' room.*

This dream appeared to serve as a bridge to our next session, three weeks later. Donna returned to her Jewish lifetime. Her experience was very intense. Being present at this session, I could hardly doubt that what Donna was going through was anything less than real.

My grandmother is waking me up. The house is empty. I'm a little girl, not a baby. I'm five and have long, brown hair and a fair complexion. My eyes are also brown. I have on a little plaid dress with frills at the bottom. My name is Elizabeth.

My grandmother is trying to calm me down. There's something very wrong, but I'm not scared. I think she's more scared. There are loud noises outside, made by men banging on doors and driving trucks.

We're hiding now, me and grandmother. She's very scared. The men are in the house. I don't know what they want. They're wrecking everything looking for us.

Where's my family?

Grandmother's screaming. They're beating her up.

I ask Donna to describe the men.

They're blond and tall. One's wearing a long overcoat and one's not. He has a funny hat on. It's a dark grey-green hat. He's got a gun.

My grandmother's unconscious now. He's grabbing me. He's very mean. They're throwing me across the floor. They're dragging my grandmother.

(Donna tells me she is having a lot of stomach activity.)

We're on the street now. There are so many people, and it's so dark outside.

Somebody picks me up. My grandmother's gone. Everyone looks so unhappy. These men keep yelling at us. There's fire everywhere. I see my neighbours. I can't get to them though.

We're walking a long way. I want to get to my friend. He sees me.

We're in a dark, dark place. It's so hot and so dark. They're taking us somewhere. Everybody's crying. Everyone's so tired. We're hungry. Somebody just died—an old man. He looks awful. They're keeping us here in this dark place. We're not moving anymore—just sitting here.

All the children are put together. They're shooting the adults. They're just standing there shooting them.

I'm very scared now. They're moving us again. We're being put somewhere. They're so rough.

I can see my friend. He's with another group of children. They've divided us somehow. My friend has to work. He doesn't want to though. I can see him from here. They keep hitting him.

My group doesn't have to work. They're leaving us for something. They haven't fed us. We're all so hungry. I keep watching the other children. If they don't work, they'll kill them.

They're taking some of our children. They're screaming. I'm hiding in the back so they don't grab me first. I can hear them screaming. We're here for so long. I just want to go home. I'm afraid to come out of my corner.

They're coming back. I'm hiding. I don't want them to see me. They're looking for everybody hiding.

He's laughing at me. I don't want him to grab me. No! He's taking me too. Don't! Tell him to stop that. Mommy! [Crying] *He's naked. There's two of them. They're hurting me. They've stopped. They're laughing. They raped me.*

I'm back with the children. It's so dark. I can hear other children screaming. I can see a big smokestack. I've been noticing it for days.

They've left us alone for so long with no food. I'm getting weak. I can't get up. It's getting harder to move all the time. Everyone looks awful.

They take turns in beating up all the children. I know my turn is going to come up soon too. If we cry we're beaten up — so we all are quiet.

I think they're bringing more people. I can hear the guns. They're coming back again. I want them to go away.

He keeps dragging me off the bed. He just keeps laughing. He's called away for something. Something's happened outside. I know he'll come back though.

I can see my friend again out the window. He knows I'm here too. They're beating him up because he doesn't want to work. They're throwing him in a box.

I don't like this place. I want to go home.

They're tired of us. There's too many people coming in. Some women are coming for us. We're all naked. They're throwing our clothes somewhere. We won't need them again. It looks like we're going to have a shower. We're by the place with the smokestack. I don't know where we're going. The air smells funny. It stings my eyes.

I'm flying!

What has happened?

I died! I'm going to the light. It's all over. The pain is gone. We're safe now.

Elizabeth, is there any connection between your death in the gas chamber and the issues Donna is dealing with in her present life?

It has to do with being in a small place where I know I can't get out. This even happens sometimes in a bigger place. I have no control over the situation and I panic. The elevator takes you up and up and up. It's so slow. The time it takes is the problem.

How can you let go of your fear?

By knowing why I'm afraid — because that's how I died [in the closed and crowded space of the gas chamber]. *Understanding makes the difference.*

(I asked her to breathe and let it go. She did so for 2 or 3 minutes.)

It's gone. I feel at peace.

Once more, three weeks passed before I saw Donna for the fourth and last time. She told me that her fear of heights had diminished even more and there didn't seem to be any limit to how high she could go in an elevator.

In retrospect, claustrophobia, more than acrophobia, was really the problem. This is why elevators could never move fast enough for Donna — she needed to get out of them.

> There is a crystal
>   that reflects black light
> and in it
>   I can see
>   fragments of life
>   from distant times
>   and distant space
>   it moves quickly
>   affording only a glimpse
>   except
>   when it moves so quickly
>   it stands still
>   and all my lives
>   are as one
>   and I see myself
>   as I am

A QUESTION OF GENDER
CREATING PAIN

IT WAS UNLIKE Sandra to show a lot of emotion. From time to time it did emerge from between aphorisms and smiles, but hardly was there a hint of what lay buried deep inside her.

She had come to a weekend group therapy session. It was my practise in these sessions to work with one person at a time. For this reason, the group was small, as an individual interaction could take one, two, or more hours to complete.

It was Sandra's turn to work. She was a little nervous, but overall quite composed. She lay down on the floor on a mat, with the other members of the group sitting around in a circle. She closed her eyes and began to tell us a dream relating to her childhood and her relationship with her father. Things were proceeding pretty much as expected for this early in the session when suddenly Sandra doubled up and began screaming in pain. It was not unusual for my clients to enter deep emotional states in their work with me; nevertheless, I became somewhat alarmed when, after several minutes, Sandra was still experiencing excruciating pain. She could not contain her screams, nor her tears. When approximately twenty minutes had passed and no relief seemed in sight, I decided to not take any chances and asked one of the group to call an ambulance, suspecting that somehow an attack of appendicitis had been triggered. Sandra also felt this was the case. The ambulance was called, and we anxiously awaited its arrival.

On the off chance that this wasn't appendicitis but rather a severe emotional disturbance expressing itself in a physical way, I decided to continue working with Sandra until the ambulance came. She was in great pain, and I wanted to see if some further processing could bring relief.

As we started to work, I noticed that the pain subsided and then returned. A pattern began to emerge. The deeper she moved into her feelings and started to express what was bothering her, the more the pain subsided.

I feel so stupid! I've given in again! I can't believe that this pain is just my mind! I can't believe it! But it makes perfect sense. I can't believe the mind is that strong that I can give myself this sort of pain. It's like having a baby. [She begins screaming again.]

Help me! Help me! God, help me! The pain's coming back. I can't do it. It hurts — the pain. Please love me! I'm not so bad! Honest! I'm not so bad! I tried hard to be good but it didn't work. Daddy, please love me. You wanted a boy and you hated me. I just wanted to be an ordinary little girl, but I wasn't good enough.

I tried so hard to be a boy. I climbed trees; I ran races; I stood on my hands — that's the nearest I could be to a boy — an upside-down girl.

Sandra began to laugh and continued for several minutes. Then, with a look of satisfaction on her face, she said,

That's stupid! Eleven years old — an upside-down girl — the nearest she could be to a boy!

I can't be a boy!

I can only be a girl!

I can only be me!

I just want to be a girl!

I'm a good girl, and I'm a good woman!

It's strange how you can get rid of appendicitis. There's no more pain. There's no more yearning.

The ambulance had not yet arrived. We cancelled it.

THE *MAGIC TOUCH* stories, and many more like them, have served to underscore my belief that even in the darkest of moments there is always hope. So much more transpires in the healing process, and in the dying process, than what we commonly envision. It is this mystery that sustains me and declares to me that Shakespeare knew something very special when he had Hamlet tell Horatio, "there are more things in heaven and earth than are dreamed of in your philosophy, Horatio."

WHEN DISCUSSING PAST-LIFE regression with people, I am often asked if I have ever had this experience myself. I answer in the affirmative, and I would like to share with the reader my personal adventure in this realm.

In 1984, I had a very deep emotional and spiritual relationship with Dona, a beautiful, highly sensitive woman who, as mentioned, was also an astrologer. She agreed one day to conduct a past-life regression with me. As she had never done this before, I gave her some basic guidelines and then surrendered to her love and care for me, trusting that she would know what to do. I was not disappointed.

> Dona: What do you see?
> Jerry: A beach — smooth sand. It feels like the Mediterranean.
> Dona: Is there anything else?
> Jerry: I see a temple with pillars. It's white.
> Dona: Go on.
> Jerry: I'm wearing sandals with a thong between the toes. I'm experiencing a muscle spasm at the base of my spine — a fluttering sensation. I'm wearing a loose, white toga-like garment with some brown in it. I go into the temple. It's another time.
> . . . Now, I'm in a tent in a desert. People are brought to me and I put my hands on them. I know where to go. When my hands are there I know what to do. I'm working with a man who is a little older than me. My hand is on top of his head. He closes his eyes. I very gently put my thumb and first two fingers on his eyes and I can feel through that. It plugs me in. I pick up where I have to go and what I have to do. He has a problem with his liver. Strange! I put my forehead on his body where his liver is and keep it there, and I generate through my third eye. There is a power or force that moves into the organ and the surrounding area. This begins to reverse the condition and removes the pain. I keep it there for ten to fifteen minutes. He stays in the area for the next few days. He comes in once a day for me to

repeat the treatment. By the end of the fourth day, there is no more pain, and he leaves. He comes back a few months later, healed and well, with gifts of food and animals. He thanks me.

I put my hands on some people and on others, my forehead. Some I don't even touch. I just sit with them. I generate such a force that it goes into them and helps begin a healing process in them. Thereafter, for a period of time, they visualize my face and feel that force of energy coming from my forehead and healing them. They do this until they are well.

Dona: Tell me about your home.

Jerry: My home! I have two sons. My wife is not clear, but she is there. She has a role of caring for me and allowing me a place of quiet and sanctuary. She's proud of me. She's quiet and unobtrusive, and we have a quiet understanding. There is a deep bond between us. Her name is Leah. The house is made of brick and white stone with wood inside. It is primitive, reasonably comfortable, and very simple. It feels quite ancient, three to four thousand years ago.

Dona: What is your name?

Jerry: My name is Jacob.

Dona: What is the saddest time of your life?

Jacob: The saddest time of my life? Nothing really hard or sad. My powers of healing manifested at a young age, and I got a reputation as a young child. People came from all over, and I would heal. That's what I did every day. I would be restored to heal during sleep. It was during sleep that I would be guided and directed, my doubts assuaged, my power renewed and regenerated. There was the occasion, not often, when the night did not restore me, when I needed a rest. People would be restored to health just by looking at me. An emanation or vibration, very healing. People even healed without me actively doing anything. My aura extended for many feet and yards beyond me. I could sit in the centre of my tent, and people at the furthest places and even beyond would feel healing. Sometimes, people coming to see me, within a few miles, would begin to feel the healing. Sometimes they would just get close and turn around and go home healed.

I feel very fulfilled while doing this. I died in good health. I was old and it was time to go. I just blended with my teachers. Leah was no longer around. My sons are also healers, doing my work, carrying on. I can leave without abandoning people. My sons will carry on my work. I will begin again as a dream teacher or sleep teacher with my sons.

Dona: What is your purpose in this lifetime?

Jerry: My purpose in this lifetime is to heal.

Dona: What is your most important lesson in this lifetime?

Jerry: My lesson in this lifetime, my fulfillment is in being true to my nature, doing and cultivating that which is most natural to me, no matter how odd or strange it seems to others. This is what brings me peace and fulfillment. It removes any fear, even of death. It makes my life worthwhile. There is harmony.

Three years after this regression I was with another woman, June, who was also highly sensitive and intuitive. June was willing to help me reconnect with Jacob and explore more fully the relationship between Jacob and Jerry.

Sunday, March 29, 1987

June: Take yourself back to the time you were Jacob. Allow yourself to resonate with him and that time.

Jerry: There is no time when I am Jacob. I am Jacob. I'm always Jacob. Jacob in one segment lived many centuries ago in the desert, in the wilderness.

June: What is he doing now in the desert, in the wilderness?

Jerry: Again he sits near the tent. He spends his days sitting and many people come. With some he touches and with some he scans with his forehead. Others look upon him, and just to be in the presence of Jacob is healing. There are those who reach out to touch him, feeling that by touching him they will be healed. This is true. But what they don't know is that they don't have to touch him — just let him into their hearts.

Jacob is a reflection of the wholeness of each person. When they see him and touch him, they experience their own wholeness, and that is why they are healed. He is like a mirror, a very pure, very clear, highly polished mirror that reflects back brightly one's essence. That essence is beauty and joy and love. People are sick because they have forgotten that, and when they are told that, they still forget it, because they are not in touch with it. Words are not sufficient.

They are not Jacob, because Jacob is them. Jacob is them in the pure sense, without the dross, without all the disturbing thoughts and negative energies. Jacob reflects back to them their own divinities. When they let their light shine throughout their being, they are healed. That is why they don't have to touch Jacob. They don't even have to see him. It is the pureness that is reflected back into them, and they are healed.

They praise Jacob and deem him a holy man and attribute their well-being to him, but this is really a delusion, for what they are experiencing is their own holiness. But they are not able, with few exceptions, to accept it as such, so they must experience somebody exterior to them if they would recognize the truth of this; then they would know they wouldn't have to go to someone other than themselves to be healed, but they are not ready for that.

June: What will make them ready?

Jerry: They will simply have to continue to grow. They will have to shed the kind of doctrine that makes them less than God. That is why Jacob heals, because he knows that he is not less than God and he expressed this in his silence, in his movement, in his voice and his eyes. And he touches, through this, the souls that come to heal. He touches their divinity without their being aware, and they are healed, and they think it is him. It is not him. He is but a reflection — a powerful reflection.

June: What gifts can Jacob give to the Jacob in Jerry Steinberg to continue this healing?

Jerry: Jerry Steinberg does not yet have the confidence and the trust.

June: What can he do to attain the confidence and the trust?

Jerry: He needs to dream of Jacob.

June: How can he do this?

Jerry: By thinking of Jacob often — before he goes to bed and when he wakes up, and in doing so he will bring Jacob more fully into his consciousness and into his heart. Jacob will begin to come to him more strongly in his dreams. In a sense, Jerry is no different than many who come to Jacob encumbered by veils. Now Jerry has to take off these veils to let Jacob come forth.

June: How can Jerry take off his veils and let go of his fears?

Jerry: By healing. He needs to do it more, and with his heart more open. It needs to be more and more a part of his life, his expression. He is not to be afraid to feel love for those that he touches with his soul or his hands.

June: What fears does he have to release first?

Jerry: What comes to mind is the fear of being laughed at, but that is pretty well gone. Ridicule. It is not really an issue. He has to let go of the fear of being swamped and of being in touch with his own power.

June: What exercises can Jerry do to help him overcome these fears?

Jerry: There are not really any exercises. Just be more frequently, consistently aware of Jacob as Jacob. That is all.

June: Is there anything else you would like to tell Jerry?

Jerry: Be in your stillness. Stay in your stillness and beings will come to you. For in your stillness will they be still. Value the stillness, for it, too, is healing.

June: Now allow Jerry to feel close to Jacob. Aspire to that closeness and stillness. Abandon all negativity. Feel only the love, the joy and the peace that is Jacob. Move closer so there is no longer any separation, so that you and Jacob are one. [Long pause] How do you feel?

Jerry: Fine. Perhaps a bit sleepy.

June: Would you like to sleep?

Jerry: Perhaps for a little while. Is there something you would like to know?

June: How can I become closer to my joy, to my healing self?

Jerry: You need to sing. Not just tunes that you know, but do some training with your voice for singing. The process of song produces a vibration in the bones of the skull, which, in turn, stimulates the cortex of the brain, and this produces an opening and a joy and a health. If you wish to know the effects of this briefly, then practise humming five minutes every day and observe yourself in the minutes, possibly hours, after the humming, and you will begin to see a change. And when you hum, feel the resonance.

June: Thank you.

Jerry: You're welcome.

[June adds a note: "Jerry sleeps."]

This was the last time I had my own personal regression.

NOT LONG AFTER my move to Toronto I became involved with a group of people who strongly advocate Kundalini yoga as a practice that might result in a spiritual paradigm shift that would make the world a better place. Earlier in this book I discussed Kundalini yoga mainly in a sexual context, but its implications are broader, encompassing the totality of the human experience. It is for this reason that my new group of friends studied and practised Kundalini and put forth the proposition that this spiritual practice could have a salutary effect on human consciousness, they hoped on a global scale. They believe, as do I, that Kundalini forms the roots of the world's religions and is the foundation from which many spiritual experiences emerge. In Judaism it is known as the *Ruach HaKodesh* (Holy Spirit), a term also mentioned often in Christian literature. Kundalini, in my view, is also at the root of Kabbalah, and I often talk about this in my lectures, describing some of the similarities and differences. Briefly, Kundalini has a more practical side than Kabbalah, emphasizing many specific practices for attaining higher states of consciousness, such as breathing techniques, visualizations, and the chanting of mantras. While Jewish mystical literature does touch upon these practical aspects from time to time (see, as an example, works by Rabbi Abraham Abulafia), it is generally more oriented toward the theosophic, giving descriptions of higher states rather than the techniques for getting there. When techniques are mentioned, they are intellectual in approach, with an emphasis on the study of Torah. Exceptions to this include the use of the *nigun* (melody), a parallel to the mantra, and prayer accompanied by focus or *kavanah* (intention). Both Kundalini and Kabbalah have connection to God (*deveykut* in Hebrew) as their goal and are grounded in moral and ethical principles.

Perhaps the best-known modern progenitor of Kundalini yoga is Gopi Krishna, a Hindu holy man of the mid-1900s. Some of the Toronto group studied with Gopi Krishna (who has since passed on) and follow his teachings, but with an openness to other spiritual systems and teachers. In this spirit, I was welcomed into the group and continue to have rich and meaningful contacts with its members. I have spoken frequently at their local conferences and once at their international conference in Philadelphia. The local group is known as FIND (Friends in New Directions) and ICR (Institute for Consciousness Research).

I have been listed on the Web as one of numerous therapists who work with kundalini experiences, and from time to time I receive calls from people across North America who believe they have had a Kundalini experience and don't know what to do with it or are having difficulty managing its effects. Most of my conversations with those who contact me are on the telephone. Sometimes I can offer callers advice or insights into their experience, and other times there is very little I can say. Most often I suspect that the experience being conveyed to me is not Kundalini as I understand it, but rather the emergence of psychological issues, which perhaps have been triggered by some kind of unusual stimulus such as a dream or an emotional or physical trauma. Whatever the case, the telephone is not the medium for dealing with experiences that have the potential to change one's life, although I do what I can to help the individual. I am also not hesitant to suggest, where appropriate, that the person seek professional assistance. Sometimes the information given by the caller goes beyond common psychological issues and not only leaves me in doubt about whether they are experiencing a Kundalini phenomenon but suggests to me some kind of mental aberration. In these instances I ask callers if they are able to meet with me personally, so I can ascertain, to the best of my abilities, what the problem is and try to help.

This was the case with a woman I will call Doris who was referred to me by a rabbinic colleague. I suspected, from what he told me and from speaking to Doris on the phone, that she might be experiencing a kind of Kundalini aberration, although she believed that she was possessed by some kind of malevolent spirit and that an exorcism was in order. Doris arrived in Toronto, prepared to spend up to a week working with me. I told her that I would only attempt an exorcism if, after working with her for at least two days (more, if necessary), I determined that it might be of benefit to her. After two days I had ruled out Kundalini but still had doubts about her being in a state of possession. However, I felt that if the exercise of exorcism could bring her a measure of relief from her suffering, even if only at the psychological level, then it was worth a try. With this in mind, I enlisted the help of two other rabbis in the community, Rabbi Danny Gottlieb and Rabbi Lori Cohen, who were open to forming a rabbinic tribunal, or *Bet Din*, and working with me to see if we could help the woman. Rabbi Gottlieb offered his synagogue as the venue for the ritual.

We gathered together at 8:00 p.m. on a Wednesday evening. I had told my colleagues that much might happen, or very little, and that they should prepare themselves for either possibility. They were gracious, and although neither had any experience in this area, they were willing to follow my lead wherever it would take us. I introduced Doris to my colleagues and allowed her some time with them, so they could chat and feel comfortable with one another. Then we assembled on the *bimah* in a semicircle and seated Doris directly in front of the ark, with me on one side of her and my colleagues on the other side.

A Jewish ceremony of exorcism has perhaps never before been presented to the public in detail. I have tried to find precedents for this, but other than very brief references such as the blowing of the *shofar* and whisperings into the supplicant's ear by a rabbi, I could not find anywhere in the Jewish sources a detailed account of a step-by-step procedure for an exorcism. I have put together Jewish liturgy and my thoughts on what might be meaningful and effective for such a ritual. Where the text is in Hebrew, all of us, including Doris, whenever possible, recited together. Where Doris was not able to read the Hebrew, the *Bet Din* read it and then Doris joined in with the English.

It is not uncommon in exorcisms (and similar events, like seances) for the supplicant to speak in a voice quite different from his or her normal voice.

For those attending such an event for the first time, this can be quite disconcerting.

EXORCISM CEREMONY AND RITUAL
(Some liberties have been taken with the Hebrew translations)
1) Song
"Eli Eli" ("My God, My God") sung twice by all, the first time in Hebrew and then in English.
English translation: Oh God, My God, may these things never end — the sand and the sea, the crash of the waters, the sound of thunder in the heavens, the prayer of man.

2) Creation
(Excerpts from the traditional evening service in Hebrew and English)
Hebrew — All
English translation: Praised be the Lord our God, Ruler of the universe, whose word brings on the evening. His wisdom opens heaven's gates. His understanding makes the ages pass and the seasons alternate and His will controls the stars as they travel through the skies.
Hebrew — All
English translation: He is Creator of day and night, rolling the light away from darkness, and darkness from light. He causes day to pass and brings on the night. He sets day and night apart. He is the Lord of Hosts.
Hebrew — All
English translation: May the living and eternal God rule us always, to the end of time. Blessed is the Lord whose word makes evening fall.

3) Declaration of purpose
Jerry: Creator of all, we come together this night to ask your help for Doris [full name of supplicant, in English and then in Hebrew]. Whatever distraught or harmful forces there are that possess Doris, may Your presence manifest strongly through Your servants [all members of the *Bet Din* speak aloud their full Hebrew name, in my case, Yona ben Kalman V'Beyla], together with the soul that You have implanted in Doris [surname and full Hebrew name], that these distraught and harmful forces may be withdrawn and leave her permanently, and that these distraught and harmful forces, which also are Your children, may be elevated to a place of holiness, that they

may ascend to levels of purification and be cleansed by Your blessed angels, thereafter to go on to a good path and fulfill their destiny as blessings to all whom in the future they shall encounter.

Hebrew — All

English translation: We praise You O God, Ruler of the universe, Who bestows blessings upon distraught spirits and brings them to levels of supernal holiness.

4) For the soul

Hebrew — All

English translation: The soul that You have given me, O God, is a pure one. You have created and formed it, breathed it into me, and within me You sustain it. So long as I have breath, therefore, I will give thanks to You, O God, my God and God of all ages, Master of all creation, Lord of every human spirit. Blessed is the Lord, in whose hands are the souls of all the living and the spirits of all flesh.

5) Song

"Hashiveynu"

Hebrew — All

English translation: Help us to return, help us to return O Lord our God, and we shall return to You. Renew our days as in former times.

6) Hebrew prayer

Hebrew — All

English translation: Blessed is the One whose compassion covers the earth and all its creatures. Blessed is the living and eternal God, Ruler of the universe, divine source of deliverance and help.

7) Half Kaddish

Hebrew — All

English translation: Let the glory of God be extolled and let His great name be hallowed in the world whose creation He willed. May His kingdom soon prevail in our own day, our own lives and the life of all Israel, and let us say Amen. Let His great name be blessed forever and ever. Let the name of the Holy One, blessed is He, be glorified, exalted and honoured, though He is beyond all the praises, songs, and adorations that we can utter, and let us say, Amen.

8) God's power
Hebrew — All
English translation: Eternal is Your might, O Lord; all life is Your gift; great is Your power to save!
Hebrew — All
English translation: With love You sustain the living and with great compassion give life to all. You send help to the falling and healing to the sick. You bring freedom to the captive and keep faith with those who sleep in the dust.
Hebrew — All
English translation: Who is like You, Master of might? Who is Your equal, O Lord of life and death, Source of salvation? Blessed is the Lord, the Source of life.

9) 23rd Psalm
English — All
The Lord is my shepherd, I shall not want
He makes me to lie down in green pastures
He leads me beside the still waters
He restores my soul
He guides me in straight paths for His name's sake
Yea, though I walk through the valley of the shadow of death
I will fear no evil for You are with me
Your rod and Your staff, they comfort me
You prepare a table before me in the presence of my enemies
You have anointed my head with oil
My cup overflows
Surely goodness and mercy shall follow me all the days of my life
And I shall dwell in the house of God forever.

10) Addressing of spirits
Jerry: O spirit or spirits who are presently inhabiting the body of Doris [name of supplicant in Hebrew and English], tell us for what reason you have come to dwell in the body of Doris [name of supplicant in Hebrew and English]? Why have you chosen her and what do you hope to gain from her?

(At this point in the exorcism, Doris spoke, and the voice that issued from her throat was not her normal one. This took my two colleagues by surprise. The voice stated that it needed a body to express itself, and that Doris's body was open to it.

I then addressed the spirit.)

Jerry: O holy spirit, you are in the presence of three rabbis and four Torahs, and you must now leave Doris in peace. I am now going to open the ark, and we are all going to stand before the Torahs, and you, O holy spirit, are going to feel the presence of God and be blessed by God's presence.

(My colleagues, Doris, and I stood up and came before the ark, which I then opened, making the Torahs clearly visible to all. I then gave Doris the following *Mi Shebayrach* [prayer of blessing]:)

O God who has blessed our fathers, Abraham, Isaac and Jacob, and our mothers, Sarah, Rebecca, Leah, and Rachel, let Your blessings of light and protection be with [Hebrew and English name of supplicant], and may You draw from her the entity that inhabits her body and bring it into Your presence, that it may be freed from its turmoil and enter higher spiritual realms, where it will find peace beneath Your sheltering wings.

11) Prayer by supplicant to be free of the inhabiting spirit(s). This prayer is spontaneous and in the supplicant's own words. (I did not record Doris's words.)

12) *Kedusha* (Sanctification)
Hebrew — *Bet Din*
English translation: We sanctify Your name on earth, even as all things to the ends of time and space proclaim Your holiness and in the words of the prophet, we say — Holy, holy, holy is the Lord of Hosts, the whole earth is full of His glory.

13) Exhortation — for spirit(s) to leave, done while continuing to stand before the open ark.
Jerry: Go now, O spirit(s), into God's holy presence and find peace in the arms of *Shechinah* [God's indwelling presence].

(My two colleagues recited the *Kedusha* in Hebrew and English three times.)

14) The Torahs are taken from the ark by the *Bet Din*, who then circle the supplicant as they adjure the spirits to depart:
Bet Din: Be gone fallen spirits! Be gone!
           Return to God.
           Return to your home.
           Do not anymore inhabit the earth plane.
           Do not anymore possess any human form.
           Be gone!
           May God's blessings be upon you.

[Supplicant is given one of the Torahs to hold]
and upon you [supplicant's name in Hebrew and English], now clean of all possessing spirits, we, the holy *Bet Din* of [each member of the *Bet Din* gives their Hebrew name] bestow our blessings upon you.
Hebrew—*Bet Din*
English translation: Hear our voice, O Lord our God; have compassion upon us and accept our prayer with favour and mercy, for You are a God who hears prayer and supplications. Blessed is the Lord who hearkens to prayer.
[The *Bet Din* place their hands upon the supplicant's head and/or shoulders and offer the Priestly Benediction:]
Hebrew—*Bet Din*
English translation: May God bless you and protect you.
May God's light shine upon you, and may God be gracious unto you.
May God lift His countenance upon you and grant you peace.

15) Supplicant's prayer of thanks
[This is a personal and spontaneous prayer of gratitude for being released of the visiting spirit. It is followed by a more formal prayer of gratitude from the liturgy:] I gratefully acknowledge that You are the Lord my God and God of my people. You are the Rock of my life, the Power that shields me in every age. I thank you and sing your praises, for my life which is in Your hand; for my soul which is in Your keeping; for the signs of Your presence which I encounter every day; and for Your wondrous gifts at all times, morning, noon and night. You are Goodness; Your mercies never end; You are compassionate; Your love will never fail. You are always my Hope.

16) Return Torahs to ark and close ark

17) Oseh Shalom
Hebrew—All
English translation (sung by all): May He who makes peace on high, grant peace to us and all Israel and let us say, Amen.

18) *Mikveh* (Ritual immersion)
Supplicant is taken to *mikveh*, which is presided over by the *Bet Din*. Supplicant immerses three times, with the blessings of *T'vilah* (immersion), *Sh'ma* (proclamation of faith), and *Shehecheyanu* (praise of the occasion).
    (Note: Only the female rabbi, Rabbi Cohen, accompanied Doris to the *mikveh*. The other two rabbis, being male, remained outside the *mikveh* room,

out of view but within hearing range of the supplicant. This procedure would, of course, be reversed if the supplicant was male and a female rabbi was present.)

19) *Kiddush* (celebration)
English — All
Wine is a symbol of joy
As you drink from this cup of wine, may your life be filled with joy
May any bitterness be sweetened
May you go from strength to strength

Blessing over wine — Hebrew — *Bet Din*
English translation: Praised are You O Lord our God, Ruler of the Universe, Who creates the fruit of the vine.

The supplicant is given some wine to drink.
Blessing over bread is made by all, in Hebrew and then English.
English translation: Praise are You O Lord our God, Ruler of the Universe, Who brings forth bread from the earth.

The supplicant, who has been fasting since lunch, eats some bread and is joined in the eating by the members of the *Bet Din*. Any other food provided is then eaten.

I CONTINUED TO work with Doris for the next three days to process her experience and to deal with any relevant issues; then she returned home. I continued to have follow-up telephone conversations with Doris, who held her own and was well for about two weeks, after which, unfortunately, other issues not directly related to possession began to return.

My experience over the years with possession has been that most individuals who believe they are possessed have associated psychological problems, and while an exorcism may offer temporary relief, it does not usually help in the longer term. I agree to do an exorcism only rarely, in the hope that some good can come of it on a permanent basis. More often than not I am disappointed in this regard, but, from time to time, a profound change for the better occurs and lasts. Still, as long as I feel there is a hope of something positive being accomplished, even if only for the short term, I think it is worthwhile. Movies and popular literature on the topic of exorcism do not tell the whole story and almost always leave out what happens to the individual in the weeks, months, or years afterwards. They also play up the more sensational aspects of exorcism; in fact, I have never encountered anything more dramatic than changes in voice and demonstrations of psychic abilities (as with the young woman from North Dakota who wrote down my Hebrew name).

The best-known story of exorcism in Judaism is the stage play known as *The Dybbuk*, written by the Russian playwright S. Ansky in 1914. Originally in Russian, it was translated into Yiddish and has been presented on the world stage in many languages as recently as 2008.

> Demons abound
> on night paths
> unlikely warriors
> for the spoil of souls
> flitting about
> groundless in their dance
> without mercy
> without love
> without life
> shadows upon shadows
> drifting
> seeking release

As a rabbi living in a large metropolis, I am frequently called upon by my colleagues to cover for them when they are away for various reasons. It is always my pleasure, although most of the time my services are not needed. Occasionally, however, I do get a call from a member of the congregation, if for instance there is a death. Once, while a colleague was away, one of his congregants, a woman in her early forties with four children, passed away. Their rabbi was informed; he wanted to be there for the family and to conduct the funeral but couldn't get back for two days, so I attended to the family until he returned. I went right away to the deceased's home and offered what information and comfort I could.

I noticed that one of the children, a boy of about ten, looked very lost, confused, and distressed; he couldn't find a place for himself among the many visitors who had come to pay their respects. I took him aside and asked him what he liked to do, and he replied that he liked to play hockey. I asked him what position he played, and he said he was a goalie. I told him that I used to play hockey when I was his age and I also played goal. One thing led to another, and before long we were in the basement, he with his portable net and equipment, and me with a hockey stick and a tennis ball. We played together for about a half hour as different members of the family came down to check on him but left when they saw what we were doing. On succeeding evenings, when I came over, we would go downstairs and play. By the third evening, when I entered the house, someone said, "Here's the hockey rabbi." The young man and I developed a warm bond, and once in a while, when we would see each other at services, we would talk about hockey. To this day, I am still occasionally referred to as "the hockey rabbi."

IN THIS BOOK I have mentioned in several contexts the possibilities of healing outside of conventional medicine. I wish to make clear, if I have not yet done so, that I have a great respect for medicine and the many doctors who practise this noble science. I'm sure they, much more than I, are well aware of medicine's limitations and their own as practitioners. If I have a criticism in this regard, it would be that most physicians I have met are not open to hearing about or exploring alternate healing modalities such as naturopathy, the self-regulation of bodily processes (for example, biofeedback), and spiritual healing (for example, dreams and prayer), even though many studies within the parameters of good science have been conducted in these and related areas. I have been fortunate to know a few physicians who are interested in these avenues of healing and who are either active in promoting them or willing to support patients who want to pursue them in addition to conventional medical care. Let me give an example of this from my own life.

Sometime around 1999, I noticed that the little finger on my left hand was becoming crooked. At the same time, I was feeling some stiffness and discomfort in my joints. Fearing that I was developing arthritis, I went to see my physician, who referred me to a rheumatoid arthritis specialist, who had me undergo a number of tests. When I came for the results, she told me that in order to slow down further deterioration from arthritis, I would have to go on anti-inflammatory medication and that I could expect possible side effects, such as ulcers and gradual deformity in my body and posture as I aged. This was not good news! I returned to my physician and told him I did not want to go on anti-inflammatory drugs and asked if he had any other suggestions. My physician is a close friend and a man who has studied first-hand the healing practises of many cultures worldwide. He is interested in approaches to healing other than those of conventional allotropic medicine, although his practise is that of the Western model. He informed me that he himself had, not long before, had a small medical problem that his doctor friends were unable to treat successfully. He went to see a certain naturopath, and the problem went away. He said I might want to see this same man, since his usual medical resources for my situation were exhausted. I therefore made an appointment and a few weeks later was in the office of Dr. Mikhael Adams.

Mikhael Adams, a man of considerable expertise in the art of healing and a person of high spiritual integrity, set me on a path of healing that brought results in just six weeks. The discomfort in my joints diminished and, not long after, disappeared entirely. In addition, I began to generally feel better, both physically and emotionally. It is ten years since my first appointment, and I see Dr. Adams every six months, just to be sure my health is on track. I continue to feel very good and very young. Also, my other nine fingers have remained straight. I have over the years referred many friends and acquaintances to Dr. Adams, with excellent results in most cases. The trick, of course, is doing exactly what he asks you to do; those who have deviated from his recommendations have always paid a price and lost ground. I continue to this day under his care, and that of my physician friend and, I might add, a very fine chiropractor and an equally fine dentist. This is my health team, and, as my physician friend tells me, I'm a good patient. As for my crooked finger, Mikhael Adams suggests I try a hammer.

IN THE LATE winter of 1999, I received calls from Harley Saltzman and Michael Chasler, two of the founders of a congregation called *B'nai Shalom V'Tikvah* (Children of Peace and Hope), located in Ajax, an eastern suburb of Toronto. They wanted to know if I was interested in being their rabbi, to which I replied that I had no particular interest in entering the pulpit again. They said that the congregation they were representing was very small, and they would appreciate if I would at least come and meet with the board before giving a definite no. I was reluctant to do so, but something in their voices spoke to me at a deeper level, so I agreed to come to a meeting. However, I cautioned them that neither they nor the board should expect much.

I was interviewed by about ten board members, possibly at that time the entire board, and was impressed by what I saw and heard. I felt that the group had a strong commitment to Judaism, as evidenced by the fact that for several years they had sought the help of various rabbis in the community to keep their congregation alive and vibrant. But they had never had one rabbi consistently over a period of many years. I left the meeting feeling I had to do some serious thinking, as I still felt a reluctance to be a congregational rabbi again, having not forgotten the sting of my experience in Winnipeg.

A few days later, Harley called and told me that the board had decided they would like me to be their rabbi. I eventually agreed to come on a one-year contract, with the understanding that the congregation or I could end the arrangement at the end of the year if it proved unsatisfactory for either of us. I also told them at one of my first services that if I was going to stay on for any length of time, they would have to feed me lox (smoked salmon) for breakfast before every service. They have rarely missed an occasion.

It is ten years later, and I'm still with *B'nai Shalom V'Tikvah*. My experience with the congregation has been more than satisfactory. I usually give services on the first Saturday morning of each month, the High Holidays of Rosh Hashanah and Yom Kippur, and some of the Jewish festivals. On my Saturdays, after a communal breakfast, I begin with a one-hour discussion of that week's Torah portion followed by a full service. The service is followed by lunch for everyone, which is always sponsored by one of the families in the congregation. I also do life-cycle events for the temple, such as *bar* and *bat mitzvahs*, weddings, and funerals, and I am the sponsoring rabbi for anyone in the region who wants to convert to Judaism. Over the years I have often represented the congregation in interfaith gatherings with Christian and Moslem groups. In general, I have enjoyed myself immensely at Temple *B'nai Shalom V'Tikvah* and find a feeling of family among the members and their enthusiasm for all things Jewish. They have treated me well, and I look forward, God willing, to many more years of service on their behalf.

On the second day of Rosh Hashanah, I have what I refer to as my *kavanah* bag, a burlap bag containing a collection of sayings from various rabbis over the centuries, each saying printed on a small piece of paper. At present the bag contains one hundred and fourteen sayings. I explain to my congregants that this is an exercise in synchronicity, meaning that if they say a prayer asking for guidance in selecting a saying, then this prayer or *intention* (the meaning of the word *kavanah*) will direct their fingers to a paper that will help guide them in what they need to work on in their lives over the next year. This is, I explain, God's homework between this Rosh Hashanah and the next one. As the cantor sings, the bag is passed around until each person who wants to has selected a paper. (If someone does not wish to participate, they simply pass the bag on.) When everyone else has had a chance to pick, I take my turn, and then everyone reads their selection to themselves. Most of my congregants look forward eagerly to this event, and each year some tell me how meaningful and appropriate their selection is.

Here are three of the sayings that I have selected over the past few years as my homework from God:

The Meaning

When Rabbi Bunam lay dying, his wife burst into tears. He said: "What are you crying for? My whole life was only that I might learn how to die."

The Verse Within

Once when Rabbi Mordecai was in the great town of Minsk expounding the Torah to a number of men hostile to his way, they laughed at him. "What you say does not explain the verse in the least!" they cried.

"Do you really think," he replied, "that I was trying to explain the verse in the book? That doesn't need explanation. I want to explain the verse that is within me."

The Great Crime

Rabbi Bunam said to his *Hasidim* [followers]: "The sins which man commits — those are not his great crime. Temptation is powerful and his strength is slight. The great crime of man is that he can turn at every moment and does not do so."

These sayings, and most in the *kavanah* bag, are from *The Early Masters* and *The Later Masters*, collected by Martin Buber.

MY FASCINATION WITH guns has persisted. In 2005, I received a birthday present from my partner, Shelley, that reflected this. I opened the envelope containing her birthday card, and inside it was an invitation for Shelley and me to spend half a day at a gun club. She had seen an advertisement in the paper and, knowing my love of guns, decided to register both of us. It was probably the most unusual birthday present that anyone has ever given me, and I was excited to receive it.

A week later Shelley drove me out of the city to the gun club, about a half hour from where I live. To get in, we had to identify ourselves as being on the guest list, which was checked carefully, and we were then buzzed in through a large and very secure door. Once inside, we were warmly greeted and ushered into a large room, where we joined about thirty other guests. For the next hour, detailed instructions were given on the use of handguns, with a special emphasis on safety. Among other things, I was interested to learn that if we wished to join the club, we needed three different licences: one to purchase a gun, another to purchase ammunition, and a third to transport the gun. Even with the relevant licence, we would only be allowed to transport the gun in a locked case, and only directly from home to the gun club. Side excursions were not allowed, and the gun had to be secured in the trunk of the car. Of course, before a permit to purchase was issued, a background check would be conducted. We were then told that after the class, we would be taken to a waiting room near the shooting range, and when our turn came, each of us would be given a qualified and experienced instructor. Then we would have the opportunity to fire fifty rounds each from two different kinds of guns — a revolver and an automatic nine-millimetre (the kind many police forces use).

I waited anxiously for my turn to come. Finally my name and Shelley's were called out, and we were introduced to our instructors and given goggles and ear protectors. The range was a very large, barnlike room. Each of us stood behind an opening, with a shelf separating the two sides of the opening. Upon my shelf lay a gun, and I was told that I mustn't touch it until told to do so by the instructor. In front of the opening was perhaps forty yards of open space, with targets whose distances could be changed by remote control. There were about eight of us at a time, all standing in our designated spaces waiting for instructions to pick up our guns and begin firing. Then we were coached on how to hold the gun and how to fire it. For example, when I first picked up my gun, I aimed the barrel toward the ceiling and then slowly lowered it until it reached the point where I had my sight lined up with the target, at which point I pulled the trigger. My instructor told me not to do this in case I accidentally fired before the barrel was level, which would have meant putting a hole in the ceiling. I quickly corrected my firing procedure.

It was the first time in my life that I had ever even held, let alone fired, a handgun. Holding the weapon in my hands gave me a feeling of power and at the same time scared me. I could understand why someone carrying a gun would feel well protected, and I understood just how dangerous a handgun can be in the hands of the wrong person, and how easy it would be to kill someone, even unintentionally. Just moving my trigger finger a fraction of a centimetre could end another person's life. Yet there was a thrill in holding the gun and firing it. Also, I began to understand how spending time on a gun range could be good therapy for someone who needed to get aggressive feelings out in a safe manner. The thought of joining the club was appealing.

I began to think about which kind of gun I would choose if I became a member. While the nine-millimetre, referred to sometimes as a semi-automatic pistol, was less fuss — all you had to do was fill the handle with ten or twelve bullets and shoot away — the revolver was more to my liking. First, it almost never jammed (I was told this by a rabbi friend of mine, who is an expert in handguns). Second, I was more able to relate to the revolver and the process of slowly rotating the drum and filling each opening with a bullet, known as a *round* — even though the revolver would hold only five or six rounds. Perhaps my years of attending many cowboy movies in Regina and watching how the cowboys handled their weapons had an influence on my choice of weapon. As a young man I always had a desire to pack a revolver on each hip and, like Wild Bill Hickok, fire them both at the same time, with a quick draw and deadly aim.

After I'd shot fifty rounds with each gun, my instructor told me that he felt I was a natural, since I had scored high on the targets. I didn't feel that he was just telling me this in order to get me to join the club: there never was any pressure in this direction from anyone. I was allowed to take my bullet-ridden targets home with me, and for days afterwards I admired my expertise (or perhaps my beginner's luck).

For the next several months I thought on and off about joining the club, but finally realized that the visit had satisfied whatever vestige of my childhood desire for guns was still lingering in my subconscious. I look back on the experience as very satisfying and, except for the occasional tinge, no longer feel any strong need to fire a handgun. It was a great birthday present on many levels.

I have sometimes wondered what connection, if any, exists between my love of guns and my passion for spirituality. Recently I tried doing some word association on *guns* and came up with *power, control, life and death,* and *warrior.* While I have never explored this in a regression, I have frequently sensed that in another lifetime I was a military commander. Perhaps this explains my love of war movies as a child, and of almost anything military as I grew up. Of the words I came up with, *warrior* stands out most strongly, and even in the spiritual realm, my exploration of the literature indicates that to pursue a spiritual path, one indeed needs to be a warrior and learn from both victory and defeat. The *Bhagavad-Gita*, Hinduism's most sacred work, is all about a scene that takes place on a battlefield just before the two sides are about to engage. Krishna says to Arjuna, "Bodies are said to die, but that which possesses the body is eternal. It cannot be limited or destroyed. Therefore you must fight." Given my interests in the martial arts, I find it interesting that eventually I ended up choosing karate, a discipline that combined both physical aggression and spirituality. Preceding this by about fifteen years was my brief involvement in tai chi, which some consider the basis of all martial arts, and which I studied while in the intense spiritual atmosphere of the ashram. So perhaps weapons of some sort were a past-life imprint on my soul that carried over to this lifetime, manifesting early in the form of guns and later in martial arts with a spiritual dimension. In the dojo where I studied karate, we always began with a brief period of meditation, and our *sensei*, Masami Tsuruoko, repeatedly emphasized the power of *Chi*, an intangible force with spiritual roots.

In the bible, many battles are won on the basis of a spiritual presence — that of God, or of Moses, or other prophets. In one such instance, the simple act of Moses raising his arms over a battlefield brought the Israelites victory: "But Moses' hands grew heavy; so they took a stone and put it under him and he sat on it, while Araron and Hur, one on each side, supported his hands; thus his hands remained steady until the sun set. And Joshua overwhelmed the people of Amalak with the sword."

Does any of this adequately explain my lifelong fascination with guns? I cannot say with certainty. What I do know is that my interest remains, although it has waned, yielding to the increasing strength of my focus on the spiritual. And throughout, the warrior image prevails.

GIFTS COME IN many forms, and I was blessed in 1997 to meet Susan Wehle at a week-long conference in Fort Collins, Colorado, sponsored by Jewish Renewal. She had just lost her mother a few weeks before and was in a state of mourning. Something clicked between us, and at the beginning of the week, I was a source of comfort to her in her grief. Then I got very sick and Susan nursed me, making sure that I received proper medical attention. By the end of the week, we were very close, and before parting at the end of the conference, I gave her a copy of my poetry book, *Melting: Poems of a Frozen Man*. A few days later she called me from her home in Buffalo to tell me how much the book meant to her. This was the beginning of a rich and delightful four-year relationship.

Susan worked as a cantor at a congregation in Amherst, a suburb of Buffalo. She had a magnificent voice and was a great teacher of music and Judaism in general, her beautiful demeanour, along with her voice, uplifting countless people. Toward the end of our relationship, as we were both struggling to save it, Susan pushed me to a place deep within myself where I broke down in tears, followed by her tears. It was a place of love unlike anything either of us had ever experienced, the kind of love one reads about and hears about, and, if the person is lucky, has the privilege of experiencing, even if only once in a lifetime. We were left trembling, in awe of what had just transpired. In retrospect, I believe we had a profound spiritual experience in which the hand of God brought our hearts together, but only too briefly. The experience frightened Susan, and within a week she had withdrawn from me. Shortly thereafter the relationship ended. Two years later, we had a conversation in which, to her credit, she acknowledged that she had been frightened and unable to keep her heart open to me. By then I was with Shelley, and Susan, too, had other interests, so there was no possibility of us getting back together at the time. Having said that, I have always longed for the kind of connection we had on that special day, and I hope again to find it. She left an imprint on my heart that remains firmly planted and is always with me.

We touched the recesses of our being
                                    that day
                treading on hallowed ground
                the wings of our souls unfurled
                        shaken to realms of disbelief
                        merging into the oneness
                                        of sacred joy
                                            we trembled
        We were cleansed that day
                                the dross taken from our essence
                                our hearts born to feelings
                                        of awe and purity
                        while our minds tried to grasp
                        what minds cannot grasp
        We were blinded that day
                        unable to see the pastures of plenty
                                        that awaited us
                        fearful of remaining too long
                                        in a strange place
                                without walls
                                without darkness
                                without signs
        Blind and afraid
                        we hesitated
                                bidding Eden
                                        farewell

In November 2008, I found myself single once again; my relationship with Shelley had come to an end after six years. I was aware that Susan was not in a committed relationship either, although she was occasionally seeing a very fine man whom I knew. My thoughts, therefore, began to move again in her direction, with the hope that something might be rekindled between us. Our communications during this time were encouraging — at least, that's the way I saw them — though by no means clear or conclusive. I decided that I needed to keep the channels open between us and wait to see what, if anything, would happen. Then, on the evening of February 12, 2009, while I was celebrating my son's fortieth birthday in Toronto, Continental Airlines Flight 3407, with Susan aboard, crashed a few minutes before landing at the Buffalo International Airport.

Susan

There are no words, except pain, despair, and disbelief, to describe my anguish, and even now, more than two years after her death, I write these words with tears in my eyes. I drove to Buffalo with my son a few days after the accident to attend and participate in a memorial service for her. Just before the service, the fine man she had been seeing and I embraced and wept on each other's shoulders. We had both lost someone precious beyond description, and I'm sure he continues to grieve and hold Susan's memory in his heart and soul, as do I. And I can only guess what might have been, for him or for me.

A few months later, two women who had been very close to Susan attended a conference in the southern United States. On one of the evenings of the conference, Susan appeared in a vision to each woman independently (they were not standing together), and, looking very radiant, gave each one the same message, that she was okay, and since she no longer needed all of the energy in her possession, she was giving each woman a portion of it. One of the women immediately approached the other excitedly to tell her about what had just happened, only to learn that she had received the same vision and message. Upon hearing of this from one of the women, I could only marvel once more at the wonders of the universe and take comfort from their visions. There is a biblical parallel to this in the Book of Numbers, when a portion of Moses' spiritual energy (while he is still alive) is given to seventy of the elders of Israel. A later, post-biblical parallel in Jewish mystical literature postulates that the departed soul of a great person, such as Abraham or Moses, can fragment and return to earth to inhabit many bodies in what is known as *gilgul* (reincarnation).

My final tribute to Susan took place on December 18, 2010. The background to this began one September day in 1999. I was travelling on a back road from Thornhill to Newmarket to conduct a Rosh Hashanah service. As I was driving, I began singing one of the High Holiday melodies, and my mind wandered from one tune to another in a random fashion. Suddenly a tune came into my mind for the closing hymn to many Jewish services throughout the year, *"Adon Olam."* Only it was a tune I had never heard before. I sang it over and over so I wouldn't forget it, as I had no means for recording it. When I got home later that evening, I immediately put the tune on tape. A while later, while visiting Susan, I played the tune for her and asked if she could write down the notes for it. She said that would not be a problem, and a few minutes later gave me a sheet of music paper with the tune written down.

I did not pursue this any further until November 2010. I asked Tara Abrams, the cantor at Temple Har Zion in Thornhill, if she would mind looking at the tune and telling me what she thought. She showed it to Eleanor Rice, the music director at the temple, and a few days later I received an e-mail from both of them telling me how much they enjoyed the tune. They offered to debut it at a forthcoming service. Included as an attachment to the e-mail was a recording of Tara singing it and Eleanor playing on the piano. So, on the morning of Saturday, December 18, with twelve members of my congregation in attendance to celebrate with me, along with a good turnout from the members of Har Zion, the concluding hymn was *"Adon Olam"* by Jerry Steinberg, dedicated to the memory of Cantor Susan Wehle. I don't know if I will ever again be graced with a creative piece of music, especially since I have no competency in this field. I am satisfied to have received this one piece and to have been able to dedicate it to someone I loved very much.

FOR A PERIOD of time in the '70s and '80s, a phenomenon called "channelling" was prevalent in the United States. Certain rather extraordinary individuals such as Seth and Ramtha would go into unusual states of consciousness, contact entities believed to be from another dimension of reality, and bring messages from these entities to human audiences. Channelling was like hearing a voice from a soul who had passed on, who was privy to vast stores of information and wisdom, and was eager to educate those who were willing to listen. Audience members would ask questions, and the channeller would usually respond in a voice different from his or her normal voice — similar to what I've described in cases of possession, but from a vastly different place. Unlike Edgar Cayce, who was able to deliver very precise messages in the form of medical diagnosis and prescription, the channellers focused primarily on spiritual, philosophical, and psychological topics. I refer to them as "soft" channellers because their material was broad and general and seldom lent itself to empirical verification. (With Cayce, the person either got well or didn't.) In my opinion, some of the more interesting of these "soft" messages were delivered by Jane Roberts (Seth), and evolved into her book *The Nature of Personal Reality*.

I found the subject of channelling fascinating and, over time, came to wonder if I could do something along these lines. After all, I had received valuable information for healing others in my dreams, as evidenced with Shula and her headaches. I had also tried to do some psychic diagnosing and prescribing with Swami Radha as my ground, but with only moderate success. I thought that if I prayed for messages from beyond and then tried to open myself to other realms of reality, perhaps something would come through me that could be of interest and use to others as well as myself. So, one day in 1989, I said a prayer asking God or an angel to bless me with some words that I could record and perhaps pass on. Within minutes, words, phrases, and whole sentences, even paragraphs, came pouring out. Although external entities are the more common source of such transmissions, I could not identify any particular entity from which these messages might be coming, and it felt more like I had tapped into another dimension from which I was being fed material from an undisclosed source.

Regularly over the next several years, I would either pray for a message or spontaneously find myself in a state of heightened awareness and know that I was in touch with something beyond my normal self. Sometimes a topic would be on my mind and I would ask for clarification; at other times, I would present to a higher self (for lack of a better term) a question posed to me by a friend or acquaintance. None of this seemed to be the "channelling" I was familiar with from the literature and from what I had witnessed in person in my encounters with self-described channellers. I also felt that since no entity was identifying itself to me, I had to take responsibility for the material I produced; I could not simply attribute it to someone or something else. One unusual aspect of my channelling was that once I had committed the material to paper, I immediately forgot what I had written. When I read the transmission later, I had the strange feeling that I was reading words written by someone other than myself. Over time I accumulated a volume of readings, to which I have given the title *Contact*. Here are excerpts from the table of contents of this work and a few selections.

From the table of contents:

God
"Dangerous Encounters in the Place of God"
. . . gods whom you have not experienced
Some Practical Aspects of Making Contact

Religion
Penetrating the Membrane
On the Origin of the Universe

Soul
On Depression
On Passion
Soul Mates

Spiritual — Mental — Physical
The Regeneration of Limbs
The Non-Necessity for Illness
Physical Stimuli as Catalysts to Spiritual Awakening

Unity
On Changing Human Nature

Love — Sexuality — Relationships
Communication
On Orgasm
The Tactile Element in Relationships

Techniques of Healing
The Nature of Visualization
On Humming

Death
On Communicating with the Dead
On the Fountain of Youth

Psychotherapy
Past, Present and Future in Psychotherapy

Expansion
The Exceptional
Growth Without Pain
The Tower of Babel

Other Aspects
On Cancer
On Laughter
On Miracles

SELECTED PASSAGES

Immunity and the Soul

Much is said about the importance of the immune system in maintaining good health. That a strong immune system is vital in supporting a healthy body can be considered axiomatic. Yet the immune system itself is difficult to define, medical knowledge notwithstanding.

An essential aspect of the immune system, and one seldom mentioned, is the soul. A healthy body and a well-functioning immune system will break down, if for some reason the soul decides it is time to leave. This is sometimes called "the will to live." The will and the soul are inseparable.

Many mysterious deaths can be attributed to a soul that wishes to leave. And many persons who achieve longevity against formidable odds do so because the soul is tenacious.

Longevity can be enhanced by bringing soul-consciousness into mind-consciousness. Being aware of the strivings of the soul allows us to take measures which will make our lives both longer and richer.

An example of this would be someone who has an illness that does not respond to medical treatment. By coming into touch with his soul through meditation, dreams or other means, and by being made aware that a certain change is necessary in his life before healing can take place, the individual can take steps to effect that change. In so doing, the illness is mitigated or totally alleviated, depending on how full the change is.

Many persons, however, will not make the necessary change, as it is too disruptive to their lives. They would prefer suffering to change, excusing themselves with the question, "How do I know the change will do me any good?"

Being aware of the soul's needs and acting to fill these needs is the focus that will most benefit an individual. It is also an area of major importance for those wishing to help others find and meet their souls' needs, such as psychotherapists and the clergy.

Just as white cells move through the blood stream protecting our health, so too the soul moves through every cell and intercellular space, promoting the well-being of the entire person.

On Changing Human Nature

There is no physical body without needs. Each being, human or otherwise, requires sustenance. Yet sustenance does not guarantee the quality of that being, particularly with regard to our species. Other factors constantly come into play and an individual may be tossed and buffeted in many directions during the course of a lifetime.

Being deprived of sustenance, especially physical sustenance (food and shelter), does not always produce the same results; some perish, others rebel, while still others are innovative and create, seemingly from nothing, what they need.

So varied are the circumstances of those with and those without, that it is difficult to predict the behaviour of persons benefiting or suffering from abundance or deprivation. In particular does this apply to moral behaviour. If we are to learn from history, then let it be that circumstances do not produce long-lasting benefits, "long-lasting" being measured in centuries. In terms of the status of the human heart, there is little evidence to show that, as a race, we have advanced over our biblical ancestors. One might even argue, given the events of this century, that we have regressed.

It appears that neither technology, nor constitutions, nor laws, make much difference when it comes to the workings of the human heart. Nor, for that matter, does religion and philosophy.

The question may therefore be asked: is there anything that makes a long-term difference?

History would tend to answer "no" to this question. Intuition, at least as it comes through this person, would answer, "yes!"

The "yes" comes in the form of a fundamental shift in consciousness resulting from a personal experience of God. This is not the God of any particular religion. This God may, in fact, be defined as the infinite number of dimensions in the universe and beyond.

The fundamental shift I am referring to here is the movement of consciousness into the next most immediate dimensions that are accessible to us. These dimensions are not different from those experienced by our greatest mystics in the bible and in the sacred literatures of all peoples.

Nor are we to be restricted or limited by the experiences of others. To begin with, we need only learn that such dimensions do indeed exist, and every human being has access to them.

The nature of these dimensions is such that the more one experiences them, the greater is the feeling of unity and love with all creation. Herein lies the fundamental shift of which I speak. It is not only a shift in concept, but a shift in being. Even our cells are affected in such a shift.

The achievement of this state of consciousness will come about eventually as we evolve. Evolution, however, is a slow process and untold suffering will ensue en route to this goal. To shorten the process, research is needed in the areas of human consciousness, with particular emphasis on the phenomenon of sleep. Here our hearts and souls are most open.

It is possible to alter our states of being while we are sleeping. This can be done by directing our dreams, either internally or externally. Internal direction means lucid and directive dreaming — we become aware of our dreaming while in the dream state and make decisions about where we want to take the dream. Our dreams may also be altered externally by input from others, through sensory or extrasensory stimuli. As sleep research progresses, the ability to influence our sleep states will increase.

The question arises: how do we know that our sleep state is being influenced, either by internal or external means, in a manner that will produce a beneficial shift, one where the individual and others will be enhanced?

In the short term, there will be mistakes, as is the case with any research endeavour. In the long term, however, the mere exploration of other dimensions, as stated above, will result in a greater feeling of unity and oneness, a greater interconnection with all beings and all existence, and consequently, a fundamental shift in our hearts. The major benefit will be a sustaining love and the writing of a new chapter in the evolution of human consciousness.

On Orgasm (excerpts)

Just as war is the frustrated and misdirected attempt of men to express their higher consciousness, orgasm is a very direct experience of contact. Even the most base of humans experience, in orgasm, a sense of contact, however fleeting this may be. There is no experience so universally powerful as the experience of orgasm. It is the physical expression of the soul's yearning for contact, yearning to be reunited with the realm of higher awareness.

The more full and intense, the more deep the experience of orgasm, the more lasting the impression on man's higher nature. Orgasm is a moment of holiness, expanded in the context of love and diminished in the context of abuse.

At times, orgasm does produce physical death, but this occurs when the individual is ready to make this transition, and need not be feared in other instances. There are times when orgasm, if encouraged, is an aid to healing a debilitated body. In health, orgasm is a thrust towards death [death here being understood as the state or experience of not having a physical body] and in sickness it is a thrust towards life [life here being understood as the state or experience of having a physical body]. Both instances interface with each other and both move the soul towards greater fulfillment.

It is physically beneficial to promote orgasm in humans for as long as possible. There is no age at which orgasm cannot occur, and no matter the age, it is an elixir for youth and health.

The movement into new dimensions of being brings one further along the road of spiritual growth. Orgasm stimulates the soul. It's as if our very essence is being gently massaged; gently, even if the orgasm is powerful.

Orgasm brings one to a place of wholeness and promise. It connects us with the greater self and brings a deeper awareness of God. It is a sublime spiritual experience when it occurs in the context of love.

Orgasm is a universal phenomenon. It is experienced in all life forms and also in the inanimate world. It is an expression of celebration. From the explosion of genital juices to the eruption of a volcano, to the birth of a new star, orgasm is a statement of the affirmation of existence. It is being rejoicing in being. Even the least noticeable of orgasmic expressions—a new cell coming into existence, a new leaf being formed, a drop of water crystallizing—all state that the creative force at work in the universe is working well.

The moment of orgasm is a moment of accessing our soul. So sweet is this moment that, once having had the experience, we long for it over and over again for most of our lives. This experience, therefore, is the other reason for being endowed with a sexual drive (along with procreation).

The desire to prolong orgasm is the desire to remain in touch with the soul at a deeper level and thus in closer contact with God. The deep fulfillment and satisfaction experienced by the individual during orgasm, and during a mystical experience, are either similar or the same.

On Commitment

Reference here is to commitment within the context of a male-female relationship, although aspects of what is to follow may also apply to other situations involving commitment.

Fear of commitment is based on restriction. If the individual perceives that he or she may be restricted through commitment, there will be a reluctance to commit. The soul is outward-bound, desiring always greater and greater measures of freedom. Whatever appears to limit this freedom is seen as a threat. When one perceives that another will limit her/his freedom, one will pull back. On the other hand, if one perceives that the other will allow for a greater expression of freedom, then one will move forward into a relationship. Relationships run into difficulty when the initial perception of greater freedom turns into limitation. One then wishes to withdraw, sometimes temporarily, sometimes permanently.

If two individuals are aware of what is being said above, and apply their efforts towards unbinding themselves and each other, then the relationship will flow more easily and has a better chance of lasting.

A commitment is only as good as the degree to which each partner endeavours to free the other from limitation. In the beginning, limitation may be desired, boundaries giving a sense of security. Before long, however, boundaries stifle, and the partners struggle for more air. If a deeper breath cannot be provided in the relationship, one or both partners will seek it outside of the relationship. If too much is sought outside the relationship, there is no longer a relationship.

The thrust is always towards greater freedom, it being understood that within our awareness as human beings, there is no perfect or absolute freedom. Thus, in any human situation, there are always limitations. In a relationship, some limitation is to be expected and can be lived with. It depends on the nature of the limitation and its extent.

In my introduction to *Contact*, I make the point that just because the information I am presenting appears to come from another dimension, there is no reason to assume it is more or less authoritative than information derived in the normal manner. In other words, the information is just as subject to scrutiny as any other information and, indeed, should not be excluded from criticism. The purpose of this information, as I see it, is to stimulate thought and experimentation, with the hope that it will contribute to a better world.

Since completing *Contact* I have begun a second volume, which is moving along rather slowly and seems to have a different feel to it than the first volume, suggesting that perhaps I have no more to say on this level. Time will tell.

OTHER WRITINGS

WHAT A PERSON writes beyond memoirs and autobiographies helps further define and modify his character. For this reason, I felt the reader might find interesting the titles of other works I have done, which perhaps reflect aspects of my personality not mentioned in the main body of this book, although excerpts from some of these works have been included here. All of these writings were penned between the mid-'80s and 2011, a particularly productive time in my life.

I have produced two manuscripts on dreams: one for the layperson on techniques of interpretation (*DreamTime One*) and one for the professional on doing in-depth psychotherapy using the Re-Dreaming and Figure Identification technique (*DreamTime Two*). An early novel, *Amelia*, addressed the interface between sexuality and spirituality, while a later short story, written as a birthday gift to an intimate friend, reflected one of her favourite sexual fantasies. A series of six very short children's stories, *The Adventures of Herbie the Hippopotamus*, was built on a bedtime tale I made up one night for Dahlia while we still lived in Ottawa. *The Magic Touch* is a collection of unusual true stories about healing and hope, based on encounters in my practice as a psychotherapist and in my travels. *Contact* was written over a period of years, with very occasional entries still being made. For fun, one week I wrote a long series of humourous, semi-humourous, and a few serious epitaphs entitled *The Last Word — Epitaphs Out of the Box*. *Melting: Poems of a Frozen Man* was published in 1992 by ECW Press. Two additional volumes of poetry have been written since: *The Heart Rising* and *The Thornbury Poems*. An article, "Voices and Visions — The Roots of Kabbalah," appeared in the fall 2007 edition of the *Journal of the Central Conference of American Rabbis*. Most recently, I have completed a summary of my theological views in a work entitled "The Unlikely Nature of God — A Kabbalistic Perspective." A few small articles have appeared in the *Canadian Jewish News*, *Reform Judaism Magazine*, and other publications. An article, "Meditation — A Perspective," a treatment of meditation from Jewish sources emphasizing techniques and practice, is pending.

CURRENTLY

AS OF THIS writing, my life is quiet and normal. My small congregation of about sixty families, *B'nai Shalom V'Tikvah*, continues to give me much pleasure. They are a committed family of individuals and, I sometimes think, a model for what a small congregation can and should be.

Although my children are grown up and on their own, I continue to find great joy in being a parent and count my blessings to have two such wonderful and interesting kids.

I have always felt most fortunate to have great friends, and this is no different today than it was when I was a child. Their love, caring, and loyalty are treasures to which no words can do justice. Unfortunately, three of my friends have passed on.

I continue to find a lot of satisfaction in lecturing, conducting *Shabbatons* (weekend retreats) with congregations around Canada and the United States, and covering for my rabbinic colleagues when they are away — doing Torah study at their congregations and sometimes conducting their services. Interfaith work with Christian and Moslem communities and performing weddings and other life-cycle events round out my activities. I do not enjoy conducting funerals but nevertheless find it an honour to be able to offer some comfort to the bereaved. And I like very much taking a week off whenever I can and going away to a quiet place to write.

I swim three times a week, bicycle (outside or indoors) twice a week, and I am back to the love of my life — curling. Every Monday morning from October to April, three of my rabbinic colleagues and two cantors and I go out for an early breakfast together and then head for the curling rink, where we are in a clergy league. Once every year we are all together on the same team (I won't mention how we fare), but otherwise we compete against one another. Our other clergy colleagues are all Christian. Occasionally an announcement is made that someone is ill, or someone's wife or kin has passed away, and we are asked to offer our prayers. Once on the ice, however — and even before, during warm-up — curling takes over and religion does not exist. Neither does swearing. We call ourselves "The Frozen Chosen."

All that is lacking in my life at the moment is a deep, loving relationship with a woman. I was married for fifteen years, and I have since been in relationships lasting up to six years with wonderful female partners. Some of these relationships I have ended, some the woman has ended, and one or two have ended by mutual understanding and agreement. In most cases, I have continued to remain friends with the women, though this has sometimes taken a while to accomplish. What lies in store with regard to relationships I have stopped trying to determine or guess. Sometimes I think my destiny is to remain alone, but I have thought this before only to be pleasantly surprised by the appearance of someone quite wonderful. Either way, with or without a woman, my life is rich and intriguing, and I look forward to living fully and meaningfully for many years to come. (Since the above was written, I have had a very pleasant surprise and, in November of this year, a wonderful woman by the name of Laurie came into my life. Although the relationship is still young, the future looks promising.)

PERISCOPE:
BELIEFS, LEARNINGS AND OBSERVATIONS
AS I LOOK back upon my life

1) The Broad Picture
The Prairies imbued in me an appreciation for space and freedom. Being able to see from one horizon to another in all four directions has inclined me to always want to see the larger picture, whether in politics, history, religious experience, or life in general. Not that I don't appreciate details and recognize their importance, but that which contains and gives form to the details has always been the greater attraction.

2) God
I define God as the sum total of all dimensions of reality, there being an undetermined but very large number of realities. The purpose of religion is the expansion of consciousness into these realities.

While we may never be able to fully know the nature of God, it is nevertheless vitally important that the participants in any discussion of God define what God is for them. This can be done with humility, acknowledging that while any definition is inadequate, nevertheless it provides a more clear basis for discussion, since at least each person knows what the others are thinking. I have observed that most discussions of God never define the subject, and people argue and debate about what they think others mean without actually inquiring. The result is not only disagreement but often anger and frustration. On important matters, definitions should mark the starting point.

3) Love and Sex
Love between a man and a woman is not dependent on good sex.
Good sex is not dependent on love.
When both good sex and love are present, this is a gift.
When both good sex and love are present for many years, this is a blessing.

4) Friendship
Friendship is about a quiet love that may get rattled but never gets thrown.

5) Holism
The whole man or woman exists when reason and non-reason abide harmoniously in the same person.

6) The Primitive
The primitive person lives life with passion.
The passionate person is in debt to his/her primitive side.

7) Longevity
Longevity is a matter of will with a little help from science.

8) Forgiveness
Forgiveness is not always healthy or helpful.

9) Reality
There are many dimensions of reality, and some are inhabited by intelligent beings.

10) Dreams
Many a dream is a portal through which the soul is nourished and/or disturbed, disturbance often being nourishment in disguise.
Working with dreams engenders a relationship with the non-material and can be a factor in developing spiritual awareness.

11) Anger
Anger can be a force for good.

12) Science
Science is the evolution of mystery.

13) The Soul
The soul is the essence of a human being and has its own integrity, whether in the body or apart from the body.

14) Death
Death is when the soul leaves the body — even if the body is still alive.

15) Life
The difference between life and death is a matter of perception.

16) Intelligence
Intelligence is the creative assembly of knowledge.

17) Spirituality
Spirituality is the belief in the existence of non-physical intelligence.

18) Education
The purpose of education is to integrate the mind and the soul.

19) Moral Relativism
Moral relativism is the uncertainty that anything is good or bad.

20) Sexuality
The two-fold purpose of sexuality is procreation and the expansion of consciousness.

21) Truth
Truth is relative and not always what it seems.

22) Psychic Awareness
Psychic awareness enhances spirituality.

23) Suicide
Suicide is the failure of desperation.

24) Intimacy
Intimacy is becoming acquainted with another's soul. It is only for the fearless.

25) Humour
Humour is not necessarily funny.

26) Suffering
Suffering should not be rationalized.

27) Foreplay
Foreplay is what lovers do off and on twenty-four hours a day.

28) Laughter
Laughter is not a universal panacea, but it comes close.

29) Prayer
Prayer is talking to God.

30) Meditation
Meditation is listening to God.

31) Mistakes
A person who believes he or she has not made any mistakes in life has a poor memory.

32) Leaping
Sometimes one has to leap before one looks.

33) Bible Stories
Bible stories depicting unusual and extraordinary phenomena reflect the possibilities inherent in the soul and point to the future of human evolution.

34) Kabbalah
Kabbalah is the essence of Judaism. A Kabbalist embraces three beliefs: the existence of a soul independent of, but related to, the body; the existence of other dimensions of reality, some of which are inhabited by intelligent beings with which we can interact; and acceptance of non-rationality as a factor in the pursuit of expanded consciousness.

35) The Possible
 Not everything is possible, but everything has possibilities.

36) Silence
An aphrodisiac for the soul.

RETROSPECTIVE

AS I LOOK back upon my life, what stands out most prominently for me is my spiritual pursuit. In one way or another, spirituality has woven its way through the fabric of my years and continues to push me into new frontiers. While I have finally arrived at a definition of God that satisfies me—God is the sum total of all realities — many questions remain: the nature of the soul; the reality that preceded the big bang; the nature of sexuality beyond procreation and pleasure; the nature of spiritual intelligences such as angels; the limits, if any, of perception while still in a physical body; what happens to the soul between lifetimes (Sylvia Browne, a renowned psychic, notwithstanding); the greater meaning of sleep; the end point, if any, of evolution; and a good definition of love — at least, one that satisfies me. Not that this list is exhaustive.

From the Jewish perspective, what I have learned that is most important to me is that reason and mysticism are compatible. Some of our greatest rabbis who were consummate rationalists, such as the Vilna Gaon and Joseph Caro, were also mystics and saw no contradiction in harbouring both in one body and soul. This is perhaps one of Judaism's greatest gifts — the harmonious blending of reason and non-reason to make what I consider, and what I believe Judaism considers, to be the whole person.

My task, as I see it in the years ahead, is four-fold: to bring to whomever will listen an awareness of the harmony between science and mysticism, reason and non-reason; to encourage a greater appreciation of the vast potential of the soul; to further explore the interface between spirituality and sexuality (the theme pursued in my novel *Amelia*); and to plant a seed that the prevalent concept of God, anthropomorphism (God envisioned in the image of man), must be changed. For reasons I expand upon in my manuscript "The Unlikely Nature of God — A Kabbalistic Perspective," to perpetuate anthropomorphism is to perpetuate religious misunderstanding and the violence that has issued from this misunderstanding. In my view, only a new, pluralistic, and inclusive concept, mine or someone else's, that does not claim to have *the* truth has a chance of helping to bring to fruition the prophetic dream of peace for all mankind. However, whether or not the type of concept I'm advocating comes to be, at the very least it is my hope that each religion will disclaim having *the* truth and recognize the efficacy and beauty of other religions as vehicles for mankind to transcend the limits of cognition and materialism.

I left medicine to become a rabbi. As the years have passed, I have come to realize that no profession was better suited for me than the one I ultimately chose to pursue. My life has not been without difficulties and pain, but I have been blessed in many ways — children, friends, good health, and loving companions. God willing, the years ahead will be fruitful, and I will continue to serve the sum of all realities, the *Ribone Shel Olam*, the One who is all creation.

— Yonah, the son of Kalman and Bayla, this 24th day of Nisan,
in the year 5771, the 28th day of April, 2011.